KT-230-317

Adam Ruck

 Publishing

Cover (front a): enjoying a glass of red;
cover (front b): bicycle racing is a major sport in France;
cover (front c): an old street in Saint-Paul-de-Vence;
cover (back): the old town of Morlaix;
cover (spine): boules is a favourite pastime;
page 2: farmhouse flowers;
page 3: a view of Chateau de St Ulrich from Ribeauville;
page 4: trading at Chauvigny market;
page 5 (a): fine old house in Rennes;
page 5 (b): view of the Alps from Argentière
pages 6–7: Perigordian landscape;
page 8: Pesmes on the River Ognon;
page 9: Beynac-et-Cazenac.

Written by Adam Ruck
Additional writing and research: Fiona Dunlop, Lindsay Hunt, Michael Ivory, Ingrid Morgan, Judith Samson, David Shepheard

Revised fourth edition 1999. Reprinted 1999, 2000
First published 1993
Edited, designed, produced and distributed by AA Publishing, Norfolk House, Priestley Road, Basingstoke, Hampshire RG24 9NY.
Maps © The Automobile Association 1993, 1995, 1997, 1999.

The contents of this publication are believed correct at the time of printing. Nevertheless, the publishers cannot be held responsible for any errors or omissions or for changes in the details given in this guide or for the consequences of any reliance on the information provided by the same. Assessments of attractions, hotels, restaurants and so forth are based upon the author's own personal experience and, therefore, descriptions given in this guide necessarily contain an element of subjective opinion which may not reflect the publishers' opinion or dictate a reader's own experiences on another occasion. We have tried to ensure accuracy in this guide, but things do change and we would be grateful if readers would advise us of any inaccuracies they may encounter.

A CIP catalogue record for this book is available from the British Library.

ISBN 0 7495 1886 3

Published by AA Publishing (a trading name of Automobile Association Developments Limited, whose registered office is Norfolk House, Priestley Road, Basingstoke, Hampshire RG24 9NY. Registered number 1878835).

Colour origination by Fotographics Ltd
Printed and bound in Italy by by Printer Trento srl

Titles in the Explorer series...
Australia • Boston & New England • Britain • Brittany California • Caribbean • China • Costa Rica • Crete • Cuba Cyprus • Egypt • Florence & Tuscany • Florida • France Germany • Greek Islands • Hawaii • India • Ireland • Israel Italy • Japan • London • Mallorca • Mexico • New York • New Zealand • Paris • Portugal • Provence • Rome • San Francisco Scotland • South Africa • Spain • Tenerife • Thailand • Tunisia Turkey • Turkish Coast • Vietnam

AA World Travel Guides publish nearly 300 guidebooks to a full range of cities, countries and regions across the world. Find out more about AA Publishing and the wide range of services the AA provides by visiting our web site at www.theaa.co.uk

ORGANISATION

France Is, France Was

Discusses aspects of life and living today, from traditional ways to modern times, and places the country in its historical context and explores those past events whose influences are felt to this day

A–Z

The book begins with sections on Paris, and is subsequently divided into geographical regions. Places of interest are listed alphabetically within each section. Suggested walks, drives and Focus On articles, which consider a variety of topics in greater detail, are included in each section.

Travel Facts

Contains the strictly practical information that is vital for a successful trip.

Hotels and Restaurants

Lists places to stay and places to eat alphabetically by region. Entries are graded budget, moderate or expensive.

ABOUT THE RATINGS

Most places described in this book have been given a separate rating. These are as follows:

 ►►►   Do not miss

 ►►   Highly recommended

►   Worth seeing

MAP REFERENCES

To make the location of a particular place easier to find, every main entry in this book is given a map reference, such as 176B3. The first number (176) indicates the page on which the map can be found, the letter (B) and the second number (3) pinpoint the square in which the main entry is located. The maps on the inside front cover and inside back cover are referred to as IFC and IBC respectively.

Contents

How to use this book 4

Contents pages 5–7

My France 8

FRANCE IS, FRANCE WAS 9–47

France Is 9–29
The Republic 12
Society 13
Multicultural 14–15
The economy 16–17
Fashion 18–19
Words and pictures 20–1
Cuisine 22–3
Work and play 24–5
Architecture 26–7
Paris vs regions 28–9

France Was 30–47
Early days 31
Roman 32
Feudal 33
Medieval 34–5
Religion 36–7
The King 38–9
Revolution and empire 40–1
Expansion and growth 42–3
At war 44–5
Modernising 46–7

A–Z
Paris 48–71
Shopping 66
Food and drink 67
Nightlife 68
Accommodation 69
Practical points 70–1
Drives
The Forest of Fontainebleau 62

Walks
Concorde to the Palais Royal 53
Pont des Arts to rue Soufflot 55
Beaubourg to the place des Vosges 57

Normandy 72–89
Focus On
Bayeux Tapestry 75
La Côte Fleurie 76
Invasion beaches 79
Norman churches 82
Mont-St-Michel 83
Drives
A tour of the Perche 88
The Lower Seine Valley 89

Brittany 90–105
Focus On
Islands and capes 93
Megaliths 95
Parish closes 97
Pont-Aven 103
Drives
Visiting the hill country: Monts
d'Arrée 100

The Loire 106–25
Focus On
Tapestries 109
Renaissance châteaux 112–13
The French garden 125
Drives
Discovering the River Vienne 115
Tributaries of the Loire 122

The Atlantic Coast 126–33
Focus On
The Landes 130
Bordeaux vineyards 132
Drives
Entre-Deux-Mers and Sauternes
129
Churches, beaches and the Gironde
estuary 133

Dordogne 35–51
Focus On
Fortresses 137
Prehistory 142–3
Drives
River valley and open land 140
Exploring Périgord Vert 147
Along the Aveyron Valley 149
Between the Dordogne and the
Corrèze 151

The Pyrenees 152–67
Focus On
The Basque country 156–7
Cathars and fortresses 159
The High Pyrenees 164–5

Romanesque churches 167
Drive
Pays de Foix 161

The Provence Coast 168–93
Focus On
The Camargue 170
Modern art 174–5
Perched villages 177
The Riviera 182–3
The Maritime Alps 186
Roman Provence 188–9
Drives
The Dentelles de Montmirail and
Mont Ventoux 179
The Vaucluse plateau 181
Vaison-la-Romaine, Nyons and the
Baronnies 193
Vence, Col de Vence and Gourdon
193
Walk
The Fort de Buoux 181

Massif Central 194–207
Focus On
Volcanoes 201
Romanesque Auvergne 203
The Grands Causses 206–7
Drives
The Cévennes and Mont Lozère 197
Mont Mézenc and the source of the
Loire 205
Walks
Footpath across the massif 197
Mont Mézenc and the Gerbier de
Jonc 205

The Alps & Rhone Valley 208–23
Focus On
Mountaineering 215
The Rhône Valley 221
Rural architecture 223
Drives
The Croix de Fer and Glandon
passes 219

Over the mountain from Morzine 219

Burgundy & the Jura 224–39
Focus On
The Burgundy vineyards 228–9
Beaune 230
Medieval monasteries 231
Drives
The Auxois 233
The Charollais and the Brionnais 238

Alsace-Lorraine & the North 240–59
Focus On
Gothic churches of the North 243
Nancy 251
Reims and champagne 253
Battlefields of the North 256–7
Drives
Route des Crêtes 246–7
Route du Vin d'Alsace 247
La Thiérache 252

TRAVEL FACTS 260–73

HOTELS AND RESTAURANTS 274–83

Index 284–8

Picture credits and contributors 288

Maps and Plans
France IFC and IBC
France 10–11
France in 1603 30
Paris: the Périphérique 48
Central Paris 50–1
Drive: Forest of Fontainebleau 62
Normandy 72–3
Tour of the Perche 88
Drive: Lower Seine Valley 89

Brittany 90–1
Drive: Monts d'Arrée 100
The Loire 106–7
Drive: River Vienne 115
Drive: Tributaries of the Loire 122
The Atlantic Coast 126
Drive: Entre-Deux-Mers and Sauternes 129
Drive: Gironde estuary 133
Dordogne 134
Drive: River valley 140
Drive: Périgord Vert 147
Drive: Aveyron Valley 149
Drive: Between the Dordogne and the Corrèze 151
The Pyrenees 152–3
Drive: Pays de Foix 161
Provence and the Mediterranean Coast 168–9
Drive: Dentelles de Montmirail and Mont Ventoux 179
The Vaucluse Plateau drive 181
Drive: Vaison-la-Romaine, Nyons and the Baronnies 193
Drive: Vence, Col de Vence and Gourdon 193
Massif Central 194
Drive: The Cévennes and Mont Lozère 197
Drive: Mont Mézenc and the source of the Loire 205
The Alps and the Rhone Valley 208
Lyon 217
Drive: The Croix de Fer and Glandon passes 219
Drive: Over the mountain from Morzine 219
Burgundy and the Jura 224–5
Drive: The Auxois 233
Drive: The Charollais and the Brionnais 238
Alsace-Lorraine and the North 240–1
Drive: Routes des Crêtes 246
Drive: La Thiérache 252

Adam Ruck is the author of *The Holiday Which? Guide to France* and *The Holiday Which? Guide to Greece*. He is a regular contributor to British national newspapers, including *The Daily Telegraph*, *The Sunday Telegraph*, *The Guardian*, *The Sunday Times* and *The Observer*.

My France by Adam Ruck

My first trip to France was avoidable after a French boy, who was somewhat older than me, stayed with us repeatedly. A mulish 12-year-old, I went predisposed to have a bad time to prove myself right for not wanting to go. This was quite easy. Having travelled from Paris to Provence via Lourdes, my hosts were delayed and reached Marseille airport four hours after I did. A few minutes later we had a head-on collision with a truck and I spent my first evening sitting outside Aix en Provence hospital.

The following fortnight seemed longer than a school term. Encouraged to drink wine in the evening, I found it helped me to sleep. The question was: to drink it neat (foul taste) or diluted (more of it)? Excursions were offered, but after the crash I was terrified of the car and said I was quite happy at the house. 'France and I do not agree,' I wrote pompously to my mother, revelling in my unhappiness.

The best part of the trip was when the Baron, my host, who had broken his chest on the steering wheel, summoned me to his bedside in order to explain that owing to his incapacity I would have to take the train to Paris, where the last days of my stay were to be spent. Hooray! I was shown the Eiffel Tower but not allowed up. 'No true Parisian goes there,' said my friend with a sneer.

I was glad to get home but kept the language up, and came to love France through its literature. I soon developed an unhealthy interest in old buildings and discovered sightseeing as a good wet-weather alternative to tennis, and an equally useful distraction from constructive activity. After school I spent six months in Paris.

Once I could drive, I discovered the user-friendliness of France for a touring holiday, whether your budget confines you to le camping municipal or extends to the village hotel, and gradually my interest in the country broadened to include food, wine, landscape and even people. Slavishly devoted to guidebook star ratings, I would become furious when a long detour, or even a voyage, to a top-rated spot proved unrewarding. Sitting at the top of the Mont Beuvray, surveying one of the world's most boring views after a long drive through the only dull part of Burgundy, I almost exploded with rage. 'I could do better than this!' I shouted. 'Go on, then,' my passenger said. 'Since you seem to want to spend your whole life sightseeing, you might as well.'

France Is
France Was

France

11

Unruly, rebellious, the French nature is such that their revolutions and uprisings once came and went as often as their governments. After two centuries of changing constitutions, political stability is only a recent phenomenon, introduced by De Gaulle with the Fifth Republic, relayed by the sphinx-like Mitterrand, and now steered by the more impulsive Chirac.

Monarchies, republics and empires have all had their turn over the last 150 years, interrupted by the traumatic four-year German occupation during World War II. Yet today France is regarded as one of the most powerful Western democracies, and a pivotal force within the European Union.

WHO GOVERNS? Far from being a mere figurehead, the French President in the Fifth Republic has considerable powers. Head of the army, responsible for nuclear force, nominator of the Prime Minister, he can call referendums or dissolve Parliament. Strangely aloof in the gilded cage of the Elysée Palace, he is not allowed to set foot in the National Assembly and is only answerable to the Conseil Constitutionnel, an independent elected body which judges the validity of every law passed and guarantees the Rights of Man. The Prime Minister, who leads a Council of Ministers, answers to the National Assembly (lower house) and Senate (upper house), which together make up the body of Parliament.

Elected for seven years, the President's mandate can adversely cross the fortunes of Parliament, whose deputies are elected every five years. Twice during Mitterrand's reign (1986 and again in 1993) slumps in his Socialist Party's popularity forced him to 'cohabit' with right-wing prime ministers.

One of these, Jacques Chirac, was elected president in May 1995 after Parliament had radically swung to the right in 1993. Two years later, his popularity had plummeted, strikes and demonstrations were escalating, unemployment was still growing, Algerian fundamentalists were bombing Paris and the franc was shuddering. He dissolved Parliament and after the ensuing massive victory of the left, was left musing on the irony of having been the first right-wing prime minister to cohabit with a left-wing president as well as the first right-wing president to cohabit with a left-wing prime minister.

France meanwhile continues to move towards the Euro and into the high-technological age whilst struggling with the angst of unemployment and social exclusion. Plus ça change?

Many worlds make up the Republic: a delightful rural idyll near Chartres

Of all Western European countries, France has possibly undergone the most radical social transformations since the 1950s. Previously an agriculturally based society and economy, slowly undergoing industrialisation, its top stratum was a highly intellectualised, culti-vated middle class. The nobility had all but disappeared with the Revolution, but certain of their values had been adopted by the haute bourgeoisie, one of which was an abhorrence of commercialism. This left the field open for the rise of the petit bourgeoisie.

Property-owning, relatively well educated, set in their ways, the petit-bourgeoisie were also xenophobic, proud of their regional identity and suspicious of intrusion. Since the 1950s rural areas have lost both the lower middle classes and the land-working peasantry to the big cities: today less than 5 per cent are employed in agriculture (before the war the figure was 33 per cent). Moving into urban areas, like nearly 75 per cent of the population, they have renounced their historic individualism and become wage-earners. Highly conformist, their materialistic values are centred around the family and many embrace the National Front.

RELIGION AND MORALITY

Traditionally and still nominally a Catholic nation, France separated the Church from the State in 1905. Today maybe 14 per cent of the population are church-goers, and religion is no longer a burning issue. Yet the moral character of the nation remains Catholic and sensual.

❑ Over 46 million French people belong to the Roman Catholic Church. Other major denomina-tions include the Protestants (about 900,000), Jews (700,000) and over 4 million Muslims, concentrated in urban areas. ❑

EVER PLEASURE-LOVING The French were as influenced by the swinging '60s as the rest of the world. Although women only obtained the vote in 1946, their movement had its effect, legalis-ing the Pill and, in 1974, abortions. Over two-thirds of women now work and many hold key posts in govern-ment and business aided by a nursery school system which welcomes 2-year-olds. Yet, unlike Anglo-American fem-inists, they cling to a feminine image while adroitly manipulating a still male-dominated society. Diane de Poitiers, Pompadour, Marie-Antoinette, Joséphine – the tradition is a long one. French morality is very much an individual's private business. The whole nation is often aware that a public figure has a mistress – but who cares? Or, 'et alors?'

The suicide rate among farmers is the highest of all professions

The tapestry of France's population, which has always included regional identities (Bretons, Alsaciens, Corsicans) is becoming increasingly rich. Xenophobia and racism have come to the fore, as the immigration issue is tossed to and fro by political parties, each trying to win maximum electoral support. The 1990 census recorded a foreign population of 3.58 million (out of a total of 56.6 million), which does not include 1.8 million with French nationality and countless illegal immigrants. Well over 10 per cent of the French population is of foreign origin – a proportion that demands attention.

As elsewhere in Europe, immigrants were brought in after World War II to cope with unwanted low-paid jobs. Portuguese, Italians and Spaniards were joined by people from the former colonies, particularly the Maghreb: Algeria, Tunisia and Morocco. Lesser numbers arrived from Central and West Africa, while French citizens from the DOM-TOM (overseas départements in the Caribbean, Indian Ocean and Pacific) also left their shores searching for work. The 1960s suburban bidonvilles of cheap pre-fabs were soon replaced by badly planned towerblocks which in their turn became immigrant ghettos.

RACISM Today the situation has hardly improved, despite various government attempts to rectify an incendiary situation. Politicians of every party try to divert support from Le Pen and his overtly racist tirades, via Chirac's bungled sympathy for those 'driven crazy' by their immigrant neighbours, or via Edith Cresson, as the then Socialist Prime Minister, talking of the need to 'fly planeloads home'. Phenomenally high unemployment, soulless

> ❏ In 1995, the French unemployment rate was 11.6 per cent; for an Algerian immigrant under 25, it was 54.1 per cent. ❏

suburbs, police harassment, attacks on immigrants, 1995's spate of terrorist bombs and endless tinkering with immigration and nationality laws has hardly cooled racial tensions.

NO MAN'S LAND Rarely socially welcome, France's naturalised North Africans find themselves stranded between two cultures. Women, more than men, suffer from restrictive Muslim laws which separate them from French society.

> ❏ In October 1989 a French headmaster banned three Muslim schoolgirls because they insisted on wearing their scarves. The incident developed into a major political confrontation. ❏

Support for the extreme right National Front runs high enough, particularly in the south-east, for them to have started winning control of town councils. Immigrants feel understandably threatened. Assimilation, however, takes time and all is not negative: mixed marriages are on the increase and the third generation now speaks almost exclusively French. In the 1980s, SOS Racisme created a forceful lobby that led to a seriously increased awareness of the problems.

Young Algerians born in France in particular are also forging a new identity, calling themselves les beurs and successfully creating their own alternative music – le Raï. Full integration, though, is a long way off.

JEWISH COMMUNITIES Although France's oldest immigrant group, the Jewish population, has played a major role in French culture and politics over the last two centuries, it too suffers from racism. About 700,000 Jews (the largest community in Europe) originated from central Europe, and they were joined during the 1960s by an influx into France of Sephardic Jews from North Africa.

As well as revitalising the Jewish community, the Sephards have underlined their distinct identity. Jewish sense of separation from 'mainstream' French history can only be heightened by the memory of the deportation of over 117,000 Jews to concentration camps during World War II.

THE AMERICAN FACTOR Since World War II, the French have been at odds about the Americans. They rail against their insidious influence on French culture, their economic dominance and brash commercialism; but they admire and espouse many of their commercial and cultural inventions (media styles, westerns, soap operas, rock 'n' roll, jazz, fast food and Internet). However much French politicians may rant about the spread of American cultural hegemony and support the Académie Française in its unyielding crusade to keep all words pure French, much of the US influence is welcomed and imitated by the general public.

The well-known rue des Rosiers, in Le Marais, Paris...

15

❏ Sylvester Stallone and Sharon Stone figure among US citizens solemnly decorated by the French Minister of Culture in the last few years. ❏

speaking a different language or not – but not always quite so eager to accept those who are regarded (rightly or wrongly) as society's losers.

The victory of France's football team in the 1998 World Cup may have helped, making heroes of its multi-cultural team.

...is the heart of the city's lively Jewish quarter, and is packed with Mediterranean-style restaurants and specialist shops

❏ At the beginning of 1998, there were 630 McDonald's in France and the Académie Française decreed that the word mél should be used instead of e-mail. ❏

With their newly acquired self-respect and high-tech society, the French are ready to accept the 'winners' – whether foreign and

For France the 1970s and 1980s were decades of economic progress by leaps and bounds, reaping rewards from the near past and establishing a new, high-profile identity. State dirigisme and centralised planning proved hard to maintain in the complexities of this newly wealthy society, despite the fact that the decade kicked off with a spate of nationalisations and rigorous controls.

16

Yet the face of both society and the economy was transformed, bringing prosperity on most levels. In the early 1980s, industrial strategy was still tightly controlled by central government. Countless banks and mega-industries were nationalised, and the state share of industrial production rose from 15 to 30 per cent virtually overnight.

REVERSED POLICY After these initial steps, Mitterrand did a volte face, leading to fiscal and monetary rigour, tax reductions, some privatisations (under Chirac's two-year government) and, above all, much financial deregulation. The French franc was locked into the Deutschmark, supported by an all-powerful Bundesbank.

A new breed of entrepreneurial French managers also appeared – a

contrast to the old élitists of the Grandes Ecoles. Not least, modern high-tech industries benefited as much from government aid as from real market effectiveness.

FLUX It couldn't last. Recession (la crise) hit, deeply affecting the Gallic ego; unemployment soared to over 12 per cent with a lot more people depending in one way or another on state aid; corruption scandals rocked the higher echelons of industry and politics; the requirements to join the Euro loomed larger and larger; social unrest and strikes broke out; and government went through a double flip from left to right and back again.

Nor can the gilded face of France conceal a widening rift between rich and poor: although the number of poor hasn't changed much over the last decade, the poor are getting poorer and the rich, helped in some cases by corruption, richer. The compulsory minumum wage stands at around 50 per cent of the average wage but exorbitant social security charges discourage employers. Nevertheless, the social security debt is cavernous and the Socialist government's proposals to introduce a 35-hour working week have not been welcomed by industry.

And yet, the recession seems to be easing, the criteria for joining the Euro have been met, inflation is well under control, unemployment has stabilised, growth is patchy but respectable, France is still the fourth industrial power in the West and the French are past masters at bouncing back, which may, or may not, explain their status as the world's greatest consumers of tranquillisers.

A nuclear power station at Civaux. Nuclear power now provides most of the energy which is required in France

FUTURE STRATEGIES Known today as much for the TGV, Minitel, Ariane and Concorde as for camembert and Château Margaux, France has caught up with a vengeance on the 20th century. Moving to the forefront of modern technology – whether fast-breeder nuclear reactors or off-shore oil techniques – it has become a pace-setter in Europe.

Telecommunications, transport, bio-technology, computing and aerospace are fields where French know-how is recognised, although there is often a chasm between the world of pure research and its industrial applications. Less inspiring was France's obstinate insistence on perfecting nuclear war-heads through controversial tests in the Pacific, in late 1995. Following the American example, French firms have invested heavily overseas. St-Gobain has factories in over 40 countries while Renault, Peugeot, Michelin, Total and Aerospatiale all have a strong overseas presence. Between 1990 and 1997 the trade balance rose spectacularly to leave France

❏ France's greatest industry is tourism: in 1997, an estimated 67 million visitors mingled with the 60 per cent of French who take their holidays in France. The result: a net income of 65 billion francs. ❏

US$ 22 billion in the black, partly due to the efforts of the armaments industry (its influence often reflected in French foreign policy), to France's near self-sufficiency in energy and to the tourist industry.

NEW ENERGY For years France depended on coal, gas, hydro-electricity and imported oil. When the oil crisis hit France in 1973, it was importing nearly 75 per cent of its energy needs.

Home-grown nuclear power now accounts for three-quarters of national electricity requirements. Curiously, despite the ominous presence of over 50 nuclear power stations throughout France, there is little public outcry. Even after Chernobyl (when French authorities solemnly declared that the radioactive cloud dispersed at the French border) 70 per cent of the population remains in favour of continuing with nuclear power, though not, paradoxically, of building any new power stations.

Somehow, the EDF (French electricity board) public relations department convinces the public that French reactors are more sophisticated and less prone to accidents. Only time will tell whether they are right.

It was Christian Dior's 'new look' which set the tone for post-war Paris fashion hegemony: women all over the world tossed away the masculine, practical clothes that had dominated the war years and bowed to Dior's new feminine style. Despite repeated offensives from Milan, New York, London and Tokyo, high French style still maintains a monopoly on the successful marketing of thousands of signed accessories – the bread and butter of every top couturier. And the French remain supreme in street chic.

Twenty-three fashion houses make up the Chamber of Parisian Couture. But for many couturiers their collections are simply a necessary public relations parade, all the better to sell their perfume. For your average punter, life is far from the gilded chairs surrounding the catwalks. Luckily, another stratum of high fashion designers was officialised in 1974 to keep up with the growing rejuvenation of the fashion industry. Much influenced by England's Biba and Mary Quant, the new group of 24 members was labelled créateurs de mode and now includes Chloë, Kenzo, Montana, Gaultier, Mugler, Chantal Thomass, Cerruti, names whose fame is often greater than that of the more obscure couturiers (ever heard of Lecoanet Hemant?). Wilder, racier, younger, the fashion creators' style can be outrageous, but when their twice-yearly collections are presented in the Carrousel du Louvre (a specially designed space beneath the pyramid), Parisian hotels are taken by force.

MIXED INFLUENCE French shrewdness in realising the scope and power of fashion extends to the acceptance of talented foreigners into their midst. Among the grands couturiers are four Italians, one Spaniard, one Japanese and one Norwegian, not to mention the ubiquitous Karl Lagerfeld, of German origin. The fashion creators include the Japanese Kenzo, influential Issey Miyake, several Italians and two Englishmen, Alexander McQueen and John Galliano. Strict rules govern production and marketing, and only those with a strong businessman behind them succeed. Yves St-Laurent would never have survived without the astute Pierre Bergé nor Dior without the textile giant, Boussac.

In total the prestigious French fashion industry manages to generate an annual turnover of around 20 billion francs, though the number of regular haute couture customers is estimated at only 2,000 worldwide. Skilled craftsmen dedicated to the creation of luxury can only be found in Paris. But as their ages advance, fewer young people come forward to replace them in a laborious and traditional field.

A glimpse of Parisian style, worn off the catwalk

18

CUT OF THE CLOTH The rest of French fashion is heavily dependent on impetus and inspiration from the upper echelons. No designer can exist outside Paris, but textile manufacturers are scattered all over the country. Much of French elegance depends on the fine quality of fabrics and the 'backward' French textile industry specialised for years in producing small runs of divine, costly cloths. Lyon was until relatively recently the centre of the silk industry, though cheaper foreign suppliers are now stepping in.

However chic the average Frenchman or woman seems to be, much of their style emanates from a high degree of self confidence. Head high, a good strut, and over half-an-hour a day spent on a

❏ The sturdy denim actually originated in Nîmes (hence the name de Nîmes). Today Nîmes is ruled by the fashion industry of Cacherel, and Hong Kong seems to supply the rest. ❏

careful toilette – the result is assured.

Keeping up with the latest trends is an expensive affair but most manage to acquire the latest accessories. It is this innate sense of what is suitable and an eternal desire to seduce that ensures an impeccable turn-out.

Good to look at, but it might break the budget: a stylish display in the Boutique Christian Dior

'*France is the most brilliant and dangerous nation in Europe, best suited to become in turn an object of admiration, hatred, pity, terror, but never of indifference.*' *The words were those of Alexis de Toqueville from the 19th century, but the thought is still relevant today. Student idealism is as potent in France as it was in the 1960s, as this nation spawns thinkers from generation to generation, most of whom end up in Paris and on the Left Bank. Joined by artists, film directors and diverse literati, they should be providing some hot discussion towards the end of the millennium...but are they?*

20

Ever fashion conscious, the French are drawn to new abstract ideas like moths to flames; the national passion for debate starts at school, where verbal dexterity is encouraged. Post-war thought was governed by Camus and Sartre's existentialism.

Shakespeare and Company: English words for sale in the Latin Quarter of Paris

Every intellectual was strongly influenced by their disenchanted voices and expressions of man's freedom to choose his destiny. But by the late 1960s a new approach began to take over, broadly called structuralism, bringing to the fore theorists such as Barthes, Foucault, Lacan and Lévi-Strauss, all of whom rejected the bourgeois view of history and saw man as the prisoner of a determined system. Philosophers such as Derrida, Kristeva, Deleuze and Lyotard relayed this rationalist approach, exploring the concept of 'post-structuralism' but remain well beyond the bounds of general understanding and concerns.

FIN DE SIECLE After Glucksmann and Bernard-Henri Lévy in the late 1970s, no new figures emerged during the 1980s and early 1990s, creating a gaping void, linked with a general mental apathy and the erosion of left-wing ideology: after all, world economic crises were monopolising attention and communism was dead. Meanwhile, historians, economists and sociologists, such as the hugely influential Pierre Bourdieu, filled the void. Philosophy, however did not die. A scattering of disparate names is starting to appear: Debray with his mediologie, Honfray with 'new hedonism', Roméro, young and brilliant, and Finkelkraut, steady and serious. Millenniums, apparently, concentrate the minds.

> ❏ Intellectuals in France still have clout, though. During the 1994 European elections, an ad hoc group led by Bernard-Henri Lévy managed to drag Bosnia on to the political agenda; and in 1987, a group of 100 film-makers and intellectuals forced the government to water down its proposed immigration reforms. ❏

LITERARY LOW The world of literature has followed a similar pattern. The famous old literary reviews, through which you could hear the rattle of gun-fire between intellectuals, have given way to fact-based news magazines. Authors with the universal appeal of Flaubert, Zola, Maupassant, Proust, Camus, Colette or Sartre have not been replaced, and the exponents of the nouveau roman of the 1960s have virtually retired.

Publishing is monopolised by three major companies which also control the juries of the main literary prizes. Despite this, the influence of Les Editions de Minuit, who refuse to publish anything other than new, intellectual, original and avant-garde books, continues to grow.

CINEMA is still going strong and channels much of French creative talent. Since Louis Lumière directed the first moving pictures in the 1890s, the French have maintained a monopoly on a specific genre: poetic, intimate, intelligent and sensitive, they focus on human relations and life. Although the heyday of recognisable styles such as the 1960s nouvelle vague is over, the cinéma d'auteur is still buoyant. Godard, Chabrol, Rohmer, Resnais and Malle have all left their indelible stamp, while more recently, Besson, Berri, Serreau, Annaud, Corneau and Téchiné continue to innovate. On screen, Gérard Depardieu, Catherine Deneuve and Isabelle Huppert have achieved international status. Benefiting from substantial state subsidy, French cinema retains a strongly Gallic flavour despite inroads from Hollywood, and is still the third largest producer in the world.

Cinema is still big business

ART IN CRISIS After dominating the world, Paris lost to New York when World War II broke out. Since then the hoped-for come-back has never quite happened, despite public interest and government backing. Galleries and museums carpet the country but there is a crisis of creativity and few contemporary French artists have achieved world renown. Buren? César? Boltanski? Garouste? Although big at home they mean little abroad. As in literature, it is almost as if the French are waiting for the 21st century.

French cuisine epitomises the complexities of the national character. Science, sensuality and creativity combine to produce, at its best, food fit for the gods. Every region of France has its specialities, proudly refined from generation to generation, and in the 1990s these are being enthusiastically revived by chefs weary of the two-carrot nouvelle cuisine. Hearty, so-called 'peasant' dishes are now widely available.

Twenty years of invasion by a lighter, fresher diet has left its mark: the nouvelle cuisine school has been assimilated into a new approach to cooking which puts as much emphasis on nutrition as on inventive flavours and presentation.

QUICK CUISINE Don't believe that every French family sits down to a gastronomic orgy every evening. The advance of the 20th century has brought with it a rushed lifestyle and the French have adopted convenience foods like every other Western nation. Food is no longer the priority it once was.

Over the last decade fast-food joints have invaded every town centre and the young, ever attracted

French bread comes in many delicious varieties

to the American way of life, find these budget victuals the ultimate in trendiness.

Old habits of lengthy, elaborate preparation do survive, above all in rural working-class homes, whereas the more monied urban strata, if not dining in a restaurant, are more likely to knock together some pasta and a salad than indulge in preparing a blanquette de veau.

DINNER TALK Food and wine are still serious topics, talked about at length and with at least 15 national magazines devoted to them. Diners are choosy about the restaurants they frequent, whether the world-famous havens of top chefs like Joël Robuchon, Paul Bocuse, Guy Savoy and Michel Guérard or a neighbourhood bistro.

Foreign influences have made themselves felt, too, and the recent assimilation of nouvelle cuisine has led to a boom in Japanese restaurants, and avant-garde treatments of seaweed. A new consciousness of ecology and dietetics in the 1960s and 1970s nurtured Michel Guérard's famous cuisine minceur, but countless Japanese apprentice chefs in the top Paris kitchens emphasised texture and meticulous presentation. The largest cookery school in the world is now in Tokyo.

> ❑ Only 30 years ago the French spent an average of 40 per cent of their household budget on food; today it is half as much. ❑

FOODIES' NEWS However easily this new style of cooking was adopted by France's most famous chefs, it would not have been so widespread without the influential gastronomic magazine and guide, the Gault Millau, launched in the 1970s. Daring to confront on its own terrain the long-standing little red book, the Michelin Guide, the innovative Gault Millau preached and praised an innovative approach, setting the pace with its own journalistic style. Chefs were encouraged to sweep away old rituals and prejudices, take risks, marry the unmarriageable; and thus a new generation of diners was brought up on flourless sauces, fish, delicate vegetable mousses and harmoniously arranged plates. Classic table service disappeared and a more balanced, nutritious gastronomy shifted into top gear.

GOOD OLD DAYS Some may look back with nostalgia to the last days of grande cuisine, which really ended with World War I. But who has time these days to sit down to a five-hour, 16-course lunch? The line of illustrious historic chefs is long, from Taillevent (who wrote the first treatise on cooking) to Beauvilliers and the master of modern French cooking, Carême, author of five volumes about 19th-century French cuisine. Today's

masters can no longer doggedly follow tradition: they must invent and personalise, while returning to products and techniques born from regional cooking. Now-adays you can forget the turbot aux kiwi or the rouget à la framboise.

HOME GROUND Paul Bocuse, unofficial French gastronomic ambassador, is himself descended from a line of chefs going back to 1765. After the necessary apprenticeship at Paris's top restaurants he returned to Collonges-au-Mont-d'Or, just outside Lyon, where diners still lap up his black truffle soup. France's gastronomic capital, Lyon, has the most varied supply of fresh produce at its doorstep. As the French couturier uses the richest fabrics, so the chef's priority is to show off the fresh, flavoursome, perfectly ripe ingredients of his region.

La nouvelle cuisine de terroir led by Roger Vergé, Jacques Maximin, André Daguin or Lucien Vanal is to be found scattered all over this varied country and even if your purse doesn't stretch to the greats, there's little to beat a traditional regional dish in a family restaurant.

Eating at a bistro: not necessarily a very intimate affair

Although their priorities apparently lie firmly in the camp of pleasure and leisure, the French are actually a hardworking nation. Since the working week is officially 39 hours long, and there are five weeks' holiday a year (the longest in Europe), as well as 11 days of public holidays, this can be hard to believe. Yet executives often start work at 8am and finish 12 hours later. Weekends have thus become sacrosanct, often spent at a weekend home, and holidays are calculated to the minute. 'Work hard, play hard' seems to be the maxim for every French family.

24

It was not until the 1936 Front Populaire government that social reforms were made stipulating two weeks' annual paid holiday, a 40-hour week and compulsory collective bargaining. The new congés payés changed the face of the nation and, when extended after the war, led to that familiar sight of entire cities closed down for August with main roads taken by storm on the 1st and 31st. Changes in school holidays and state encouragement have now spread holidays over July and August and the traditional month's duration is often reduced to allow for an increasing number of shorter breaks such as skiing holidays in February and/or a break over the Christmas period.

Further short holidays are astutely concocted by bridging a public holiday with a nearby weekend (le pont). This means that May, which carries three separate holidays, becomes a complete wipe-out in terms of economic productivity.

HOMELY HOLIDAYS Where do all these itchy-footed French go? They are not particularly adventurous: most stay at home or at least never leave France. A small but growing percentage cross the border to Spain, Italy or Britain. A faster growing percentage, the more affluent classes in particular, are opting for more exotic destinations.

Begun in 1950, the Club Méditerranée holiday villages have been influential in opening up destinations where previously no Frenchman dared to tread. This formula of controlled individualism suits French needs: once a year they let their hair down in some exotic spot without running any risks. And more recently the charter company Nouvelles Frontières has successfully herded groups of retired and/or middle-class people round Indian temples or paddled them up the Amazon.

SPORTS HOLIDAYS are increasingly popular. Cycling has always been a French sport, followed closely by football and, in the south-west, rugby. But along with the rise in leisure time and spending power, the French have taken up tennis – inspired by idols Yannick Noah and Henri Leconte – horse-riding, sailing, golf and the ubiquitous urban gyms. Previously their only national sport had been boules and leisure time was spent mainly over long voluble meals, in dance-halls, at the cinema or chatting at a local café.

Cinema attendance is back on the rise but elsewhere TV continues its relentless rise: boules is now more a retirement sport, night-clubs attract only a very young urban crowd and even cafés are losing their clientele and being forced to close.

LE WEEKEND Conversely, with one family in nine owning a weekend home, the French are returning to their rural origins and the joys of nature. But not to church: even before the war the French were losing their faith and seeing Catholicism merely as a form of social conformism. Although 75 per cent still describe themselves as Catholic, instead of genuflecting in church, the French now spend their Sundays, and Saturdays, hiking, gardening, eating of course and indulging in the new national pastime of bricolage (DIY), filling sleepy little villages with the happy sounds of hammers and drills.

FOLLOWING THE RULES Back at work the French are a law-abiding lot on the whole. The number of days lost to strikes is low and, at nine per cent, union membership is the lowest in Europe but, as it is concentrated in the public sector, it does not stop even token strikes paralysing the transport, tax or education systems.

When this fails, the French revert to the spirit of 1789 and take to the streets. Doctors, nurses, students and car workers demonstrate; farmers burn British lamb and tip Spanish

Weekend leisure: punting on the Charente river

wine onto motorways; fishermen deliver tons of fish to elected representatives; and lorry drivers bring the whole country to a grinding halt for weeks on end. Even the unemployed, with nothing to lose, joined in the fun in 1998.

The French grumble, but rarely complain, viewing the right to demonstrate as absolute. The government usually intervenes with an amendment and/or a hand-out or two and everything returns to normal – 13 million private gardens and 64 milllion window-boxes require attention, after all.

After two post-war decades of frenetic growth and mindless modernisation, France has finally developed a more rational approach to town planning and, above all, consideration for the 'quality of life'. Since the 1970s, numerous town councils have switched their emphasis from build-ing monolithic housing estates to concentrating on schemes of a more ecological or aesthetic nature.

With more power in the hands of local authorities, architecture and urbanism have become political status symbols: throughout France towns vie with each other to design the most avant-garde pedestrian zone, museum or conference hall, or to carry out the most ambitious programme of restoration.

CHANGING CONDITIONS Somewhat belatedly, the French have recognised the importance of welfare and leisure amenities and the dangers of tower-block ghettos. Earlier this century millions moved from the land to embrace city life, but very often their housing conditions were basic: in 1954, for example, only 10 per cent of French homes had a bath or shower and only 27 per cent had flushing lavatories. But a crash programme of public housing (called HLM, habitation à loyer modéré), which by 1975 peaked at 550,000 homes a year, soon encircled every French town with modern blocks. The nouvelles villes around Paris pursued the same policy on a larger scale. Today basic home comforts are available in nearly all houses: by the mid-1980s only 12 per cent were without a bath or shower. Public housing now looks to individual pavillons springing up on the outskirts of every town, and to more intelligent inner-city projects, while some of the early blocks have been unceremoniously dynamited.

CHANGING TASTES It was really in the 1980s under President Mitterrand that public awareness of architecture blossomed. Visitors to Paris are unlikely to miss seeing what has become the granddaddy of them all: the controversial Centre Pompidou. Built in 1977, of British/Italian design, its polychromatic high-tech design, rising out of the heart of historic Paris, upset many. But it set the tone for a new generation of architects and a new attitude towards public building, and today attracts more visitors than the Eiffel Tower.

BIG IDEAS At his election Mitterrand immediately announced plans for his grands projets while completing others initiated by Giscard d'Estaing (La Villette, Musée d'Orsay). As Paris became a building site and a new billion-franc project hit the drawing-board daily, the French realised that 'modern architecture' was not just a rectangular block. It was becoming more subtle, as were its implications. Accused of harbouring a 'Louis XIV complex', Mitterrand commissioned monument after prestigious monument, while his arch-rival, Jacques Chirac, as Mayor of Paris, played a vanguard action with less visible urban projects, many of which are finally bringing some green to the city. As a result, Paris has become a window of contemporary design – not only by French architects. La Grande Arche looms in the west; Dominique Perrault's Bibliothèque de France rises over eastern Paris. At the same time, behind the scenes, gentrification continues, as districts like Le Marais and Bastille are renovated, rents rise and Paris becomes an increasingly bourgeois city. But will this activity turn it into a stultified museum and strip it of its essential local colour?

REGIONAL STYLE Not slow to follow the capital's example, the provinces have also scrubbed their façades and invested heavily in presenting a modernised image to the rest of Europe. Since the autonomy of the 22 regions was increased in the 1980s, their self-consciousness and individual ambitions have rocketed.

Obsessed by city status, towns such as Montpellier, St-Etienne or Bordeaux compete with each other in attracting foreign investment and in exporting a contemporary image. Every city seems to have its technopole, a concentration of high-tech skills, or its 'international' airport, while modern art museums mushroom.

Apart from massive rebuilding of city centres, many places throughout France were spruced up for the 1993 European ball.

❏ The most extraordinary city project to be found in France is that of Montpellier, where the Catalan architect Ricardo Bofill has designed neo-classical medium-rent social housing that is, in the local Mayor's words, 'the Rome of tomorrow'. ❏

Rouen has been superbly restored, with the omnipresent pedestrian precinct, while the medieval streets of Rodez are gentrified to an almost absurd degree. And this is the danger: if renovation and rebuilding continue at such a rate, France risks losing much of its unique character for the sake of a bland, pristine Euro-face.

La Géode, the spherical cinema in the Parc de la Villette, Paris

If Napoleon, let alone Louis XIV's minister Colbert, could see the political structure of France today, he would certainly turn in his grave. Decentralisation gathers momentum and devolution is a reality in a nation that was once the most centralised of all. This policy really came to fruition in 1982 when Mitterrand's administration granted far greater autonomy to the restructured 22 regions, further increased by direct elections for regional councils in 1986. At the same time, the reorganisation cut across traditional and cultural boundaries, causing bitter controversy throughout the country but particularly in rural areas.

28

CITY SCENE Today, France has a handful of burgeoning cities that are able to stand on a par with European equivalents, from Barcelona to Turin, while at the same time containing any separatist sentiments.

The French provinces were long seen as sleepy, narrow-minded, bourgeois backwaters where only the priest or boule-playing mayor had any importance. Inhabitants of any intelligence were destined for instant intellectual death in what was known as le désert français. Anyone with ambitions or initiative headed straight for Paris, leaving the provinces to Madame Bovary and co.

INDUSTRIAL MAGNETS This rural exodus continued until the last war and well into the 1950s, leaving behind an already under-populated countryside, as people flocked to the growing industrial centres and, of course, to the cultural and economic metropolis of Paris.

But the tide had started to turn under German occupation, when the government was moved to Vichy and the southern provinces, cut off from the north, were forced to act for themselves. This was also the chance for the provincial press to play a role in daily life.

Post-war policies concentrated on catching up, modernising, urbanising and gearing up a

backward industrialisation. Communications were one of France's greatest drawbacks: even in 1970 she had fewer telephone lines than Greece and half as many as the UK or Germany.

Tunnels (Mont Blanc), bridges, motorways and railways were built which opened up new investment possibilities and increased mobility. Today nearly all French households have not only a phone but a Minitel as well, the railway system is one of the most technologically advanced in the world and motorways, though expensive for the user, radiate across the former désert.

A new look: modern civic buildings in Carnac

> ❏ In 1992 Strasbourg set an example of new 'clean city living' by creating a car-free centre and, two years later, by introducing trams. ❏

ABOUT TURN Thus the pattern has changed and even Parisians are moving to the provinces. Increasing inner-city congestion, urban tensions, pollution and a high cost of living have lessened the appeal of the big centres. Looking for a calmer, less neurotic rhythm and more living space at a lower cost, the French are transferring to Montpellier, Lyon, Bordeaux, Toulouse or Grenoble.

Government schemes initially showed the way for the post-war shift: atomic and space research centres were set up in Brittany, mass tourist projects in the Languedoc, Aérospatiale developed the Concorde and Airbus in Toulouse and France's own 'silicon valley', Sophia Antipolis, grew up out of the lavender fields of Provence. Aid often came from the government agency DATAR, created in 1963 to stimulate new economic ventures and help with the infrastructure for these emerging regions. In La Rochelle, an experiment started in 1995 enables you to hire an electric car to take you round in an eco-friendly way.

LIVING OPTIONS However rich the economic life of a town may be, few people want to live there without a reasonable choice of leisure activities. Here, again, the map of France has been radically transformed, first with Malraux's famous Maison de la Culture in the 1960s and more recently with a flood of prestigious new musuems, concert halls and cultural centres.

Jack Lang, Socialist Minister of Culture throughout most of the 1980s, stimulated local decision-making and created specialised schools and major arts festivals throughout the country. Montpellier is now seen as the centre for contemporary dance, Arles and Lyon for photography, Montbéliard for video, Grenoble and Bordeaux for contemporary art. Even so, every artist, however well he is received in the provinces, has to come to Paris for the ultimate consecration.

REGIONAL REDISCOVERY
Psychologically, provincial towns have thrown off the cloak of central state influence and in some cases their populations have trebled over the last 30 years. As the government transfers entire departments of civil servants to the regions and exorbitant rents create a surfeit of empty office space in Paris, the relationship between capital and regions continues to adjust.

ANGLIAE

PARS

London

Douer

Mid...

Duyncke...

Calis

Roan

Ficar...

die

Con stanc

...ay

...ranches

Caez

Paris

Fra

S. Malo

Alencon

Vendofme

nce

...ret aigne

Mans

Loir...

...nnes An

Tours

Orleans

...Jou

Loire flu

...Angiers

Bourges

Nantes

Poictou

Poictiers

Molit...

Rochelle

Limog...

Saintes

Clermo...

Limofin

...ordeaulx

Guien

...rcaxon

ine

Agen

Cahors

Montau ban

...rol

Baiona

Monreal

Toulouse

Carcas fone

Gualcoigne

Narb...

30

The first evidence of human life in the area now known as France goes back nearly half a million years, to a time when the ancestors of modern man left traces of their occupation in the form of stone tools and weapons. Eventually, these people were replaced by the first Neanderthals.

Neanderthals were skilled hunters and workers in stone, but they were unsophisticated in comparison with the next wave of migrants, known now as 'Cro-Magnon' people after the cave where a skeleton was excavated in 1868. The subtlety of Cro-Magnon culture is revealed in the still vibrant wall paintings of the Lascaux caves in Dordogne. This society was gradually subsumed into an age known as Mesolithic, when the nomadic way of life probably gave way to permanent settlements. Some time around 4500 BC, men began to grow food rather than gather it, and to enclose and tame animals rather than manage wild herds. All of this was made possible by the cultivation of grains to feed humans and animals all year. This, the Neolithic Revolution, led to the transformation of the landscape into something approaching the one we know today. The most obvious legacies of the Neolithic era are the complex ceremonial sites such as Carnac, in Brittany.

These monuments were developed by Bronze Age settlers, who introduced metalworking skills. The Neolithic and Bronze Ages spanned nearly 5,000 years, and much of that time was peaceful: the bronze weapons that remain may only have been ceremonial.

The disruption of this peaceful society seems to coincide with the arrival of Celtic tribes. Their culture and ironworking skills mark the beginning of a much more fully documented period of history – due largely to the written records of a new wave of invaders: the Romans.

ROMAN VS GAUL The Celts became known as Gauls to the Romans, who set out to halt their advance into

❏ A famous Gallic uprising against the Romans was led by the chieftain Vercingetorix, who in 52 BC was captured at Alesia, and taken to Rome and executed. Caesar came to be both ally and conqueror of the Gauls, at once helping them to defend themselves in their turn against invaders from across the Rhine and enabling Rome to exploit new territory with trade and taxation. ❏

31

Carved megaliths in Gavrinis

northern Italy. In 190 BC, the Romans came to the defence of the then Greek-owned port of Marseille, and advanced to Narbonne, Aix, Arles and Nîmes. In 58 BC, Julius Caesar finally crushed the Gauls.

In 43 BC, the Romans established their central government at Lyon, and trade to the north, with Britain, and to the south, with Spain and Italy, flourished. The new conquerors built stables (Arles), amphitheatres (Nîmes), circuses (in the Latin Quarter at Paris), baths, aqueducts (Pont du Gard), and founded schools (Autun and Reims), and the whole country was criss-crossed by an efficient network of roads.

The Gauls themselves became increasingly Romanised, benefiting from the new political and economic stability. Many educated Gauls, now speaking a form of Latin, were assimilated into the Roman Empire, and held positions of power within the imperial administration, later being entitled to Roman citizenship.

CHRISTIANITY It was during the Roman period that Christianity was first introduced into France, from the second century AD. Early Christians were persecuted: the great Saint Denis of Paris was beheaded at Montmartre (Martyr's Hill) in AD 262. The turning-point came, however, with the conversion of the Emperor Constantine in the year AD 312, when Christianity became the official state religion. Priests such as Martin of Tours were then eager to drive out the old pagan ways of the Celts, and many monasteries and churches were founded. By the year AD 500, the Church had established itself as a powerful presence alongside the state, and exerted an influence which has continued to the present day.

BARBARIAN INVASIONS From AD 300 onwards, the Roman Empire was in decline, and successive emperors were hard pushed to secure Gaul against the incursions of the Barbarian tribes from Germany. The Romans repeatedly fought back, but when, after AD 400, the great invasions of the Vandals began, the collapse of the empire was inevitable.

Attila the Hun advanced into eastern France and the Romans withdrew to Orléans, Tours and Bordeaux, so that when Rome itself was sacked and finally overrun in AD 455, Gaul was abandoned to the conquering tribes of Visigoths, Burgundians, Alemanni and Franks. In AD 481, Clovis became the first Merovingian king of the Salian Franks, who ruled the area between the Rhine and the Seine, and the foundations were laid of a recognisably modern France.

❏ The Vandals overwhelmed the Romans with their brilliant horsemanship; they fought with bow and arrow from horseback – but according to Saint Jerome they 'could not walk on foot, and once dismounted, count themselves dead'. ❏

The Roman theatre in Orange

During the 500 years of Frankish rule, there was a constant struggle to expand territorial control. The south remained Romanised, with local aristocrats holding most of the land. The walled cities were governed by bishops, and religious schisms showed Christianity's hold was only skin-deep until Charlemagne was crowned in Rome by the Pope in 800.

Clovis' own conversion to Christianity and his political marriage to Clotilda, a Burgundian princess, helped to secure Frankish power over a broader area. This power was under the feudal regime, in which vassals pledged allegiance to their overlords and provided services, taxes and military support in return for protection and benefices. After Clovis, civil strife between warring robber barons was rampant, and successive Merovingian kings, like Dagobert I (628–37), tried in vain to impose law and order. The Frankish kings became rois fainéants ('do-nothing kings') as power was effectively passed to their administrators, the so-called 'mayors of the palace'.

THE CAROLINGIANS In 732, one of these mayors, Charles Martel, usurped royal power, and became the first of the Carolingian kings. Martel led forays against the Arabs,

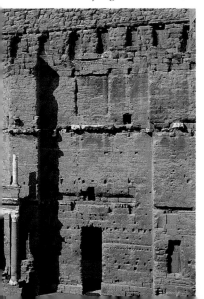

the Burgundians, the Aquitanians and the Saxons, and by confiscating lands and giving these out as fiefs to his followers, established a wide influence.

The long-term project of uniting Gaul was virtually realised by Martel's grandson, Charlemagne, who was crowned in Rome by the Pope on Christmas Day 800, and became the founder of the Holy Roman Empire, an entity which was to last officially for 1,000 years.

Charlemagne was a great warrior and cunning politician, and it was his own personal energy and frequent ruthlessness which held together a vast amalgam of lands in central and western Europe. His capital at Aix-la-Chapelle became the centre of a cultural Renaissance, whose reputation attracted scholars from many lands.

DIVISION OF EMPIRE The feudal cohesion which Charlemagne imposed on Gaul, with a set of counties and marches, was short-lived. On his death in 808, the empire was divided among his sons, and the western section, Francia, fell prey to the ambitions of neighbouring dukes.

Meanwhile, a flourishing civilisation had arisen in the Languedoc, around the counts of Toulouse, and Viking Norsemen, or Normans, as they became known, established themselves at Rouen. The Church had also acquired tremendous authority and great wealth, often using its assets to thwart the policies of the kings. A state of aristocratic anarchy prevailed, and only lip-service was paid to the sovereignty of the Carolingians.

In 987, Hugh Capet was anointed King of France, founding a new dynasty of Capetian kings. Like his predecessors, his range of influence was largely confined to the Ile de France, and for three centuries, royal power was relatively limited. The Church, meanwhile, came under pressure to put an end to corruption. The order of Benedictine monks at Cluny, founded in 909, tried to provide a new moral discipline, claiming a direct link to the Pope in a bid to side-step the powerful bishops.

The Papacy itself had reformed and in 1095 Pope Urban II launched the first Crusade to 'liberate' Palestine from the domination of the Saracens. The Crusades galvanised thousands of French men and women from all classes in a renewal of faith and devotion, in which princes and kings often participated for a mixture of religious and political purposes. Louis IX (1226–70), later canonised, was himself taken captive in Egypt on a crusading expedition and ransomed at an exorbitant fee.

AGE OF LEARNING The Church also promoted learning and scholarship in the new schools and universities. The University of Paris was set up around the year 1200, and soon became the intellectual centre of Europe, attracting famous teachers and

La Rochelle 1372: medieval France was a nation at war

scholars, including Peter Abelard and Thomas Aquinas. And it was during the Middle Ages that Gothic architecture came into its own in superb cathedrals like those at Reims, Amiens, Chartres and Notre Dame in Paris.

HARD TIMES In the 10th and 11th centuries, although trade and commerce had blossomed, the costs of war at home and abroad forced princes to raise taxes. In the early

❏ The Holy Order of the Knights Templar, founded in 1120, had its headquarters in Paris; the Templars' wealth was a coveted prize, and Philip IV brutally suppressed them in 1307 amid appalling torture and execution, seizing their assets for himself. ❏

14th century, poor harvests led to famine and disease; meanwhile, a new class of mercenary knights emerged, regularly switching allegiances between lords.

STRUGGLE FOR SUPREMACY Philip Augustus (1180–1223) consolidated royal power, driving the English out of their Angevin Empire, which had grown up in Aquitania, Brittany, Gascony and Normandy. The King strengthened Paris as his capital city and backed the Church against the Albigensian heretics (Cathars) in the Languedoc. When, in 1245, under Saint Louis, the siege of the hilltop fortress at Montségur ended in the burning of hundreds of Cathars, the independence of the south was broken. From 1309 onwards the popes were in exile at Avignon, a city under the control of the French king. So the Capetians were looking strong at the start of the 14th century. But in 1328, Charles VI died with no male heir. At first the crown passed to Philip IV of Valois, but soon the young King Edward III of England, a grandson of Philip IV, also laid claim to the throne. This dispute led to the devastating Hundred Years' War.

THE HUNDRED YEARS' WAR The war had three main phases. In 1338, Edward seized back lands in Gascony. The English advanced into Poitou, took Caen, and won the historic battle of Crécy in 1346. To add to French misfortunes, the Black Death now swept the land, killing nearly a third of the population and leading in turn to peasant uprisings,

or jacqueries. In 1360, the new king, John II, was captured at Poitiers, and the French were forced to cede Aquitania and Calais to the English.

The second phase of the war followed the death of Edward III and his son the Black Prince, when the English position had begun to weaken. In 1415, Henry V returned to defeat the French at Harfleur and Agincourt, and Aquitania, Normandy, Brittany and Anjou became English territories. Henry married the French king's daughter, but both he and his wife died in 1421, and the quarrel over the throne passed to their infant son, the future Henry VI, and the Dauphin, the future Charles VII.

The third phase of the war brought the shepherdess and saint, Joan of Arc, to raise the siege of Orléans and help Charles to be crowned in the cathedral at Reims. Soon after this, Joan was captured and burnt at the stake in Rouen in 1431, but Charles went on to win decisive victories over the English. When the English eventually withdrew from Normandy in 1453, the Hundred Years' War was finally over.

THE AFTERMATH War and disease had shaken the foundations of feudalism. Aided by a civil service drawn from the emerging bourgeoisie, Louis XI was now able to end the factionalism of the Middle Ages. When he died in 1483, Burgundy, Normandy, Brittany, Picardy, Anjou, Provence and Roussillon were all subdued, and France had begun to develop into a modern nation-state.

The Renaissance was the time of an explosion of tremendous creative energy in the arts, literature, philosophy and science. The city-states of 15th-century Italy had been its birthplace, but the revived knowledge of the ancients and the developing concerns of humanism, together with a new consciousness of exploration and experiment, spread across the whole of Europe.

François I (1515–47) presided over the patronage of the arts in France. Many of the beautiful châteaux of the Loire Valley, like those at Chambord, Chenonceau and Azay-le-Rideau, were built at this time. Art collections and libraries were expanded and artists were attracted to the court, including the Italians Benvenuto Cellini and Leonardo da Vinci (who spent the last years of his life working in France and is buried at Amboise). Literature also flourished, under a group of poets known as the Pleiade; the love poetry of Ronsard and Du Bellay is among the most beautiful in the French language. Rabelais wrote his farcical novels Pantagruel and Gargantua during this period, and the retired mayor of Bordeaux, Michel de Montaigne, composed his essays on knowledge and the enigmas of the human condition.

THE WARS OF RELIGION François built France into the new system of European diplomacy, and negotiated a set of carefully arranged marriages to check the age-old rivalries with England and the powerful Habsburg dynasty which ruled Spain, the Netherlands and the Holy Roman Empire. The picture became more complicated, however, once the Reformation in Germany gained momentum. When, in 1517, Martin Luther was excommunicated, the many German princes took sides in theological debates on trans-substantiation and Papal authority – by championing the Protestant cause. For political reasons, many opposed the Habsburg Emperor, Charles V, who was a Catholic Spaniard.

This political dimension was slow to emerge in France because of the tradition of Gallicanism, which meant that the clergy were more directly linked to the king than to the Pope. Nevertheless, in 1523, the Parlement of Paris seized and burnt Luther's books, and, after some hesitation, the king decided that the Lutheran heretics were a threat to be stamped out.

REPRESSION of the Protestant Huguenots remained ineffectual. In 1536, Jean Calvin published his Institutions of the Christian Religion, and many Frenchmen sought instruction in his teachings in the independent Swiss state of Geneva. Protestant churches continued to spring up throughout France, and in 1560, Charles IX went so far as to issue an amnesty against religious persecution.

However, civil war eventually broke out as the members of the royal household divided between the two faiths in a fight for power. The Prince de Condé headed the Huguenot Montmorency faction against the Duc de Guise, who defended the royalist Catholic cause. The war was fought at different levels, with some full-scale military engagements (at Dreux and Jarnac), and a terrorist campaign of political murders (the Duc de Guise, the Prince de Condé and Henry III were assassinated). But the frequent outbreaks of crowd violence were the most horrifying; on 24 August 1572, thousands of Huguenots were murdered in riots in what became known as the Saint Bartholomew's Day Massacre.

Cardinal Richelieu by Henri Toutin

HENRY IV Supported by the traditionalist Catholic League, Henry of Navarre became the first Bourbon king (1589–1610). He was an ex-Huguenot turned Catholic, and, with his chief administrator Sully, he tried to restore political and social harmony. In 1598, he issued the Edict of Nantes, which guaranteed the right of worship to the Protestants. Although this helped to heal the wounds of civil strife, Henry was himself assassinated by a Catholic extremist while out one day in his carriage.

The reign of Louis XIII (1610–43) saw the rise to power of the great Cardinal Richelieu. Richelieu was a wise and wily statesman, whose strength lay in a dedication to the French national interest. Richelieu set about creating a complex balance of power in Europe, negotiating often secret treaties with different heads of state, playing off the German Protestants against the Catholic Habsburgs during the Thirty Years' War, and contracting alliances via royal marriages, including Charles I of England. At home, he helped Louis cultivate the patronage of dukes and princes, overrode the various parlements and sent out his intendants, or agents of the crown, to collect taxes and manage the fiscal affairs of the state. Richelieu was a prime mover in assuring a strong central government, and did much to resolve the centuries-old antagonism between the nobility and the crown by paving the way for absolute monarchy.

Louis XIV (1643–1715) was France's most glorious and longest reigning king. Only five years old when he ascended the throne, his first task was to secure his position against La Fronde, an alliance of discontented nobles who sought to overthrow him. Louis successfully broke down the opposition and from 1661 onwards he was determined to exercise absolute power. He believed in his God-given right to govern the country and saw the welfare of the state as embodied in his own person: L'Etat, c'est moi became the motto which characterised the Sun King's attitude to his role and to his country.

38

Under his rule, France rose to new heights of prosperity and glory. The rise of mercantilism, masterminded by his minister of finance and loyal supporter Colbert, saw new industries grow up, and imports from the colonies in Canada, Louisiana (named after the king) and India brought massive wealth to the country. By contrast, however, much of this affluence was squandered by the lavish lifestyle of the royal household and by the wars which Louis waged against his European neighbours.

In the 1670s, work began on the construction of the huge and magnificent palace at Versailles. Versailles became the new seat of the court and a symbol of national unity. Everyone jostled to take up residence there and enjoy the endless round of feasts, balls and concerts, the elaborate rules of etiquette and social frivolities which Louis staged to divert the aristocratic families from more serious political concerns. Everything good, it seemed, emanated from the Sun King.

WARRIOR KING Louis also headed an impressive war machine, built up by General Vauban, which he launched into several ill-fated campaigns. In 1672 Louis declared war on Holland, and in 1685 he revoked the Edict of Nantes. These actions incensed the Europeans. The Germans rose up at the hostility

which Louis, a staunch Catholic, had shown towards Protestants; in 1688, William of Orange, himself a Dutch Protestant, became king of England, and soon most of Europe was ranged against France. Yet, in 1689, Louis invaded the Rhineland, and many years of war ensued, in which France suffered eventual defeat.

Undeterred, Louis sparked the War of the Spanish Succession, by insisting that his grandson be settled on the throne of Spain as Philip VI. The Europeans again objected, and after a series of humiliating defeats in the years 1701–13, notably at Blenheim, the French were forced to retreat. The terms of the Treaty of Utrecht involved permanent renunciation of Bourbon claims to rule Spain and the loss of France's main colonies in the Americas.

AGE OF ORDER Louis's reign saw the rise of classicism, in which order, reason and elegance were major features. René Descartes, in his *Discourse on Method* (1637), had laid the foundations for modern science by emphasising the importance of rational argument from observable facts. Love of order is reflected in all the arts of the period, whether in the architectural symmetries of baroque 'hôtels' and 'châteaux', in the layout of parks and ornamental gardens, in Pascal's mechanical 'computers', or in the harrowing precision and logic of Racine's tragedies.

THE ENLIGHTENMENT These trends in science, culture and the life of the mind led, in the 18th century, to the Age of Enlightenment. French philosophes such as Voltaire, Diderot and Rousseau turned their thought to the practical applications of knowledge and the possibilities of social change. The absolutism of the monarchy had grown out of the 1,000-year-old traditions of feudalism, but now its structures were outliving their usefulness. The established Ancien Régime of kings and princes was increasingly alarmed by the spread of revolutionary ideas.

But the storm was brewing. Under Louis XV (1715–74), France was brought closer to the brink of chaos. Rivalries between noble families, the corruption of officials, the widespread abuse of privileges, the division between Paris and

The Sun King: a miniature of Louis XIV, the longest-reigning French king

❑ One of the most unpopular of the many taxes in the 17th century was the salt tax, la gabelle. In some provinces, where salt was a government monopoly, it was compulsory to buy a fixed amount. ❑

the provinces, the incompetent management of the economy, all contributed to the widening gap between rich and poor. Taxation was high, famine and squalor were rife across the land, while a privileged minority lived in the lap of luxury.

In the early years of the reign of Louis XVI (1774–93), food riots were commonplace, the monarchy was bankrupt, the financial and bureaucratic institutions were becoming increasingly rickety and ineffectual, and the time was ripe for massive social and political upheaval.

In 1789 began one of the most dramatic episodes in France's history. In a last-ditch effort to resolve the country's pressing problems, Louis XVI summoned the Estates General, representing the three states of the nobility, the clergy and 'the rest'. The Estates had no real political power, and had not convened since 1614, so their negotiations soon got bogged down over questions of procedure. The Third Estate, representing over 95 per cent of the 20-odd million people of the country, decided to form a breakaway National Assembly.

One morning, finding the door to the meeting-hall inexplicably locked, the Third Estate withdrew to a nearby tennis court and swore an oath not to disperse until they had founded a new constitution. The King, in a panic, dismissed them, and in the ensuing unrest, the crowds in Paris, fearing a military crackdown, stormed the prison of the Bastille on 14 July.

THE REVOLUTION The National Assembly, composed mainly of liberal Girondins and radical Jacobins, issued the Universal Declaration of the Rights of Man. France was divided into a set of administrative départements, and feudal duties and hereditary titles were abolished. At first, the King went along with this new order of things, but in June 1791, he foolishly tried to escape.

❏ Legend has it that Louis XVI was captured at Varennes, because he was recognised from his likeness on a coin. ❏

In September 1791, a constitutional monarchy was officially declared, but there was a growing fear that the émigrés (exiled aristocrats), helped by European heads of state, were going to invade. To pre-empt this, France declared war, and won an immediate, astounding victory at Valmy against the Austrians and Prussians.

FIRST REPUBLIC The imprisoned Louis could no longer be trusted. A new Convention abolished the monarchy and proclaimed the First Republic. In 1793, Louis was put on trial for treason, convicted and guillotined. Unfortunately, none of this revolutionary activity had really helped to solve the severe domestic problems of food shortages and money. In April 1793, a Committee of Public Safety was created to impose social reforms, ensure law and order and protect the Revolution. A power struggle among the Revolutionary leaders led to the Jacobins ousting the Girondins. Robespierre, who emerged as virtual dictator, unleashed a Reign of Terror.

The Revolution now spun out of control and turned into a bloodbath of executions, wiping out thousands of former nobles, clergy and ordinary 'citizens'. Even the original leaders, Desmoulins, Danton, Saint-Just and the incorruptible

The Emperor Napoleon

Robespierre himself, were sent to the guillotine. In 1795 a Directory, politically conservative and backed by the army, attempted to restore order, but its efforts remained futile, until an opportunistic Corsican, General Napoleon Bonaparte, mounted a surprise coup d'état in 1799.

NAPOLEON AND EMPIRE Napoleon immediately established his own brand of personal dictatorship. He was immensely successful. At home, he reformed taxation, confirmed the post-Revolutionary property rights, set up a Bank of France to help the economy, developed the Code Napoléon to administer the law of the land, and restored the Church. He then launched into a series of brilliant military campaigns which swept across Europe. In the decade 1800–10, the French won victories at the battles of Marengo, Austerlitz, Jena and Wagram, and gained control over Italy, Spain, Germany and Poland. In 1804, Napoleon had himself crowned Emperor in Rome.

Napoleon at the head of his staff

Europe fought back. Britain and Spain counter-attacked in the Iberian Peninsula, while a sea blockade starved France of important trade and supplies. In 1812, Napoleon launched an ill-fated Russian campaign, prevailing at the hard-fought battle of Borodino and marching into a tactically deserted Moscow. The severe Russian winter proved fatal. Napoleon's lines of communication and supplies were badly overstretched, and the grande armée was forced into ignominious retreat. Thousands of soldiers perished in the snow. At Leipzig, the French suffered a crushing defeat, and eventually in March 1814, Napoleon abdicated.

EXILE Even this was not the end of the irrepressible petit caporal. In 1815, Napoleon escaped from exile on the Mediterranean island of Elba, and staged a brief comeback, only to be conclusively overcome at the Battle of Waterloo. This time, his captors banished him to remote St Helena in the south Atlantic, where he died in 1821. The man was dead, but the Napoleonic legend, and the legacy, lives on.

> ❏ During his crowning ceremony, Napoleon seized the imperial crown from the hands of the Pope and placed it on his own head. ❏

After Napoleon, the Bourbon monarchy was restored. Under Louis XVIII (1814–24) France settled into a period of much-needed peace, while Charles X (1824–30) tried to turn the political clock back to reinstate the old ways. Such reaction was in vain, however, for the bourgeoisie were hungry for power, and the momentum of industrialisation created new aspirations which backward-looking policies could not hope to fulfil. In the summer of 1830, the barricades went up in Paris, the King abdicated, and Louis-Philippe was made head of the 'July monarchy'.

Now a rapid industrial revolution took place. Output in coal, iron and textiles multiplied, and a national railway system was developed. As the money-grabbing middle classes grew rich, however, the working classes felt increasingly oppressed. Romanticism gave expression to the complex feelings of dislocation France was experiencing. Writers such as Châteaubriand, Vigny and Hugo evoked a nostalgia for the past, and the value of individual imagination and emotion was invoked against the constraints of reason and routine. Socialist philosophies also sprang up, with thinkers like Saint-Simon and Fourier offering visions of an alternative social order often prefiguring much in Marxism.

THE 1848 REVOLUTION By 1848, the spectre of revolution again haunted Europe. Food shortages and a recession had starving peasants on the rampage in the countryside, and the crowds in Paris again took to the barricades. Armed insurrection forced Louis-Philippe to abandon his throne, and the Second Republic was proclaimed. Once again, heady idealism failed to effect any substantial changes; then out of the turmoil emerged Louis-Napoléon, the emperor's nephew, who managed to get himself elected France's first president. He first took steps to enhance his popularity, and then, in 1851, seized his chance to mount his own coup d'état and crowned himself Emperor.

Napoleon III, as he now was, steered a course between competing political factions and enabled France to prosper. The right to vote was extended, trade unions were made legal and schools educated more of the young. In 1869, the Suez Canal, a vast engineering project backed by the French, opened the way to increased trade with the Far East. Baron Haussmann undertook the systematic modernisation of the capital, clearing slums and laying out the boulevards, squares and gardens which have made Paris so renowned a metropolis.

TIPPING THE BALANCE Across the Rhine, Chancellor Bismarck was busy unifying Germany and

Henri Toulouse-Lautrec...

destabilising the balance of power. In 1870, diplomatic provocation gave way to war. France lost battles at Metz and Sedan, and Napoleon III was himself taken prisoner. Paris fell to the advancing Prussian army. After the calamity of defeat, a new National Assembly clung to nervous conservative policies. In March 1871, a more radical municipal council was elected in Paris; the 'Commune' rose up against the national government, who sent in troops to besiege the capital. After six weeks of fierce guerrilla-style urban warfare, the uprising was crushed, and some 20,000 communards were either summarily shot or deported.

FIN DE SIECLE In 1875, France made a new start with the Third Republic. The political division between left and right persisted. Socialism gained ground, with a growing labour movement led by Jaurès, and for a time it was feared that the conservatives, under General Boulanger, might try another coup. Meanwhile, investment abroad brought great wealth from the colonies in Indo-China, northern and Black Africa, and the Near East. France boasted an empire second only to Great Britain's.

Deep social divisions became manifest in the Dreyfus affair. In 1896, Captain Dreyfus, a Jewish army officer, was accused of espionage. On forged evidence, he was deported to the notorious penal colony at Devil's Island. The whole of France split into two camps over the question of his innocence. Among the traditionalist Catholics, anti-semitic feelings ran high, while Emile Zola, in his famous article J'accuse, denounced a miscarriage of justice. Eventually, Dreyfus was acquitted, but the bitterness the affair aroused was long-lived.

REVOLUTIONS IN ART During this time, a wave of experimentation broke in the arts. In literature, the realism of the great novelists, Balzac and Flaubert, gave way to Proust's meditations on time and memory, while the sensual poetry of Baudelaire was followed by the ethereal symbolism of Mallarmé's sonnets. In the visual arts, Impressionism outraged the traditional salons, as new techniques in composition and colour were developed by Manet, Monet, Cézanne, Gauguin, Pissarro, Renoir and Van Gogh. In music, too, new textures of sound and tonal harmony were introduced by Debussy, Satie and Saint-Saëns; and the new arts of photography, developed by Daguerre, the cinema, developed by the Lumière brothers, and the commercial poster-art of Toulouse-Lautrec, captured the popular imagination as the century moved into a mood of fin-de-siècle decadence.

Meanwhile, super-power rivalries loomed large. Germany's attempts to isolate France were outmanoeuvred by a defence pact with the Czar and the entente cordiale with Britain. Austria–Hungary's interventions in the Balkans threatened access to Suez, and to oil. The spiral of the arms race brought the European imperialists to an unavoidable showdown.

...celebrating a new age in French art and decadence

The assassination of Archduke Franz Ferdinand of Austria, in Sarajevo in June 1914, was the trip-wire which plunged Europe into war. Austria declared war on Russia; and when Russia responded, Germany in turn declared war on Russia, and then Britain and France declared war on Germany. The well-rehearsed Schlieffen Plan allowed German forces to move swiftly through Belgium and penetrate into north-eastern France.

The battle of the Marne halted the German advance, and years of trench warfare followed. Thousands fell, at Ypres, at Passchendaele, defending a few yards of mud in fields where once poppies blossomed. In 1916, Marshal Pétain held the symbolic stronghold of Verdun against persistent attack, before launching a counter-offensive on the Somme. The stalemate was only broken by the intervention of the Americans, who entered the war in 1917, finally forcing the Germans to capitulate in November 1918.

THE COST OF THE WAR A

generation of young French men had been sacrificed, with over a million dead and 3 million wounded. Large areas of Flanders and the Ardennes were devastated. Inflation and the national debt had rocketed. The gains were comparatively slight: Alsace and Lorraine were returned to France, and the Treaty of Versailles, signed in 1919, imposed massive war reparations on the Germans.

After the horrors of the trenches, many Frenchmen turned to promoting the cause of peace, and France contributed significantly to the newly created League of Nations and international conferences on disarmament. In the 1920s, reconstruction was initially paid for out of the reparation money from Germany; when the Germans stopped paying, French troops were sent to occupy the Ruhr. In spite of a series of unstable governments, things were relatively buoyant, until the Wall Street crash of 1929

provoked a world recession. In the 1930s, unemployment rose, and the French economy nosedived. Some feared, and others hoped, that there would be a Communist takeover, but the socialist Front Populaire, elected in 1936 under Léon Blum, was shortlived.

APPEASEMENT AND WAR

Meanwhile, the Nazis were gaining strength in Germany. In 1935, Hitler broke the terms of the peace and ordered German rearmament. The French, fearing a collision course, sought to contain Germany with a series of fragile alliances, and even agreed to German expansion in the east. In 1938, Hitler annexed Austria

Greed, Revenge and other devils sign the Treaty of Versailles, 1919

General de Gaulle makes his come-back in 1946

and the Sudetenland in Czechoslovakia, and, signing a non-aggression pact with the Soviet Union, invaded Poland. Finally, both Britain and France abandoned their policy of appeasement and declared war.

WORLD WAR II The quiet months of the so-called 'phoney war' were shattered by the Blitzkrieg of April 1940: Hitler invaded Belgium, Denmark and Holland, and dodged the Maginot Line, in which France had invested heavily after 1918 to prevent another German attack. After the panic evacuation from the beaches of Dunkerque, Nazi stormtroopers marched into Paris.

> ❏ 'The French will only be united under the threat of danger. Nobody can simply bring together a country that has 265 kinds of cheese.' – Charles de Gaulle ❏

The collapse of France was a deep humiliation. The country was divided into occupied territory in the north and a 'free' zone in the south, with a seat of government at Vichy headed by Pétain. Many fell into collaboration with the Nazis; the authorities deported Jews to the concentration camps and betrayed agents working in the French resistance. On the other side, underground resistance groups, like Combat and Libération and the famous Maquis, courageously helped prisoners of war to escape or planned attacks on military installations. They were aligned with the Free French Forces headed by General Charles de Gaulle, based in London, who acted as rallying point and a symbol of hope.

LIBERATION As the war progressed, Hitler's forces were worn down on the eastern front, and the Americans and British united to prepare an invasion. In June 1944, the first landings on the beaches of Normandy were launched and the Nazis were steadily driven back out of France.

In August, Paris was liberated, and de Gaulle led a victory parade along the Champs-Elysées. Former collaborators were shot or publicly humiliated or, like Pétain, sentenced to prison. De Gaulle founded a provisional government to bring back to life a country once more ravaged by war. A national referendum opted for the creation of a new state, and in May 1946 the constitution of the Fourth Republic was declared. After 40 years of strife, France was ready to set itself on the road to reconciliation and recovery.

In the aftermath of war, France had to rebuild its infrastructure but also its entire economy and a new national identity. This involved a constant tension between the desire for traditional independence and the harsh realities of the modern world. It was with the aid of the Marshall Plan, that Jean Monnet's Four Year Plans were able to relaunch French industry.

In 1951, the European Coal and Steel Community linked France to West Germany, Italy and the Benelux countries, and this formed the basis of the European Economic Community. In the realm of defence, French wishes for a European 'column' were overridden by the American-led NATO, which held sway as the Cold War developed.

OVERSEAS France now entered the traumatic era of decolonialisation. French paratroopers were routed at Dien Bien Phu in 1954, dealing a severe blow to the nation's morale. In 1956, Egypt seized the Suez Canal. Britain and France invaded to protect navigation rights, but this turned into a fiasco after American intervention and Soviet threats persuaded them to withdraw. And then there was Algeria.

ALGERIA Although Syria, Lebanon, Tunisia and Morocco were all granted independence peacefully, it was Algeria which focused political tensions. Since 1945, the Algerian National Liberation Front had kept up a campaign of terrorism, but the large number of settled French colons were unwilling to relinquish power. More and more troops were despatched to keep law and order, though there were sinister reports of unlawful torture and bombings. The generals commanding the army in Algeria threatened rebellion, and even for a time seized Corsica. The crisis caused the collapse of the government, and with it the Fourth Republic.

THE FIFTH REPUBLIC General de Gaulle was recalled from retirement to help solve the dilemma. He instituted the Fifth Republic, giving him, as president, increased powers, and opted first for a version of Algerian 'self-determination'. His decision proved unpopular among the members of the Organisation de l'Armée secrète, composed of disgruntled officers and colons, who mounted a terrorist campaign of their own. But de Gaulle stood his ground and in 1962 Algeria was granted independence.

Under de Gaulle, the 1960s became a time of rapid modernisation. A wilting economy was boosted as France espoused consumerism. De Gaulle himself was all for traditional grandeur. His dream was for a united Europe stretching 'from the Atlantic to the Urals'. He resented American influence, and in 1966 he withdrew from NATO and forged ahead with the development of the independent nuclear force de frappe. He ensured that France would continue to play a leading role in the Common Market by twice saying Non! to entry by the United Kingdom.

UPRISINGS For all his experience and political astuteness, de Gaulle was unprepared for les événements of May 1968. Students and workers took to the streets to protest against the Vietnam War, wage settlements and the 'system'; riot police stormed the barricades with tear gas and truncheon charges, and within days a general strike brought the whole country to a standstill. Somewhat at a loss, de Gaulle called for fresh elections, but when his proposals for reform were rejected in a national referendum, he retired from the stage.

In the 1970s, both Presidents

François Mitterrand addresses the Socialists in 1973

Georges Pompidou and Valéry Giscard d'Estaing continued to pursue broadly Gaullist policies. The oil crisis of 1973 brought inflation and recession, and the alliance between the socialists and the communists gained ground. In 1981, finally, the Socialist François Mitterrand was elected to the presidency. Sweeping social changes were expected, and new legislation provided for more nationalisation, ensured a minimum wage, and ended capital punishment. But harsh economic realities forced the government to backtrack into a policy of austerity, and disillusionment set in. In 1986, France weathered another constitutional crisis when a conservative prime minister, Jacques Chirac, was appointed to 'cohabit' with a socialist president. In 1988, Mitterrand was elected to a second term. The political situation remained stable until 1993 when the electorate swung massively to the right, elected Chirac president in 1995 and then swung even more massively to the left in 1997, leaving Chirac to 'cohabit' from the other side of the fence.

In recent years, France has adopted a thoroughly modern outlook, building high-speed trains, a Channel Tunnel, nuclear reactors and space rockets, while not neglecting to restore its Gothic cathedrals, tend its vineyards and expand its art galleries. This is a country which has settled into its new role as a major post-industrial nation with long traditions and a rich culture.

Part-Dieu station, Lyon. The national rail network symbolises modern France

PARIS - PERIPHERIQUE

Paris

PARISIANS are a country if not a race unto themselves, notorious for their superiority complex, high fashion, argumentative qualities and speedy approach to life. Paris is certainly not where the expression douceur de vivre originated. But it is an intellectual and artistic hotbed that has always enjoyed exporting its ideas, while happily importing and absorbing those of visiting foreigners. Although long vilified for their off-hand attitude to tourists, Parisians have actually become more approachable.

And the face of the city itself is also being transformed: scrubbed, renovated, relandscaped, rebuilt, it has hardly stopped to breathe over the last 20 years and looks ambitiously to the future.

CHARMED CIRCLE Nestling in the thickly forested saucer of the Ile de France, the intramuros population of Paris is just over 2 million; but if you count a growing number of satellite towns and the suburbs of the Ile de France it exceeds 10 million. Yet however accessible the suburbs become, Parisian snobbery reigns supreme; the 'true Parisian' lives inside the circle of 19th-century portes which contain its 20 arrondissements. Outside that limit are the banlieusards, the suburbanites, commuting into the centre by RER.

Over 75 per cent of suburban dwellers use cars, since their local transport, excluding the limited RER network, is totally abysmal and there is no other choice. Monstrous traffic jams build up in Paris and on the périphérique (ring-road) are part of their daily lives – sometimes stretching the 25km as far as Roissy airport. Amenities are still being developed and much

Opposite: the Arc de Triomphe is spectacular at night
Below: Notre-Dame, one of the world's most famous monuments

thoughtless suburban planning of the 1960s and 1970s has left a generation of lost souls and a few delinquents. Many of France's North African immigrants live in these characterless areas and have become targets for increasingly frequent racist attacks.

THE NEW LOOK At the same time, some of the most controversial architecture of Paris is appearing in satellite towns such as Noisy-le-Grand, St-Quentin-en-Yvelines or Cergy-Pontoise. Cultural facilities have grown from the days of Malraux's famous Maisons de Culture and inner suburbs such as Bobigny, Gennevilliers, Nanterre or St-Denis now boast modern theatres staging international productions.

For visitors driving around the Ile de France and coming into Paris, the landscape is not always as expected. Often resembling a New Jersey freeway peppered with an unplanned array of hoardings and advertisements, the routes nationales can be a shock. But turn off suddenly to follow the road to a château and you may find yourself in rolling, forested terrain. When not a spread of instant bungalows, villages are spruce, no stone out of place, and more than likely half the houses belong to Parisian weekenders. Avoid routes entering the capital on a Sunday night: traffic jams are guaranteed.

PARIS LIFE In the centre of Paris getting about is easy if you stick to the excellent public transport system or your own two feet. Distances are not great and by metro it is unlikely to take more than 30 minutes from one end of a line to the other. Join in the Parisian way of life in the cafés of St-Germain or the new haunts of the Bastille; dine in animated brasseries or bistros where shared tables give an opportunity to chat with fellow diners.

Parisians lead fast lives, spending freely, and in consequence have to earn well to keep up. Time is valuable, and at the end of the day tempers can be frayed. But underneath the gruff exterior is a converted peasant dying to crack a joke, or a radical intellectual ready to chew the cud. The spirit of Paris, as well as its illuminated monuments, well deserve the description 'city of light'.

▶▶▶ CITY HIGHLIGHTS

Arc de Triomphe
page 52
Arts Décoratifs, Musée des *page 52*
Beaubourg *page 56*
Concorde, Place de la *page 52*
Eiffel, Tour *page 55*
Louvre *page 52*
Le Marais *page 56*
Montmartre and Sacré Cœur *page 59*
Notre-Dame *page 57*
Orsay, Musée d' *page 54*
St-Germain *page 54*
Tuileries, Jardins des *page 52*

PARIS

50

Cimet
de
Montm

Station
Pont Cardinet

Square des
Batignolles

AVE DE CLICHY

AVE DE ST-OUEN

BLVD BERTHIER

AVE DE LA PORTE DE CHAMPERRET

AVENUE DE VILLIERS

17

BOULEVARD DES BATIGNOLLES

RUE DE CLICHY

RUE D'AMSTERDAM

BLVD GOUVION ST-CYR

Porte des
Ternes

Palais des
Congrès

AVENUE DE WAGRAM

BLVD DE COURCELLES

Parc de
Monceau

St-Augustin

Gare
St-Lazare

RUE ST-LAZARE

Porte
Maillot

AVENUE DE LA
GRANDE ARMEE

AVE DE FRIEDLAND

Musée
Jacquemart
André

BOULEVARD MALESHERBES

RUE DE LA
PEPINIERE

RUE ST-LAZARE

RUE DU HAVRE

BOULEVARD HAUSSMANN

Arc de Triomphe

Lido

AVENUE FOCH

PLACE CHARLES
DE GAULLE
ETOILE

VICTOR HUGO

AVENUE

16

AVENUE D'IENA

Office
du
Tourisme

AVENUE DES CHAMPS-ELYSEES

8

Palais de
l'Elysée

Ste-Marie
Madeleine

PLACE
DE LA
MADELEINE

Opéra

BLVD DES
CAPUCINES

PLACE
VENDOME

RUE TRONCHET

St-R

Palais
Galliera

Palais de Tokyo

AVENUE MARCEAU

Grand
Palais

Petit
Palais

Jeu de
Paume

RUE ROYALE

RUE DE RIVOLI

Palais de
Chaillot

COURS
ALBERT 1er

COURS LA REINE

PLACE
DE LA
CONCORDE

Orangerie

Jardin des
Tuileries

Con

QUAI
DES
TUILERIES

Jardins du
Trocadéro

QUAI DE NEW YORK

Seine

PONT
D'IENA

QUAI D'ORSAY

QUAI D'ORSAY

PONT
ALEXANDRE
III

RUE DE BOURGOGNE

QUAI
ANATOLE FRANCE

QUAI
VOLTAIR

Tour Eiffel

AVENUE BOSQUET

Esplanade
des
Invalides

Assemblée
Nationale-
Palais
Bourbon

Musée
d'Orsay

RUE DU BAC

Parc du
Champ
de Mars

7

BLVD DE
LA TOUR-MAUBOURG

Hôtel des
Invalides

Musée Rodin

RUE DE VARENNE

RUE ST-GERMAIN

Ecole des
Beaux-Ar

St-Germain
des Prés

B

AVE DE TOURVILLE

Hôtel
Matignon

RUE DE BABYLONE

BOULEVARD

Ecole
Militaire

AVE DE LOWENDAL

BLVD DES INVALIDES

AVE DE BRETEUIL

RUE DE RENNES

6

UNESCO

BLVD GARIBALDI

BOULEVARD
DE GRENELLE

QUAI DE GRENELLE

AVENUE EMILE ZOLA

2

15

RUE LECOURBE

BLVD PASTEUR

RUE DE VAUGIRARD

BOULEVARD DU MONTPARNASS

BLVD RASPAIL

RUE
LEBLANC

BOULEVARD VICTOR

Porte de
Sèvres

Parc des
Expositions

BOULEVARD LEFEBVRE

Porte de la
Plaine

RUE DE VAUGIRARD

Gare
Montparnasse

BLVD
DE VAUGIRARD

Tour
Montparnasse

Cimetière
du
Montparnasse

RUE FROIDEVAUX

14

PERIPHERIQUE

RUE
ERNEST
RENAN

0   ½   1 km

0   ½ mile

A   B   C

Viewing one of the 30,000 works of art in the Louvre...

Beat the queues by booking your entrance ticket in advance at any FNAC store in France, or on Minitel 3615 Louvre, or by calling 01 49 87 54 54.

...and recovering near the Arc de Triomphe

Rive Droite

Covering a much greater area than the Rive Gauche, the Rive Droite governs the north, east and west of Paris in a curved sweep north of the Seine. This is where most museums and monuments are concentrated as well as regal squares and boulevards, often the results of Baron Haussmann's frenetic urban transformations in the mid-19th century. Less intimate in scale, more disparate in style, it ranges from tackiness to high luxury.

The Louvre▶▶▶ Hard to miss in its central riverside location is the Louvre, now face-lifted and expanded to be the world's largest museum and entered through IM Peï's controversial glass pyramid (a new entrance is under construction in the Denon Wing facing the Seine). Symbol of seven centuries and 17 rulers, the Louvre developed from 12th-century fortress origins, and was rebuilt and extended in Renaissance style by François I and classical style by Louis XIV, who completed the awesome Cour Carrée. The royal art collection was first displayed to the public during the Revolutionary period; today 30,000 works are exhibited, while many more remain in storage. Archaeological treasures found during recent excavations have added to the permanent display. The marble entrance under the pyramid skylight leads to the three wings, with categories and 'hit' exhibits (*Venus de Milo, Mona Lisa,* etc) well signposted.

In the same Louvre complex is the less frequented **Musée des Arts Décoratifs**▶▶, (entrance 107 rue de Rivoli) with furniture, decorative objects and reconstituted period rooms from the Middle Ages to the present (closed until 2000 except for Medieval and Renaissance rooms). Its immediate neighbour is the **Musée de la Mode et du Textile**▶. In contrast the arcades of the **rue de Rivoli** outside offer wares designed solely for the visiting masses.

Unique Viewpoint Looking through Napoleon's **Arc du Carrousel** due west, you see one of the city's great perspectives: through the **Jardins des Tuileries** to the **Concorde**, up the **Champs-Elysées** to the **Arc de Triomphe** and beyond to the new office blocks of **La Défense** and the **Grande Arche**. The Tuileries house both the **Orangerie**▶▶, with Monet's spectacular large-scale series of Nymphéas, and the renovated **Jeu de Paume**▶, now a contemporary art exhibition centre. The terrace outside provides an unbeatable view across the Concorde with its swirling, snarling traffic, its Egyptian obelisk, neo-classical mansions and across the Seine to the **Palais Bourbon**, home of the National Assembly, while in the distance looms the **Tour Eiffel** and the glass domes of the **Grand-Palais**.

The Grand-Palais was built for the 1900 Exposition Universelle, and epitomises the soaring domed iron and glass architectural style, while the **Petit-Palais** opposite is more baroque in style. Both are used for major historical retrospectives while the sheer scale of the Grand-Palais (undergoing repairs) accommodates a permanent science museum, the Palais de la Découverte. **The**

Concorde to the Palais-Royal

Starting at the Concorde, walk up to the Jeu de Paume, then back to the terrace where steps lead to road-level. Turn left off the rue de Rivoli up the rue de Castiglione to the place Vendôme. Cross the square and turn right down the rue Casanova which becomes the rue des Petits-Champs. After the Bibliothèque Nationale, turn right to the rue de Beaujolais, which leads to the Palais-Royal; pass the 1806 restaurant, Le Grand Véfour. Walk through the gardens, past the back of the Comédie Française. Emerging on the place du Palais-Royal, either enter the Louvre or turn left along the rue St-Honoré to Les Halles.

Champs-Elysées is no longer what it was. Invaded by fast-food joints and shopping arcades, its main attraction lies in large-screen cinemas and Napoleon's Arch which crowns the crossroads, **L'Etoile**. Its summit platform is accessible by lift. Immediately to the north of the Louvre, on the **place du Palais-Royal**, stands the famous theatre, the **Comédie Française**, and behind this are the **Palais-Royal Gardens**. The palace was built in 1642 and the adjacent apartments in 1780, their arcades soon sheltering fashionable cafés. In the front courtyard are Daniel Buren's controversial 1986 striped columns.

Running northwest from the Palais-Royal, the avenue de l'Opéra culminates in the **Opera House▶▶**. Garnier's lavishly ornate design, completed in 1875, comes into its own inside, with a *grand escalier* of breathtaking magnificence. Leading off the place de l'Opéra is the **rue de la Paix**, lined with top jewellers; this runs into the place **Vendôme▶▶** (1715), home to the Ritz and crowned by a column commemorating Napoleon's victories.

The nearby **rue St-Honoré** epitomises the Rive Droite: its western end, the Faubourg, boasts luxury boutiques, while to the east are echoes of the 'belly of Paris', **Les Halles**, a meeting point for itinerant youth.

Above: the skylit Forum des Halles was part of a controversial 1970s redevelopment of the old central market of Les Halles

60,000 BULLOCKS
In pre-Revolutionary days the Parisian population was 600,000. Its annual consumption was the following: 60,000 bullocks, 15–20,000 cows, 200,000 calves, 420,000 sheep: estimated total of 42 million kilos of meat.

Rive Gauche

Stretching from the **Quartier Latin** (5th) in the east across the increasingly bourgeois hub of **St-Germain-des-Prés** (6th) to the sedate 7th *arrondissement* and its pinnacle, the **Tour Eiffel**, the heart of the Rive Gauche is part official-dom, part academia, part bohemia and part aesthetics. Some inhabitants claim never to cross the Seine and it is easy to understand why. Narrow streets lined with fasci-nating shops, cinemas, galleries and inviting bistros combine with academic monuments and literary cafés to create an atmosphere more of *far niente* than of a hectic capital city.

The Sorbonne Students have traditionally mono-polised the 5th since the Sorbonne's foundation in 1257. Now joined by other colleges, it seems impervious to time: twisting streets full of bookshops, cheap eateries and his-toric churches, culminating in the **Panthéon** at the summit of the Montagne Ste-Geneviève. To the east lies Jean Nouvel's striking **Institut du Monde Arabe**, and the Jardin des Plantes, home to botanical gardens and the superbly renovated **natural history museum▶▶**.

Musée de Cluny On the crossroads of boulevards St-Michel and St-Germain, the **Musée de Cluny▶▶▶** clearly represents the span of the Quartier Latin's early history: don't miss the Roman baths integrated into this superb Gothic mansion. Its collections include the famous *Dame à la Licorne*, a series of six allegorical 15th-century tapestries; the Gallery of Kings, sculpted heads lopped off Notre-Dame by an angry mob in 1793; and a rich panorama of other medieval treasures.

St-Germain Beyond boulevard St-Michel, the atmos-phere changes as the 6th *arrondissement* begins. Rising above the central crossroads of the rue de Rennes and the boulevard St-Germain is the Romanesque tower of the 1163 **church▶▶**, worth visiting for its architecture and evening concerts. Once a powerful Benedictine monastery, its fortifications disappeared in the late 17th century to make way for the residential Faubourg St-Germain. Close by are the **Brasserie Lipp**, the **Café de Flore** and the **Deux Magots**, all intellectual havens. Beyond streets of fashion boutiques is the church of **St-Sulpice**, famous for its gigantic 6,588-pipe organ and murals by Delacroix.

Ideal for promenading, jogging or sun-bathing, the **Jardin du Luxembourg▶▶**, redolent of *nouvelle vague* films, stretches south from Marie de Médicis' **Palais du Luxembourg**, now home to the Senate, as far as the boulevard du Montparnasse.

Musée d'Orsay Back down at the Seine, linking the 6th and 7th *arrondissements*, is the **Musée d'Orsay ▶▶▶**. Once a hotel and railway station, it is now a spectacu-larly renovated museum devoted to art and applied arts,1848–1914. Beneath Laloux's soaring 1900 shell are galleries taking you from Romanticism through monu-mental academic works to Symbolism, the Ecole de Barbizon and finally to the jewel in the Orsay's crown – the Impressionists.

54

Art: the street version, as practised on the Left Bank

The sculptor Auguste Rodin (1840–1917) has his own delightful museum, south of the boulevard St-Germain. Set in one of the 7th *arrondissement's* loveliest gardens, the **Musée Rodin**▶▶ has a strong collection of bronzes and marble works. The **Assemblée Nationale** lies to the north, glowering across the bridge at the Concorde.

Les Invalides The most impressively scaled monument of the Rive Gauche was built under Louis XIV to house 6,000 invalid soldiers – hence its name. Inside this massive group of buildings is the vast military collection of the **Musée de l'Armée**, while towering over it all is the magnificent baroque church, **l'Eglise du Dôme**▶▶. Some of France's greatest soldiers are entombed here, including Napoleon, encased like a Russian doll in six coffins. Leading elegantly west from the military academy are the formal gardens of the **Champ-de-Mars**, crowned at their end with the **Tour Eiffel**▶▶, built for the Exposition Universelle of 1889 by the engineer Gustave Eiffel. Much criticised at the time, its technical ingenuity was soon recognised. Walk below it, climb it, dine at it, gaze over Paris from it, day or night: you won't forget it.

Inside the Musée d'Orsay

Pont des Arts to rue Soufflot

Starting from the Pont des Arts, walk east along the Quai de Conti, past the Institut de France, home to the Académie Française, and turn right at the Hôtel de la Monnaie. The narrow rue Guénégaud leads past galleries to the rue Mazarine. Turn left here, following it to the boulevard St-Germain, passing Paris's first café, Le Procope. At the three-pronged fork leading south from Odéon, take the left street, the rue Monsieur-le-Prince, which winds uphill to the rue Racine. Turn right here to arrive at the Théâtre de l'Odéon, behind which unfolds the Jardin du Luxembourg. Return to the north-east corner and emerge on to the boulevard St-Michel. Straight ahead is the rue Soufflot, which conceals a Gallo-Roman forum and ends at the Panthéon.

Floor-level shopping at Les Halles: buskers, street artists, tramps, fashion victims and sub-urban youth share this central urban park

Bateaux-mouches ply the Seine day and night, taking in Notre-Dame on the circuit

Le Marais and the Ile de la Cité

The transformation of Les Halles and Le Marais is a phenomenon barely 20 years old. Stretching from Les Halles eastwards to the Bastille, the renovated **Marais** has almost completely recovered the fashionable identity of its mainly 17th-century origins. Although geographically bordered to the south by the Seine, its historic character spills over on to the **Ile St-Louis**. The other, larger island, the **Ile de la Cité**, is the historic heart of Paris.

Beaubourg Officially known as the **Centre Pompidou►►**, its twentieth anniversary in 1997 foresaw its total closure until 2000, for a much-needed facelift, worn out by 20,000 visitors a day (5,000 at most were anticipated). Its multicoloured high-tech architecture reigns over a completely renovated *quartier* which includes the site of the former vegetable market, now an underground shopping and leisure centre. Beaubourg itself shelters the **Musée d'Art Moderne►** and other cultural activities, while its precinct below (also being restored) buzzes with crowds drawn to a ragged army of street artists.

Le Marais Immediately east starts **Le Marais►►**, now bristling with trendy restaurants and bars, art galleries and boutiques. Propelled to its zenith in the 17th century when aristocrats vied with each other to build the most elegant mansion, it became home to literary salons, duels and power struggles. Today some of its narrow streets shelter mainly Chinese jewellery wholesalers (notably Rue de Temple), replacing traditional craftsmen, and a lively Jewish quarter dating from the 13th century, the **rue des Rosiers**. The **Musée d'Art et d'Histoire du Judaïsme►** in the Hôtel de Saint-Aignan is fascinating. The **rue Rambuteau**, leading into the **rue des Francs-Bourgeois**, is the main east–west axis along which are located monuments such as the magnificent **Hôtel de Soubise►**, housing the Musée de l'Histoire de France, and the **Hôtel Carnavalet►►**, which contains a fascinating museum covering the history of Paris, as well as superb period rooms, including those of illustrious former resident Madame de Sévigné. One block north stands the beautifully renovated Hôtel Salé, which in 1985 opened as the **Musée Picasso►►**.

Place des Vosges Le Marais culminates in the east in the perfect symmetry of the **place des Vosges►►**, completed in 1612. Once the site of a royal palace, its 36 red-brick mansions soon housed the *crème de la crème* of Parisian aristocracy and literati, today replaced by successful designers and artists. One former resident, Victor Hugo, has left a museum well worth a visit. Across the rue St-Antoine, Le Marais claims further landmarks such as the medieval **Hôtel de Sens**, the **Hôtel de Sully** and, behind the **Hôtel de Ville**, the church of **St-Gervais-St-Protais**.

Bastille Indelibly marked as a Revolutionary symbol, the **Bastille►** is today an animated district dedicated to a youthful avant-garde, whether in its galleries, night-clubs or bars. Only 15 years ago it was resolutely working-class,

Walk

Beaubourg to the place des Vosges

Starting from Beaubourg, take the rue Rambuteau and cross the rue des Archives. On your left is the vast courtyard of the Hôtel de Soubise. Continue along rue des Francs-Bourgeois past the 1510 turret of the Maison de Jean Hérouët before turning left into the rue Payenne by the Musée Carnavalet. Walk past some typical Marais gardens and the Parc Royal. Turn left, then right to enter the rue de Thorigny and pass the Hôtel Salé (Musée Picasso). Walk round to the garden at the back, turn left down rue Vieille du Temple as far as the rue des Rosiers on your left. Walk to the end, turning left up rue Pavée and right back into the rue des Francs-Bourgeois. Continue to the end of the street and the place des Vosges.

home to furniture craftsmen, but its identity changed as artists moved into abandoned workshops and the new 'people's' opera opened in 1990. A landscaped marina, the Port de l'Arsenal, terminates the canal St-Martin.

The islands Floating mid-stream between the Rive Gauche and Rive Droite, the Iles are as different in character as the two banks they separate. The village-like **Ile St-Louis▶▶** grew up as a successful property development in the 17th century and has always been densely inhabited by wealthy business people and successful writers, from Helena Rubinstein to Baudelaire and Balzac. The adjoining **Ile de la Cité**, famous for **Notre-Dame**, **Sainte-Chapelle** and the **Conciergerie**, is a bizarre mixture of the sublime and the banal. Alongside its medieval monuments stand government symbols such as the **Palais de Justice**, the **Hôtel Dieu** (a massive hospital) and the **Préfecture**, the central police station. The spectacular stained-glass windows of the 13th-century **Sainte-Chapelle▶▶** and **Notre-Dame's▶▶** intricate sculpture and rose windows attract millions every year.

FORMER PRISON
Monopolising the northern stretch of the Ile de la Cité, the turreted walls of the Conciergerie are a grim reminder of the Revolution, when over 4,000 citizens, including Marie-Antoinette, were imprisoned there.

Paris

*Grandeur, 1930s-style –
the Palais de Chaillot is
home to the Musée de
l'Homme, a wide-
ranging ethnographic
collection, as well as the
extraordinary replicas of
the Musée des
Monuments Français
(re-opening in 2000 as
the Centre National de
l'Architecture)*

58

Beyond the centre

The winding path of the Seine, lined with blissfully shady quais and massive monuments, tends to monopolise visitors' attention. But don't forget that there is more to Paris than the Louvre and Notre-Dame. Today's city gates, encircling the 20 *arrondissements*, were built in the mid-19th century, while Haussmann was still busy laying out a modern city, and included what were then outlying districts such as **Montmartre**, **Montparnasse** and **Père-Lachaise**. As the years pass, Paris spreads further. Urban developments have provided new poles of attraction at **La Villette** and **La Défense**, where La Grande Arche now stands as the western gateway to the capital. Meanwhile, **Vincennes** and **Boulogne**, former royal hunting-grounds, are lungs for the west and east of the city.

Palais de Chaillot Built for the Paris Exhibition of 1937, the grandiose Chaillot completes a monumental axis sweeping across from the Ecole Militaire, down the Champ-de-Mars, under or over the Tour Eiffel and across the Seine to the gardens below. Its other façade dominates the **place du Trocadéro**, a famous haunt for well-heeled local residents. Inside Chaillot are no fewer than four museums, a theatre, a cinema and a restaurant. Close by stand the twinned forms of the **Palais de Tokyo**, with Paris' excellent **Musée d'Art Moderne** in the east wing; the rest still lies empty after abandonment of the costly Palais du Cinéma project.

Bois de Boulogne Immediately to the west, through Passy, beyond the Impressionists of the **Musée Marmottan►►**, is one of the many entrances to the extensive Bois de Boulogne. Donated by Napoleon III to the city, it was remodelled by Haussmann to resemble London's Hyde Park. Hire bicycles or rowing-boats, wander in the rose gardens of the **Jardin de Bagatelle►►**, amuse your children in the Jardin d'Acclimatation or recuperate in the luxurious restaurant of the pretty Pré Catalan.

La Défense Western Paris no longer ends here. Since the late 1950s the business centre of **La Défense** has sprouted anarchically skywards, leaving as many architectural horrors as marvels. The monumental **Grande Arche►►**, completed in 1989, has at last given a focus to the high-rises and its roof views are stupendous – as is the ascent in transparent lifts.

Montparnasse Another tower dominating Paris' skyline is the Tour Montparnasse, a 1970s hiccup, which was part of a massive urban development, signifying the birth of an entirely renovated quartier which includes the city's most confusing railway station. Although no longer the artists' mecca that it was in the 1920s, it retains a few symbols, particularly the rebuilt bar and brasserie of **La Coupole**. Side-streets like the **rue Vavin** or **rue de la Gaieté** are essential relics of this epoch.

La Villette Attempts at creating another cultural island have, over the last decade, been concentrated in the northeastern corner of Paris at **La Villette**. Completed in 1993, this multicultural park complex contains an impressive museum of science and technology, a spherical cinema (**La Géode**), the renovated 19th-century cattle market christened **La Grande Halle** (used for concerts and exhibitions), a music academy and concert halls.

Eastern Paris Here are two more popular promenading areas: the cemetery of **Père-Lachaise▶▶** and the Bois de Vincennes. The former, spreading over a hillside, must contain the greatest density of celebrated writers, musicians and artists in the world. Armed with a plan, visitors set off in search of the tombs of Edith Piaf, Jim Morrison, Modigliani, Chopin or Oscar Wilde. More mundane, the **Bois de Vincennes▶** is the eastern equivalent to Boulogne, and is similarly equipped with lakes, woods, rose gardens, a zoo and, its pride and glory, a severe medieval fortress once home to French kings. Vincennes will no doubt regain popularity with the important urban developments currently taking place in nearby Bercy and immediately across the Seine in Tolbiac, where Dominique Perrault's controversial new **Bibliothèque Nationale de France** now stands.

Montmartre Montmartre's charming winding streets and steps climb up to the white Roman–Byzantine cupolas of **Sacré-Cœur**. Built as atonement for the massacred victims of the 1871 Franco-Prussian War, it attracts millions for its **spectacular view▶▶** across Paris. Montmartre also means throngs of fake artists, but its leafy back-streets and vineyard cannot shake off a unique, peaceful character. At the bottom of the hill, tourist buses line the boulevards and sex-shops ply their trade – more proof of the city's eternal contrasts. Here, too, the famed Moulin Rouge is a reminder that over 30 windmills once ground silex from underground quarries – bringing the hill to near collapse.

VIADUC DES ARTS
Running the full 4.5km between the Bastille and the Bois de Vincennes is a walkway-cum-garden with cycle path, the Promenade Plantée. For 1.5km it runs along a viaduct whose converted red-brick archways below house workshops for numerous craftsmen and restorers as well as providing a showcase for contemporary artists. This is the trendy end of the vast develop-ments changing the face of eastern Paris.

59

Montmartre lights up at night with bars and cafés spilling on to the cobbled streets

TUMBLING SPIRE
Building started on Beauvais Cathedral in 1227 but the choir collapsed a few days after completion under the weight of its ambitious design. A replacement was completed in the late 14th century, but remained roofless for two centuries. More disaster struck in 1573 when the new 153m spire tumbled, leading to the closure of the cathedral in 1605.

The Temple of Love, one of the ornaments to be found in Le Nôtre's grounds of the Château de Chantilly

Ile de France

▶▶ Anet, Château d' *240A2*

28260 Anet, on D928 south of Rouen
Open: Easter–Oct, 2–6.30. Closed Tue. In winter – open weekends 2–5
No direct train line

In 1548, Diane de Poitiers, Henri II's ambitious mistress, commissioned the architect Philibert Delorme to expand and rebuild Anet. Some of the greatest Renaissance artists, Jean Goujon, Germain Pilon and Cellini, created a magnificent home for this powerful woman. She later moved to the fabulous Loire château of Chenonceaux, but after Henri's death in 1559 she was ousted by his widow, Catherine de Médicis, and returned to Anet. An extravagantly decorated chapel containing her tomb is one of the few remaining features alongside one wing, the beautifully sculpted front entrance and a lovely park.

▶ Astérix, Parc *240B2*

60128 Plailly
Open: daily Jul–Aug. Opening erratically at other times. Closed winter

Only 35km north of Paris, this park, based on the antics of the Gallic cartoon hero, Astérix, created by Albert Uderzo, is packed with replica Roman monuments, gladiators, slaves and an imaginative range of related games, fun-fair rides and gastronomy (fancy a head of wild boar?). Nor is his fat, devoted friend Obélix forgotten. It is well organised and very popular at weekends, so be prepared for queues.

▶ Beauvais *240A3*

In the flat Picardy landscape, the bulky medieval cathedral of Beauvais rises above the surrounding roofs. Apart from the incredible scale of the choir, its most astonishing features are the stained glass, the sculpted stone portals and the remains of the 'Basse Oeuvre', a rare 10th-century Carolingian church incorporated into the cathedral. Beside the cathedral, the old bishop's palace houses the renovated and expanded collections of the Musée Départemental de l'Oise, the principal museum of the Oise *département*.

▶▶ Chantilly, Château de *240A2*

Musée Condé, 60500 Chantilly; take Survilliers exit off A1
Open: Wed–Mon, 10–6; 10.30–12.45, 2–5 in winter
Rail: Chantilly

Famous for its forests, racecourses and whipped cream, Chantilly also boasts a château. Its attractive and mixed architectural styles reflect a lively history, from Renaissance origins through destruction in the Revolution to rebuilding in the 19th century. The magnificent grounds were transformed by Le Nôtre, who added lakes and canals. Inside the château, the **Musée Condé** displays Italian and French Renaissance furnishings, a remarkable art collection ranging from Raphael to Delacroix and a facsimile of the illuminated medieval manuscript, the *Très Riches Heures du Duc de Berry* (original not on view).

▶ ▶ ▶ Chartres
240A2

A11 southwest of Paris
Rail: Chartres

'The acropolis of France' (Rodin), Notre-Dame de Chartres, replaces five successive churches, the last built in 1021 to house the relics of the Virgin Mary. Numerous fires culminated in the devastating flames of 1194, which inspired the community to build a new cathedral – accomplished in 25 years. The lower half of the façade remains pure 11th-century Romanesque, while the rest of the cathedral represents the transition to Gothic. Inside the cathedral, 176 luminous stained-glass windows of classical and modern designs attest to the talents of the Chartres craftsmen. The crypt dates mainly from the 11th century and is the largest in France (entry charge).

▶ Compiègne
240B2

Château de Compiègne, 60200 Compiègne; on A1
Open: Wed–Mon, 9.15–6.15, 4.30 in winter (last entries 5.15 and 3.45)
Rail: Compiègne

Surrounded by the glorious Forêt de Compiègne, the elegant town of Compiègne was a favourite retreat for French kings from the 14th century onwards. Louis XIV gave some spectacular parties there; both Louis XV and XVI extended the château and Napoleons I and III also enjoyed its splendour. The lavish rooms are arranged according to period, the most impressive being Empress Josephine's bedroom, the Grand Salon and the ballroom.

▶ ▶ Disneyland Paris
240B2

77777 Marne-la-Vallée; autoroute A4 east of Paris
RER: Line A from central Paris

The fourth Disney theme park opened its doors in 1992, an American paradise in the heart of Europe. Hotels grouped round a lake allow visitors to explore the Magic Kingdom, its attractions ranging from the vaguely medieval castle of Sleeping Beauty to a science fiction environment à la Jules Verne. Despite catastrophic losses, this plastic universe is undeniably big-time entertainment and was recently reinjected with US $400 million by a Saudi prince.

Dreux
240A2

Its forest long preserved as hunting-ground, Dreux became the personal property of the royal family in the 16th century and still has strong royalist connections. In recent years it has controversially supported the extreme right party, the Front National. The main monument of this market town is a hilltop chapel built by Louis-Philippe's mother as the mausoleum for the Orléans family, still the French pretenders to the throne.

▶ ▶ Ecouen, Château d'
240A2

Open: Wed–Mon 9.45–12.30, 2–5.15

This superb château, on the edge of the Parisian suburbs, was built in the mid-16th century for the Constable Anne de Montmorency. Artists Jean Goujon and Jean Bullant were among those employed in the château design. Today it houses a museum devoted to the Renaissance period.

The odd mismatched towers of Notre-Dame de Chartres are a result of lightning striking the north tower in the 16th century, decapitating its spire

61

MONSIEUR PLATE-SNATCHER
In the outskirts of Chartres lies an extraordinary house and garden, created by an eccentric. Using thousands of multicoloured fragments of smashed plates, glass, mirror and ceramic, he plastered the walls and even his wife's sewing-machine with mosaic murals. The garden even contains a mosaic throne. The Maison Picassiette (literally plate-snatcher) is at 22 rue du Repos. *Open* Apr–Oct: 10–12, 2–6 (*Closed* Tue and Sun morning).

memorabilia in the houses of Millet and Rousseau.

From Barbizon follow the D64 to Arbonne-la-Forêt. Take a tiny road on the right to reach Courances.
The château is sometimes open to the public, and the pure classical gardens and canals are exceptional (Open Apr–Oct at weekends and public holidays 2–6.30).

Drive south to Milly-la-Forêt.
Milly-la-Forêt was once the home of Jean Cocteau; he is buried in the 12th-century church. The enormous beamed wooden market-hall in the main square is 15th-century.

Leave Milly, passing the church, via the D16 and drive to Le Vaudoué.
On your left is the 124m hill of Les Trois Pignons, one of the most beautiful parts of the forest.

Continue to Achères-la-Forêt, from where you can either circle back to Fontainebleau via the Gorges de Franchard, another notable climbing and panoramic spot, or continue towards the very pretty River Loing. Drive south of the Loing on the D40 to Moret.
This fortified medieval town was once home to the Impressionist Sisley. Its Grande Rue is lined with medieval and Renaissance houses.

Return to Fontainebleau via Champagne-sur-Seine.

The Forest of Fontainebleau

Start your tour at the sprawling Château de Fontainebleau.
The largest forest in the Ile de France is that of Fontainebleau. Rich in natural wonders (6,000 species of insects, 200 birds), as well as a wide variety of flora and fauna, it was originally a 12th-century hunting lodge. The château was transformed in the 16th century by François I and later used by Napoleon (Open Wed–Mon 9.30–12.30, 2–5; 9.30–6 in summer). The gardens, re-landscaped by Le Nôtre in the mid-17th century, are criss-crossed by canals.

Leave Fontainebleau by the N7 which takes you to Barbizon.
On your left are the Gorges d'Apremont, which invite a halt to climb up. Below stretches a spectacular gorge. Barbizon itself was home between 1825 and 1870 to landscape painters who created their own movement. Corot, Millet, Rousseau and Daubigny all worked here, painting in the open air and spending their evenings at the Auberge du Père Ganne. Today it is full of commercial galleries, but remains pretty; and there are

▶▶ Rambouillet, Château de   240A2

Château de Rambouillet
Open: only in the president's absence; hours are limited
Lying about 55km southwest of Paris, the Château de Rambouillet has been the country retreat for French presidents since 1897. Dating from the 14th century, it really came into its own when François I died there after becoming ill while hunting in the forest. It was later much appreciated by Louis XVI. Marie-Antoinette was less impressed and described the château as a 'toad-pond'; to appease her a dairy was built inside an English-style garden. The magnificent park has been landscaped over several centuries with rare trees, canals and islands. Guided tours of the château include rococo bedrooms and Napoleon's bathroom, decorated with neo-Pompeii frescoes.

▶▶ Saint-Denis   240A2

Open: daily 10–5; till 7 in summer
The daunting necropolis of French kings, a metro ride from the centre of Paris, is often overlooked by visitors. The Christian martyr St-Denis, who was decapitated at Montmartre, is said to have staggered northwards carrying his head to a rural burial. A church rose on this site in the 5th century, but today's basilica was built by the leading churchman and royal counselor Suger in the early 12th century. Its Gothic beauty inspired similar edifices at Chartres, Meaux, Senlis and Notre-Dame. Following the example of the 7th-century Dagobert, Saint-Denis was for over 12 centuries the royal burial ground. Restored from Revolutionary pillaging, it remains an incredible museum of funerary sculpture and a showcase of Gothic architecture.

▶ St-Germain-en-Laye   240A2

The main interest of this chic Parisian suburb lies in its medieval fortress, much rebuilt by François I in the 16th century. The château now houses the **Musée des Antiquités Nationales**▶ (*Open* Wed–Mon 9–5.15), a virtually unrivalled showcase of archaeological artefacts with one of the richest prehistoric collections in the world. The home of the late 19th-century artist Maurice Denis is now a museum with a superb collection of Symbolist and Nabi works of art.

LIKE A WOMAN
'Many men, not all of them French, have loved France like a woman, seeing in it, according to each context, their mother, their mistress or the woman of their dreams.' – André Fontaine, Le Monde, 1982.

63

The Grande Terrasse of St-Germain-en-Laye's fortress was designed by Le Nôtre in 1668–73 and stretches for 2.4km. The view from the terrace across the valley of the Seine inspired the Impressionist painter Sisley

The Musée National de Céramique in Sèvres displays valuable examples of porcelain from Sèvres, Vincennes and Dresden, and copies of Oriental pieces, Italian majolica and Islamic ceramics

64

VAUX'S HIGHLIGHTS
Inside Vaux, don't miss the Salon des Muses with ceiling paintings by Le Brun of nine different muses. Here Molière and his troupe first staged L'Ecole des Maris with Queen Henrietta-Maria of England and Fouquet as audience. Upstairs, the superb Chambre du Roi was subsequently copied at Versailles and throughout Europe

▶ Sceaux   240A2

The well-tended park at Sceaux once surrounded a 1677 château which was used for lavish receptions and has become a favourite for promenading or picnicking Parisians today. Those early days ended with the Revolution when the original château was completely destroyed. Today's château was built in 1856; the grounds were restored to Le Nôtre's design earlier this century. Inside, the **Musée de l'Ile de France** (*Open* Wed–Mon 10–6, 5 in winter) displays paintings, costumes, royal porcelain and other objects relevant to the history of this region. The park is open from sunrise to sunset. The Orangerie has a summer programme of music recitals.

▶▶ Senlis   240B2

Formerly a Roman settlement, Senlis became home to a remarkable Gothic cathedral in 1153; building was not completed until 1560. The sculptures of the main entrance are devoted to the Virgin Mary and the lateral porches are typical of the Flamboyant Gothic style. Full of original Renaissance houses and 17th- to 18th-century town houses and devoid of a railway thanks to local lobbying in the 19th century, the cathedral town exudes a timeless atmosphere.

Numerous Gallo-Roman ruins remain too. Some have been integrated into the remains of the medieval castle (*Open* Wed pm–Mon 10–noon, 2–6; 5 in winter); others (such as the fortified wall) are still visible: 16 towers have survived from this period.

▶ Sèvres   240A2

Between Versailles and Paris lies the pretty old suburb of Sèvres (the baroque composer Lully lived here, as did Balzac) which borders on the 392-hectare park of St-Cloud, with its Le Nôtre-designed waterways and infinite views over the city. Home to the royal porcelain factory, moved from Vincennes in 1756 by Madame de Pompadour, Sèvres has become synonymous with exquisite French craftsmanship, examples of which can be seen in its museum   (*Open:* Wed– Mon 10–5).

▶▶ Vaux-le-Vicomte, Château de   240B2

Domaine de Vaux-le-Vicomte, 77950 Maincy
Open: Mar–11 Nov 10–1; 2–6 daily
Without Vaux, Versailles would never have happened. It was here that Louis XIV's shrewd, power-hungry Minister of Finance, Fouquet, decided to build a monument to the artists of the epoch – and to himself. Between the architect Le Vau, the painter Le Brun and landscape gardener Le Nôtre, a château and park of unrivalled extravagance and beauty were created between 1656 and 1661. Unfortunately for Fouquet, Louis XIV was only too aware of its value and soon clapped his minister into prison, then proceeded to build Versailles. A victim of the vagaries of French history, Vaux-le-Vicomte was saved by an industrialist and has undergone extensive restoration over the last century. The formal gardens are a masterpiece of French style with terraces, fountains, statues and ponds leading away towards a concealed canal.

The Water Gardens in Versailles are best seen in full action ('les grandes eaux') from early May to early October on Sunday at 3pm (tel: 01 39 50 36 22)

▶ ▶ ▶ Versailles

240A2

Château de Versailles, 78000 Versailles

Every imposing avenue of Versailles converges on the palace, the town's *raison d'être*, Louis XIV's greatest creation and a world unto itself. In 1661, Louis decided to move his court and government to this swampy area, an astute way of isolating them but also of marking the flowering of French baroque in an area with unlimited space for expansion.

The garden façade best epitomizes the Sun King's ambitions. Faced in stone, lined with Ionic columns and capped with ornamental balustrades and carved trophies, the central section is part of the 'envelope' Le Vau designed around the original hunting lodge.

The Royal Apartments are divided into the 'Grands' and 'Petits' (*Open* Tue–Sun 9–5.30, till 6.30 in summer). The 'Grands', laid out in the 1670s by the King's chief painter, Le Brun, were the luxurious public rooms. The jewel of this stretch is the Galerie des Glaces, the largest, most magnificent and last public room to be completed. Le Brun's painted ceilings depict the King himself, while the 17 great mirrors once reflected candelabra, damask and precious furniture. Beyond is the Queen's Apartment and a series of dull picture galleries built later by Louis-Philippe.

Before entering the 'Grands', don't miss the **Royal Chapel**, a perfect combination of elegance and grandeur, laid out on two levels. The 'Petits Appartements' can only be seen with a guided tour. These were the royal family's real living quarters.

The gardens The severe symmetry of the largest palace gardens in Europe, another of Le Nôtre's masterpieces, is relieved by hundreds of statues, 'follies' and fountains, not to mention the canals. If your time is limited, a small train will take you through the park (*Open* sunrise–sunset) to the **Trianons**, two more modest kingly residences (*Open* Tue–Fri 10–12.30, 2–5.30; weekends 10–5.30; Tue–Sun 10–6.30 in summer). The 'Grand Trianon' was built for Louis XIV to escape from the palace routine; the neo-classical 'Petit Trianon' was built by Gabriel for Louis XV. Its grounds were later entirely transformed for Marie-Antoinette to play at milkmaid in a theatrical village, the *hameau*. For visitors similarly wanting to escape palace tedium, bicycles and rowing-boats are for hire at the Grand Canal.

EUROPE'S LONGEST
In 1678, Hardouin-Mansart filled in the terrace to create the almighty Galerie des Glaces (Hall of Mirrors), the most famous room in the palace, and added two blocks north and south to make the garden front of Versailles the longest (570m) in Europe.

LE POTAGER DU ROI
A stone's throw from the château lie nine hectares of impeccable kitchen gardens-cum-orchards, virtually unchanged since their creation by La Quintaye between 1679 and 1683. Micro-climates within the 29 walled gardens surrounding the central sunken gardens and terraces enabled La Quintaye to develop methods of growing produce out of season, as well as new pruning techniques still used for the 5,000-odd fruit trees. Unusual vegetables flourish such as blue Hungarian pumpkins, 50 varieties each of apple and pear – such was the choice set at the king's table (now sold to the public). Guided tours: Wed–Sun at 2.30pm, 6 rue Hardy (Jun–Sep extra tour at 4.30pm at weekends).

For the best in fresh food, go to market

Shopping

The perennial problem of Paris is how to escape without running up an almighty overdraft. Temptations lie in wait round every corner, many outrageously expensive but some just within a normal budget.

Markets For food and wine, go straight to the main market streets (closed on Mondays), which have a vast array of fresh produce and clusters of specialised shops. The most touristy, the **rue de Buci** (*6th arrondissement*), is the least impressive. Go instead to the **rue Montorgueil** (1st), traditionally part of Les Halles; the popular **rue Mouffetard** (5th); the **rue Poncelet** (17th); the picturesque **rue du Poteau** (18th); or the **rue Lepic** in Montmartre (18th). For North African specialities, head for the back streets of Belleville or try the colourful **Marché d'Aligre** (12th). Nearby, at the **Bastille**, an immense, generous Sunday morning market is held. Lovers of Asiatic delicacies should go to **Chinatown** (13th), where numerous shops and supermarkets are concentrated among the restaurants south of the place d'Italie.

Fashion For cheap and cheerful, always stylish clothes, your best bets are the boutiques of the **rue de Rennes**, not forgetting the ubiquitous, unbelievably cheap **Tati** at No 140, and the **boulevard St-Michel**, a favourite with students. Slightly more up-market, the boutiques of **boulevard St-Germain** and **Les Halles** always stock the latest crazes. Designer *prêt-à-porter*, from Kenzo to Mugler, is best chased around the **rue Etienne-Marcel** and the **place des Victoires** (1st); go straight to the Boutique Victoire itself. Top shoe designers such as Stephane Kélian have also homed in here. And for the very top end of the market go to the **Faubourg St-Honoré** and the **avenue Montaigne**: you may even find some affordable gifts at Hermès or Au Bain Marie. But don't forget **Galeries Lafayette**.

Bric-à-brac and antiques are relegated to the flea markets, from the **Porte de Clignancourt** (*Open* Sat–Mon) to the **Porte de Vanves** (weekends only) or the daily auctions held at **Drouot**. Valuable pieces can be seen at the enormous **Louvre des Antiquaires** (metro: Palais-Royal) or in the world-famous **Carré Rive Gauche**, a grid of streets behind the Quai Voltaire (7th) chock-a-block with priceless objects and paintings. Antiquarian book- and print-lovers could spend a lifetime exploring the back streets of the **Quartier Latin** and the *bouquinistes* lining the *quais*.

Food and drink

The choice of eating places in Paris is almost disarming – where to start? All depends on your budget: you could spend every evening in the 3-Michelin-star restaurants of the 8th *arrondissement* – **Taillevent, Lucas Carton** and **Pierre Gagnaire** – or just head straight for the smokey bistros of the Quartier Latin and St-Germain.

Even if your pocket does not stretch to **Michel Rostang** or **Guy Savoy's** establishments, you can try their more affordable bistros, both near the Etoile. There is a gamut of famous brasseries from **Flo, Julien** and **Terminus Nord** in the 10th to the **Vaudeville** or the **Grand Colbert**, both near the Bourse in the 2nd, **Bofinger** at the Bastille, the art deco artists' monument in Montparnasse, **La Coupole**, or the **Brasserie Lipp** in boulevard St-Germain.

If your aim is for a more intimate tête-à-tête that is not ruinous, go straight to **Le Marais**, where reasonably priced bistros and restaurants offer very acceptable cuisine. The side-streets of **St-Germain-des-Prés** have equally inviting pickings, particularly near the metro Mabillon. For limited budgets try the **rue de l'Echaudé**, the **rue St-Benoît** and the **rue Monsieur-le-Prince**. In the 5th, low-budget travellers should go to the **rue des Boulangers**, while the **rue St-Séverin** and **rue de la Huchette** have lots of Greek and middle-eastern restaurants.

Night Food The Bastille area has become a nocturnal haunt for trendy young Parisians (20 to 30 age group). Small restaurants and bars abound along the **rue de la Roquette**, the **rue de Lappe** and the **rue de Charonne**. Les Halles is more downmarket but very colourful. Other age groups may prefer the **boulevard St-Germain** and its side streets.

Ethnic food enthusiasts should go for Asiatic food to the 13th (**Chinatown**) or 20th (**Belleville**), for Japanese the **rue Ste-Anne** (2nd) and for North African any of the couscous restaurants scattered all over the capital. See also **Hotels and Restaurants**, page 276.

FRENCH TASTES

In 1991, 63 per cent of French people thought they ate too much compared with only 50 per cent in 1971. Today, 66 per cent think they drink too much. Of all foreign cooking, 66 per cent of the French prefer Italian, 51 per cent North African, 35 per cent Chinese, 32 per cent Vietnamese, 20 per cent Greek, 17 per cent Indian, 16 per cent Japanese and a mere 6 per cent English cooking.

Café-terraces are the ultimate Parisian institution, ideal for people-watching, penning a novel or a discreet rendezvous

HAIR OF THE CHIEN!

It's six in the morning, you've been dancing all night: it's time for breakfast. Try the freshly-baked goodies at Chez Jean-Mi, rue de d'Ancienne Comédie (6th); La Maison d'Alsace, avenue des Champs-Elysées (8th), for a dozen oysters; the Mustang Café (until 5am only), boulevard du Montparnasse (14th), for tacos; Le Dépanneur, rue Fontaine (9th), for a follow-up tequila; some onion soup, tripe or a pig's trotter at the aptly named Au Pied de Cochon, rue Coquillière (1st).

CELLAR RATS

The rhythms of 'be-bop' started in post-war St-Germain at the Tabou Club in rue Dauphine, which opened in 1947 with Juliette Greco, Boris Vian and Jacques Prévert. Sacrilegious in tone, exuberant in expression, these infamous night-owls were reacting to the severe restrictions of the war years. They were soon named the 'cellar rats'.

Parisian nocturnal fidelities may be fickle, but the Moulin Rouge survives – thanks to tourists

Nightlife

It is unavoidable: when in Paris you have to partake of the nocturnal forbidden fruits. Part of the myth and part of the fun, there are haunts for all generations and tastes.

Pigalle is still hot, still changing since the days of Toulouse-Lautrec. Around the **place Blanche** and the **place Pigalle** is a multitude of haunts, from the classic **Moulin Rouge** to nightclubs like **Folies Pigalle**, trendy bars like **Le Moloko** or **Divan du Monde**. Try the kitsch of **Lili La Tigresse** followed by a more leisurely belly-dance at **Shéhérazade**. Ballroom dancing (without the dress) is back in style at the **Elysées-Montmartre**: big bands, varied programme for all types and ages.

Late night Les Halles offers plenty of jazz-bars and late-night haunts. For peep-shows and tackiness the northern section of the **rue St-Denis** has it all, but for a late drink with good live or recorded music go to the **rue des Lombards**: **Le Duc des Lombards** is always buzzing, as is **Sunset**, a few doors away. **Le Petit Opportun**, round the corner, is still hot for jazz if you can find a seat. The rue Berger has another stretch of popular music bars: **Eustache** at No 37 is cheap and friendly. Then there's always the long-standing, ultra-trendy nightclub, **Les Bains**.

Another nocturnal zone circles around **Le Palace**, the notorious theatrical disco in the Faubourg Montmartre. Not far away is the **Folies-Bergère**, and downstairs is the more select **Privilège**. The **Rex** pulls in crowds for its rap and major concerts, while jazz aficionados still track down the **New Morning** live jazz bar or swing to Dixieland at **Le Petit Journal** in St-Michel.

Light fantastic Concentrated around the **rue de la Roquette** and the **rue de Lappe** at the Bastille are renovated old dance-halls (**Le Balajo**) and busy bars open till the early hours. Gentrification of the area has moved some of these bars north to the **Oberkampf** area: same crowd, different place. Try **Cithéa** on the rue Oberkampf itself.

For more mature visitors the **Champs-Elysées** area has several rather select nightclubs, including **Régines**, **Villa Barclay** and the up-market **L'Arc** (with garden) as well as smart cocktail bars away from the flashing lights guiding tourists into the **Lido** and the **Crazy Horse Saloon**.

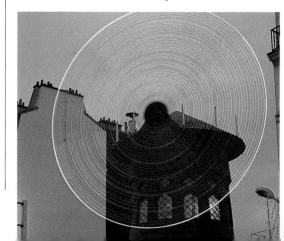

Accommodation

With nearly 1,500 hotels and an average of 20 million tourists spread between them annually, Paris caters for all tastes and budgets. It is one of the rare European capitals which offers quite acceptable and affordable accommodation in central areas, while a dozen or so establishments maintain standards of luxury straight out of another epoch. Unfortunately, France has the smallest minimum legal size of bathrooms and bedrooms in Europe, and in Paris, where real estate does not come cheap, many hoteliers exploit this standard to the full.

High Style The 8th *arrondissement* (**Champs-Elysées, avenue George V**, **avenue Montaigne**, **Faubourg St-Honoré** and surrounding streets) is by far the most chic neighbourhood, with a high concentration of luxury and 4-star hotels. This is where you stay if you need to pop out for another fitting at Dior's or to shop at Hermès. Some of the top hotels are also renowned for discreet call-girl systems.

Following closely in the luxury stakes is the 1st *arrondissement* (**Tuileries, Louvre, place Vendôme**), convenient for high-class jewellery and for culture, yet whose back streets have a sprinkling of affordable 2- and 3-star hotels. The adjacent 9th (**Opéra, Grands Boulevards**) has the densest concentration of hotels, over half of which are budget 2-star establishments. The **Faubourg Montmartre** claims the majority; many are used by tour operators, but further north towards **Pigalle** and **Montmartre** are some characteristic family-run hotels.

What's Left The area most visitors should and do head for is the Rive Gauche, the 5th, 6th and even 7th *arrondissements*. Less business-like in atmosphere than the Right Bank, the **Quartier Latin** and **St-Germain-des-Prés** house a host of reasonable 1-, 2-star and some very attractive 3-star hotels. In general, prices are lower on this side of the Seine. Becoming increasingly similar in style is the Rive Droite's **Marais** district (3rd and 4th): lively, full of history, restaurants, galleries, boutiques and bars and within easy reach of other *quartiers*. More youthful in temperament, it also borders the **Bastille**, where new hotels are opening yearly.

May, June, September and October are the hardest months to find rooms – be warned! See also **Hotels and Restaurants**, pages 274–6.

Visitors with fat wallets will head for a handful of the world's most luxurious and historic hotels – from the Ritz to the Crillon

A TERRIBLE PLACE
'Paris is a vast studio of putrefaction where misery, plague and disease work together, where neither air nor sun penetrates. Paris is a terrible place where plants wilt and perish, where out of seven children, four die within the year.' – Victor Considérant, 1848.

1- and 2-star hotel comforts can be surprising but are unlikely to include Van Gogh originals

Paris

CANAL TRIPS

Take a three-hour trip along Paris' canal Saint-Martin, above and below ground and through a couple of locks. Boats run between the Bastille's Port de l'Arsenal or the Musée d'Orsay and La Villette, taking you along a leafy partly underground itinerary in eastern Paris, past the famous Hôtel de Nord and around the Parc de la Villette (from Port de l'Arsenal, daily, 01 42 39 15 00; or from Musée d'Orsay, Apr–Nov daily and weekends in winter, 01 42 40 96 97).

BATOBUS

Re-launched in 1997, this boat service plies the Seine between Easter and mid-October, providing a quick and pleasant way of getting around Paris, whilst enjoying its riverside architecture. Three boats operate daily services between the six docking points at the Tour Eiffel, the Musée d'Orsay, Saint Germain-des-Près, Notre Dame, l'Hôtel de Ville and the Louvre (departures every 25 minutes, 1 or 2-day passes available).

MUSEUM PASS

Museum and monument admission charges can mount up dramatically, as do queues, so if you are planning intense cultural sightseeing it is worth investing in a Carte Musée et Monuments. This is available at major museums and metro stations, valid for 1, 3 or 5 consecutive days and covers 70 destinations in the Paris region.

Practical points

Air Paris has two international airports: **Orly** (14km south) and **Roissy/Charles-de-Gaulle** (23km north). Both are served by international and domestic airlines. The terminals of **Orly-Sud**, for international flights, and **Orly-Ouest** for domestic flights, can be reached by Air France bus from the Invalides or Montparnasse; by Orly-bus from Denfert-Rochereau; by Jet Bus from Villejuif-Louis Aragon; by RER line C from Austerlitz; or by Orlyrail from Châtelet. **Roissy I** (foreign airlines) and **Roissy II** (Air France) can be reached by Air France bus from Etoile or Montparnasse; by Roissybus from behind the Opéra; or by RER line B (Roissy-Rail) from Gare du Nord.

Car If you arrive in Paris by car you will eventually end up on the *boulevard périphérique*. This ringroad encircles the city centre with exits at each of Paris's gates – the portes – and avoids crossing unnecessary stretches of the centre. However, it can get disastrously jammed up, particularly during the evening rush-hour (between 6 and 7). If arriving from the west of Paris follow signs for *voie express Georges Pompidou*: this expressway is what you should follow to be spirited along beside the Seine into the heart of Paris.

Driving in Paris is not advisable, nor will it save you time. Parking has become a real problem and even if you imitate Parisian pavement parking, it is still difficult. There is an increasing number of central underground car parks where you can safely leave your car for a few days while touring the city by public transport. If you insist on driving, keep out of the bus lanes and remember to give priority to the right.

Train Paris is served by six main-line stations, each covering a different part of France or Europe. The **Gare du Nord** is for northern France, Belgium, Holland, Germany, Scandinavia and Britain; the smaller **Gare St-Lazare** serves Normandy and its channel ports For eastern France, Germany, Austria, Switzerland and onwards, the **Gare de l'Est** will be your destination. The **Gare de Lyon** speeds you south to the Côte d'Azur and south-east to Italy and Switzerland. Trains for south-west France, Spain and Portugal leave from the **Gare d'Austerlitz**, but not the TGV services; these leave from the **Gare Montparnasse**, a modernised station seemingly without any logic, along with trains to western France, Brittany and the Atlantic coast. All are on the Paris metro and close to the centre. Be careful about choosing the correct section of the station: *banlieue* means suburbs; *grandes lignes* designates main-line trains. And always punch (*composter*) your ticket before boarding.

Inside Paris Finding your way around Paris is not complicated. The *arrondissement* system starts at the heart (Louvre, Châtelet) and curls outward, snail-like, to end in the 20th, the eastern *quartier* of Belleville. Street numbers start at the Seine, working outwards. Walking around Paris is a pleasure, and safe; for longer distances the Métro is easily mastered. Buy a *carnet* of 10 tickets or a *Paris-Visite*, valid for one, two, three or five days.

Mobilis is an alternative one-day pass across different zones. Métro tickets are also valid for central sections of the RER and for buses; punch them (*composter*) as you board. Most buses stop at 8–9pm, but Noctambus night buses run from 1–6am. The Métro runs from about 5.30am to around 30 minutes past midnight. Be very careful about wallets and handbags: skillful pickpockets abound, particularly on Line 4.

Taxis are not Paris's greatest asset. Be prepared for extras to be added to any fare from stations or airports and don't be surprised if they refuse to take four passengers. Several radio-taxi firms exist (**Taxis Bleus**: tel: 01 49 36 10 10; G7: tel: 01 47 39 47 39; **Alpha**: tel: 01 45 85 85 85) but this makes for a more expensive ride.

Emergency Purchases Very useful is the network of 'drugstores, hardly changed since the 1960s'. Open till 2am daily, they sell items ranging from newspapers, books and records to medicine, camera equipment, gifts, wine, cigarettes, a snack or a meal. You can find them at the top and bottom of the Champs-Elysées, and at l'Opéra.

Few of Hector Guimard's original art nouveau metro entrances remain: the best are at Abbesses and Porte Dauphine

NORMANDY

0   20   40   60 km

0   10   20   30 miles

GBA

Cap de la Hague

Goury • St-Germain-des-Vaux

Nez de Jobourg

Pointe de Barfleur

Féca

Cherbourg

Barfleur

Cap d'Antifer

Et

• Flamanville

• St-Vaast-la-Hougue

Valognes

Montivilliers

Barneville-Carteret

LE HAVRE

Cap de Carteret

Utah Beach

Ste-Mère-Eglise Omaha Beach

Baie de la Seine

Hai

GBG

Carentan

Port-en-Bessin

Courseulles Deauville Trouvil

Hor

Isigny

Arromanches

Ouistreham Houlgate Villers-su-Me

Lessay

Bayeux

Fontaine-■

Cabourg Dives-sur-Mer Eve

Pont

Cérisy

Ihory

Beuvron-en-Au

GBJ

Ballerov

Cambremer

St-Lô

Villers-Bocage

Caen

Coutances

Crèvacoeur-en-Auge

Lisi

St-Germain-de-Livet

Pays d'Aug

A13

A84

Livaro

Hambye

Clécy ■ Suisse Normande

Vimoutiers

Golfe de St-Malo

Villedieu-les-Poéles

Pont d'Ouilly

Falaise

Granville

Vire

Condé-sur-Noireau

Camembert

Lucerne

Roche d'Oetre ■

Pte du Grouin

Sourdeval

Putanges

Argentan

Gace

Cap Fréhel

Paramé Cancale

Avranches

Flers

Erquy

Dinard St-Malo

le-Mont-St-Michel

St-Hilaire-du-Harcouet

Mortain

St-Servan

Domfron

Bagnoles-de-l'Orne • la Ferté-Macé

Sées

Plancoet

Dol-de-Bretagne

Pontoçson

Louvigné-du-Désert

Forêt d'Ecouves ■

Carrouges

Lamballe

Antrain

Mayenne

Dinan

Combourg

Lassay

Alpes Alençon

Sartbe

les Iffs Montmuran

■ Lanrigan

Fougères

St-Céneri-le-Gérei •

Mamers

St-Méen-le-Grand

Ernèe

Mayenne

St-Léonard-des-Bois •

Mancelles

Mauron

Montfort Rennes

Vitré

les Rochers-Sévigné

Evron •

Sillé-le-Guillaume

Bonnétab

Châteaugiron

Laval

A81

A11

le M

Janzé

■ la Roche-aux-Fées

A   B   C

Ploërmel

Guer

Retiers

▶▶▶ REGION HIGHLIGHTS

Bayeux *pages 75*

Caen *page 77*

Château Gaillard
page 80

Deauville *page 76*

Dieppe *page 78*

Etretat *page 74*

Giverny *page 80*

Honfleur *page 76*

Mont St-Michel
page 83

Pays d'Auge *page 84*

Rouen *page 86*

NORMANDY emerged from an long era of conflict and invasion. Viking invaders sailed up the Seine in the 9th century, wreaked their usual havoc and won themselves a handsome duchy, from which their vigorous descendants exported well-ordered Norman rule and striking architecture to England and the Mediterranean.

After William the Conqueror's invasion of England in 1066, Normandy was passed to and fro between English and French rulers. More recently, Normandy was the setting for the 'D-Day' landings in 1944. The Battle of Normandy inflicted terrible damage on many old towns and villages.

ART AND BEAUTY Northwest of Paris, the Seine meanders through the heart of Normandy past fortresses, abbey ruins and the beautiful old city of Rouen, as if in no hurry to reach the sea. This is a region rich in artistic associations (Impressionists, Flaubert, Proust) from the period when the Normandy coast, easily accessible by train from Paris, was the height of fashion. To the west of the mouth of the Seine, the resorts of the Côte Fleurie still have plenty of chic, especially Deauville, with its golf and horses. Inland, the Pays d'Auge is Normandy at its most fruitful: Camembert and Calvados territory, with colourful timbered manor houses, fat cows in the orchard, and a diet of cream and butter, with no skimming.

POORER COUNTRY Western or Lower Normandy is poorer, more rugged land, geologically of a piece with Brittany. It keeps its quiet charms to itself – fortunately for those who love it.

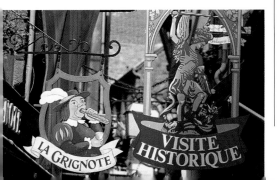

ETRETAT
Fashionable seaside resort in the 19th century, inhabited by writers such as Dumas, Leblanc and Maupassant., as well as by two Spanish queens (at Château Les Aygues), and oft-painted by Boudin, Corot, Courbet, Delacroix and Monet, Etretat's 'pilgrim's' today are mainly hikers (maps and all details from the tourist office).

BENEDICTINE
Benedictine is still made to the original recipe first concocted by a monk in 1510. The Palais Bénédictine was purpose-built in the 1880s, five minutes from the abbey, by Alexandre Le Grand, a wine wholesaler, for the commerical production of the liqueur. Visitors can see the distillery and cellars where it matures in oak casks, as well as tasting it (*Open* daily).

The museum in the Benedictine distillery includes a rich collection of medieval objets d'art

▶ Albâtre, Côte d'   73D3

This 100km stretch of once fashionable coastline between Dieppe and Etretat was named after its chalky cliffs and milky waves. **Etretat▶▶▶** is the best place for cliff walks, beautifully set on a shingle beach with pillars and arches on both sides and immortalised by Monet. A small museum commemorates the fatal first attempt to fly the Atlantic by two French aviators in 1927. **Fécamp** is a larger town and busy commercial port, famous for the Benedictine liqueur based on an elixir made by the monks of its abbey. The drink has a museum to itself and the great abbey church (La Trinité) has interesting works of art. Pilgrims venerate a marble tabernacle said to contain the blood of Christ (behind the altar). A stone in the south transept has an 'angel's footprint', imprinted in 943.

▶ Alençon   72C1

A handsomely restored old market town in fertile agri-cultural and horse-breeding country north of Le Mans, Alençon has interesting Gothic buildings: a fat feudal fortress with bulging towers, now a prison; the 14th- to 15th-century church of Notre-Dame, with a beautiful porch and good stained glass; and the 15th-century mer-chant's town house Maison d'Ozé, now the Tourist Office. But Alençon's great fame is its lace industry, by appointment to Louis XIV. Both the art museum and the **lace museum▶▶** have superb lace collections. Musée Leclerc focuses on World War II.

▶ Alpes Mancelles   72C1

Considering no summit rises higher than 417m, 'Alpes' overstates the mountainous nature of this part of the Normandy/Maine Regional Nature Park, south-west of Alençon around the Sarthe Valley. But it is a picturesque and colourful region of fast-flowing streams, rocky gorges and slopes covered in heather and broom. **St-Léonard-des-Bois** is the best base: a picturesque village with accommodation, a very old church, good walks and fishing. Interesting frescos can be seen at the former her-mitage of Ste-Céneri-le-Gérei.

▶ Balleroy, Château de   72B2

This supremely elegant low 17th-century château was lucky to survive the last war intact. The château remained in the family for three centuries until bought by an American multi-millionaire, the late Malcolm Forbes. It has sumptuous interior decoration and con-tents, and a hot-air balloon museum in the stables.

Having beaten off French invaders in 1054 and 1058, William, Duke of Normandy, turned his attentions to lands across the Channel. In 1066, England's new king, Harold, was crowned; in the same year he was defeated and killed by William's forces at the Battle of Hastings. On Christmas Day 1066, William the Conqueror was crowned King of England.

A few years after the conquest of England, Bishop Odo of Bayeux commissioned a work of embroidery to adorn the choir of the cathedral on feast days, illustrating the Battle of Hastings and events leading up to it: a moral tale of Harold's perfidy punished. Traditionally known as Queen Matilda's Tapestry, the 70m-long work (coloured wool on linen) was in fact produced in 10 years (1070–80) by English nuns.

Touring tapestry The story is told in 58 scenes bordered by friezes of mythical beasts and enlivened by a wealth of incidental detail, with captions and names of the main actors in Latin. Napoleon so appreciated the story, with its stylised depiction of the English as long-haired villains and the Normans as clean-cut heroes, that he took the tapestry on a tour of France as part of the marketing for his planned invasion of England.

Bayeux itself, a few miles inland from the 'invasion beaches' of the Calvados coast, was the first town to be liberated in 1944 and came through World War II unscathed. The centre is correspondingly pretty and a popular holiday base, with good hotels and old timbered houses. The tourist office is in the old fish market, Pont St Jean. The beautiful cathedral is mostly 13th-century Gothic, but has Romanesque towers and arches in the nave, decorated with splendid reliefs. The carvings over the south doorway tell the story of the murder, by Henry II of England's soldiers, of Thomas à Becket, Archbishop of Canterbury, in 1170.

THE TAPESTRY
Political propaganda, exquisite work of Romanesque art, medieval comic strip or valuable historical document: the tapestry can be enjoyed on many levels – provided you can get near enough to see it. It has a museum to itself in Bayeux and is one of the town's main sights. The strip of linen is surprisingly narrow (only 50cm wide) and although it is well displayed, queues are often a problem. But there is an excellent slide show, audio guides and a photographic replica.

The Duke of Normandy's fleet lands at Pevensey – as depicted in the Bayeux Tapestry

The short stretch of coast from Honfleur at the mouth of the Seine to Cabourg at the mouth of the Dives is the smartest, indeed about the only remotely fashionable section of the north coast of France. The landscape is less rugged than to the north of the Seine, with long sandy beaches briefly interrupted by mini-cliffs, and a lush hinterland of orchards, thatch and timbered manor houses (the pays d'Auge).

MONET'S MENTOR
The son of a Honfleur ferryman, Eugène Boudin (1824–98) was the young Monet's mentor at Le Havre, and influenced Impressionism through his methods (painting outside and often recording the date, time and wind speed) and subject matter: bright, breezy Normandy seascapes, with a fore-ground of doll-like figures, indulging the new taste for seaside leisure. Boudin's use of colour remained more traditional.

Apart from the view of Le Havre across the estuary, **Honfleur**▶▶▶ is at heart a picturesque fishing port and artists' colony, with tall slate-hung houses overlooking the old harbour. St-Cathérine is an unusual 15th-century wooden church built by shipbuilders (it shows); and there are several good museums, one devoted to Boudin and other local marine artists, who got together at the Ferme St-Siméon (now an exclusive hotel). The sea has receded and Honfleur now has gardens where once was a beach.

Different styles Separated only by the waters of the Touques, Trouville and Deauville lie at the heart of the Côte Fleurie. Both have big sandy beaches with duckboard promenades and ornate turreted villas, but there is a marked difference of style. **Trouville**, the first to become fashionable (in the 1850s) is now the poor relation, but does have a year-round community. **Deauville**▶▶▶ grew from nothing in the last quarter of the century, an affluent sprawl of big hotels in typically Norman timbered style, with a casino, spa, airport and other trappings of high society. It likes to be known as the Monte Carlo of the north, but bears a closer resemblance to Biarritz.

Quieter scene West of Deauville lies a series of quieter resorts, all with good beaches: **Blonville**, **Villers-sur-Mer** and **Houlgate**, the last two separated by cliffs which force the road inland. The former port of **Dives-sur-Mer**, where William the Conqueror set sail, has kept its 15th-century wooden market hall near the Guillaume le Conquerant shopping mall. On the opposite bank lies **Cabourg**, a stiflingly pretentious resort where most things are dedicated to the memory of Marcel Proust, who stayed often at the Grand Hotel, and wrote about Cabourg (as Balbec). At the Grand, time is not lost: merely arrested.

The pretty port of Honfleur takes pride in its maritime past

►► Caen 72C2

A big city and river port, mostly rebuilt after intense bombardment in 1944, Caen is not an obvious tourist magnet. It has its appeal, however: great churches, albeit more imposing than endearing, and excellent museums, including the Caen **Memorial-Musée pour la Paix►** (at the northwest edge of town, near the D22 exit to Creully), a presentation of life during World War II.

Town sights Caen owes its importance to William the Conqueror and his wife Matilda who made it their base. William and Matilda were cousins, and their marriage led to excommunication, lifted only when they founded an abbey each, for men and women at Caen. The two churches, St-Etienne (gentlemen) and La Trinité (ladies), survive, sited well apart to the east and west of the central fortress. Both show Norman Romanesque architecture at its most severe. A plaque marks William's empty tomb at St-Etienne. Both abbey buildings offer daily tours (the men's one is now partly occupied by the Town Hall).

Between the two abbeys, reconstructed fortress ramparts, with a walkway, now enclose gardens and the outstanding fine arts and regional museums. Outside the walls (via the porte sur la Ville) the 15th- to 16th-century church of **St-Pierre►** contrasts sharply with the abbey churches, with a wealth of Renaissance ornament. A few old timbered houses, including the tourist office, survived the war, as did much of the 18th-century place St-Sauveur, near St-Etienne. In the same part of town the deconsecrated 11th-century church of St-Nicolas is worth a visit. Rue du Vaugueux (east of the ramparts) is good for cafés and restaurants.

Carrouges, Château de 72C1

This vast brick château of many periods seems like a moated village turning its back on intruders. As well as the guided tour of the château itself, there is an information centre for the Normandy/Maine Regional Nature Park and a good crafts centre in the old chapel.

► Champ-de-Bataille, Château de 73D2

This is not a landing beach, but a magnificent late-17th-century château, comprising twin symmetrical brick and stone wings – one for the duke, the other for guests. There is varied decoration and contents, and a fine park.

MEDIEVAL MANNERS
Originally reluctant to accept a bastard's suit, Matilda was persuaded to change her mind when William dragged her round Lille by the hair, a wooing tactic that even then must have seemed primitive.

77

CAEN STONE
The creamy whiteness of Caen limestone gives it the appearance of being too soft for building material, yet it has created magnificent monuments, not just in France but also in England. The stone was taken down the River Orne and across the English Channel for use in the cathedrals of Canterbury and Winchester, as well as Westminster Abbey.

Dieppe's attractive fishing port flourished in the Middle Ages before being overtaken by Le Havre

LES MOUTIERS
Five kilometres west of Dieppe at Varengeville-sur-Mer lies one of France's most beautiful private gardens. It was landscaped at the turn of the century by the English architect, Sir Edwin Lutyens, in consultation with the great garden designer, Gertrude Jekyll. It is open to the public daily, mid-March to mid-November (tel: 02 35 85 10 02).

IVORY CARVING
Dieppe's trade links with Africa and the Far East led to the rapid growth of ivory carving in the home port. At the height of its 17th-century prosperity, 350 craftsmen were engaged in transforming tusks into portrait medallions, crucifixes, fans, caskets and other luxury baubles. The museum has a splendid collection, and a model workshop.

Cherbourg   72B3
A vast harbour for naval and passenger ships at the head of the Cotentin Peninsula, Cherbourg was efficiently destroyed by its occupiers in 1944, but remained a vital supply line for the Allied forces. Buildings and setting are equally uninspiring but respite is offered at the century-old **Parc Emmanuel Liais▶**.

▶ Cotentin   72B3
The rocky head of this anvil-shaped peninsula is at its most impressive in the west, with granite cliffs at **Cap de la Hague** and **Nez de Jobourg** and a splendid sandy bay between them; accommodation at **St-Germain-des-Vaux** and tiny **Port Racine**. In the sheltered north-east, **Barfleur** and **St-Vaast-la-Hougue** are fishing ports with some charm. To the south stretch the dunes of Utah Beach (see opposite). There is better bathing on the peninsula's west coast, on either side of the Flamanville nuclear power station. The best base is **Barneville-Carteret▶**, a merger of villages on an estuary sheltered by the Cap de Carteret: good cliff walks, beaches and excursions to the British island of Jersey. There are bigger resorts (notably **Granville**) further south, without much charm. The best thing about the Cotentin interior is the town of **Bricquebec▶** – unpretentious, unspoiled and with an excellent market on Saturdays.

▶ Dieppe   73D3
A Roman sea-water spa and the leading port of Renaissance France, Dieppe developed into a seaside resort in the 19th century. Today it is a busy fishing port, with an excellent Saturday market and good shopping. A free bus service runs the 2km from the cross-channel (Transmanche) ferry terminal to the heart of the old town, near the pedestrianised Grande Rue. The long pebble beach is overlooked by the 15th-century **castle▶▶** (*Closed* Tue in winter), now a museum showing ivories and items illustrating Dieppe's seafaring history. More marine interest is explored at the **Cité de la Mer**. The Square du Canada has memorials to the thousands of Canadians who died in the ill-fated Operation Jubilee raid of August 1942.

Domfront   72B1
This former fortress town in Lower Normandy commands a river gorge. Castle ruins stand in public gardens at the top of the town. There are remains of old ramparts, and picturesque streets around the modern church (St-Julien). Across the river stands the truncated Romanesque church of Notre-Dame-sur-l'Eau.

As early as the summer of 1943, Churchill and Roosevelt decided that Normandy would be the bridgehead for the liberation of France under the joint command of Generals Montgomery and Eisenhower. After months of intensive air attacks to destroy the occupying army's communication lines, and a day's delay because of bad weather, a fleet of more than 4,000 landing craft set sail from England during the night of 5 June 1944 for the beaches of the Calvados and Cotentin coast, landing at dawn on the 6th, D-Day.

The Maison Gondrée café, Pegasus Bridge

Airborne troops were simultaneously dropped behind the coastal defences at both ends of the invasion front. On the beaches, initial losses were heavy but the defenders lacked air support and a vital toehold was soon won.

RETRACING HISTORY
Eight signposted circuits covering over 1,000km across the departments of Calvados, Manche and Orne, lead you from one history-packed place to another, tracing each step in the Battle of Normandy: Overlord, the assault; D-day, the onslaught; Objective, a port; the Confrontation; Cobra, the breakout; the Counter-attack; the Encirclement and the Outcome. A special pass is available offering access to the numerous museums along the circuits at considerably reduced rates.

Joint landings With Caen as their objective, British, French and Commonwealth forces landed in the east, on beaches code-named Sword (**Colleville-Plage**, **Lion-sur-Mer** and **St-Aubin**), Juno (**Bernières** and **Courseulles**) and Gold (**Ver-sur-Me**r and **Asnelles**). On D-Day itself the invading force took Arromanches and began to install an enormous artificial or 'mulberry' harbour, towed across the Channel. Two and a half million soldiers and 4 million tons of equipment landed at Arromanches in the next three months.

Further to the west, American forces landed at Omaha Beach (**St-Laurent**, **Colleville** and **Vierville-sur-Mer**) and Utah Beach on the Cotentin coast. Fierce defensive resistance resulted in very heavy American losses, especially in the area around **St-Laurent** itself (Omaha Beach).

Coastal route The D514 runs the length of the Calvados section of the 'Invasion Coast', passing numerous memorials, small museums and eloquent graveyards. War debris still litters the dunes and beaches and visitors are advised to tread very carefully.

Museums and memorials The 50th anniversary of D-Day in June 1994 refocused the world's attention on the area. Both Caen and Alençon have new World War II museums as does Ambleteuse, near Boulogne. Others can be seen at Bayeux, Cherbourg, Pegasus Bridge and Arromanches, all of which played a key role in the Battle of Normandy. At **Arromanches**, remains of the mulberry harbour are still visible, and a British graveyard lies between Ryes and Bazenville. **Colleville** and **St-Laurent** have monuments by the sea and the biggest US grave-yard (Omaha Beach). **Utah Beach** has an impressive American memorial at La Madeleine.

WHERE TO STAY
Arromanches and the lively fishing port of Port-en-Bessin are the best places to stay in this area; Courseulles, best known for its oysters, and Riva Bella are beach resorts with numerous hotels.

CLAUDE MONET

Claude Monet was born in Paris in 1840 but grew up at Le Havre, where Boudin persuaded him to paint landscapes. After studying in Paris and soldiering in Algeria, Monet settled in Paris in the 1860s, escaping to London during the Franco-Prussian war. His Le Havre painting *Impression, Sunrise* (exhibited in 1874) prompted a critic to coin the term Impressionism. Monet moved to Giverny in 1883 and died there in 1926. His dedication to his art was total. When his wife was dying, he painted her. 'Just an eye, but God what an eye!' said Cézanne.

▶ Ecouis 73D2

This small village north of Les Andelys is grouped around the 14th-century collegiate church of Notre-Dame, an unusual, broad, brick-vaulted building with many beautiful sculptures and carved wood panelling.

▶ Evreux 73D2

The departmental capital of the Eure has risen from the ashes many times, most recently after 1944 air raids. The cathedral spires melted, but the rest of the building survived, a surprisingly elegant mixture of styles from all periods from the 12th to 17th centuries, with richly decorated north and west façades, beautiful windows, an iron grille and carved wood screens in the choir. The old bishop's palace is now the town museum, and the former abbey church of St-Taurin has a marvellous 13th-century reliquary of Taurinus, Evreux's first bishop.

▶ Falaise 72C2

The birthplace in 1027 of William the Conqueror, son of the 17-year-old Duke of Normandy and a tanner's daughter, Arlette, was devastated in August 1944. But impressive castle ruins have survived, with the restorers' help. The guided tour reveals the window from which the lustful prince watched Arlette washing clothes at a riverside fountain below, and the room where William the Bastard was born. The main round tower dates from the 13th century.

▶▶ Gaillard, Château 73D2

Superbly sited castle ruins command a meander of the Seine and the pretty little town of **Les Andelys**, which has two small riverside hotels. Richard the Lionheart built the castle in less than a year (1196–7) to defend the Seine against the King of France. There is a steep path up to the ruins from the river, and a long way round by car, passing Grand Andelys' interesting late Gothic and Renaissance church (Notre-Dame).

▶ Giverny 73E2

In this small village near the confluence of the Seine and Epte, Monet spent the last 43 years of his long life, turning out countless paintings of his gardens, including the water lilies displayed at Paris' Orangerie and Musée Marmottan. Only reproductions of Monet's paintings are on display, but the pink and green house is an original, with spectacular gardens and lily pond. An attractive **museum**▶ nearby, opened in 1992, displays the works of American disciples of Monet. (Both *open* Apr–Oct.)

Monet's two-storey pink and green house in Giverny. The rooms have been restored to the artist's original designs and retain his personal furniture, mementoes and collection of Japanese prints

Le Havre 72C3

Built in the 16th century for François I when the port of Harfleur became unnavigable, Le Havre was all but obliterated in 1944 and in its reconstructed form is no place to linger, except for the **art museum**▶ at the port entrance, with works by Boudin and by Dufy, a native of Le Havre, and the Espace Oscar Niemeyer. Avenue Foch leading from the beach to the place de l'Hôtel de Ville is Europe's widest avenue.

▶ Lassay, Château de 72B1

This imposing, well-preserved 15th-century military fortress, complete with barbican, drawbridge and pepperpot towers, is on the main road from Bagnoles de L'Orne to Mayenne. The château's contents include the oven which baked the first porcelain from Alençon clay.

▶ Laval 72B1

The departmental capital once known for its linen, is a textile town. The old quarter, huddled around its cathedral and château, has picturesque walls, gateways and buildings. The naïf painter Henri (Douanier) Rousseau was born in a tower of the Bucheresse gate (his father's workshop) in 1844; the château has a naïf art museum.

Lisieux 72C2

This market town is a great place for cheese lovers on market day (Saturday). The grey Gothic cathedral **(St-Pierre)**▶ houses the tomb of Bishop Cauchon, who executed Joan of Arc. But Lisieux's focus is the vast pilgrimage basilica of Ste-Thérèse. Millions come to ride the Petit Train (summer only) linking Thérèse's family home of Les Buissonnets with the Carmelite chapel and basilica.

▶ Lyons-la-Forêt 73D3

This flower-filled village in the thick of splendid beech woods was chosen as Yonville in Claude Chabrol's film of *Madame Bovary*. Flaubert's original model, Ry, lies to the west near Vascoeil, where the historian Michelet's château **(Martainville)**▶ has interesting works of art. Lyons-la-Forêt is a good base for exploring Normandy and the immediate forest. Its sights include the 40m Bunodière beech (signed from the N31), the ruined Cistercian abbey of Mortemer (south of Lyons) and the château of Fleury.

SAINTE THÉRÈSE
Born in Alençon in 1873, Thérèse Martin moved to Lisieux aged four and entered the Carmel there at 15 by special papal dispensation. The body was as fragile as the spirit was strong and responded badly to the hardships of life in the convent, where in winter only one room was heated to 10°C. After Thérèse died of TB in 1897, her autobiography, *The Story of a Soul*, was published. Its poignant account of pain and sacrifice in the quest for spiritual perfection ('my little way') proved enormously popular consolation, especially during World War I. Pilgrims came to Lisieux as early as 1899, miraculous cures were reported, and Thérèse was canonised in 1925.

81

Château de Lassay – a near-perfect fortress

In Normandy as elsewhere in France, Benedictine monks of the Cluniac persuasion provided the main impetus for a wave of church-building which followed the year 1000. Duke Richard II persuaded the Abbot of St-Benigne at Dijon to found a new monastery at Fécamp in 1003, and from then until the mid-12th century there was a frenzy of building in a distinctive style which spread to Britain, southern Italy and Sicily.

The basic elements of the architectural style, christened Romanesque (*roman* in French) in the 19th century because of its similarities with Roman (*romain*) architecture, are the barrel vault and round arch. Compared with some of the highly decorative styles which developed in the south of France, the Norman version was based on a sobriety verging on the austere.

Places to visit Caen's two abbey churches (St-Etienne and La Trinité) are fine examples on a grand scale, as are the abbeys at **Jumièges** and **St-Martin-de-Boscherville** (see page 89), and, simplest of all, **Lessay's** reconstructed abbey church (north of Coutances). The truncated abbey church of **Cérisy** (southwest of Bayeux) is all the more impressive for its isolated setting at the edge of the village. **Lucerne** and **Hambye** are ruined sandstone abbeys in tranquil settings on the Cotentin Peninsula, between Coutances and Avranches. **Bayeux** Cathedral has typically Norman decoration of geometric and foliate patterning. This is the style that was exported to England after the Norman conquest; in Britain all the Romanesque architecture is known as Norman.

Rouen (above and below) – filigree stonework

Norman Gothic From the late 12th century the Gothic style (pointed arches, flying buttresses and bigger expanses of glass), born in the Ile de France area around Paris, gradually replaced the Romanesque style in Normandy.

    Coutances Cathedral, famous for its splendid octagonal lantern tower, and the later cathedral-sized church of St-Ouen at **Rouen** are superb examples of Norman Gothic at its most elevating and harmonious. Many other churches, if less admirably proportioned, have richer and more decorative detail to enjoy from the exuberant Late Gothic (or Flamboyant) period, which continued to be used well into the 16th century: **St-Maclou** and the cathedral at **Rouen**, **Mont-St-Michel**, **Caudebec-en-Caux** and **Evreux** Cathedral are all worth inspecting.

An 80m granite island rises from the muddy estuary of the Couesnon river, whose tortuous course at low tide, to the west of the rock, now places Mont-St-Michel in Normandy, rather than Brittany. It has been a site of importance since prehistoric times. There are quicksands in the notoriously treacherous estuary and water races across the 16km of mudflats, occasionally flooding the car park. Explore the bay on foot at your peril. Land is encroaching, but a massive redevelopment of the bay (1995–2002) aims to reverse its fate.

The rock may have been a place of worship in pre-Christian times: its early name, Mont Tombé, suggests use as a burial ground. In the 8th century the Bishop of Avranches built St Michael's Chapel there. Legend has it that it was designed according to the instructions passed on to the Bishop by the Archangel Michael in a vision. This was followed by increasingly splendid Carolingian, Romanesque and Gothic buildings, crowning the summit of the rock and supported by massive buttressed walls. A monastery was founded in the late 10th century, and throughout the Middle Ages played a dual religious and military role. As a fortress, Mont-St-Michel resisted the English throughout the Hundred Years' War.

Place of pilgrimage The pilgrim traffic began before the foundation of the monastery. Today, just under three million visitors a year file up the steep and narrow Grande Rue to La Merveille, as the abbey is known. The buildings are a combination of the finest sacred Gothic and Romanesque architecture. The most beautiful elements are the church itself (the incomplete nave is Romanesque, the choir soaring Gothic), the cloister and refectory. At the top of the 157m spire, the 19th-century figure of St Michael has recently been rearmed, having lost his sword in a thunderstorm. This forms the apex of a multi-tiered citadel whose outlook alone is breathtaking, offering views of both Normandy and Brittany coastlines.

Between the souvenir shops is a limited amount of accommodation and an overnight stay is recommended and well worthwhile, giving the chance to explore the sanctuary at its most evocative and least crowded – at dawn and dusk, or join the itinerant *son-et-lumière* (Jun–Oct, nightly except Mon).

Visitors crowd into the narrow streets of Mont-St-Michel

84

The Pays d'Auge village of Le Bec-Hellouin presents typically well-maintained, timbered façades

▶▶▶ Pays d'Auge   72C2

The fertile hinterland of the Côte Fleurie, between the Rivers Risle and Dives, is Normandy at its most delightful: the heartland of cider, Calvados and cheese. There is also plenty for the eye to enjoy, notably colourful manor houses like toy châteaux with moats, red tile roofs and patterns of timber, brick and stone. Traditional thatched roofs planted with flowers are less common than tourist office pamphlets suggest, but they do exist. **Cambremer** (west of Lisieux) and **Livarot** are at the hub of cider and cheese routes. Local tourist offices can supply maps of the routes and details of farms you can visit on the way.

The towns of the Auge did not escape war damage and cannot match the charm of their surrounding countryside. **Lisieux** is the main industrial and market centre of the region (see page 81). **Pont-Audemer**▶▶ is prettier: an old tanning town with timbered houses on its central island between branches of the Risle. The church of St-Ouen is a mixture of Romanesque and Renaissance, with beautiful 16th-century windows.

In the Middle Ages, the abbey of **Le Bec-Hellouin**▶ was an important centre of learning and supplier of eminent churchmen, including Lanfranc, William the Conqueror's right-hand man and first abbot of St-Etienne in Caen. Only one tower survives of the medieval buildings. The rest is modern restoration of 17th- and 18th-century buildings, but the visit is interesting, the abbey being very much alive. Other village attractions are the Musée de la Musique Mécanique and an excellent hotel/restaurant.

Manor Houses For a good manor house tour (combining sections of the cider and cheese routes), head south from Lisieux along the river before turning west to Livarot

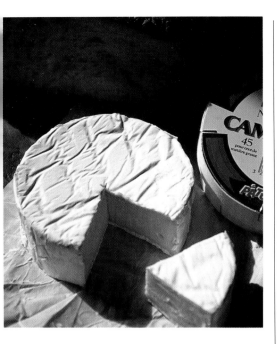

LITTLE ANGEL & COLONEL

Perhaps the best-known Normany cheese, Pont l'Evêque, was already renowned in the Middle Ages, known as 'angelot' (little angel). During the 19th century, Livarot, known as 'poor-man's meat', was the most popular Normandy cheese. It is still made traditionally, working the curds by hand, salting with dry salt and hand-tied with 5 paper 'stripes' (originally strips of willow, hence its nickname, 'colonel'). Free tours and tastings, Apr–Sep, at the Fromageries Graindorge in Livarot.

and Vimoutiers (see below) and returning north to the coast at Dives, via Crèvecoeur-en-Auge and Beuvron-en-Auge. The jewel of the manor houses is **St-Germain-de-Livet**▶ ▶ (*Closed* Tue) (south of Lisieux), a fairy-tale vision with pepperpot turrets, arcaded courtyard and pink-and-white check stonework like a gingham tablecloth. The timbered wing is older than the rest (15th-century), but discordant. There are guided tours of the interior.

The manor crawl continues south to **Fervaques**, its moat also fed by the Touques; **Bellou**▶, **Coupesarte**▶ (a delightful moated farmhouse, with patterned brickwork and corner towers supported on wooden buttresses) and **Grandchamp**. **Crèvecoeur**▶ ▶ assembles a moated manor house, timbered dovecote, gatehouse, chapel and farm buildings, a museum devoted to the Schlumberger family's oil business, and Norman architecture (*Open* Apr–Sep). On the way north to Cabourg, **Beuvron-en-Auge**▶ is an exceptionally pretty, timbered crafts village, strong on cider; there is also a 16th-century manor house at **Cricqueville**.

Cheese Country Normandy produces over a quarter of the nation's meat and dairy produce, including the celebrated pungent cheeses of **Livarot** and **Pont-l'Evêque** and the more recently elaborated and milder **Camembert**, which is now produced throughout France in insipid imitation of the real thing. You can watch the manufacture of all three at the Musée du Fromage in Livarot (Mar–Nov). **Vimoutiers** (south of Lisieux) has a Camembert museum and a statue to Marie Harel, who launched Camembert after sheltering a priest during the Revolution in exchange for his cheese recipe. Cheese lovers will head for the hamlet of Camembert itself, south by the D16/246, where farms offer tastings.

APPLE SPIN-OFFS

Cider orchards proliferate in the Auge, thanks to the dampness and clay soil. Normans prepare meat and fish in cider sauce and drink cider, corked and wired like champagne, with their food. Calvados, the best known of many local apple brandies, does not reach its best for 15 years. Normans no longer pour 'calva' down their infants' throats in the hope of producing another Conqueror (or perhaps to get some sleep), but still drink a nip with coffee, between courses (a habit known as *Le Trou Normand*), and after the meal. A distillery at Coquainvilliers (north of Lisieux) offers tastings.

Rouen's remarkably restored historic centre is full of arresting details

▶▶▶ Rouen   73D3

The capital of Normandy is a big industrial port spanning the Seine with a fascinating centre of tall, timbered houses and great Gothic churches, all carefully restored since Rouen was bombed during the war.

City Centre The two focal points of the city are the cathedral and the place du Vieux Marché, where Joan of Arc was burnt at the stake on 30 May 1431. As well as a memorial cross and a modern church with 16th-century stained glass, the square has a car park; it makes a good starting point for a tour on foot.

The pedestrian rue du Gros-Horloge, a main shopping axis, is spanned by a one-handed gilt 14th-century clock mounted on a sumptuously carved Renaissance arch. The nearby **Palais de Justice**▶▶ (take rue Thouret), much restored after war damage, is the city's most splendid Renaissance palace.

One of the great churches of France, from all periods of Gothic (mostly 13th- to 15th-century), the **cathedral**▶▶▶ has a wealth of intricate carving on the outside. Inside, there are superb Renaissance tombs in the lady chapel (weekends only, admission charge). Take the rue St-Romain to St-Maclou, a masterpiece of late Gothic (15th- to 16th-century) art on a cobbled square of timbered houses. A covered alley leads to the Aitre St-Maclou, a 16th-century court, originally a cloister used as a charnel house. Timbers are decorated with skulls and other death motifs.

Rue Damiette leads north to the 14th- to 15th-century St-Ouen, which purists consider the most harmonious and elegant of Rouen's churches. Apart from the 19th- century façade, little ornament interrupts the soaring architecture.

Museums Another of Rouen' picturesque streets, rue Ganterie, leads west to a cluster of the city's best museums: fine arts, ceramics, and metalwork (Le Secq des Tournelles). To the north looms the **Musée des Beaux Arts**▶▶▶ housing 4,000 paintings from Velázquez to Renoir. Rue Jeanne d'Arc leads back to the clock. The **Museum of Antiquities**▶, north of St-Ouen, has a rich and varied collection, including tapestries and mosaics; the **Flaubert/History of Medicine Museum** is west of Vieux Marché; and the **Corneille Museum** (dedicated to Rouennais playwright Pierre Corneille, 1606–84) is near Vieux Marché.

A MAN AND HIS PARROT
Gustave Flaubert (1821–80), misanthropic and merciless chronicler of his age (*Madame Bovary, Education Sentimentale*) was the son of a surgeon at Rouen's Hôtel Dieu, where young Gustave observed disease and death at close quarters. After giving up law for literature, he based himself in a riverside villa at *Croisset* (right bank, a few kilometres downstream of Rouen), now a museum, as is Flaubert's birthplace in Rouen, which doubles up as a museum of medical history. Both have a stuffed parrot purporting to be the bird Flaubert kept on his desk while writing *Un Coeur Simple*.

Sées   72C1

A peaceful, small town on the River Orne north of Alençon and the Ecouves forest, Sées scarcely seems to justify a grand 18th-century bishop's palace and **cathedral►►**. This is a fine twin-spired 13th- and 14th-century Gothic building with good stained glass in the crossing and a sweet 14th-century marble Virgin. A spectacular *son-et-lumière* highlights it from June to September. Over the river is a no-less-surprising 19th-century market hall, in grand classical manner. Several good hotels make Sées ideal for an overnight stop.

► Suisse Normande   72C2

The likeness to Switzerland is not unmistakable, but on its way north to Thury Harcourt (château park and gardens open May–Sep afternoons) the Orne dives and weaves through gorges and wooded valleys, and energetic visitors indulge their taste for a wide range of Alpine activities, from rafting to rock-climbing. At a more leisurely level, there is good fishing and attractive walks to rocky belvederes above the river. For campers this is a good area. The main tourist centre is **Clécy►►**, a good base for exploring the valley on foot, on horseback, by car or in a canoe. It also has Europe's biggest miniature railway. **Pont d'Ouilly** is a possible alternative, a few miles downstream from the **Roche d'Oëtre►►**, about the most impressive of the viewpoints in Norman Switzerland, overlooking the wooded gorge of the Rouvre valley. To the south, the Orne is dammed near **Putanges** to form the long **Lac de Rabodanges** (bathing and watersports).

Vire   72B2

Vire is the not very interesting capital of the not very remarkable *bocage* area, which is characterised by hedges sited on raised earth banks. These proved effective defences and made the area a nightmare through which to advance during the Battle of Normandy. Vire's speciality is a sausage (*andouille*) of pigs' intestines, the small wrapped in the large. Scanty castle ruins command a good view of the River Vire winding through a wooded gorge known as the Vaux de Vire. A medieval labourer and songwriter of the locality gave rise to the term *Vaux de Vire* (later Vaudeville) songs. There is a museum of bocage crafts and traditions in the 18th-century Hôtel-Dieu (*Closed* Tue).

TAKE A WALK
The long-distance path GR36 follows the Orne from near Argentan to Caen. The section on the right bank opposite Clécy makes a good half-day's walk from the village. Take the minor road north from Clécy to join the GR36 just before the river bridge and railway crossing. The path forks right and climbs to the Pain de Sucre (sugar loaf), a good viewpoint high above a river bend, before descending south to the bridge and riverside cafés at Vey. Legs permitting, you can continue south to the Rochers des Parcs cliffs, popular with rock climbers.

87

The 19th-century market hall at Sées comes second only to the town's grandiose cathedral

A tour of the Perche

Start from Sées.
The Perche is a region of forests, undulating hills, powerful Percheron workhorses and manor houses.

Take the N158 to Château d'O.
Built on an island in a lake, the **Château d'O's** fanciful turrets would not be out of place in the Loire (*Open* Jul–Aug).

D16/26 to Haras du Pin.
Haras du Pin is the national stud founded in the 17th century and housed in gracious buildings and park.

N26 to l'Aigle; D930 to Abbaye de la Trappe and Mortagne-au-Perche.
La Trappe's 17th-century Abbot de Rance launched the strict Trappist rule of abstinence, silence and hard labour. The abbey's setting is beautiful but the buildings are of little interest. **Mortagne-au-Perche** has an interesting Renaissance church.

D938 to Bellême; circuit to Courboyer, l'Angenardière and Les Feugerets.
Southeast of Bellême, **Courboyer**, **l'Angenardière** and **Les Feugerets** are among the finest of Perche manor houses.

Returning to Bellême, take the forest road and D210 to Mamers; the D311 to Alençon; and the D26/226/908 to Sées via the Ecouves Forest.
The biggest and most impressive of the Perche forests is part of the Normandy/Maine Regional Nature Park (information centre at Carrouges), well provided with marked paths. Denizens include boar, deer, snakes and multitudinous insects, so walkers should set off prepared (for the insects, anyway). Near the D26 and D226 crossroads, where there is a war memorial, the **Signal d'Ecouves** (417m) is the summit of Normandy. The GR36 path leads south from here to the Croix Madame crossroads, whence another path descends (east) to the Vignage rocks (good views), rejoining the D26 5km south of the war memorial.

See pages 74 and 87 for **Alençon** and **Sées**.

century and since used as a quarry. But the roofless ruins of the 11th-century church (the porch and the towers survive) and its still older neighbour (St-Pierre, 10th-century) are wonderfully romantic.

Take the D982 to St-Wandrille.
After centuries of changing fortunes, during which it was used as a mill and a private home and was much damaged, altered and restored, **St-Wandrille** abbey is once more inhabited by monks, known for their singing (open to the public for daily services) and jam. The present church is a medieval barn brought from La Neuville, 50km away in the Eure.

Continue to Caudebec-en-Caux.
Caudebec-en-Caux has a lively Saturday market beneath the beautiful late Gothic church (Notre-Dame), which has good stained glass.

Take the D81 to Norville (Etelan).
The late Gothic **Château d'Etelan** is open in summer (mid-Jul–Aug: afternoons).

❏ At Villequier, just over 4km from Caudebec, Victor Hugo's daughter and son-in-law were killed in a boating accident in 1843, victims of one of the fierce tidal currents that were a feature of the river at this point. There is a Hugo museum in the house on the quay, where Hugo used to live (closed Tue). ❏

The Lower Seine Valley

Start from Rouen.
The Seine probably derives its name from its sinuous course, nowhere more evident than on either side of Rouen: from Elbeuf to Jumièges is about 20km as the crow flies, but 75km for a fish. This tour follows the main road along the right bank, passing abbeys founded as early as the 7th century. It does not follow the meandering river, but there are minor roads that do. There is no bridge across the Seine between Rouen and Caudebec-en-Caux, but there are ferries at La Bouille, Le Mesnil-sous-Jumièges, Duclair, Jumièges and Yainville. On the outskirts of **Rouen**, Flaubert's no longer rustic pavilion at Croisset has memorabilia.

Take the D982 from Rouen to St-Martin-de-Boscherville.
At **St-Martin-de-Boscherville**, the 12th-century abbey church (St-Georges) has typical Norman geometric decoration on the façade and interesting capitals within, including jousting knights.

D143 to Jumièges and back.
Quietly set away from the main road, **Jumièges** is the greatest of the Seine Valley abbeys and the most ruinous, having been sacked in the 17th

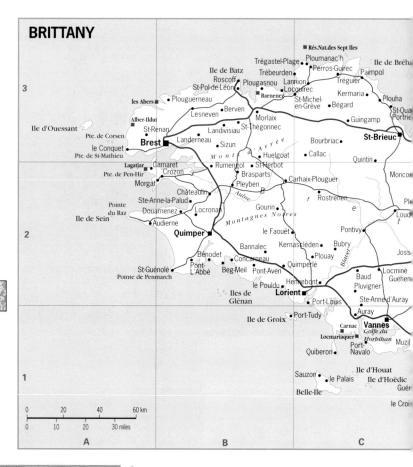

BRITTANY

Rés.Nat.des Sept Iles
Trégastel-Plage • Ploumanac'h
Ile de Bréha
Trébeurden • Perros-Guirec
Paimpol
Ile de Batz • Lannion
Roscoff • Plougasnou • Tréguier
St-Pol-de-Léon • Louguirec
Barnenez • St-Michel-en-Grève • Bégard
Kermaria • Plouha
Plouguerneau • Berven
Morlaix
Guingamp
St-Qua
Portrie
Lesneven • Landivisiau St-Thégonnec
Ile d'Ouessant
Alber-Ildut • St-Renan
Bourbriac • St-Brieuc
Pte. de Corsen • Brest Landerneau • Sizun • Huelgoat • Callac
Pte. de St-Mathieu Monts d Arrée
Quintin
Lagatjar Camaret Crozon • Rumengol • St-Herbot
Carhaix-Plouguer Monco
Pte. de Pen-Hir Brasparts
Morgat Pleyben B
Châteaulin Aulne
r Rostrenen e
Ste-Anne-la-Palud • Gourin Montagnes Noires
Loud
Pointe du Raz Douarnenez • Locrona
t
Ile de Sein • Audierne le Faouët Pontivy
Quimper
Bannalec Kernascléden • Bubry
Joss
Bénodet • Concarneau • Plouay Blavet
St-Guénolé • Pont-L'Abbé Beg-Meil Pont-Aven Quimperlé
Locminé
Pointe de Penmarch le Pouldu Hennebont Baud Guéhen
Iles de Lorient Pluvigner
Glénan • Port-Louis Ste-Anne d'Auray
Auray
Ile de Groix • Port-Tudy Carnac Vannes
Golfe du
Locmariaquer Morbihan Muzil
Port-Navalo
Quiberon •
Sauzon • le Palais Ile d'Houat
Ile d'Hoëdic
Belle-Ile Guér
le Crois

0   20   40   60 km
0 10   20   30 miles

A   B   C

90

▶▶▶ REGION HIGHLIGHTS

Belle-Ile page 92
Cap Fréhel page 98
Carnac page 94
Concarneau page 94
Corniche Bretonne pages 96
Dinan pages 98
Locronan page 99
Morbihan, Golfe du page 101
Quimper page 102
St-Malo page105

BEFORE IT WAS NAMED 'Little Britain' by invading Franks in the early Middle Ages, Brittany was called Armorica: the land of the sea. For the visitor, the region's great attractions are its long coastline of golden sandy beaches, muddy estuaries with fascinating wildlife, small fishing ports, villages of low grey and white houses; and, in the extreme west, rocky capes battered by Atlantic storms.

Inland Brittany is no longer a wasteland of heath, rocky hills and subsistence farmers, but one of the most dynamic agricultural regions of France. This is good news for the Bretons, though it does not make compelling tourism and they still top the tables for regional alcoholism. Brittany's big towns are dull and incursions from the coast are for specific points of interest – richly decorated village churches and fortresses marking the long-disputed frontier between France and the Duchy of Brittany, independent until 1547.

A LAND APART As part of France, Brittany has been a backwater, physically remote (Brest is further from Paris than are Bordeaux and Grenoble), poor and ignored. As a result, Brittany has kept, and recently tried hard to revive, its culture, traditions and the Breton language

Traditional Breton dress

Attractive Breton stone dormer window

which, although scarcely flourishing, survives in western Brittany.

This is a region of deep religious feelings, interwoven with a rich tissue of pagan myth and Arthurian legend. The combination of an intricate coastline, intriguing folklore and a good climate makes the south-west, around Concarneau and Quimper, the most picturesque corner of Brittany today.

Brittany

Remarkable shutters in the village of Les Abers – a rare display of contemporary creation

LANDMARKS
Aber Ildut marks the boundary between the Channel and the Atlantic, and the nearby Pointe de Corsen is the westernmost point of mainland France.

FAT FLAT OYSTERS
Bélons de Bélon is an increasingly rare entry at the top of a French menu, promising a plateful of slithery delight. Bélons are the most prized of flat oysters. The estuary of the Bélon river, which joins the Aven at the sea, is their traditional but not their only place of origin – hence the distinction between Bélons de Bélon and any old Bélons.

Les Abers   90B3

On the northwest coastline of Finistère, the many estuaries and shallow muddy inlets are known as *abers*. It is a low-lying, bleak and somewhat drab stretch of coast, rich in seaweed, artichokes and cauliflowers. But the small port of **Aber Wrac'h▶**, on a promontory between the two main *abers*, has charm, small hotels and dunes at the end of the peninsula.

▶▶ La Baule   91D1

No longer officially part of Brittany, La Baule is the last resort before the mouth of the Loire, and the most fashionable of the long Breton coastline. Its 5km crescent of south-facing pine-sheltered sands, promoted as the best beach in France, boasts 2,000 hours of sunshine a year. The sprawling resort behind the beach is geared up to the young, affluent and sporty.

▶▶▶ Belle-Ile   90C1

The largest of the Breton Islands is also the most lively and varied, with rocky coastal scenery on one side, good beaches on the other and picturesque villages, notably the little yacht harbour of Sauzon and fortified **Le Palais▶**, the main port and island capital. On the so-called Côte Sauvage (fairly tame, unless you coincide with a storm), Port Goulphar has two good hotels. The biggest sandy beach is Grands Sables, south of Le Palais, but there are prettier sandy coves (Herlin, near Bangor). The ferry from Quiberon is very busy in high season. Car hire can be arranged on the island, but this needs advance booking in season. (See also page 93.)

Bélon see panel.

Brest   90B3

France's great Atlantic naval base has little to offer tourists except the beauty of its setting, on a huge natural harbour: the bridge over the Elorn linking Brest and Plougastel Daoulas is a good viewpoint. Rebuilt since World War II, the city is modern and grey, but its history, including the building of the 17th-century port by forced labour, is well evoked in the waterside château and the Tanguy Tower on the other side of the river Penfeld (Old Brest Museum). A 'sea centre', the **Oceanopolis▶**, at the Moulin Blanc Marina, Port de Plaisance, has some 2,600sq m of exhibits and aquariums.

The many islands dotted along the Breton coast-line are rich in fascinating legendary, folklorish and historical associations but, in general, fairly unrewarding to visit. The wilder the island, the more intriguing the folklore, as a rule. Belle-Ile (see page 92) is the great exception, its size according it more life and variety.

Sein► (access from Audierne, and Brest in summer) is no taller than a big wave and will be an early victim of global warming. A druids' refuge and burial ground, the island's entire active male population (130) answered de Gaulle's call by setting sail for Britain in 1940. Island produce is coquilles-St-Jacques, lobster and crayfish.

Storm-lashed **Ouessant** (access from Brest, and Le Conquet in summer) is the westernmost point of France and notorious for shipwrecks. One of its lighthouses can be climbed; another contains a museum. Here, as on some of the other islands, women work the land (little of which is workable) and make the marriage proposals.

In the more sheltered waters off the south coast, Belle-Ile's neighbours **Houat►** and **Hoëdic►** (Duck and Duckling) are also accessible from Quiberon; Duck has excellent beaches and neither has cars.

Groix (access from Lorient, and Doëlan in summer) is like a smaller Belle-Ile, with a similar mixture of rocky and sandy coast. Its main village, Port Tudy, once a tunny fishing port, sees a little tourism.

Desert isles Off Concarneau, the nine uninhabited Glénan islands are a nature reserve with a big sailing school. Despite its northern location, **Bréhat►►** (access from L'Arcouest, near Paimpol) has a famously mild climate and exotic vegetation. With an intricate coastline of pinkish rocks, it is a better island for gentle walks than bathing.

The two most spectacular capes of three pronged Finistère (which means 'the end of the world') are **Pointe de Pen-Hir**, on the cross-shaped tongue of the Crozon Peninsula, and the more celebrated Pointe du Raz, at the tip of Cape Sizun in the extreme south-west. There is not much to choose between them: cliffs of about 70m in both places and an overall effect whose savagery depends chiefly on the weather and crashing waves.

LEGENDARY MERMAID
Between the Pointe du Raz and the less visited cliffs of the Pointe du Van, the little Baie des Trépassés is one of the candidate sites of the legendary city of Is, which was swallowed up by the sea as a result of King Gradlon's beautiful daughter Dahut's carrying on with the devil. She has since haunted the coast in mermaid's guise, luring sailors to their deaths.

93

Belle-Ile's town hall lies in the port of Le Palais, dominated by a 16th-century citadel

Investigating the centre of Concarneau

▶ Brière Regional Park 91D1

North of St-Nazaire, the D50 runs from Montoir up through the Grande Brière – an area of peaty bogs, canals and villages on granite mounds which are islands in winter when the bogs flood. There are several of these around St-Joachim, which has accommodation and an information centre for the regional park in summer. The most interesting is **Ile de Fédrun**, a ring of white cottages, each with a punt berth. Punting excursions on the reedy canals can be organised. Much of the Brière is a bird reserve.

▶ Cancale 91D3

Cancale is a cheerful port and gourmet pilgrimage, with fine views of the bay of Mont-St-Michel. It has the most extensive oyster beds on the Channel coast, well viewed at low tide from the harbour jetty or on the tables of its many restaurants. A museum just outside the town is devoted to oysters (*Open* Mar–Oct, must reserve: 02 99 89 69 89). Cancale's flat oysters, which were appreciated by Julius Caesar, Louis XIV and Napoleon, are now brought in from southern Brittany and planted at Cancale.

▶▶▶ Carnac 90C1

Famous for its lines of standing stones (see page 95), Carnac is also a busy seaside resort with a splendid beach. Between Plage and Préhistoire is an ordinary town centre, with an excellent museum of prehistory (*Closed* Tue).

Combourg 91D2

This is a small lakeside town beneath a mighty **feudal fortress**▶▶ (*Open* afternoons Apr–Oct, except Tue). The great romantic author Chateaubriand spent a short but gloomy period of his youth here, sleeping in a tower haunted by a previous lord of Combourg's cat. A few rooms have been made into a Chateaubriand museum, but the view is the main thing. A number of other châteaux and churches nearby make an interesting outing from Dinan: Lanrigan, Montmuran and Les Iffs, with its Renaissance stained glass.

▶▶ Concarneau 90B2

One of the great fishing ports of Europe, and one of the great tourist centres of Brittany, Concarneau's walled old town (*ville close*) sits on an island within the port. The *ville close* has 17th-century walls to walk round and an interesting fishing museum with its own floating *chalutier* (traditional fishing boat) and numerous fishy curiosities. The outer town is less special, but there are plenty of good fish restaurants around the port. The Iles de Glénan (see page 93) are one hour away.

Megaliths (big stones) are a Breton speciality, although by no means unique to the region. There are many in the north and west, but the main concentration is on the Gulf of Morbihan in the south-east.

Carnac, on the Gulf of Morbihan, has a unique series of over 3,000 stones in three alignments. The stones were raised over a long period, possibly beginning in 5500 bc, and lasting until about 1000 bc. It also has an interesting tumulus and an excellent museum about prehistoric civilisation.

Mystery system It is argued that the Morbihan megaliths form an integrated system of astrological observation points, established over a period of hundreds of years and centred at **Locmariaquer** (east of Carnac), where the greatest of all standing stones, weighing over 350 tonnes, stood 20m high. The argument leaves many experts unconvinced, and the significance of the standing stones remains a mystery. Several theories have been put forward for the alignments at Carnac; the most colourful, include windbreaks for Roman tents, and petrified legionnaires miraculously arrested while in pursuit of an early Christian pope, Cornelius, the patron of Carnac church.

Selected sites Apart from Carnac, sites include:
Barnenez (eastern side of Morlaix estuary). Tumulus.
Gavrinis Island (access from Larmor Baden). A half-covered tumulus here has beautiful patterned carving.
Lagatjar (Crozon Peninsula, near Camaret). Alignments of 100 stones.
Locmariaquer. Doubters say the great menhir never stood, but a 17th-century sailor's description confirms that it did, before crashing and breaking into five pieces (four still *in situ*). There is a fine dolmen (Merchants' Table) with carvings nearby.
La Roche Aux Fées (at Retiers south-east of Rennes). A massive 42-stone monument, one of France's largest.

MENHIRS AND DOLMENS
Brittany has no circles to compare with Britain's Stonehenge, but large numbers of menhirs (standing stones, from the Celtic *maen hir*, 'long stone'). These either stand on their own or in lines. Dolmens are structures with roofs, probably used as graves, and tumuli are earth-covered burial mounds with stone-walled tunnels and chambers.

Dolmens are collective burial places with horizontal slabs over upright stones

CRÊPES AND CRÊPES...
Ask most visitors to France where crêpes come from, and the most likely answer is the boulevard St-Michel in Paris, where street vendors smear them with gooey chestnut purée (or whatever), roll them into floppy cones and serve in a paper napkin. The buckwheat pancake is, however, a Breton export, and every village on the coast has its crêperie, where pancakes with a variety of fillings are served at table, preferably with Breton cider. Wheat flour is often used instead of traditional buckwheat flour.

The beaches of the Corniche de l'Armorique are sculpted by cliffs and rocks: tides leave plenty of interest in rock pools

►► Corniche de l'Armorique 90B3

This short stretch of scenic wooded coast road runs round a W-shaped bay, from **Locquirec** – a white-washed resort with beaches on both side of its narrow promontory – to **St-Michel-en-Grève**. The great feature of the bay is the enormous (4km) beach at **Lieue de Grève►►**, punctuated by the **Grand Rocher**. This is a good viewpoint which can be reached by a short but steep path from the road. There are interesting churches at **Plougasnou** (on the coast west of Locquirec) and **Ploumilliau**, east of St-Michel. The **Pointe de Primel** is an impressive granite headland in the manner of the Breton Corniche (see below), which adds to the confusion between the two Trégastels. **Primel-Trégastel** is a more modest resort than Plage of that ilk, but has a good beach. **Lannion►**, the main town of this area, is not a bad place for a rainy day, with picturesque old houses around the central square and a fine hilltop church. A few miles south of the town, the isolated 16th-century Kerfons chapel has a calvary and beautiful rood loft.

►► Corniche Bretonne 90C3

Scenically, the best thing about the north coast of Brittany is the zone of strangely eroded pink granite rocks between **Trégastel-Plage►** and the fishing port and busy beach resort of **Perros-Guirec►►**. The locals, inspired by the curious eroded rock formations, have conjured some evocative names for them: Napoleon's Hat, Death's Head, the Pancake, the Torpedo, and so on. There are good views of the shoreline from the light-house at **Ploumanac'h** – a small fishing port between Trégastel and Perros – and from the coastal path '**Sentier des Douaniers'►►**, between Ploumanac'h and Perros, a beautiful 5km walk. Ploumanac'h itself is divided by a municipal park – a kind of rock reserve. From Trégastel-Plage, the coast continues to **Trébeurden**, a small resort with good beaches split by a rocky promontory. From Perros-Guirec there are boat trips to the bird sanctuary archipelago of the **Sept Iles►►**. The largest of the group is the Ile aux Moines whose lighthouse and fort can be visited.

Breton sightseeing has its limitations but the parish close (enclos paroissial) is a fascinating local speciality, best seen in Léon (northern Finistère). In 16th- and 17th-century Brittany, as nowhere else in France, the buildings around the village graveyard developed into an elaborate architectural complex.

Traditionally, the parish close consists of a triumphal arch (the churchyard gate); a highly decorated church porch, where parish councils met; a separate ossuary or a charnel house, where old bones were stored to make room for the new dead; and, as the focal point, a free-standing calvary swarming with carved granite figures in modern dress, illustrating Bible stories and popular morality tales.

St-Thégonnec offers a particularly elaborate example of the traditional Breton parish close

Origins To the obvious question – why? – the best answers are probably local rivalry between villages, the survival in Brittany of passion plays, the use of the calvaries for popular religious instruction, and the singular Breton preoccupation with death. Many church interiors have richly carved and painted wooden altarpieces, pulpits, glory beams or complete rood screens.

Close competition Rivalry played an important part in the development of the two most spectacular and complex parish closes, at **St-Thégonnec** and **Guimiliau**. Other outstanding examples (not all complete parish closes) are at **Lampaul-Guimiliau** (wood carvings in the church); **La Roche** (ossuary, screen); **St-Herbot** (screen and ossuary); **Sizun** (arch and ossuary); **Le Folgoët** (pilgrimage church with a magnificent 15th-century granite screen); **Brasparts** (carved Virgin in the church); **Berven** (screen); **Plougastel-Daoulas** (calvary); **Ploumilliau** (a wooded sculpture of Ankou, the Breton Father Time, with scythe) and **Kerfons** chapel (rood loft and calvary).

CHURCH TRAIL
Making a church route from west to east, notable closes can be seen at Pleyben (church and calvary); Notre-Dame du Crann (stained glass); St-Fiacre, near Le Faouët (an outstanding screen) and Kernascléden (15th-century frescos). Guéhenno, south of Josselin, has a parish close with a remarkable story. Its great calvary was destroyed during the Revolution and pieced together laboriously and expertly by the villagers. In the north, near Paimpol, the chapel at Kermaria has a remarkable series of Dance of Death frescos.

97

Brittany

Dinan's harmony arises as much from its riverside setting as from its fine granite buildings

RURAL ROAMING
One of Brittany's loveliest rural areas lies inland from the Emerald Coast and can be explored starting from Dinan. Don't miss the Roman ruins at Corseul, the charming back roads radiating from Plancoët or the powerful fortress ruins of the Château de la Hunaudaye overlooking the Arguenon river.

ONE-MAN DEFENCE
Dinan's favourite son is Bertrand du Guesclin, who defended the town against the English by winning a single combat against a Canterbury knight in 1364. Du Guesclin's request to be buried at Dinan was complicated by the distant location of his death (caused, after a lifetime of heroics, by drinking icy spring water), in a remote region of the Massif Central. Bits of him were laid to rest in Paris, Le Puy, Le Mans and Montferrand, but the great soldier's big heart made it back to the basilica of St-Sauveur at Dinan.

▶▶ Dinan   91D3

Dinan is a wonderfully preserved medieval town, surrounded by 600-year-old ramparts and guarded by an impressive fortress, high above the Rance. Its few museums are a less powerful magnet than the cobbled streets, timber-fronted houses, craft shops and weavers' workshops. There are good views from the Jardin des Anglais (Dinan had a large 19th-century British colony) and the small port.

The Rance estuary▶▶ One of the longest and most beautiful of Breton inlets, the Rance sees huge tides of up to 13m. A short distance upstream of its mouth at St-Malo and Dinard, it is bridged by the world's first tidal power dam, which uses both ebb and flow to generate electricity. You can walk along the dam, which makes a long narrow reservoir of most of the steep-sided inlet, drive over it, and sail through it. Boat trips go up the Rance from St-Malo to Dinan.

▶ Dinard and the Emerald Coast   91D3

Facing St-Malo across the mouth of the Rance, **Dinard**▶▶ was crowned 'Queen of the Emerald Coast' by English Victorians, who 'discovered' the resort and its sheltered crescent of white sand. Its claims to rival La Baule as a fashionable Breton resort should be treated with some scepticism, but Dinard retains a certain style, with neo-Gothic villas, formal hotels, lush Mediterranean-type gardens, coastal walks and well-heeled visitors.

Between Dinard and Cap Fréhel the coast weaves an intricate course up inlets and back along rocky promontories, with the finest cliff scenery between the medieval **Fort de la Latte** and **Cap Fréhel**▶▶▶. To the east and west lie a succession of bucket and spade resorts: **St-Cast-Le-Guildo** and **St-Quay-Portrieux** (both mergers) are the liveliest, both good for watersports. **Sable d'Or Les Pins**▶ lives up to its name with shady pines and long golden sands, and **Erquy** is a small fishing port with everyday Breton charm, good seafood, and a beach into the bargain. The big town of the area, **St-Brieuc**▶, has an unusual fortified 14th-century cathedral.

Dol de Bretagne   91D3

Once a bishopric, once beside the sea, Dol now overlooks land reclaimed from the Bay of Mont-St- Michel since the Middle Ages. **St Samson's Cathedral▶** is a massive 13th-century granite structure, with splendid views from the tower. Champ-Dolent is a fine **menhir▶** (see page 95) to the south, near the Rennes road.

▶ Fougères   91E2

One of the most impressive of all **fortresses▶▶** marking the medieval border between France and Brittany is eccentrically located below this substantial town. Perhaps for this reason its defensive record was not spotless. The ruined interior has open-air concerts. One of the best views of its turreted structure is from the garden terrace of the place aux Arbres.

▶ Josselin   90C2

This old town was named after the younger son of the baron who began building its castle**▶▶** in the early 11th century. In striking contrast to the powerful round towers and wall rising from the waters of the Oust, most of the building is in ornate Renaissance style, much restored.

▶▶ Locronan   90B2

Between Quimper and the Crozon Peninsula, the small village of Locronan has a grand ensemble of Renaissance buildings around its central square, a reminder of the days of wealth derived from sail-making. Every second Sunday in July, Locronan has a *pardon* (pilgrimage) following the course of Saint Ronan's daily barefoot walk. The village is now a thriving arts centre.

Lorient (see panel) is a large fishing port and naval base. The arsenal and submarine base are only open to French citizens.

JOSSELIN'S RULER
The first Rohan at Josselin was the wife of Jean de Beaumanoir, who captained the winning side in 1351 when the forces of Josselin and pro-English Ploërmel agreed to a hand-to-hand fight.

LORIENT'S MARITIME PAST
Lorient prospered with the Compagnie des Indes, which built its shipyards on the Blavet estuary. Louis XVI and Napoleon transformed the port into a naval base. The German garrison held out until May 1945 and little remained standing. A festival of Celtic culture is held in August.

Dol de Bretagne's main street is flanked by timbered houses supported by 11th- and 12th-century pillars

shows the interior of an 18th-century peasant home. South of St-Cadou is the **Ménez-Meur** Wildlife Reserve and Regional Park information centre.

D130/342/42, Forêt du Cranou, to Le Faou.
Le Faou is an attractive estuary port, with good hotels to be found on the main square.

D791 Corniche de Térénez road; excursion to Ménez-Hom (D60/47/83).
Ménez-Hom (330m) is the western bastion of the Monts d'Arrée, a splendidly isolated hump at the base of the cruciform Crozon peninsula. A steep road climbs to a viewing platform. At a crossroads near **Trégarvan**, north of Ménez-Hom, the old village school hasbeen restored (Musée de l'Ecole Rurale). There are sandy beaches along the south side of the peninsula, between **Ste-Anne-la-Palud** and **Morgat**.

D47/21 to Brasparts, D14 to St-Herbot and back to Huelgoat.
Brasparts has a crafts centre and an interesting church with Renaissance porch and calvary. **St-Herbot's** Gothic church has a 16th-century ossuary and calvary and carved wooden screen. Herbot is the patron saint of horned beasts; hoping for protection for their cattle, farmers traditionally deposit locks of tail hair in the church on pardon day.

Visiting the Hill Country: Monts d'Arrée

Start at Huelgoat.
Huelgoat is a rare inland resort, beside a lake at the heart of Brittany's hill country, the **Monts d'Arrée**, now one section of the fragmented Armorique Regional Park. The 'goat' in the name, meaning forest, is no longer appropriate after centuries of deforestation and severe storm damage in October 1987. The main walking area is to the north-east of the village; Arthur's camp is genuinely ancient if not Arthurian.

D764 to Roc Trévézel; D785/30 to St-Rivoal and St-Cadou.
The route skirts the reservoir and much resented nuclear power station of **St-Michel**, a surprising landmark at the heart of a regional park. Near the crossroads of D764 and 785, the **Roc Trévézel** (384m) is the summit of Brittany, a wild and bleak rocky crest. Millions of years ago these mountains stood as high as the Alps do now. A few miles west, on the Sizun road (D764), the old hamlet of **Kérouat** has been restored as a rural ecomuseum. The Maison Cornec in nearby **St-Rivoal**

▶▶ Morbihan, Golfe du   90C1

Morbihan is the only one of Brittany's *départements* with a specifically Breton name: it means 'Little Sea', a reference to the vast mud-rimmed tidal lagoon known as the Gulf of Morbihan. The gulf forms an almost complete circle, including the **Vannes** and **Auray** estuaries and enclosing 40 inhabited islands: the entrance to the inland sea between Locmariaquer and Port-Navalo is less than 2km wide. In the 1st century bc the gulf was the site of a sea battle between the local Veneti tribe and the forces of Rome. Julius Caesar watched from the summit of a prehistoric tumulus on the shore near Arzon, on the southern arm of the entrance to the gulf.

Oyster Country The best way to see the gulf is by boat, either a private yacht (tricky currents in the strait) or on a boat trip, for which Vannes is the main base. Low tide reveals huge expanses of mud flats and oyster beds. The gulf (especially the area known as the the Auray Peninsula) is the breeding ground for flat oysters, which grow on lime-washed tiles until they are big enough to be transported to parks all round the Breton coast.

Driving round the gulf is long and not particularly rewarding. Of the two main towns, Vannes is more interesting to visit than Auray, except for one of the big *pardons* at **Ste-Anne d'Auray. Locmariaquer**, the Island of **Gavrinis** (from Larmor Baden) and Carnac are the highlights of Breton prehistory (see page 95). On the southern arm of the gulf, the main points of interest are the old monastery of **St-Gildas-de-Rhuys▶**, with a part-Romanesque church (St Gildas' tomb); and the splendidly wild 13th- and 14th-century fortress of **Suscinio▶▶**. **Port Navalo** provides accommodation and has summer boat trips.

The cobbled streets of Auray climb up from the banks of the River Loch

THE VAGARIES OF ABÉLARD
After his amorous adventure with a young pupil, Héloïse, in Paris, the philosopher Peter Abélard withdrew to the lonely job of abbot of St-Gildas-de-Rhuys in 1126. In a letter to Héloïse he expressed his hatred of Brittany and his suspicion of the Breton monks. Abélard's attempts to impose discipline in the abbey went down very badly with men he referred to as savages, who spoke a language he was unable to understand. In 1138 the resentful monks rebelled and tried to poison Abélard, but he survived and escaped.

Sailing on a private yacht or an organised trip is the best way to see the sights of the Golfe du Morbihan

Brittany

DARK PAST
Nantes' history has its darker moments. Gilles de Rais, the original Bluebeard, was tried and burned at the stake in the Ducal castle in 1440. Nantes later made fortunes out of the slave trade. And in 1793, it saw macabre ceremonies known as Republican Weddings, when Royalists were stripped naked, bound together in pairs and dumped in the Loire in order to make room in the city's prisons.

PAIMPOL
In the 19th century, Paimpol was the main base of France's long-haul cod fishing fleet, immortalised in Pierre Loti's novel *Pêcheur d'Islande*. On 20 February, most of the town's men would set sail for six months in the North Atlantic, returning in late summer. Refrigeration technology hit the industry and Paimpol is now a busy pleasure port and agricultural market place.

▶▶ Nantes 91D1
The former capital of Brittany is no longer a city of much charm. The old town is now encircled by fast ring roads, and its chief monument, the 15th- and 16th-century Dukes' castle, stands among tall modern blocks. Closed for 14 years, it will re-open in 2008 as one large château-musée covering the history of Nantes and the region. The **fine arts museum**▶▶ displays outstanding works by Perugino, Ingres and de la Tour; and the late Gothic cathedral has the beautiful Renaissance tomb of the last duke of Brittany, François II. Take time to explore the 18th-century colonial quarter which lies west of the cours des 50-Otages.

▶ Quiberon 90C1
This lively port and resort with a good beach lies at the end of the long sandy isthmus linking the former island to the mainland. There are good walks along the rocky west coast. Fresh sardines used to be a speciality, but supply has dwindled recently. There are ferries to Belle-Ile and the other Quiberon islands (see pages 92–3).

▶▶▶ Quimper and Cournouaille 90B2
Cournouaille's 6th-century King Gradlon made Quimper his capital after the destruction of Is and a statue of him stands between the twin spires of the Gothic cathedral, which changes direction at the crossing. Quimper takes tradition seriously, and is full of well-kept charm: cobbled streets, timber-framed houses, costumed and coiffed old ladies making lace. It has a moderately interesting fine arts museum, a Breton museum and a faïence museum representing Quimper's 300-year-old tradition of hand-painted pottery. There are boat trips down the Odet Estuary.

At the mouth of the river, **Bénodet** is the largest of several family beach resorts in the camper's favourite corner of Brittany. **Beg-Meil** is the other favourite focus for camping.

The rest of the south-west corner of Brittany is disappointingly dreary. **Pont l'Abbé** is a town of needle-workers and the home of the tallest of all Breton *coiffes*, here not kept for special occasions. **St-Guénolé**▶ has a good beach, a prehistory museum and splendid rocky coast at the back of the port and at the nearby Pointe de Penmarch. **Audierne** is ideal if you prefer fishing ports to beach resorts. Masses flock to the celebrated **Pointe du Raz**▶▶ with its 70m cliffs, Brittany's most spectacular rocky cape (see page 93).

A stall selling lace in Quimper, also known for its hand-painted faïence, best seen at the Faïenceries H. B. Henriot (visits Mon–Fri)

The name of Pont-Aven has become inextricably linked with Paul Gauguin, the 38-year-old Paris stockbroker who gave up everything (job, wife and five children) to spend the summer there in 1886, with his fellow artist Emile Bernard.

103

Gauguin and Bernard did not discover Pont-Aven (southeast of Quimper), which was already full of artists, mainly Scandinavian and British. It was picturesque then as now, with walks in the Bois d'Amour by the river, and watermills outnumbering dwellings 15 to 14. There were several inns: the Julia (French academic artists), des Voyageurs (Americans, some of whom stayed all year) and the more bohemian Pension Gloannec, where Gauguin and friends holed up at 60 francs a month, including two good meals a day and cider; more often, paintings were accepted in lieu.

Model neighbours Pont-Aven was a thoroughly pretty place, added to which the locals readily agreed to pose in their quaint costumes for a few sous a day. Gauguin, Bernard and disciples, including Sérusier and Maurice Denis, were not insensitive to these aspects of Breton charm but looked beyond them and the naturalistic aims of Impressionism. They launched a new, more mystical art, using the local chapels for their sense of rural piety, interwoven with myth and superstition. Within walking distance of the village, the Trémalo Chapel's wooden Christ inspired Gauguin, as did Nizon's calvary (*Yellow Christ* and *Green Christ* paintings).

Grand exit In 1889, Gauguin and friends moved from Pont-Aven, which they found overrun, to Le Pouldu on the coast, where Gauguin surprised walkers by his rough appearance – naked, with long hair and a spear at the ready. This caused less of a stir in Tahiti, which was the artist's next move.

Paul Gauguin's Gossipers

'When my wooden shoes ring on this granite, I hear the muffled, dull, powerful tone I seek in my painting.' – Paul Gauguin

PONT-AVEN PAINTINGS
Pont-Aven still has its walks, restored mills and various galleries, but go to Rennes' Musée des Beaux Arts to see original Pont-Aven paintings

SEA CURES
The whole Léon coast is rich in seaweed: Roscoff has over 70 varieties, which it puts to medical, chemical and agricultural use. Ordinary seaweed is an excellent natural fertiliser for artichokes, cauliflowers and onions.

►► Rennes 91D2

The capital of Brittany was almost entirely demolished by fire in 1720 and subsequently rebuilt in a severe classical style. Only the area between the market square (place des Lices) and the city's two waterways escaped and remains old and higgledy-piggledy. Sadly, the sumptuously decorated 17th-century law courts are closed for restoration, but the rue St-Georges presents harmonious architecture; the cathedral has a fine carved wooden altar; and the hilltop Jardin du Thabor offers verdant respite.

► Roscoff 90B3

This port and pretty seaside resort, once renowned for its pirates, is now known for the sea cure. Beautiful alabaster altar reliefs adorn the church near the harbour, whose Renaissance belfry bristles with cannon to warn off the English. Roscoff's 'Johnnies' (itinerant onion sellers) regularly crossed the channel in the 19th and early 20th century (their museum is open Jun–Sep). The creation of a deep water port was a key part of the strategy to revive Breton agriculture in the 1960s under the dynamic leadership of Alex Gourvennec. Re-establishing their old Celtic links, the farmers' ferry company, Brittany Ferries, exports vegetables to south-west England and Ireland, and welcomes ferry-loads of British tourists on the return leg. Day trips go from the old port to the sandy island of **Batz** (pronounced Baa).

► Ste-Anne-la-Palud 90B2

West of Plonevez-Porzay is the sandy beach and seaside hamlet of Ste-Anne-la-Palud, which hosts the most famous *pardon* in Brittany, on the last weekend in August.

Roscoff's harbour at low tide reveals the seaweed used in local thalassotherapy centres

▶▶ St-Malo 91D3

St-Malo is a port with a long and proud history of nautical explorers, traders and swashbuckling corsairs (licensed pirates, effectively) who took the name as far as the distant Falkland Islands (Malvinas to the Argentinians; Malouines to the Malouins). The heart of their home town at the mouth of the Rance is a walled citadel (St-Malo-Intra-Muros) at the entrance to the harbour. Although the town had to be rebuilt after destruction in 1944, the job was faithfully done, and Intra Muros deserves a **rampart tour▶▶** and a wander. An impressive aquarium lies under the ramparts.

● **Stroll** *At low tide you can walk to two islands: a Vauban fort and Grand Bé, where the 19th-century author Chateaubriand, who spent his formative years at St-Malo, is buried.*

▶ St-Pol-de-Léon 90B3

This vegetable market town near Roscoff has two beautiful **churches▶▶**, the cathedral and slightly later Kreisker chapel, famous for its slender 77m belfry. St-Pol is one of the seven old Breton bishoprics, a tour of which every Breton should traditionally make at least once. The saint in question is the 6th-century missionary Paul Aurelian, who lived here before retiring to the island of Batz, where he is said to have tamed and expelled the local dragon.

▶▶ Tréguier 90C3

An old hillside town, well set above a deep oyster-rich inlet near busy north coast resorts, Tréguier has a celebrated pilgrimage in honour of Brittany's beloved St Yves, a 13th-century lawyer and poor man's champion. A splendid cathedral is set on the market square. Tucked into the rocky coast to the north, little **Port Blanc** has great charm, and was appreciated by H G Wells and Bernard Shaw, among many other escapists.

▶▶ Vannes 90C1

This important town in Breton history (the act of union with France was finalised here in 1532) has old walls and fortified gateways intact, commanding the Gulf of Morbihan. A canalised waterway reaches the foot of the town walls. The old town centre is touristy and picturesque, with timbered and gabled houses overhanging the narrow streets around the cathedral. Thirty kilometres north lies **Kerguehennec▶▶**, a superb 19th-century park dotted with site-specific contemporary sculptures (*Open* château Apr–Oct, park all year).

▶▶ Vitré 91E2

Set at the foot of a fine turreted 14th-century castle on the River Vilaine, Vitré rivals Dinan as a medieval time warp. Lots of interesting old houses line the streets which run between the castle and the church of Notre-Dame, which has an external pulpit for open-air religious debate. Literary tourists may want to visit the nearby **Château des Rochers-Sévigné▶** (*Closed* Tue), home of a great letter-writer of the 17th century, the Madame de Sévigné.

PARDONS
Pardons are a mixture of religious and pagan festival: pilgrimages undertaken to seek anything from forgive-ness to a bumper harvest. These remain serious religious occasions, but also provide a chance for a costume display and, afterwards, a bunfight. The most important are at Rumengol (15 August and Trinity Sunday), Perros-Guirec (15 August), St-Jean-du-Doigt (23/24 June), Ste-Anne-la-Palud (last weekend in August), and Tréguier (3rd Sunday in May). The biggest pilgrimage centres are Le Folgoët (main event in early September) and Ste-Anne-d'Auray (last Sunday in June). Locronan has an extra-large pardon every six years.

105

'Vannes and his wife' look out over their home town

One of the most popular of the Loire Valley châteaux: Azay-le-Rideau

THE VAL DE LOIRE, in the form of the ancient provinces of Anjou, Touraine, Orleanais and Berry, is the historic heart of France. As capital of the Plantagenet kings' Angevin Empire, which at its zenith stretched from the north of England to the Pyrenees, it was the focus of almost three centuries of war between the French and English, which culminated in the expulsion of the English in 1453.

GRACIOUS LIVING The resulting ascendancy of French pride engendered a period of fervent building, and as a result the countryside around the Loire Valley is incomparably rich in Renaissance châteaux, built of milky-white tufa. With their turrets and towers, steep, grey-slate roofs, galleries and pleasure gardens, they are a perennially popular part of the tourist itinerary. It may come as a disappointment to realise, during a lengthy guided tour (in French), that for many châteaux the main interest is in their historical associations. It pays to make a careful selection and to include one or two of the more intimate, inhabited châteaux.

THE RIVER The wide, shallow Loire flows sluggishly between mud banks and silt islets, past looming nuclear power stations and busy towns and highways. Its prettier tributaries are punctuated with white and grey villages and fringed by forests, orchards and fertile cultivations, justifying the area's claim to be the garden of France.

The Loire

Detail from the entrance of Angers' St-Maurice cathedral. Inside are 12th-century stained-glass windows

▶▶▶ REGION HIGHLIGHTS

Amboise *page 108*

Azay-le-Rideau *page 113*

Blois *pages 110, 113*

Chambord *pages 111, 113*

Chenonceau *pages 111, 113*

Cheverny *page 114*

Chinon *page 114*

Loches *page 116*

St-Benoît-sur-Loire *page 121*

Villandry (Garden) *page 124*

LEONARDO'S RETIREMENT

In 1516, François I, determined to lure to Amboise as many distinguished Italian artists as he could, persuaded Leonardo da Vinci to enjoy a quiet retirement as *premier peintre et ingenieur et architecte du roi.* He thrilled the court with dramatic *son-et-lumières,* firework displays and pageants, using mechanical special effects; he also drew up plans for a new Venetian-style town. The museum set up in his former home in Amboise, the manor of Le Clos Lucé, contains models constructed (fairly recently) according to his designs – including a parachute, helicopter and tank.

▶▶ Amboise   106C2

This small and attractive town was one of the earliest Loire settlements, and an important bridgehead in the Middle Ages. It became the site of one of the greatest royal châteaux after Charles VIII (who was born here in 1470), inspired by the exuberant Renaissance buildings he had seen on an otherwise unsuccessful campaign in Italy, embarked on building a new style of palace – a far cry from the usual fortress strongholds which had hitherto characterised royal buildings.

Only fragments of the château remain today, but a guided tour is well worth taking in order to visit the superb Flamboyant chapel of St-Hubert, on the former ramparts, and the extraordinary Tour des Minimes, the château's original entrance, with a spiral ramp said to have been able to accommodate horses and carts. It is also worth visiting the **Pagode de Chanteloup▶**, an oriental folly, situated just south of the town.

▶▶ Angers   106B2

A large town on the banks of the Maine, Angers lies in the area known as Black Anjou on account of the local rock, which in contrast to the white tufa of Touraine, further east, lends a forbidding tone to the buildings. The black shale fortress walls of the Château d'Angers are relieved by white stripes; 17 drum towers remain to evoke its military past, when Angers was an outpost of the French kings on the border of hostile Brittany.

Angers is well endowed with buildings of interest. Around the powerful early-Gothic cathedral are many fine old houses including the 16th-century Maison d'Adam and the Renaissance Hôtel Pincé. Across the river lies the Doutre district, cradle of contemporary tapestry, and full of architectural curiosities worth exploring.

▶▶▶ Azay-le-Rideau see page 113   106C2

▶ Beaugency   107D3

Another important Loire bridgehead, delivered from the English by Joan of Arc in 1429, Beaugency is now a compact small town with a cluster of sights by the river: an evocative ruined keep (*donjon*), picturesque cobbled streets, a regional museum in the château, and a Renaissance town hall.

Tapestry weaving in Europe is believed to have started in the 12th century, although the techniques were probably used in classical Greece and Rome. From the 14th to the 17th centuries the art reached its peak. The main workshops were in Paris, Arras, Bruges, Tournai and Brussels; later, royal workshops were established at the Gobelins factory in Paris, and at Aubusson.

The most famous tapestry to have survived from the early period is the incomplete but superb series of 70 works illustrating the Apocalypse of St John the Divine, commissioned by the Duc d'Anjou in 1375, and made in Paris by Nicolas Bataille from cartoons by Hennequin de Bruges. These huge works (100m long and 5m high), intended for Angers Cathedral, provide a graphic illustration of St John's writings, depicting rivers of blood and whores of Babylon against a more gentle background of *mille-fleurs*, with humorous touches such as rabbits popping in and out of holes in the border.

COVERS AND RUGS
Tapestries were used not only for wall hangings in churches and houses of the rich, but as covers for beds, chairs, tables and cushions, and as horse blankets and rugs.

109

Survival over the centuries The preservation of these tapestries is nothing short of miraculous, following haphazard storage (they were displayed only rarely in Angers Cathedral) and disposal during the Revolution. In 1843, the Bishop of Angers set about buying all the fragments he could find, and having them carefully restored. Now they hang in a gallery in the Museum of Tapestries in the **Château d'Angers**. You can appreciate the tapestries on many levels: by following the story, Bible in hand, admiring the technical details, or simply looking at the faces whose emotions are as vivid as ever, even after 600 years.

Tapestries for today On the opposite side of the river, the **Ancien Hôpital de St-Jean** is the setting for a remarkable series of contemporary tapestries created in Aubusson by the painter and designer Jean Lurçat. Inspired by the Apocalypse, Lurçat created intense and colourful symbolic works entitled *Le Chant du Monde* ('The Song of the World'). Against a black background, he depicted his fears of the future of the world; the first four panels (including *The Man of Hiroshima* and *The Great Charnel House*) are more pessimistic in their outlook than the later ones.

Originally there were to have been 17 panels; only ten were created, over a period of nine years, before Lurçat's death in 1966.

Detail from an Angers tapestry

▶ Beauregard, Château de   *107D2*

Like Chambord, Beauregard was one of François I's hunting lodges. Unlike Chambord, this château is still inhabited, and although on the popular châteaux trail, it is relatively unfrequented, and well worth visiting. There is a portrait gallery of 327 famous people, echoed in the new Jardin des Portraits, a Delft tile floor, and some fine timbered and coffered ceilings (*Closed* Wed Oct–Mar).

▶▶ Blois   *106C2*

The busy town of Blois could be considered the tourist capital of the Loire Valley. Picturesque and lively, it is a good base for visitors without a car, with a selection of sightseeing coach tours on offer from the tourist office, and bicycles to rent opposite the château (in summer) or from Velo-Cycles Leblond (all year: 02 54 74 30 13). Taking pride of place on a cliff top north of the river is the great royal **château**▶▶▶ (see pages 112–13), whose architectural variety – with parts ranging from the 13th to 17th centuries – reflects its history as the favoured royal residence until Louis XIV moved the court to Versailles.

  The hilly town has its share of pedestrianised shopping areas and picturesque old streets by the river; the tourist office organises guided walks.

Architectural detail at the royal château of Blois

JACQUES COEUR
Jacques Coeur's remarkable talents for commerce and his consequent royal honours led, in 1451, to his imprisonment instigated by a band of jealous courtiers. After a dramatic escape, he offered his services to the Pope but died soon after.

▶▶ Bourges   *107E2*

This large industrial town is notable for one of France's great Gothic **cathedrals**▶▶▶ (mainly 12th- and 13th-century), famous for its double aisles, beautiful stained glass, and richly sculpted Romanesque side doors from a previous building. Bourges also possesses one of the most perfect examples of a Gothic mansion, which combined comfort with defence – the **Palais Jacques Coeur**▶▶, built for a wealthy 15th-century financier and trader.

▶▶ Brissac, Château de   *106B2*

Between the Loire and the wine villages of the Layon, Brissac is yet another example of a château which combines medieval foundations and towers (which resisted all attempts at destruction) with a later building:

in this case the more recent addition is an elegant 17th-century central wing, richly decorated (guided tours; *closed* Tue Sep–Jun).

► **Candes-Saint-Martin** 106B2

At the confluence of the Loire and the Vienne stands the quiet farming village of Candes, where the fortified church of **St-Martin**►► (12th- and 13th-century) has much of interest, including a richly sculpted façade and soaring Angevin vaulting. The steep path behind the church offers attractive river views.

►►► **Chambord** 107D2

At the western edge of the Sologne lies the huge forest estate and hunting reserve of Chambord. There are public avenues and paths, and game observation posts (dawn and dusk are the best times for deer and wild boar). At the heart lies the memorable 440-room Château de Chambord, transformed by François I from a simple hunting lodge (see pages 112–13). (*Open* daily).

►► **Chaumont-sur-Loire** 106C2

This small riverside town is overlooked by a hillside park whose tall cedar trees almost hide one of the finest

CHAUVIGNY

On the east bank of the Vienne, east of Poitiers, the small town of Chauvigny has a fine hill-top fortress. On the same hill, the church of St-Pierre has remarkable grotesque capitals; and to the south of the town, the little church of St-Pierre-les-Eglises has interesting frescoes.

Chauvigny Market has little to do with the ruins of five enormous châteaux up above

111

early Renaissance châteaux in France, home for many years to the scheming Catherine de Médicis and her rival, Diane de Poitiers. The château appears more like a medieval fortified castle than a royal residence, and the furnished interior illustrates the rather spartan lifestyle enjoyed by its noble inhabitants. There are very fine stables in the grounds, also home to a landscape-gardening school (*Open* daily).

►► **Chenonceaux** 106C2

The village of Chenonceaux is well provided with accommodation and other tourist facilities, but not with charm. An overnight stay is worth considering, however, in order to beat the morning crowds at the château.

BLOOMS

Chaumont's flourishing horticultural school, a recently created national institution, gives rise to a blooming festival every summer (mid-June to mid-October). Thirty landscape gardeners indulge their talents by creating a thematically inspired garden.

The great age of châteaux-building in the Loire followed the campaigns of Joan of Arc and the subsequent expulsion of the English from France in 1453. With peace, a new feeling of national pride and optimism was engendered, which resulted in ambitious royal building programmes. The failure of successive military forays to Italy by Charles VIII, Louis XII and François I between 1494 and 1525 was mitigated by their exposure to the Renaissance movement in that country. Italian architects, artists, artisans and gardeners were brought to the French court, and schools were established first at Amboise, then at Tours, Blois and Fontainebleau.

112

In the Loire Valley's ancient hunting grounds of kings and courtiers, the new climate of peace changed the need for fortification, and emphasis was placed instead on comfort and elegance. Massive walls, machicolations, battlements, moats and drawbridges were gradually to give way to ornamental details: open loggias, finely sculpted exterior staircases, mullioned and dormer windows, columns and pilasters.

Chenonceau, spanning the River Cher (right) and a detail from Blois (below)

Inspired designs In the transitional period of the early 16th century, Renaissance features were grafted on to Gothic ones; later influences were the Mannerist decorative architectural arts of Rome, providing inspiration for the school of **Fontainebleau**. This period was followed (in the 17th century) by a more dignified classical approach for exteriors, combined with brilliantly profuse rococo decoration. No motif was too elaborate: scrolls, nymphs, shells, luxuriant foliage and wreaths were applied in stucco, wood or papier maché to walls, ceilings and furniture.

Four of the most beautiful and most popular Loire châteaux from the Renaissance period are **Azay-le-Rideau**, **Blois**, **Chambord** and **Chenonceau**.

Azay-le-Rideau This graceful, small white château, its image reflected in a moat formed by the River Indre, retains its medieval appearance, but combines this with the new ornamental style. It boasts a beautifully decorated internal staircase with straight flights, an innovative departure from the conventional spiral. The interior has been arranged as a Renaissance museum (Nightly itinerant *son-et-lumière*, mid-May–mid-Sep).

Blois The royal château of Blois is interesting for its variety of styles. From the 13th century onwards, a succession of buildings was erected around a central courtyard. The most impressive is the elegant François I wing (adorned by a magnificent spiral staircase tower), which was partly demolished by François Mansart in order to build the Gaston d'Orléans wing, in sharply contrasting classical style.

A guided tour of the interior features heavily restored rooms and much historical detail, including a description of the bloody murder of the Duc de Guise in 1588. More rewarding is a *son-et-lumière* performance in the courtyard or a visit to the revamped Musée des Beaux Arts.

Chambord Designed by an Italian architect, this monumental château was built as a superior hunting lodge by François I. Its size defies most camera lenses, and lends an air of fantasy to the building, which may seem to have more in common with Disney than the Renaissance. The most memorable exterior feature is the extraordinary sculpted roofscape, consisting of numerous chimneys, bell turrets, dormer windows, spires and capitals; it served as a viewing terrace from which to observe the start and finish of hunts, as well as tournaments and pageants, and was also a place for court assignations and intrigues.

Inside, the most outstanding feature is the famous double spiral staircase, by which people can ascend and descend simultaneously without meeting each other, thought by some to have been designed by Leonardo da Vinci. The château is sparsely furnished and evokes little of the life of former times, but you can visit without a guided tour.

The exterior aspect of Chambord is best enjoyed before or after popular tourist visiting hours; at dawn or dusk, it assumes an almost magical quality.

Chenonceau A supremely elegant château whose arched gallery spans the River Cher. The building work was supervised by Katherine Bohier, the wife of Thomas Bohier, royal tax collector and embezzler. Following confiscation by François I, the château came under the influence of Diane de Poitiers and then, more significantly in architectural terms, Catherine de Médicis, who added a gallery to the bridge.

The interior is well furnished and is visited without a guided tour (explanatory notes are available). There are fine formal gardens and a park; other attractions include a waxworks museum illustrating scenes from Chenonceau's past. (Note that the village of Chenonceaux is spelt with an 'x', unlike its château.)

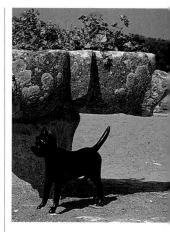

Chenonceau's gardens attract some odd visitors

A WOMAN'S WORK
Created for the financier Gilles Berthelot in the early 16th century, Azay-le-Rideau is one of several chateaux in the Loire Valley, Chenonceau included, where the building work was directed by a woman – in this case, Berthelot's wife.

The Loire

114

CHINON EXTRAS
Nuclear power fans or foes can visit France's first nuclear power station at Avoine, 12km north of Chinon. No longer in use, it houses a didactic Musée de l'Atome (tel: 02 47 98 77 77). Less stressful perhaps is a one-hour trip on the 1900s steam train from Chinon to Richelieu (services every weekend mid-May–mid-Sep). Rabelaisian-insired foodies may like to visit La Dévinière (at Seuilly, 6km west of Chinon), the birthplace and museum of the creator of Gargantua – the writer François Rabelais.

An onion-seller in Chinon

▶▶▶ **Cheverny, Château de**   *107D2*

This is a rigorously symmetrical classical château, supremely harmonious, whose interior has been largely unaltered since its completion. Sumptuously decorated and furnished in Louis XIII style, it is one of the few Loire châteaux to evoke the feel of a home; it is still privately owned and inhabited. Expect long queues for the guided tour in high season. Cheverny is famous for its liveried hunt; in the grounds of the château, the kennels and trophy room can be visited (*Open* daily).

▶▶ **Chinon**   *106B2*

A busy and interesting small town and tourist centre on the leafy Vienne, Chinon is dominated by the ample ruins of its medieval castle, a royal residence best known as the place where, in 1429, Joan of Arc first persuaded the Dauphin Charles to let her take command of an army in order to drive the English out of France.

Chinon is an attractive base for a short stay (there are several hotels and restaurants, as well as a riverside campsite). The picturesque cobbled streets of the old town are lined with half-timbered houses; the principal centre of activity is the Grand Carroi crossroads.

▶▶ **Cunault**   *106B2*

On the south bank of the Loire north-west of Saumur lies the beautiful Romanesque church of Cunault, part of a former Benedictine monastery. Tall and slender, its pure white tufa stone broken only by fragments of fresco, Cunault is renowned above all for its wealth of remarkable sculpted capitals, best admired through binoculars.

▶ **Doué-la-Fontaine**   *106B2*

Troglodyte structures of one sort or another abound here, but of particular interest are the quarry from which monolithic sarcophagi were hewn in Merovingian times, and the remarkable anonymous late 16th-century bawdy sculptures in the caves at **Dénezé-sous-Doué** (sadly unprotected). A labyrinth of caves, waterfalls and tropical vegetation in another disused quarry provides refuge for over 500 animals (mainly threatened species) at the imaginatively run **Zoo de Doué**▶.

Discovering the River Vienne

Start at Chinon.
The Vienne is an intimate and secretive river, bordered by gardens, orchards, willows and poplars.

D749 to Champigny-sur-Veude and Richelieu.
The chapel of Sainte-Chapelle at **Champigny-sur-Veude** is part of a former château demolished by Cardinal Richelieu in a fit of jealousy. Saved only by the intervention of Pope Urban VIII, it is a wonderful example of the marriage of Renaissance with Gothic. In the town of **Richelieu**, to the south, the Cardinal's own château was demolished in the Revolution. Fine parks remain; of more interest, however, are the results of 17th-century classical town planning.

D757 to l'Ile-Bouchard. Take the D760 to Crouzilles or the D18 to Parçay-sur-Vienne or the D757/D21 to Avon-les-Roches, Les Roches-Tranchelion and Crissay-sur-Manse.
The area south-east of Chinon, along the Vienne Valley, is rich in early churches. At **l'Ile Bouchard**, fine capitals remain in the ruins of St-Léonard priory. Various detours offer the opportunity to visit the Romanesque churches of **Crouzilles**, **Parçay-sur-Vienne** and Avon-les-**Roches**, the Gothic/Renaissance collegiate church of **Les Roches-Tranchelion**, or the Carolingian church of **Vieux-Bourg-de-Cravant**.

Return to Chinon direct on D21 via Cravant-les-Côteaux, or go back to l'Ile-Bouchard and take the D760 via Tavant, Sazilly and Anché; rejoin the D749 to Chinon.
The tiny Romanesque church of **Tavant** has lively frescoes, full of realism (for access apply to Mme Ferrand, who lives opposite the cemetery, or to the Mairie).

►► Fontevraud   106B2

Relatively little remains of the great 11th-century abbey of Fontevraud (even the few buildings that survived the Revolution had to serve for over 150 years as a national prison). Apart from the soaring abbey church, the most interesting part is the kitchen, a rare example of secular Romanesque architecture, flanked by apsidal chapels and topped by 20 chimneys.

Gien   107E2

A bridgehead town and useful stop on the rather dull stretch of Loire east of Orléans, Gien is known mainly for its faïence. The huge factory west of the centre contains a museum and offers tours of the fabrication process (tel: 02 38 67 00 05). Gien's red-brick **castle**► contains a well-displayed museum of hunting; next to it, the modern church of Ste-Jeanne-d'Arc fits in unusually well with its surroundings.

►► Langeais, Château de   106C2

One of the most interesting late medieval royal châteaux to have come down to us largely unaltered, Langeais illustrates the transition from Gothic (fortress exterior, drawbridge and barbican) to Renaissance (interior). Rather unusually, it contains a wonderful collection of contemporary furnishings, tapestries and works of art, which evokes the lifestyle of the time of Charles VIII and Anne of Brittany. The château (*Open* daily) lies in the busy centre of an otherwise unexciting small town.

►► Loches   106C2

Above the modern town of Loches lies the heavily fortified medieval city, whose fierce keep and dungeons, purportedly the deepest in the Loire, served for many centuries as a state prison. The château (*Open* daily) is perhaps best known as the home of Agnès Sorel, extravagant mistress of Charles VII; a guided tour reveals among other things the tiny prayer cell of Anne of Brittany. It's worth wandering around the ramparts and through the old quarter leading up to the medieval city, where there are some fine Renaissance houses.

Powder horns in the Museum of Hunting at Gien

▶▶ Le Loir   *106B2*

The confusingly named tributary of the Loire, Le Loir, meanders slowly through a peaceful agricultural countryside. Although within easy striking distance of its more famous sister, Le Loir is off the main tourist track, with the exception of the **Château du Lude▶▶**. Its towns and villages preserve an everyday charm, in the past appreciated by Ronsard and today by fishermen. Dégustations of the local wines, Jasnières and Coteaux de Vendômois, are readily available.

Church Country Le Loir is of particular interest to lovers of early churches (like the stretch of the Vienne described on page 115). Along its banks is a succession of small Romanesque buildings, most of which were on a medieval pilgrimage route leading to Santiago de Compostela in Spain. Orders of Benedictines, Cistercians and Knights Templar housed and fed the pilgrim travellers, and in **Montoire** and **Trôo** hospices and leper hospitals offered comfort to the sick.

The Loir churches are of special interest for their brightly coloured frescoes; some are remarkably well preserved. A good area for a church crawl is on the stretch of river between **Vendôme** and **La Chartre-sur-le-Loir**. Particular ones to seek out include the church in the little village of **Areines▶**, the site of a Roman settlement, on the eastern side of Vendôme (take the D917 east, followed by the first road on the left); St-Genest in **Lavardin▶▶**, which has especially fine mural paintings dating from the 12th to the 16th centuries; and **St-Jacques-des-Guérets▶**, on the south bank of the Loir just outside the village of Trôo, which also has a superb series of paintings.

Town Sights The towns along this stretch of Le Loir offer plenty of interest, too. **Vendôme▶▶** not only has a fine Gothic abbey church (La Trinité), with a rich Flamboyant west front, but is also a picturesque place built on several islands, with waterside gardens. The attractive market square of **St-Martin** has a beautiful Renaissance bell-tower. **Montoire** possesses some of the best frescoes of all the Loir churches, in the tiny chapel of St-Gilles; it is also remembered as the site of a meeting in 1940 between Marshal Pétain and Hitler.

TODAY'S CAVE-DWELLERS
The Loire Valley's soft tufa stone has long provided accommodation, in conditions of constant temperature and humidity, for wine-storage and mushroom cultivation. Along Le Loir the banks are riddled with tufa caves which are used for troglodyte dwellings. Now no longer only simple peasant abodes, troglodyte caves are sought-after second homes, with central heating to supplement the log fire (the chimney sticks out of the ground above), and conservatories tacked on to the front.

117

THE UNEXPLODABLES
River transport was once vital in the Loire region, carrying passengers, wine and other produce in flat-bottomed barges. In 1832, a steamboat service started between Orléans and Nantes, vastly reducing journey time but also leading to deafeningly exploding boilers. New 'unexplodable' steam-boats were introduced, but the development of railways in the 1850s led to their gradual disappearance.

The Loire Valley is often the cut-off point for France's varying weather: clouds stop and the southern sun starts here

In the village of Luynes

LOIRE WINES
The Loire Valley produces every style of wine. The best appellations for dry whites are: Muscadet de Sèvre-et-Maine; Pouilly-Fumé and Sancerre, and the cheaper Reuilly, Quincy and Menetou-Salon; Savennières, and the individual vineyard appellations of Coulée de Serrant and La Roche aux Moines. For reds: Saumur-Champigny; Bourgueil and St-Nicolas-de-Bourgueil; Chinon. For sparkling whites: Saumur; Vouvray and Montlouis. For sweet whites: the superb Quarts de Chaume and Bonnezeaux, and the larger area of Côteaux du Layon; Vouvray and Montlouis.

24 HOURS
The first race at Le Mans, in 1923, was won by a Chenard & Walcker which cruised at an average speed of 92kph. Prize for the fastest lap went to a Bentley which clocked 107kph.

▶ Luynes　106C2

Just off the north bank of the Loire, west of Tours, the village of Luynes is overlooked by yet another of the valley's sentinels – the Château de Luynes (not open to the public). The current building (mainly 13th-century) replaced an earlier fortress, which in turn was built on the site of a Roman castrum. The **aqueduct** which served this, and the town of Tours, can still be seen to the north-east of the village.

▶▶ Le Mans　106B3

Known mainly for its world-famous 24-hour automobile race every June, the industrial city of Le Mans, situated on the River Sarthe, serves as a crossroads town between Normandy and the Loire Valley. This ancient city still preserves its Gallo-Roman ramparts, and the beautiful Romanesque/Gothic **cathedral of St-Julien▶▶▶** is rich in interest: vivid stained glass, Renaissance tombs, and a 12th-century south doorway which could rival that of Chartres. Within the ramparts there are antique and craft-shops, more churches and several fine houses, some of which can be visited: the Maison de la Reine-Bérengère houses a local history and ethnography museum; the **Tessé mansion▶** has a rich collection of paintings.

On a different track Racing enthusiasts will not want to miss the 24-hour circuit (13.5km of track, off the D139 to the south of the city), and the **Automobile Museum▶▶** (*Open* daily, Jan–Feb weekends only), which houses an excellent collection of elegant vintage cars. Not surpris ingly, Le Mans also harbours a gigantic Renault factory.

▶▶ Meillant, Château de　107E1

South of Bourges, the Château de Meillant is the finest in the Berry. Similar to many of the Loire châteaux in its combination of fortress and palace, Flamboyant Gothic and decorative Renaissance, the still-inhabited Meillant rivals its better-known neighbours for the interest of its interior, beautifully decorated and furnished (*Closed* mid-Dec–Jan).

► Montgeoffroy, Château de 106B2

About 20km east of Angers, this elegant and harmonious 18th-century château has remained in one family since it was built, and the Louis XVI furniture, wood-panelling and wall hangings are all original. The tour of the house includes some beautiful rooms, as well as kitchen garden, saddle room and the stables, with a collection of carriages (*Open* Easter–mid-November).

► Montreuil-Bellay 106B2

South-west of Saumur, the large hulk of the 15th-century Château de Montreuil-Bellay dominates the small village above the very leafy little Thouet River; the château comprises several parts, including a pyramid-shaped kitchen reminiscent of that at Fontevraud (see page 116), complete with cooking utensils. The former chapel is now the village church (tours: Apr–Oct).

► Montrichard 106C2

This attractive little market town on the banks of the Cher has a beach, half-timbered houses by the river, and one of the many fierce keeps to be built in the 11th century by Foulques Nerra, Count of Anjou. On the outskirts of town are stretches of former tufa quarries, now housing wine or mushroom cellars, or troglodytes.

OUT OF MONTRICHARD
Twelve kilometres to the south-west overlooking a wooded valley stands the elegant Château de Montpoupon, an early Renaissance construction with a striking gatehouse. An amusing hunting museum is housed in the outbuildings (*Open* Apr–mid-Jun, Oct, weekends only; mid-Jun–Sep, daily).

The Château de Montreuil-Bellay, where the intrepid Duchess of Longueville once rode up the main staircase on horseback

►► Nohant, Château de 107D1

Near La Châtre, in the south of the Berry, this was the home of Aurore Dupin, better known as George Sand; it is now a museum, with souvenirs of Sand and her lovers and friends, who included Chopin, Liszt, Flaubert and Balzac (erratic opening hours, tel: 02 54 31 06 04). The countryside in and around the *Vallée Noire* of this stretch of the Indre features heavily in her novels.

►► Noirlac, Abbaye de 107E1

In the Berry, south of Bourges, this former 12th- to 14th-century abbey is typical of the simple, austere style of Cistercian buildings. Some of the monks' living quarters have been furnished, giving an idea of 12th-century monastic life (*Closed* Tue, Oct–Dec, tel: 02 48 96 23 64).

GEORGE SAND
Born in Paris in 1804, Aurore Dupin (alias George Sand) soon moved to Nohant. Here she lapped up the mysteries of this typical Berry countryside and transferred them to her novels. After her marriage to an uninspiring baron, she would make nocturnal escapes from the château, disguised as a peasant, to join the more rambunctious nightlife of La Châtre. She died at Nohant in 1876.

The cloisters of the Abbaye de Noirlac (see page 119)

LOIRE GASTRONOMY
Food specialities of the Loire include river fish, particularly pike (*brochet*), carp (*carpe*), shad (*alose*) and salmon (*saumon*), served with a sorrel sauce (*à l'oseille*) or a sauce of butter, vinegar, and shallots (*beurre blanc*); early vegetables, particularly asparagus, and mushrooms; game, particularly in the Sologne; cold, potted pork (*rillettes* and *rillons*), and pork with prunes, a speciality of Tours; fresh cream cheeses (*crèmets*), eaten with sugar and cream; goats' cheeses, especially from Poitou; caramelised upside-down apple tart (*tarte Tatin*).

▶ Orléans   107D3

Indelibly associated with Joan of Arc, who delivered it from the English in 1429 after a siege of eight months, the industrial city of Orléans has long been the site of decisive battles. From the early days when Orléans stopped the hordes of Attila, through the Wars of Religion and the Revolution, and finally during the last war, Orléans suffered much destruction. Now it is the regional capital and a lively university town, although it cannot be said to brim with charm. References to The Maid abound (road and house names, statues and a museum devoted to her); other sights include a much altered cathedral with fine carved panels, and an **arts museum**▶▶ (*Closed* Tue).

▶▶ Plessis Bourré, Château du   106B2

This magnificent moated fortress, north of Angers, is not only one of the finest houses in Anjou, but also one of the best examples of secular architecture of the late 15th century. Built by Jean Bourré (also responsible for Langeais), during the period which marked the transition from heavy feudal fortress to elegant abode, Le Plessis Bourré's sumptuously decorated living quarters (including an exceptionally fine painted wooden ceiling in the guardroom) surround a huge courtyard (*Closed* Dec–Jan; Wed and many mornings out of season; tel: 02 41 32 06 01).

▶ Plessis Macé, Château du   106A2

On a hill some 13km to the north-west of Angers, Plessis Macé retains much from the days when it was a strategically important fortress, including ramparts, moat and keep. The original 11th-century fortress was partially destroyed during the Hundred Years' War, but the 15th-century additions are of more interest, particularly the splendid Flamboyant Gothic courtyard balcony, which served as a ladies' viewing area during tournaments (*Closed* Dec–Feb, Tue and mornings out of season).

▶▶ Poitiers 106B1

An industrial and university city, much damaged during the last war, Poitiers is best known for its Romanesque churches, and its high-tech theme park, **Futuroscope▶**. On the great pilgrimage route to Santiago de Compostela, a distinct school of Romanesque architecture emerged in the province of Poitou; today, the finest example is the church of **Notre-Dame-la-Grande▶▶**, on Poitiers' market square. Another exceptional building is the 4th-century baptistery, which is unattractively situated but well worth seeking out for its medieval frescos. The **Musée Sainte-Croix▶** (*Closed* Mon) displays archaeological and medieval artefacts.

▶ St-Aignan 107D2

A small town on the Cher, St-Aignan has narrow streets of half-timbered houses climbing up wooded slopes below a Renaissance château (access only to the terrace). The Romanesque church has many features of interest, including beautiful capitals and frescos in the crypt.

▶▶ St-Benoît-sur-Loire, Abbaye de 107D3

The site of St-Benoît was a sacred druid place of worship before the monastery of St-Pierre-de-Fleury was founded in the 7th century. Renamed St-Benoît after receiving the relics of the saint, the abbey became an important place of pilgrimage and enjoyed increasing prosperity. The beautiful basilica which you see today was built between the 11th and 13th centuries, and is one of the finest examples of Romanesque art and architecture in the country – tall and light, with harmonious proportions and wonderfully sculpted capitals. The abbey has now been revived as a monastic community, and daily services with Gregorian chants are held.

▶▶ St-Savin 106C1

Twenty kilometres east of Chauvigny, the abbey church at St-Savin-sur-Gartempe is another very beautiful Romanesque church, notable for its extraordinarily vivid life-size mural paintings. (Binoculars are readily available and well worth renting to appreciate the detail.)

FUTUROSCOPE
The so-called 'European Park of the Image' is a vast complex of futuristic constructions offering some extraordinary technological attractions aimed at all ages. Cinema experiences include moving seats, images in relief, hemispherical screens viewed through special glasses or 360-degree screens. Interactive water-games and countless other high-tech attractions complete the range (*Open* daily 9–6, later in summer).

The village of St-Benoît-sur-Loire does not always reflect its impassioned spiritual past

Tributaries of the Loire

Start at Loches. East to Beaulieu-les-Loches, then D92 along the Indre to Châtillon-sur-Indre. D675 to Nouans-les-Fontaines.

The Indre and Indrois are quiet and beautiful tributaries of the Loire, meandering through chalky escarpments, lined with willows, alders and poplars. Despite being less well endowed with grand châteaux than other parts of the region, the area is very rewarding for an unhurried tour on minor riverside roads through sleepy villages, past small churches, ruined abbeys and mills, and troglodyte caves. **Châtillon-sur-Indre**, on the northern fringe of the Brenne marshlands, is an important market town for agricultural produce and equipment, with views from the fortress-topped old town (and a beautiful Romanesque church). The 13th-century church in **Nouans-les-Fontaines** also merits a short detour to see the large and very fine altarpiece by Jean Fouquet.

D760 to Montrésor, then the D10 to Chemillé-sur-Indrois, and a short detour to Chartreuse du Liget.

For those suffering from withdrawal symptoms, the medieval fortifications and interior manor of the **Château de Montrésor** will come as a timely architectural injection; it's beautifully furnished by the Polish family who set about restoring it in the mid-19th century. Montrésor is also notable for an elegant Renaissance doorway on the church. **Chemillé-sur-Indrois** has a small leisure complex on a lake. At the edge of the Forest of Loches lie the remains of the Carthusian monastery of **Le Liget**.

Follow the Indrois Valley west on minor roads to Genillé, and the D10 to St-Quentin-sur-Indrois and Azay-sur-Indre.

Azay-sur-Indre, **St-Quentin-sur-Indrois**, **Genillé**, **Chemillé-sur-Indrois** and **Villeloin** are all attractive villages with old houses, abbeys or small castles.

Follow the Indre south-east on the D17 back to Loches. Visitors leaving the area to head north-east via the Cher could additionally take in the Château de Montpoupon, on the D764 from Loches to Montrichard.

❏ Like several other monasteries, Le Liget was founded by Henry II in expiation for the murder of Thomas à Becket; ask for the keys to visit the frescoed Chapelle St-Jean, and take a glance at La Corroierie, a former annexe of the monastery, on the Montrésor road. ❏

► Saumur
106B2

Not one of the Loire's most attractive towns, Saumur's main fame (apart from the pepperpot-towered castle which dominates the town and surrounding countryside) derives from the tufa which gives this area its name of 'White Anjou'. The many caves and cellars carved out of the soft white chalk in and around Saumur shelter thousands of bottles of sparkling wine and around 70 per cent of the country's cultivated mushrooms. This may be reason enough for visiting the town (guided tours and tastings are offered at many of the wine houses), but an additional attraction is offered by Saumur's Cadre Noir, the corps of instructors at its famous **Calvary School**, with its annual display in July (Apr–Sep: practices can be watched). No less than three museums are devoted to various aspects of the horse and horsemanship (one in the château, which also houses a **museum of decorative arts**► ► and a toy museum).

The **château**► ► (*Closed* Tue, Oct–May) itself has been much altered since the days when it was depicted so beautifully in the book of miniatures, *Les Très Riches Heures du Duc de Berry*, and has served as a prison and barracks. There are good views from the watch-tower over the old and new towns.

Serrant, Château de
106A2

Guided tours are given of this large and very imposing domed Renaissance-style château near Angers. They reveal opulent décor and furniture; in the chapel, designed by Hardouin-Mansart, is the baroque tomb of the Marquis de Vaubrun by Coysevox (*Closed* Tue and Jan–Mar; mid-Nov–Dec. *Open* weekends).

► Sologne
107D2

This area is an infertile plain of marshland and deciduous forest, bounded by the large loop of the Loire between Blois and Gien. The D922 between **La Ferté-St-Aubin** and **Romorantin** is signed as a tourist route, passing typical Sologne countryside and lakes bright with water lilies. Attractive village features include low brick and timber houses and galleried churches: fine examples can be found at **Souvigny-en-Sologne**► ► and **Brinon-sur-Sauldre**. An interesting archaeological museum in the main town of Romorantin offers the opportunity to learn about Solognote life. The **Etang du Puis** is a large lake with watersports facilities.

Looking at the Loire across Saumur: the bridge saw a heroic stand by cavalry cadets in 1940 against the German advance

The Loire

*The quintessential
Château d'Ussé was
built in the 15th century
around a medieval
fortress*

SULLY
Henri IV's right-hand minister and shaper of the fortunes of France, Maximilien de Béthune, was given the title of Duke of Sully after he purchased the château in 1602. Always a confirmed workaholic, later in life Sully would rise at 3am to pen his memoirs and even installed a printing press in one of the towers. He also greatly embellished the fortress.

BALZAC'S TOURAINE
Born in Tours, the great novelist Honoré de Balzac (1799–1850) referred constantly to his beloved Touraine, encapsulating the charms of the countryside in *Le Lys dans la Vallée*. This novel, among many others, was written in the Château de Saché (near Azay-le-Rideau), in which he frequently sought refuge from the clamour of Parisian life. Balzac's rooms in the château have been arranged as a museum and contain manuscripts and proofs covered in such an abundance of notes that many a printer must have been driven to despair.

► Sully, Château de   107E3
This feudal fortress is notable for one of the finest medieval timber roofs in existence, which was fashioned out of chestnut (which had previously been seasoned for several years both in and out of water) by ships' carpenters (*Open* Mar–Nov).

►► Tours   106C2
The thriving industrial and university city of Tours is encircled by tower-block outskirts, but the city has managed to preserve (with much recent restoration) its historic heart, and the straight wide boulevards provide excellent shopping facilities. For tourists without a car, Tours makes a good base from which to take coach tours of the châteaux; and the lively old town is well provided with restaurants and bars. Sights include museums (devoted to medieval and **fine arts**►►, craft guilds, waxworks and wine), and a Gothic **cathedral**► with beautiful stained glass.

► Ussé, Château d'   106B2
This is the classic fairy-tale château of one's dreams, used by the writer Perrault as the model for his setting of *Sleeping Beauty*. Ussé's woodland backdrop (at the edge of the dark forest of Chinon) is appropriately romantic. Topped by turrets and tall chimneys, the outside is rather more captivating than its interior, with the exception of the Renaissance chapel (*Open* mid-Feb–mid-Nov).

► Valençay, Château de   107D2
This vast domed château, in a well-stocked park (with exotic animals) to the south of the Cher, is a very fine example of the classical Renaissance style. Most famously associated with the 19th-century politician Talleyrand, the château is richly furnished in mainly Louis XV, Louis XVI and Empire styles and has a car museum in the outbuildings (moving outside the park soon). (*Open* daily Mar–Oct, weekend afternoons only in winter.)

►► Villandry, Château de   106C2
A much altered château which retains only the keep from its original fortress building, Villandry is notable above all for the re-creation of its 16th-century gardens, one of the finest examples of the formal style known as *à la française*. Arranged on three terraces, it combines symbolic designs and decorative effects with practical use (vegetables, herbs and fruit). The planting, clipping and pruning statistics are mind-stretching (*Open* daily).

When Charles VIII returned from northern Italy filled with a desire to copy the ornamental architecture of the Italian Renaissance, he brought with him not only the best architects, artists and craftsmen, but also a very talented garden designer, Pacello da Mercogliano. French gardens before the 16th century were mainly of practical use (orchards and areas for vegetables and medicinal herbs), with only a rare concession to ornament. The châteaux gardens at Amboise and Blois were to break new ground.

Setting a trend Larger and more colourful than traditional gardens (those at Blois covered an area five or six times that of the palace), and with a greater variety of flowers, Amboise and Blois were to be the first of a series of royal pleasure gardens which became increasingly decorative and fanciful as the century progressed.

Style change The other, more subtle change concerned the composition of the garden, which became symmetrical, conceived as part of the overall design of a building. The classical garden, *à la française*, was developed with genius by the great royal gardener **Le Nôtre**; at its best it was supremely ordered, and, under Louis XIV, inescapably grand. Le Nôtre was one of the first gardeners in France to recognise the importance of trees in a landscape composition; he also used water, in the shape of tranquil ornamental ponds (unlike the Italian style of fountains or informal streams and lakes), to great effect. Three gardens sum up Le Nôtre's legacy: those at the **Tuileries**, **Vaux-le-Vicomte** and **Versailles**.

The gardens at Versailles ...

Le Style Anglais The French garden could be said to be the very opposite of the English garden (called 'romantic'), whose natural rambling style, punctuated by architectural ornaments such as fake temples, pagodas and Gothic ruins, became increasingly popular in France. The style reached its peak in the 19th-century parks created by Napoleon III as a result of his long exile in London – most famously the **Bois de Boulogne** and the **Bois de Vincennes**.

... and at the Château d'Ussé

New directions On a more modest level, in town or village, the French garden of today betrays its ancestry: formal and symmetrical patterns of bold and contrasting colours, red with blue, orange with white, are popular and widely employed; their discipline is far removed from the apparent disorder and subtle hues of the English cottage garden. In the last few years, however, a renaissance in landscape-gardening has begun to take place, producing innovatory approaches such as the **Parc André Citroën** in Paris and countless municipal replantings.

126

WHEN THE FRENCH mass-migrate for two months to the beach every summer, all roads leading to the Mediterranean are jammed, while on the Atlantic coast an infinity of pines, dunes and sandy beaches await. From Bordeaux to the Pyrenees, the map reveals only a scattering of resorts.

FAMILY FORMULA Do not expect pretty ports or charming coastal villages of the unspoilt 'hidden gem' variety. Aquitaine provides huge horizons and wide open spaces, ideal for family holidays to a formula: a simple flat or a campsite, sun and sand, lots to do but comparatively little to see. Lakes near the sea offer safe bathing and watersports. Surfers head for the ocean rollers in Biarritz.

THE NORTHERN STRETCH The **Vendée** and **Charente** coasts are more varied, with bays, fishing ports, islands and a rural economy of oysters, mussels, vineyards and salt pans. But here, too, the land is flat, and resorts are best for families requiring little more than a beach for the kids and French food and wine in the supermarket for mum and dad, who will return home with fond memories of *mouclade* (mussels in white wine) and a souvenir bottle of Pineau des Charentes, the local cognac-based aperitif. Of the towns, only the old port of **La Rochelle** has much style and *joie de vivre*.

ENGLISH LINKS Northern and southern coasts are separated by the Gironde, a deep incision where most of the rivers in southern France reach the sea. **Bordeaux** was the capital of English territory in France after Louis VII rashly lost Eleanor of Aquitaine to the future king of England, Henry Plantagenet, in 1152. The English were not chased out until 1453, by which time bibulous Albion had acquired a taste for 'claret', as the English still call red bordeaux. The region has not severed its British links of trade, blood and vineyard ownership.

WINE COUNTRY In the land of the most aristocratic of wines, connoisseurs can gaze with awe at the immaculate vineyards of **Latour**, **Lafite** and **Yquem**, whose precious grapes are picked one by one. Tasting is another matter: many of the châteaux are a bit sniffy about visitors. The wine villages are dull, with the notable exception of **St-Emilion**.

The Atlantic Coast

▶▶▶ REGION HIGHLIGHTS

Bassin d'Arcachon
page 128

Biarritz *page 128*

Bordeaux *page 128*

Ile de Ré *page 131*

La Rochelle *page 131*

St-Emilion *page 129*

Saintes *page 131*

TRAPPED AROMAS
One of the more bizarre, not to say unsavoury, traditions of Landais gastro-nomy is eating ortolan buntings. Having been caught in nets, the birds are nourished and gradu-ally poisoned by a diet of milk mixed with a daily increasing quantity of armagnac. They are roasted in their own fat, served on paper and consumed by diners with napkins over their heads to ensure that no fume of the delicate bouquet escapes.

Monolithic church of St-Jean, Aubeterre

▶ Arcachon and Côte d'Argent   *126C4*

The Aquitaine coast consists of two sandy beaches: 100km from **Soulac** to **Cap Ferret**, 125km from **Arcachon** to the outskirts of **Bayonne**. With dunes blocking the way to the sea, rivers feed a string of inland lakes. The River Eyre alone has broken through. Its estuary is the wide but tight-lipped bay of **Arcachon▶▶▶**, famous for its oysters and favoured by yachtsmen, migrant birds and Bordelais sun-seekers.

Between Arcachon and the smelly oyster capital **Gujan Mestras** is a crafts village and zoo (La Hume). **Le Teich** bird reserve has several marked walks and, if you're lucky, flamingos and storks in residence.

▶▶ Aubeterre   *126B2*

Midway between Angoulême and Bordeaux, carved out of the white cliff from which it gets its name, lies the charming town of Aubeterre. Theories abound concerning the exact origins of many of its more famous buildings – the breathtaking **monolithic church of St-Jean▶▶▶** and the so-called Couvent des Cordeliers – as well as the site's powers to cure madness! The river Dronne flowing peacefully below is a good spot for swimming and for hiring canoes.

▶ Aulnay   *126C3*

The beautiful Romanesque pilgrimage church of St Pierre is set among cypresses on the edge of a small village between Poitiers and Saintes. It has outstanding stone carving on the west and south façades and the capitals inside the church (note the Indian elephants and Delilah cutting Samson's hair).

▶▶ Biarritz   *126A1*

Biarritz was a small whaling port until Empress Eugenie brought Napoleon III for a six-week stay in 1854 and thereby launched the Atlantic coast's only rival to the Riviera. Her villa, later the Hôtel du Palais, has been sumptuously restored but other aspects of Biarritz's former splendour are sadly tarnished, and the summer population is an odd mixture of beachcombers and genteel older visitors.

▶▶▶ Bordeaux   *126B2*

A sea port 100km from the Atlantic, Bordeaux is France's most elegant provincial city, a creation of the Enlightenment dedicated to the civilised business of exporting fine wine. Like Paris, only a century earlier, it was rationalised with the creation of wide boulevards, public gardens and a colonnaded **Grand Theatre▶**. Eighteenth-century palaces line the Garonne and the place de la Bourse is a splendid gateway to the intriguing streets of **old Bordeaux▶▶**. The place du Parlement is its focus. Other sightseeing includes a vast cathedral, a well-stocked art museum and a lively contemporary art centre in a converted **spice warehouse (CAPC)▶▶**. Rue St-Catherine and cours Clemenceau are best for shopping. The tourist office Maison du Vin (with tastings) are on the cours 30-Juillet near the theatre. Adventurous urbanisation projects, particularly along the riverfront, are now underway.

The crest of the Château d'Yquem, closed to visitors but visible from the road north of Sauternes

129

Entre-Deux-Mers and Sauternes

Start at Cadillac. D11 to Cérons; N113 to Barsac, Preignac.
Cadillac, an old walled village, is at the edge of the vineyards of **Entre-Deux-Mers**, about 40km south of the medieval town of **St-Emilion**. Cross the Garonne into pudding wine country. Near Preignac the beautiful **Château de Malle** is the best Bordeaux château to visit.

D8/125 to Sauternes.
Barsac and **Sauternes** have Maisons du Vin with tastings and wine for sale. The prestigious **Château d'Yquem** is closed to visitors, but worth admiring from the road (D116E north of Sauternes).

D8 to Villandraut; D3/110 to Uzeste; Bazas; D3/223 to Roquetaillade; D125/D222 to Langon.
Bertrand de Got, the 14th-century Pope Clement V, built a fortress at

Villandraut and lies buried in the church at Uzeste. His nephew built the **Château de Roquetaillade**, whose entrance ticket also covers a rural museum. Bazas has an interesting church on an arcaded square. François Mauriac's home, Malagar, at St-Maixent, is a haven of tranquillity.

D10 to Ste-Croix-du-Mont and Cadillac.
Ste-Croix-du-Mont makes a sweet white wine modest only by Sauternes' standards. It can be tasted in caves below the church.

Wine country: Sauternes

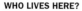

The hinterland of the Aquitaine coast, between Bordeaux and the Basque country, is a vast triangle of flat pine forest, covering 6,450sq km, planted in the 19th century to stabilise shifting dunes and to drain a marshy heath populated only by bees, mosquitoes, sheep and shepherds who went about on stilts.

WHO LIVES HERE?
Illustrious inhabitants of Les Landes have included turn-of-the-century writer François Mauriac, who described its wealthy pine forests in his many novels. Some 25,000 years earlier, the Dame de Brassempouy left her ivory image there to be unearthed in 1894 as the first female icon of prehistory (a cast of it is exhibited at St-Germain-en-Laye; the original is not on view: see page 63). More recently, former President Mitterrand and his faithful labrador enjoyed its seclusion in his forest home.

Recreating Landes life in the ecomuseum at Marquèze

New life Logging and resin tapping, followed by coastal tourism and a modest oil industry (on and around the Lac de Parentis) transformed the life of the region.

The Landes towns are on the fringe of the forest. **Mont de Marsan** is a good place to watch a *course landaise* (a race) starring nimble *écarteurs* (literally 'dodgers') who, among other tricks, leap over charging cows.

In the woods The forest itself is disconcerting, empty of spirit: no views, no flowers, little wildlife, few villages, just the smell and sight of pine trees and the piercing whine of cicadas. In small clearings there are low timber and brick farmhouses, each surrounded by a maize field, a vegetable patch and a few farm animals.

Ecomuseum The best reason to venture inland from a Côte d'Argent campsite is the Landes Ecomuseum at **Marquèze**, reached by train from Sabres. This is a fascinating all-round presentation of the pastoral life and ecology of the area in the pre-pine age, including a traditional farm. It is part of the regional park, through which runs the River Eyre, now opened up for canoeing.

Among the contents of the small museum at **Solférino**, an agricultural community founded by Napoleon III, is a cast of the Emperor's bootprint (August 1857), made to commemorate this momentous initiative to tame the wilderness. **Luxey's** ecomuseum has an old resin distillery and by-products.

▶ Marais Poitevin   *126B5*

Between Niort and the sea a maze of canals linked to the Sèvre/Niortaise drains a wide area of reclaimed marshland punctuated by 'island' villages (**Marans**, **Chaillé**). Punts are the traditional means of transport for fishermen and can be rented with or without pilot at **Coulon**, west of Niort. Eels are a local speciality. **Maillezais**, with splendid abbey ruins, also has boats for hire.

▶ Pornic   *126A6*

A fishing port on a rocky creek, Pornic has charm, unlike the notorious owner of its château, Gilles de Rais (Bluebeard), who gave up a dazzling military career for satanism and infanticide. There are summer ferries to **Noirmoutier**.

Rochefort   *126B4*

Often overlooked by tourists in favour of its larger neighbour, La Rochelle, the historic rivalry between these two ports dates back to its foundation in the 17th century, by Colbert, as France's largest shipyard. Be sure not to miss the **Corderie Royale**, the **Musée de la Marine** and the idiosyncratic home of the author Pierre Loti.

▶▶ La Rochelle   *126B4*

One of the great trading ports of Renaissance France, and a Protestant stronghold, La Rochelle is now a prosperous user-friendly city: no other French town places free bicycles at the disposal of visitors. In the old port, twin towers still guard the narrow harbour entrance. The nearby **Tour de la Lanterne**▶ (a 15th-century lighthouse and prison) gives good views. The old centre has kept its houses (rue des Merciers, rue de l'Escale), mostly 16th- and 17th-century. The Musée du Nouveau Monde relates La Rochelle's trading history; the **aquarium**▶▶▶ in Les Minimes is excellent. Plentiful local beaches include **Châtelaillon**▶.

▶▶ Saintes   *126B4*

An ancient town on one of the main pilgrimage routes (and the modern autoroute) to Spain, red-brick Saintes is a good base for visiting the highly decorative Romanesque churches along this route. St-Eutrope itself is but a fragment of a former great pilgrimage church, with the 4th-century martyred bishop's tomb in its beautiful crypt. Roman vestiges remain.

APERITIF AND DIGESTIF
Unique blends of twice-distilled eau-de-vie made from white grapes grown in the confusingly-named Grande and Petite Champagne areas around Cognac make up one of the world's most prestigious *digestifs*. If your nose doesn't lead you to one of the distilleries in the old part of Cognac, your eyes will spot the black stains caused by alcohol evaporation from the distilleries' oak barrels, fondly known as the 'angels' share'. For a fascinating dégustation-cum-history tour, head for the Château des Valois. Throughout the Charente you will find the *aperitif* known as *pineau*, made from grape juice and cognac.

HIT THE ISLANDS
Hugely popular summer holiday resorts, the offshore islands of Ré, Noirmoutier and Oléron are all accessible by toll bridge from the mainland. **Ré**▶▶▶ is the most interesting, with vineyards, farms, white-washed villages and the fortified port of St-Martin. Noirmoutier mostly consists of salt-pans, but the old village has pine woods and a good beach at hand; Oléron has vast oyster parks off the old port of Château d'Oléron. From Aix (ferries from Fouras and Boyardville on Oléron) Napoleon left France in 1815; his house displays Imperial memorabilia. Yeu (ferries from Fromentine and La Fosse, on Noirmoutier) is an island of granite cliffs, lobster pots and tuna fishing. Pétain was imprisoned there from 1945 until his death in 1951.

The Bordeaux vineyard area is one of the most productive fine wine districts in the world. The five main districts are Médoc (red), Sauternes (sweet white) and Graves (white) on the left banks of the Garonne; and St-Emilion and Pomerol (red) on the right bank of the Dordogne. Less prestigious wines (with exceptions) are produced between the rivers (Entre-Deux-Mers) and on the eastern side of the Gironde (including Côtes de Blaye and Côtes de Bourg).

HIT THE BOTTLE
Signs marked *dégustation*, *visite des chais* or *vente directe* all mean one thing – wine-sampling and potential purchasing. Watch out for the years: 1988, 1989, 1990 were excellent Bordeaux vintages; 1991 and 1992 less so; and 1993 between the two. 1995 just missed being the year of the century due to September rain but is still an excellent year, as is 1996.

Bordeaux vineyards: a treat for the eye as well as for the palate

Divisions and ranks Each region is divided into many *appellations* (**Pauillac** and **St-Julien** are two of the most famous in the Médoc, for example) and each *appellation* into estates, usually referred to as *châteaux*. The finest Médoc châteaux were ranked into five categories of *crus classés* in 1855 (from *premier* to *cinquième*); there have been only minor changes and additions since. This system of classification, which varies slightly from region to region, is not an infallible guide to quality; many wines in the lower *crus classés*, or even the supposedly lesser *crus bourgeois*, are often as good and better value. The *crus bourgeois* of the *appellations* of **St-Estèphe** and **Haut-Médoc** are worth seeking out.

Along the D2 from **Bordeaux** to **St-Vivien-de-Médoc** are some of the most prestigious wine châteaux in the world: **Margaux**, **Latour** (south of Pauillac), **Mouton-Rothschild** and **Lafite** (north of Pauillac). Not all are open to the public. Interesting châteaux in the Médoc are:

Château Batailley near Pauillac: 18th-century château with gardens and cellars open (tel: 05 56 00 00 70).

Château Cos d'Estournel at St-Estèphe: by appointment (tel: 05 56 73 15 55).

Château d'Issan near Margaux: 17th-century moated château; by appointment (tel: 05 57 88 35 91).

Château Loudenne near St-Yzans: wine museum; by appointment (tel: 05 56 73 17 80).

Château Margaux: by appointment; closed August and harvest time (tel: 05 57 88 83 83).

Château Mouton-Rothschild near Pauillac: wine museum; by appointment (tel: 05 56 73 21 29).

There are Maisons du Vin (information offices) at **Margaux**, **Bordeaux** and **Pauillac**; and vineyard tours can be taken from **Bordeaux**, **Pauillac**, **Hourtin** and **Lacanau**.

Churches, Beaches and the Gironde Estuary

Start at St-Fort-sur-Gironde.
St-Fort is 50km north of Blaye, Louis XIV's key defensive position on the Gironde. In the vineyards north of Blaye there are roadside invitations to taste and buy *pineau* (a grape juice and cognac aperitif). **St-Fort** and nearby **Talmont** have interesting churches.

D114/136 to Rioux; D216 to Rétaud; D142/N150/D117 to Sablonceaux; D117/728 to Corme-Royal; D119 to St-Porchaire; D122 to La Roche Courbon and back.
Rioux and **Rétaud** are the highlights of the inland church tour, also featuring Sablonceaux Abbey and Corme-Royal. **La Roche Courbon** is a richly decorated moated château set in lovely gardens.

N137/D18/D7/D123 to Marennes; D3 to Brouage and back; D25 to Ronce-les-Bains and Royan.
Brouage was a 17th-century salt port and mighty royal fortress, but the sea has retreated and left a somnolent village. Tablets commemorate Champlain, the locally born founder of Québec, and the sad affair of Louis XIV and Marie Mancini, who came to Brouage after being spurned in favour of a Spanish princess. At the mouth of the Seudre, **Bourcefranc-le-Chapus** and **Marennes** are the local oyster centres. There are beaches and campsites along the wooded Grande Côte and Côte Sauvage towards Royan, but bathing is often hazardous. **Royan** is a big resort which has been developed in bleakest post-war functional style, redeemed only by its shallow beach and its proximity to the excellent La Palmyre zoo.

Bergerac, on the banks of the Dordogne River

THE DORDOGNE is a river flowing from the Massif Central to join the Gironde at Bordeaux, and an administrative *département* which includes a section of this river and an area to the north fondly known to the French as Périgord – home of the truffle, the walnut and the bloated liver of force-fed geese. It is also the region of Europe that has yielded most to students of prehistory; the area is uniquely rich in cave paintings.

To its many visitors, the Dordogne embraces a much larger and more diffuse area of south-west France, stretching from the undulating farmland of Limousin to the bleak limestone *causses* of Quercy and the orchards of the Lot Valley. It signifies French country life at its most delightful: old villages of golden stone with rust-coloured roofs, fortress ruins on wooded river banks, market stalls groaning under the weight of fresh local produce, and small-scale cultivation. The typical Dordogne farmer has a handful of animals, an area of maize to feed them, fruit trees and walnuts and a small vineyard. Less idyllic, but highly significant to France's economy, are the hydro-electric power installations along the rivers.

So irresistible is the Dordogne's charm that many visitors have made it a second home, in some cases forming 95 per cent of the population. Foreign money has pushed prices up and the hunt for a cheap French ruin has moved on, but some of the prettiest villages now contain large colonies of expatriates, particularly British and Dutch. The favourite section of the Dordogne Valley, between **Sarlat** and **Trémolat**, may now seem too neatly restored, with too many foreign voices.

PROTECT AND SURVIVE In the Middle Ages the land between the Lot and Dordogne Valleys was a border zone between French territory and English-controlled Aquitaine. As well as isolated fortresses commanding the river valleys, the rival factions built fortified towns (*bastides*). Some of these survive, little changed.

Dordogne

▶▶▶ REGION HIGHLIGHTS

Albi *page 136*

Château de Bonaguil
page 137

Collonges-la-Rouge
page 151

Creuse Valley
pages 136, 141

Domme *page 141*

Grotte de Font-de-Gaume (Les Eyzies)
pages 142, 143

Périgueux *page 146*

La Roque-Gageax
page 146

St-Cirq-Lapopie
page 146

Sarlat *page 148*

Toulouse *page 150*

136

TOULOUSE-LAUTREC
Count Henri Marie Raymond de Toulouse-Lautrec was born in Albi in 1864. At the age of 14, he fell and suffered the first of two leg injuries which contributed to his deformity. Later Lautrec studied in Paris, where he immersed himself in the low life depicted in his paintings, drawings and posters. His childhood home, Château du Bosc (48km north-east of Albi, at Naucelle), has daily visits.

ARMAGNAC
The Romans brought vines to Gascony, the Arabs brought the alambic and the Celts imported casks; thus began Armagnac, the world's oldest *eau-de-vie*. Produced in only three areas of Gascony, it is matured for up to 30 years before blending according to 'recipes' secretly guarded by local distillers.

For 500 years Aubusson has been synonymous with exquisite tapestry, and remains so today. It still produces carpets and wall-hangings; the tapestry museum shows weaving methods

Agen   134A2

Prunes are not often considered a gourmet item, but the succulent *pruneaux d'Agen*, stuffed with marzipan or marinated in cognac, are in a league of their own. This market town on a fertile plain between the Lot and Garonne has a cluster of narrow streets in its old quarter, a 12th-century **cathedral**▶▶ and a handsome aqueduct. Its museum has an impressive collection of 19th-century art, including works by Goya, Sisley and Boudin, and a superb Greek marble Venus unearthed by a local farmer in 1876. See also the bastide of **Puymirol**▶▶ and its ramparts.

▶▶ Albi   134C1

This big, brick-red town beside the Tarn is dominated by its distinctively warlike Gothic cathedral. Built with funds seized from heretics or alleged *pénitents*, it formed a defensive fortress in a time of inquisition, torture and simmering popular resistance. Instead of stained glass to illuminate the faithful, **Ste-Cecile**▶▶▶ has narrow apertures like arrow slits. Only the delicate 15th-century doorway lightens the effect. Inside, gruesome Last Judgement scenes adorn the west wall. The bishop's palace (Palais de la Berbie) has a fine **Toulouse-Lautrec museum**▶▶▶. Formal gardens overlook a river spanned by an 11th-century bridge, now coping with modern traffic.

Argentat   134C3

The sleepy old village of Argentat straddles the Dordogne just before it flows into a series of reservoirs among wooded gorges. Upstream are the Argentat dam and a hydro-electric power station. The left (south) bank is by far the prettier side: a terrace of ochre-fronted, *lauze*-tiled houses with chestnut balconies hangs over the water. Nearby are the ruins of the fortress of Tours de Merle.

▶ Aubusson   134C4

The tapestry town of Aubusson nestles in the **Creuse Valley**▶▶. Weaving galleries and workshops can be visited all over the town. The Musée Départemental de la Tapisserie illustrates 500 years of weaving, including dazzling ultra-modern abstracts, and the Maison du Tapissier contains hundreds of examples of 17th- to 19th-century tapestries and a reconstructed workshop. During the summer the Hôtel de Ville holds regular exhibitions, including tapestries by the modern master Jean Lurçat.

During the Middle Ages, the English fought for centuries to gain control of this part of France. Countless reminders of this turbulent period can be seen on hilltops and strategic vantage points throughout the region, in castles, fortified churches, and bastide towns (see page 139).

War and peace Some grand châteaux date from or were rebuilt during later, less warlike centuries, and more closely resemble the pleasure palaces of the Loire. But the typical castle architecture of the Dordogne is unmistakably military. Grim fortresses glare at each other from either side of the river – English on one bank, French on the other – almost close enough to hurl insults. Much of the damage they have suffered dates not from the Hundred Years' War, but from the wars between Catholics and Protestants during the 16th century. Some castles have been restored, and are used as private residences, hotels or wineries. Others are open to the public; many of these can only be visited on lengthy guided tours (in French). There are *circuit des bastides* motoring routes: ask at the tourist offices (25 rue du President Wilson, Périgueux; 97 rue Neuve d'Argenson, Bergerac; place de la Liberté, Sarlat).

Beynac-et-Cazenac One of the Dordogne's most spectacular and memorable fortresses towers above a huddled village on a sheer cliff commanding a beautiful stretch of the Dordogne. The keep dates from the 13th century; the main building from the 14th.

Biron A massive and intimidating château perched on a volcanic crag, Biron has a huge view of surrounding countryside. The buildings date from the 12th century onwards, gradually mellowing in more gracious times.

Bonaguil One of the best surviving examples of late 15th- and early 16th-century military architecture. The cruel Berenger de Roquefeuil insisted on making his castle impregnable, even though he outlived the age when this was necessary.

Castelnaud Beynac's opposite number on the English (south) bank has almost equally splendid views. Newly restored, it houses an impressive military museum.

Coussac-Bonneval This 14th-century castle has machicolated pepper-pot towers and contains fine furnishings, tapestries and woodwork associated with Achmet-Pasha, the eccentric mercenary who was born here (*Open* mid-Mar–Oct, afternoons only).

Montbrun Dating from the 13th century, this lovely moated castle (private) was reconstructed in the 15th. It was besieged unsuccessfully by Richard the Lionheart.

Medieval siege warfare is explained in Castelnaud's military museum

Dordogne

138

PUFFERS
Tobacco first appeared in France in 1560. Powdered into snuff, it was recommended by the Portuguese ambassador as a cure for Catherine de Médicis' migraines. Louis XIII first taxed, then outlawed the habit, but the nation was hooked. And so it remains. In spring and summer the dark leaves fill plots around the valleys of Bergerac and the Lot-et-Garonne. Later they are dried before being dispatched to the newly-privatised *Régie Nationale des Tabacs* for processing into that Gallic aroma.

A cigar-holder becomes a work of art at Bergerac's Musée du Tabac

▶ **Beaulieu-sur-Dordogne**   *134C3*

This waterfront market town has as appealing a setting as its name suggests, and among its older streets are several well-preserved mansions. Its great glory, however, is the Benedictine **church of St-Pierre▶▶**, best known for its elaborate south portal, carved in 1125. Damaged in parts, this vigorous sculpture is still one of the region's best examples of Romanesque art. A *Last Judgement* takes up the tympanum. The old monastery buildings can be seen from place des Pères; the Chapelle des Pénitents from the riverside.

▶ **Bergerac**   *134A3*

Though now encased in suburbs of little interest, Bergerac's older quarter repays exploration. It is one of the Dordogne's largest towns, a former capital of Périgord, and is an important commercial and agricultural gateway to the Médoc plains. Bergerac's own wines are no mean rivals to its neighbours' products downstream, the most celebrated being the sweet dessert wine of Monbazillac, to the south.

Trading Activities Bergerac always had strong Protestant connections from its Huguenot community and its geographical and trade associations with Britain and the Low Countries, and it was much battered in the religious conflict that swept through France. Although Bergerac lost political status to Périgueux, the town made a canny entrepreneurial living through the centuries from riverborne trade. Modern preoccupations are as diverse as tobacco (a principal local cash-crop) and nitro-cellulose, used in paint and plastics. Rostand's hero Cyrano (he of the unfortunate nose) has only tenuous links with the town, but has been enthusiastically adopted as a citizen worthy of a statue.

What to See Bergerac's main sights and most picturesque buildings lie among the narrow streets north of the historic port area. The **Cloître des Récollets** is a lovely half-timbered convent where the Regional Wine

Council meets annually to deliberate the merits of the *vendange* (tours of the Salle des Dégustations, with a tasting afterwards). The museum contains an interesting section on the river and port. The turreted 15th-century Maison Peyrarède houses the intriguing **Musée du Tabac►**. Tobacco jars, pipes, snuff-boxes and cigarette-holders document the history of the weed. The Gothic church of Notre-Dame contains several valuable paintings and tapestries.

► Cadouin 134A3

This large village on the edge of the Besside Forest was once an important place of pilgrimage. Its Cistercian **abbey►►**, founded in 1115, stood on the route to the Spanish shrine of Santiago de Compostela. During the Middle Ages, kings and princes halted here to pay homage to its revered Holy Shroud, later discredited as an 11th-century Egyptian textile. The massively buttressed gold-stone monastery has now been restored. Inside, the church is severe and dark, but the cloisters are beautifully carved in a mix of Flamboyant Gothic and Renaissance styles. Bikers should head for the Musée du Vélocipède and its historical one-, two- and three-wheelers.

►► Cahors 134B2

Encircled by a natural moat, a *cingle* of the Lot, Cahors was a worthy prize to the English, who besieged it during the Hundred Years' War. They gazed at it without attacking, and the impregnable town was eventually ceded by treaty in 1360, to the great disgust of its inhabitants. The old town still bristles with ramparts, battlements, barbicans, fortified towers and no fewer than 280 ornate doorways (12th–19th century). Much more interesting, though, is the unique 14th-century **Valentré Bridge►►►** (the only one of three still standing), its curious proportions emphasised by three pointed towers from which unfriendly missiles could be directed at intruders. From a distance (the hilly banks make a good viewpoint) the seven graceful Gothic arches are magnificent.

Local specialities Within this pleasant market town, many shops display tempting local produce, particularly supplies of the robust local 'black wine'. The narrow streets leading from the main square towards the river ramparts make a fascinating area for unscheduled wandering. Worth seeing are the **Maison de Roaldès** (Henry IV's Mansion) and the **Cathedral of St-Etienne►**, with Byzantine domes in Périgord style, a fine carved north doorway and interior frescos.

► Carennac 134B3

Carennac is one of the Dordogne's most charming and peaceful villages, where medieval and Renaissance houses overlook an island in the river, and orchards of greengages flourish. François de Salignac (Fénélon) wrote his masterpiece *Télémaque* here while he was Prior in the 18th century. Not to be missed is the splendid Romanesque doorway of St-Pierre, where *Christ in Majesty* occupies the tympanum, encircled in a strange oval halo known as a *mandorla*.

BASTIDES
South-east of Bergerac, the border country of the Hundred Years' War is studded with *bastide* towns. Their purpose was military: as well as massive fortress garrisons, both the English and the French created a permanent civilian guard. Built on a grid pattern, often with an arcaded market square and fortified churchtower as a refuge during times of siege, the *bastide* towns had streets too narrow for a mounted knight to wield weapons effectively. Best of the *bastide* towns are Monpazier, Monflanquin, Villeréal, Villefranche-du-Périgord, Beaumont and Eymet. Sometimes over-restored, several of these towns now verge on the chic.

139

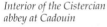

Interior of the Cistercian abbey at Cadouin

The terrace of **Belcastel**'s mighty château offers a splendid panorama of a wooded river-bend. A short way west is the **Château de la Treyne**, part 14th-century. It is now a hotel.

D23, D673, D90 to Gouffre de Padirac.
The **Gouffre de Padirac** is a giant sinkhole imbued with Satanic associations and in season spoiled by crowds. A lift descends the fern-lined walls; a boat tours the caverns.

Divert from D673 on to D14 and D118 to Loubressac or D38 to Autoire; then join D30 and D673.
Loubressac is a hilltop bastide, with a vast view from the 15th-century château. A long-distance footpath, the GR652 (480), leads through Loubressac to **Autoire**, where farmhouses have been snapped up as second homes. Near the village is a beauty spot, the **Cirque d'Autoire**.

D673 to Montal and St-Céré.
The romantic Renaissance château of **Montal** was built by Jeanne de Balsac d'Entraygues as she waited for her son Robert to return from the wars in Italy. He never did, and the heartrending legend *Plus d'Espoir* ('Hope No More') is carved beneath one of the château windows. Inside, the Renaissance staircase is encrusted with sea monsters and shells, testifying to the dedication of Maurice Fenaille, a philanthropic historian who restored the château and later gave it to the state.

River valley and open land

Start at St-Céré.
St-Laurent castle in St-Céré was the home of Jean Lurçat, the great tapestry designer of the 1930s. His work is displayed in the Casino.

D940 and D43 to Castelnau.
One of Quercy's most formidable castles is **Castelnau**. This vast 12th- and 13th-century fortified castle was saved from ruin by an opera singer whose sumptuous furniture and lapidary collection can be seen.

D43 and D30 to Carennac; D43 to Cirque de Montvalent and N140 to Gluges; D43 and D23 to Creysse and D114, D15 to Meyronne.
The River Dordogne curves through lush meadows dotted with villages. Most strikingly set is **Gluges**, at the foot of sheer cliffs; **Creysse** and **Meyronne** have castle remains.

D23 south to Grottes de Lacave.
At **Lacave**, a lift and underground railway transport visitors to limestone caverns.

D23 to Belcastel; D43 to la Treyne.

▶▶ Creuse, Vallée de la 134C5

The River Creuse rises on the Millevaches Plateau, on the granite foothills of the Massif Central. Dozens of small streams eventually form this picturesque waterway, beloved by George Sand, who set several of her novels here. From its infant course past the tapestry towns of **Aubusson** and **Felletin**, the river flows through a varied landscape of gorges, reservoir lakes and farmland. Principal landmarks include the great fortress of **Crozant**, the lovely village of **Gargilesse▶▶** and the giant dam at **Eguzon**, behind which stretches the serpentine **Chambon Lake**. At **Fontgombault▶**, an abbey founded by the hermit Gombault is worth seeing for its tall choir and decorated capitals. The Benedictine order has returned (it was suppressed in 1714) and goats' cheese is sold in some of the outbuildings.

▶ Culan 134C5

A massive fortress clings to the overgrown rocks overlooking the Arnon Gorges. Among many illustrious visitors, the castle numbers Joan of Arc, sheltering here after Orléans, and Louis XI. It is open to the public (daily Mar–Oct), and contains a collection of furniture and tapestries, as well as a 'neo-medieval' garden.

▶▶ Domme 134B3

Few fail to be impressed by Domme's picturesque location on a rocky cliff high above the Dordogne. A *bastide* town, its hilly setting proved too difficult for the classic grid-patterned rectangle, and getting around Domme, particularly in high season, is best accomplished on foot. In the main square is a covered market hall; below it is an entrance to some small stalactite caves, once used as a refuge for the townsfolk. Animal bones found in the caves are on display at the **museum▶**, which also exhibits traditional crafts and objets d'art. From the Belvedere de la Barre there are stupendous views of the river looping through fields far below. Most striking of the surviving gateways is the Porte des Tours, whose burly round towers once imprisoned many hapless Knights Templar, falsely accused of heresy and perversion by Philip the Fair.

▶▶ Hautefort, Château de 134B3

The formidable silhouette of Hautefort Château, overlord of the Ans country from the 14th century, is a striking feature of the Périgord Blanc. Hautefort has been rebuilt several times, most recently after a disastrous fire in 1968, and is now restored to its largely 17th-century grandeur. The moat is dry, the drawbridge fixed, and the grey-gold walls enclose English- and French-style gardens and a few furnished rooms (tours; tel: 05 53 50 51 23).

Basket-weaving in Domme

CUREMONTE
You really do feel a time warp when walking the two main streets of this extraordinary village, dominated by three castles in varying states of repair. Don't be put off by 'ye olde' shop fronts down the far end (intentionally left in situ from the last film set); the old ladies knotting bunches of garlic on their doorsteps, in the shadow of the castle, are for real, and the garlic is for sale!

Domme's magnificent setting high above the Dordogne defeated the traditional geometric bastide plan

The limestone caverns of the Massif Central are famous for their beautiful formations; those in the Dordogne are better known for prehistoric animal paintings. The Périgord region has been inhabited by man since palaeolithic times: the earliest skeletal traces of Neanderthal type were found at Le Moustier near Les Eyzies-de-Tayac in 1909. Many other remains (tools, tombs, bones, weapons, ornaments) have been unearthed, but by far the most exciting discovery occurred in 1940, when some boys out rabbiting with a dog stumbled by chance upon the cave of Lascaux, one of Europe's most important and most beautiful prehistoric finds.

The Museum of Prehistory, set into the rock-face at Les Eyzies-de-Tayac

The paintings at Lascaux and other caves in the Dordogne are probably between 12,000 and 20,000 years old, and were executed by Cro-Magnon man, a taller, vastly more sophisticated creature than the earliest flint wielders. The most interesting prehistoric sites in the Dordogne lie between **Les Eyzies** and **Montignac** in the Vézère Valley, and near Cabrerets on the Lot, but there are numerous lesser caves dotted all over the region, some decorated with animal drawings, others naturally adorned with stalagmites and stalactites. The best museums and exhibition centres of prehistory are at **Les Eyzies**, **Périgueux**, **Sarlat** and **Le Thot**. The major sites become very crowded in high season; advance booking is advisable.

Damaging breath Lascaux itself was thronged with curious visitors from the end of World War II, and alarmed officials soon realised that just two decades of warm, carbon dioxide-exhaling tourists had done more damage to the paintings than 17,000 years of lying undisturbed. A film of greenish micro-organisms was creeping steadily across the walls. Quickly, the original cave was closed to all but a handful of privileged researchers. Meanwhile a replica cave, **Lascaux II**, perfect down to every last contour, with all the dyes synthesised from the same ingredients, was created nearby. It is fascinating and awe-inspiring to emerge from the air-lock system amid a herd of galloping bison, deer and horses in brilliant shades of red, ochre and black. To visit the caves, you must book tickets in the attractive town of **Montignac** (tel: 05 53 51 95 03). At **Le Thot**, 7km south-west, a prehistory centre (tel: 05 53 50 70 44) houses displays of cave art, audio-visual shows, and in the surrounding park, wild animals (bison, aurochs, Przewalski horses) roam among life-size animated mammoths.

Les Eyzies-de-Tayac Further down the Vézère, Les Eyzies revels in its soubriquet 'Cradle of Prehistory' because of the archaeological riches discovered in the immediate surroundings. The **Museum of Prehistory**▶▶ (*Closed* Tue, tel: 05 53 06 45 45), housed in a 13th-century fortress halfway up a rock-face, is certainly worth a visit for background information, time-charts and displays of bones and arte-facts discovered locally. Just outside the town is the **Grotte de Font-de-Gaume**▶▶▶, where the highly sophisticated animal drawings are originals, not copies; among them are the marks of later 'artists' of modern times. Numbers of visitors are restricted, so book early in the morning (*Closed* Wed, tel: 05 53 06 90 80).

Smaller caves with animal drawings near Les Eyzies include the **Grotte des Combarelles**▶ and the **Abri du Cap Blanc**, to the east. The **Roque-St-Christophe**▶▶ is a series of rock galleries in a cliff used for millennia as a shelter from elements, wars and predators, where various traces of troglodyte inhabitants have been found. **La Madeleine** is an excavated Magdalenian village with cave dwellings. Visitors tour the caves at **Rouffignac**▶▶, north-west of Les Eyzies, in an electric train, through about 4km of galleries decorated with hun-dreds of animal engravings (tel: 05 53 05 41 71).

On a lighter note, the Disney-like **Préhistoparc** presents an everyday story of cave people. While at Le Bugue, chil-dren love the theme-park-style village of Bournat in 19th-century peasant fashion (*Closed* Jan).

PREHISTO-INDUSTRY
'Prehistoric tourism' is big business in the Périgord: over 300,000 tourists visit Lascaux II alone every year. Many sites are at saturation point, others forbid access altogether and several other facsimi-lies are under discussion (see displays at the Centre d'Art Préhistorique at Le Thot). But the flow continues and Les Eyzies is due to relaunch itself as an international centre for prehistory in the year 2000, with a new museum and research centre.

Pictures from another age: painting of a horse at Lascaux II – not an original but a faithful replica

143

Pech-Merle▶▶ Further south, above the River Célé, a tributary of the River Lot, is **Pech-Merle**, near Cabrerets: here there is a huge series of caverns contain-ing limestone formations, exquisite animal paintings, sil-houetted handprints and a frieze of bison and mammoths. Among these curiosities are the mudprints of prehistoric feet dating back some 15,000 years. The chambers adjoin a heavily didactic museum (*Open* Easter–Oct, tel: 05 65 31 27 05).

The porcelain industry in Limoges took off with the discovery of high-quality kaolin (china clay) at St-Yrieux in 1768; today Limoges produces about half of France's porcelain, mostly tableware.

LIMOGES ENAMEL
The process of firing enamel dates back to the 6th century, but it developed to a much more sophisticated art in Limoges during the 12th century with the invention of the *champlevé* technique: successive coats of enamel are spread on engraved copper, each fired at decreasing temperatures, resulting in a deep, jewel-like lustre. Painted enamels are still produced at Limoges.

▶ Limoges   *134B4*

The ancient crafts of enamelling and porcelain-making still figure largely in Limoges' economy, but the old town has now spread along both banks of the Vienne. The most interesting part is the **Quartier de la Boucherie▶▶**, a web of narrow alleys lined with half-timbered houses. Don't miss the Cathedral of St-Etienne in ambitious Gothic. Two excellent museums chart the history of Limoges's major industries: the **Musée National Adrien-Dubouché▶▶** (*Closed* Tue) is devoted to the history of ceramics; the Musée Municipal contains a splendid collection of Limousin enamels.

▶▶ Martel   *134B3*

This quiet grey truffle town on Quercy limestone is rich in history and fascinating to explore. The town is named after Charlemagne's grandfather, Charles Martel, who defeated the Saracens in the 8th century and built a church here. From the 18th-century covered market, composed of a forest of timbers on stone stilts, streets full of ancient mansions stretch past the sturdy fortified church of St-Maur, the Mirepoises Cloisters and the Maison Fabri, where Henry Short-Coat, son of Henry Plantagenet, died a painful and penitent death after pillaging the shrine of Rocamadour.

▶▶ Moissac   *134B2*

Despite Moissac's river setting, surrounded by hilly orchards and vineyards, the modern town is unprepossessing. The reason to visit it is the ancient abbey church of **St-Pierre▶▶** on the right bank of the Tarn. It has suffered many vicissitudes since its Benedictine foundation in the 7th century, but still has a remarkable Romanesque south doorway depicting St John's Vision of the Apocalypse. The ornately carved capitals in the cloisters are among the best in France.

▶ Monbazillac, Château de   *134A3*

From the lovely hilltop château with its massive pepper-pot towers, well-combed vineyards stretch as far as you can see. The luscious white wine for which Monbazillac is famous is said by some to be sweeter and richer than Sauternes. The château dates from about 1550 and, though it looks robust enough, was designed more for leisured living than defence. Today it is looked after by the wine co-operative which produces Monbazillac, and houses a tasting centre, restaurant and shop.

▶ Montauban   *134B1*

Modern suburbs do little for this pink brick bastide on the rich plains of the Garonne and Tarn, but its historical and artistic associations are impressive. A Protestant stronghold, Montauban resisted Louis XIII's besieging troops for over three months in 1621. The picturesque quarter surrounds the 17th-century arcaded place Nationale, where rose-coloured houses are linked by angled porticoes. The best thing in town is the **Ingres Museum▶▶** (*Closed* Mon) in the bishop's palace near the river, where the 19th-century artist's paintings and drawings are displayed; and the best event is the annual jazz festival in July.

▶ Montpezat de Quercy   *134B2*

Besides its agreeable old houses and arcades, this little Quercy town is worth a visit to see the Collegiate Church of St-Martin. Its main treasures are the lavishly worked tapestries in the sanctuary depicting scenes from the life of St Martin, and the tombs of the local great family, the des Prés, several of whom became famous clerics.

Moutier d'Ahun   *134C5*

A church is again the main focus of interest here: the part-Romanesque, part-Gothic building dates originally from the 12th century, but later suffered at the hands of pillaging Protestants. Between 1673 and 1681, its finest feature was incorporated: a magnificent display of oak woodcarving. See also the 14th-century bridge over the Creuse.

▶ Oradour-sur-Glane   *134B4*

Most French towns quickly repaired wartime damage, but what happened in Oradour was too dreadful to forget. So it has been left exactly as it was, an effective monument to the horrors of war. On June 10, 1944, a group of SS troops swept through the town on a mission of vengeance. They were still smarting from their humiliation after D-Day and angered by the deaths of two outriders at the hands of Resistance snipers in a neighbouring village. They rounded up all the citizens of Oradour, putting women and children in the church, men in the surrounding outbuildings, and systematically massacred them. Many died in machine-gun fire, others burned to death when the church was torched. The total death toll was 642, of whom over 200 were children. Today the old village of Oradour is just the same as when the Nazis left: bullet marks on walls, charred shutters, old – now vintage – cars parked in garages, trailing telegraph wires. The ruins and the cemetery can be visited. Nearby, new Oradour and its modern church have risen phoenix-like from the ashes.

History and tranquillity in the village of Martel

NUTS
Walnuts are best sampled when at their autumnal freshest. Originally brought by the Romans, walnut-trees are now found throughout the region. Europe's largest walnut forest is at Doissat, outside the lovely medieval village of Belvès.

Dordogne

FAITHFUL CLIMBERS
The faithful who visit Rocamadour climb the long stairway halfway up the side of the cliff to an assembly of seven chapels, where the miraculous shrine of St Amadour is believed to lie beneath the altar of a smoke-blackened Virgin. September 8 is the annual pilgrimage get-together.

CRUMBLING
In 1956, several people were killed in rock-falls at La Roque-Gageac as the cliffs collapsed. Today the village is safely shored up.

Lush countryside surrounds Périgueux at the heart of Dordogne département

▶▶ Périgueux   134A3
The capital of Périgord is a large, lively agricultural and commercial centre, where truffles, *foie gras*, walnut sweets, honey, wine and liqueurs are stacked temptingly high in the windows of chic *épiceries* in the old quarter. A regular open-air market (Wed and Sat) adds to this cornucopia. The pedestrianised narrow streets around the cathedral and the houses by the river offer fascinating architectural detail at every turn and much effort has been put into restoration. The Romans who patronised the Vésone spring have left plenty of evidence, notably Vesunna's Tower, a stumpy cylindrical structure of yellowish stone. Other finds from the Gallo-Roman period can be seen in Périgueux's excellent museum (*Closed* Tue). The St-Front Cathedral's white domes and spiky turrets evoke some Islamic Levantine scene rather than a Catholic stronghold, but it was badly restored in the 19th century by Paul Abadie, the controversial architect of Sacré-Coeur in Paris. The original cathedral, the massive St-Etienne-de-la-Cité, is now hemmed in by traffic.

▶▶ Rocamadour   134B3
Rocamadour's setting is irresistibly dramatic, particularly early or late in the day, when the light is indirect. Rocamadour clings to a sheer limestone spur rising from a dry canyon. An excellent view can be had from the belvedere at **L'Hospitalet**, across the valley. Close up, the fortified village loses some of its magic in an undignified scuffle for parking places and a clamour of souvenir cash-tills. The town hall contains fine modern tapestries by Jean Lurçat. On the skyline is a château fortress, partly 14th-century. Falconry displays at the Rocher des Aigles make an interesting diversion.

▶▶ La Roque-Gageac   134B3
The crumbling cliffs of golden limestone into which La Roque-Gageac is built make it one of the most remarkable settings on the Dordogne. Traditional flat-bottomed *gabares* (boats) take tourists downstream, passing numerous châteaux. The **Château de la Malartie** is a 19th-century folly, the **Manoir de Tarde** genuinely 16th-century.

▶▶ St-Cirq-Lapopie   134B2
Huddled on its wooded limestone cliffs over 80m above the Lot, this gold-stone village is much frequented by tourists. Formerly a wood-turners' colony, many of its houses are now owned by artists inspired by surrealist André Breton's example, and have been lovingly preserved with mullions and turrets intact. The 15th-century church juts out of the rock face to survey a dizzying sweep of Lot and Cère valley.

Exploring Périgord Vert

Start at Brantôme.
Brantôme lies in the heart of Périgord Vert. Its riverside setting and good food make it a popular draw. An imposing Benedictine abbey and 11th-century clock-tower (good view from top) hide much more ancient troglodyte dwellings and an extraordinary Last Judgement carving in the cliffs behind.

D78, D83, D82,D3 to Puyguilhem and D82 to Grottes de Villars.
North-east lies the 16th-century château of **Puyguilhem**, restored after World War II (*Closed* Jan and Mon). To the north-east are the **Grottes de Villars** (*Open* Apr–Oct), limestone caves decorated with animal engravings believed to be 30,000–40,000 years old.

D98 from Puyguilhem to St-Jean-de-Côle and D707 to Thiviers.
St-Jean-de-Côle has a typically Périgordian assembly of brown and gold stone houses. The 11th-century priory church and Château

Marthonie are its most notable buildings. **Thiviers** has a good foie gras and truffle market (Sat); and there are bizarre carvings in its 12th-century church.

N21 to Sorges; then D74 and D3 to Agonac, D3E to Château l'Evêque and D939 and D2 to Chancelade.
Sorges has a truffle museum in the local Syndicat d'Initiatif; in winter you can join a truffle trail through nearby oak woods. North-west of Périgueux lie the monastic ruins of **Chancelade**, where the abbey church and chapel of St-Jean remain of a once-great 12th-century community (Jul–Aug, afternoons).

D2 and side-road to Prieuré de Merlande; join D1 to Lisle, then D78 to Bourdeilles and Brantôme.
At **Merlande**, an isolated chapel in a woodland clearing is all that remains of an associated priory, remarkable for its Romanesque carving. Heading back towards the swift-flowing Dronne, you will encounter the town of **Bourdeilles**, dominated by a high medieval and Renaissance castle. Hastily patched up to receive a proposed visit by Catherine de Médicis (who cancelled), it has excellent views over the rocky green river. The drive back to Brantôme passes beneath spectacular overhanging rocks. This stretch of the Dronne is ideal for canoeing.

Dordogne

St-Léonard-de-Noblat

St-Junien   134B4

Glove-making has been the local industry here since the 11th century and today its factories supply much of the finely-crafted leather goods for Hermès, Dior, Cacherel, Kenzo etc. St-Junien's church is a fine Romanesque building in Limousin style. North of town lies the Vallée de la Glane, home to a pastoral view that inspired the painter Corot. Ten kilometres south-west is the impressive **Château de Rochechouart▶**, containing 16th-century murals and a contemporary art museum.

▶▶▶ Sarlat   134B3

This beautifully restored gold-stone town is now one of the most popular centres in the central Dordogne, and suffers accordingly from crowds. Sarlat stages many cultural events and holds an annual theatre festival. Its buildings are of minor interest, but they form a harmonious grouping, despite the busy road known as the Traverse which now bisects the old town. The cathedral's belfry is 12th-century; the rest was rebuilt in the 16th and 17th centuries. The strange conical-towered building is the Lanterne des Morts, a funerary chapel. On the main square is a Renaissance house where the poet Boétie was born. Other noteworthy mansions include the Gothic Hôtel Plamon, the Renaissance Hôtel de Maleville and the entire rue des Consuls.

▶ Souillac   134B3

A bustling commercial centre, Souillac is also a popular resort. Just outside is one of the smartest campsites in the Dordogne. Its old quarter is quite limited, but the prize is the domed church of **Ste-Marie** and its fine doorway, now visible inside the nave. The carvings depict episodes from the life of Theophilus, who retracted a pact with the devil. The monastery now houses a fascinating museum of automats (*Closed* Mon and Tue afternoons).

artists' colony, resuming a tradition of craftsmanship dating back to the 14th century.

Head west along the D91 and take D33 to Penne.

At one of the valley's most beautiful sections, **Penne** reveals yet another ruined and rugged fortress on a hill. This village was batted to and fro like a shuttlecock during the Hundred Years' War, and suffered during the Albigensian Crusade. Now its peaceful streets are lined with escutcheoned, half-timberedhouses, leading up to the castle ruins.

D115 to Bruniquel.

The cruel Visigothic princess Brunhilda is said to have founded the castle; she was eventually tied to the tail of a wild horse and trampled to death. The castle still retains very early sections; the Knight's Hall and guardroom chimneypiece are worth seeing (*Open* Apr–Oct).

149

Return on D115 to St-Antonin-Noble-Val.

This ancient town is set opposite a sheer rock wall, the **Rochers d'Anglars**. Its tiered merchants' houses have roofs covered in round *lauze* tiles, and its former town hall (actually a belfry), one of the oldest in France, houses a prehistory collection. Notice the 14th-century calvary on the market square.

Leaving the Aveyron to follow its tributary the Bonnette, head north on the D19 towards Caylus.

Caylus has a huge covered market and fortified church, with a striking modern crucifix by Ossip Zadkine.

An alternative route via the D75 and D33 leads to Beaulieu-en-Rouergue.

This route passes the Grotte du Bosc, a smallish cave in a dry underground river-bed displaying limestone formations. At **Beaulieu**, the abbey church dates back to the mid-13th century and has a seven-sided apse. The dormitory now houses a modern art gallery.

Return to Villefranche-de-Rouergue via the D33 and D926.

Drive

Along the Aveyron Valley

Many route variations are possible around the Aveyron Valley. This long, meandering river follows a picturesque course towards the Tarn through a southerly spur of Quercy.

Start at Villefranche-de-Rouergue; then D47 and D149 to Najac. From Villefranche-de-Rouergue, a 13th-century bastide town with a fine central square, follow the river southwards to Najac.

Of all the many medieval fortresses in France, **Najac**'s is a classic example. Set high on a cone-shaped bluff, its defensive walls are extended by a dizzy cliff plunge to one of the Aveyron's looping bends. To reach it, you walk along the one village street of ancient houses towards the castle keep on its promontory.

D564, D594 and D106; then D958 to Laguépie. D922 to Cordes.

Further south, leaving the river temporarily, the beautiful hilltop bastide of Cordes has been well preserved and is now a popular

Dordogne

DOWN THE GULLET

All over the Dordogne, cheerful, healthy-looking geese roam the fields, munching whatever they choose. These are the lucky ones – they haven't yet encountered the *gavage* process, in which maize is poured down their gullets through funnels to enlarge their livers. If you enjoy *foie gras* (goose liver) visit a pâté farm to see what happens. Force-fed geese stay inside dark sheds, for they can hardly waddle, and endure five or six weeks' involuntary gluttony.

150

▶▶ Toulouse   *134B1*

During the Middle Ages, Toulouse was an important stopover on the St Jacques de Compostela route and a centre of learning and culture, fostering some of the best lyric poets of the time. The present university is second in size only to the Sorbonne: one in four inhabitants is a student. Today, Toulouse has much high-tech industry (including the assembly plant for Airbus, visits Mon–Sat) and a new European Space Park, **La Cité de l'Espace**. With its horrific traffic problems, Toulouse is no longer a beautiful place, but its distinctive pink buildings include many attractive Renaissance mansions. The old quarter stretches south of the place du Capitole; recommended shopping streets include the rue Croix Baragnon, the rue des Arts and around the place Wilson.

The basilica **St-Sernin▶▶▶** is the biggest Romanesque church in France, dedicated to a saint martyred by bulls in ad 250. The **Eglise des Jacobins** is a stern Gothic hall church with an unexpectedly flamboyant interior. Equally unusual is the lopsided cathedral, **St-Etienne**, and its pretty square. The **Musée des Augustins▶▶**, housed in the peaceful 14th–15th century convent, contains remarkable collections including medieval sculpture rescued from wantonly demolished churches, and the **Musée St-Raymond▶▶** has a superb collection of Roman art. The fine Renaissance **Hôtel d'Assézat▶** is home to the Bemberg Foundation, renowned for its painting collections (Renaissance, 17th-century and modern French masters, including 30 works by Bonnard). The brand new **Espace d'Art Moderne et Contemporain**, housed in the former abattoir in the revitalised St-Cyprien district, is still further proof of the city's determinedly cultivated image as an important centre for visual arts.

An 11th-century relief at the basilica of St-Sernin

▶▶ Uzerche   *134B4*

The 'Pearl of Limousin' stands on a rocky spur above the waters of the Vézère, moated on three sides. Densely packed buildings sprouting belfries and turrets are linked by steps and interspersed with 14th-century fortifications. The 12th-century church of St-Pierre has capitals carved with animals and foliage, and an eerie crypt.

▶ Ventadour   *134C4*

These romantic castle ruins above the rocky Luzège gorge can be reached by foot from Moustier-Ventadour. Home of the Viscounts of Ventadour before they grew weary of feudal plumbing and decamped to Ussel, this was also where the troubadour Bernard de Ventadour developed his talents. Of humble birth (some say he was the son of the Viscount by a kitchen-maid), Bernard's courtly love songs were inspired by his illicit passion for the Viscountess.

151

Between the Dordogne and the Corréze

Start at Collonges-la-Rouge.
The buildings of **Collonges-la-Rouge▶▶▶**, fashioned from brilliant magenta sandstone, vie with each other for attention. The corbelled Maison de la Sirène bears a mermaid; whimsical turrets adorn the Hôtel de la Ramade de Friac and Hôtel de Beuges; the Castel de Vassignac sports mullions, watch-towers, and loopholes for firing missiles.
D38 and D150 west to Turenne.
Turenne is built of more typical pale limestone, but its vainglorious hilltop castle, reduced by the Revolution to two ruined towers, is striking. Turenne's bankrupt overlords were forced to sell their birthright to Louis XV in 1738, but during the Middle Ages the viscounts of Turenne held sway over 1,200 villages, minted their own currency and collected their own taxes. Today the village is full of 15th- and 16th-century houses. North-west lies the **Gouffre de la Fage**, a series of limestone caverns.

Take the D8, D38 (east), D162 (crossing the N121) and D48 to Aubazines.
The Cistercian abbey church of St-Stephen is **Aubazines'** main feature of interest, originally dating from the 12th century. The church has amusing 18th-century choir-stalls, and St-Stephen's splendid Gothic carved tomb. The restored abbey still houses a religious community but can be visited by guided tour.

D48 to Gorges du Coiroux and Puy de Pauliac.
The summit can be climbed on foot for a panoramic view.

D48, D94 and D940 to Roche de Vic, and D10 and D38 to Collonges-la-Rouge.
The Roche de Vic is a hilltop vantage point crowned by a chapel.

THE PYRENEES

Scale:
0 20 40 60 km
0 10 20 30 miles

A   B   C

E

▶▶▶ REGION HIGHLIGHTS

Bayonne page 155
La Bigorre page 155
Carcassonne page 158
Cirque de Gavarnie page 162
Niaux, Grotte de page 161
Pau page 163
St-Jean-de-Luz page 157
St-Jean-Pied-de-Port page 166
Serrabone page 167
Vallée d'Aspe page 162

CLIMBING ABRUPTLY FROM the plains of Gascony, the Pyrenees – rich in history, even richer in natural beauty – are a formidable natural barrier between France and the Iberian Peninsula. They are two mountain chains, overlapping for a few kilometres where the Garonne rises in the Valle d'Aran, a corner of Spain on the northern side of the watershed. Elsewhere, natural and national frontiers mostly coincide.

There is a marked contrast between the forests and pastures of the damp and cool Atlantic Pyrenees, and the vineyards and orchards of the sun-drenched Mediterranean flank, one of the driest corners of France.

Proud Pyreneans are hyper-sensitive to suggestions that this is France's second-best mountain range and resent comparisons with the Alps. They do not like to be told that their highest peaks only nudge the 3,000m level, while the Alps break 4,000m; that there are only a few pocket-handkerchief glaciers and that winter sports development lags behind by a long way. The Pyrenees' many thermal and mineral springs made the region fashionable in the 19th century, with the result that many of its main resorts are slightly run-down old spas, reinforcing the contrast with the state-of-the-art sports resorts in the Alps.

For many visitors, the unfashionable nature of the Pyrenees is their great appeal. Prices are low, accommodation unpretentious, the welcome warm and unaffected. The mountains are mostly uncluttered by ugly modern resorts and cable-car pylons. The flowers are spectacular, the wildlife abundant (only the Camargue is better for birdwatching), a few species surviving only in the Pyrenees. A Grande Randonnée trail follows the range from coast to coast and takes hikers into a spectacular wilderness. If the resorts are disappointing, the Pyrenees are a backpacker's paradise.

There is plenty for sightseers: pilgrimage places past and present, including Lourdes, the most popular invalids' pilgrimage in Christendom; the showpiece fortified city of

Carcassonne and dizzy citadels where medieval heretics sheltered from persecution; and a wealth of inventive art in the Romanesque churches of Catalonia. The Basque country offers a beautiful coastline, picturesque old villages, an ancient and cherished language and, the most fascinating of all, Europe's fringe cultures, unleashing terrorist activity over the border.

▶ **Andorra** *153D1*

Straddling the spine of the Pyrenees, Andorra is a small co-principality nominally subject to the French president and the Spanish bishop of Urgel. In practice it is proudly independent – and making a good living from tourism, much of it generated by Andorra's tax-free status. Almost all Andorra lies on the Spanish side of the Port d'Envalira (2,407m), the highest main road pass in the Pyrenees. Although both francs and pesetas circulate, Spanish currency and language prevail except at Pas de la Case (2,091m), an ugly modern ski resort on the French border. Villages along the main road down the Valira Valley have been ruined by messy modern development, and the capital, Andorra La Vella, is a traffic-jammed supermarket city. Andorra has some of the best skiing in the Pyrenees, in five separate areas.

Houses in Bayonne incorporate mountain chalet styles

Arles-sur-Tech *153E1*

This market town makes a more attractive base than nearby Amélie les Bains. Its old **abbey church**▶ has interesting Romanesque carving on the façade, a Gothic cloister and a baroque altarpiece which illustrates the story of the town's patrons, a pair of 3rd-century Kurdish martyrs. The Fou cascades down a narrow gorge (access only on foot) to join the Tech, 2km above Arles-sur-Tech.

▶ **Aure, Vallée d'** *152C1*

The Neste d'Aure (neste, like gave, is a local Pyrenean word for river) flows from the slopes of the 3,000m Massif de Néouvielle to join the Garonne at Montréjeau. The middle section of the valley is pleasantly rural, and the old grey town of Arreau makes a good base or overnight halt. The main alternative is St-Lary-Soulan, a fashionable and stylish resort by Pyrenean standards, with a cable-car to good ski slopes. Above St-Lary, the road narrows and climbs into wilder country on its way to the Bielsa road tunnel to Spain. From Fabian, it is a slow 14km drive up to a cluster of high lakes (dammed and natural) beneath the snowy walls of the **Néouvielle**▶▶, some of the most impressive Pyrenean scenery accessible to motorists. Marked GR hiking trails lead over the massif to Barèges.

▶▶ Bayonne   152A2

An old river port on the Nive, the capital of the French Basque country is famous for its ham, chocolate and bayonets. On the left bank, the twin spires of its fine 13th-century Gothic cathedral dominate an attractive precinct of old shopping streets. The arcaded rue du Port-Neuf has mouthwatering *confiseries* and old-fashioned tea shops (**Cazenave** is recommended); the place de la Liberté is the focus of café society. The right-bank half of the old town has the excellent **Musée Bonnat**▶ (*Closed* Tue), with a rich art collection, including works by Goya and Ingres.

▶ Bétharram, Grottes de   152B2

This 5km complex of grandiose underground chambers, rich in stalactites and stalagmites, is reached by minibus and toured by boat and train. Bétharram would be a powerful attraction in any region; so close to Lourdes (14km east), it is often dauntingly crowded (*Open* Apr–Oct daily; Nov–Mar, Mon–Fri at 2.30 and 4pm).

▶▶ La Bigorre   152B1

The Bigorre is the heartland of the high Pyrenees and its main tourist area. The route from Arreau to Luz-St-Sauveur crosses the attractively pastoral **Col d'Aspin**▶ and wilder **Col du Tourmalet**▶ (2,114m), notorious as the most punishing climb in the Tour de France. From the pass, a re-made road (open only in summer) and funicular provide alternative access to the observatory station on the **Pic du Midi du Bigorre**▶▶▶ (2,865m). **La Mongie** is a rather unsightly ski resort linked by chairlift to Barèges, a small resort with sulphur springs and summer campers. Madame de Maintenon brought the Duc de Maine to Barèges in 1677, and Napoleon sent wounded soldiers there to recuperate. **Bagnères de Bigorre** is an older and larger spa – there are impressive stalagmites and stalactites in the nearby Grotte de Médous. Cauterets and Luz-St-Sauveur are the other main resorts (see separate entries).

Le Canigou   153E1

Lonely eastern bastion of the Pyrenees, 50km from the Mediterranean, the Canigou (2,784m) is the holy mountain of the Catalans, who come annually from France and Spain to light fires on the summit on midsummer's night. From Vernet-les-Bains, jeep trips are organised up the rough forest road to the Chalet-Hôtel des Cortalets (2,175m), two hours' walk (a slog, but not difficult) from the summit. There is a longer and slightly less difficult road from Prades. The classic Canigou experience is to stay overnight and walk to the top in time to see dawn break over the sea.

155

Since the Basques swarmed down from the high passes to ambush Charlemagne's rearguard and kill Roland at Roncevaux in 778, they have been no friends of the French. Yet the beret and the rope-soled espadrille are just two Basque contributions to the national way of life. Of obscure origin, the Basques speak an impenetrable tongue, once thought to have been the pre-Babel language. The Devil is said to have mastered only three words of it after seven years of study.

156

Celebrating the Basque festival in Bayonne in August dressed in unseasonal shaggy sheepskins

Most of the Basque country lies on the Spanish side of the Pyrenees and only one in ten of the half-million speakers of the Basque language are French. Although the Basques are conscious of their cultural and ethnic solidarity – 'Zazpiak Bat' ('the seven are one') is a favourite slogan – Spanish and French Basques have evolved differently. In Spain, the mineral-rich region was quick to industrialise and Basques have been prominent in the economic and political life of the nation. In France, the Basque country, consisting of the three provinces of Labourd, Basse Navarre and Soule, was a remote backwater of farmers and fishermen until tourism reached the coast in the 19th century.

They are a humble and traditionally reserved people who leave acts of separatist violence to their Spanish cousins. Even in France, however, town centre demonstrations, usually about political prisoners, are not uncommon. It is hard not to view these processions with colourful banners and unintelligible chanting as another example of quaint Basque folklore, like the costumed displays of traditional Basque dancing and music.

The national game 'Basque pelota' is not one game but many variations of the old *jeu de paume*, featuring a hard ball hit against a wall (*fronton*) which is a conspicuous feature of every village in the south-west. The fastest version of the game (*cesta punta*) takes place in an indoor court (*trinquet*); players wear long, curved scoop-like gauntlets (*chistera*) to catch the ball and return it in a single swing of the arm. When played well, this is one of the most exciting and graceful of ball games. At a simpler level (as practised by children against the village fronton), bare hands or a wooden bat (*pala*) are used. Most of the major championships and important matches are held at Biarritz. St-Jean-de-Luz is another good place for pelota watching.

Labourd Well watered to a fault, the Labourd is the prettiest of the three Basque regions, with a beautiful coastline of cliffs and sandy coves fronting a bumpy landscape of green hills and immaculately kept, red and white timbered villages. Sare, Ainhoa and Ascain are outstandingly pretty, with typical Basque churches, of which the main characteristics are sex-segregated seating arrangements (the galleries are for men only) and small circular gravestones bearing the Basque swastika emblem. On the coast, **Biarritz** (see page 128) is the grand resort and surfing capital of Europe. The old fishing port of **St-Jean-de-Luz** has a perfectly sheltered sandy beach (a rare commodity on the Atlantic coast), lots of good fish restaurants, elegant shops and lashings of Basque charm in the colourful streets of its pedestrianised centre. The house where Louis XIV spent the month (May/June 1660) before his marriage to the Spanish Infanta Maria Teresa of Spain stands by the harbour. His fiancée stayed in the beautiful house next door. Their marriage took place in the spectacularly ornate church of St-Jean Baptiste. After the ceremony, the door used by the royal couple was blocked. The border town of **Hendaye** is dreary by comparison, but has a vast beach.

Bayonne (see page 155), the capital of Labourd, is the acknowledged capital of the French Basque country. It has a core of streets in typically colourful Basque style, and is worth a visit for sightseeing. In early August it hosts the largest Basque festival, with much dancing of fandangos and other dances to tunes played on the *txistu* (three-holed flute) and *ttun-ttun* (tambourine).

Inland From the Col de St Ignace, between Ascain and Sare, a railway (Apr–Nov) ascends the Rhune (900m), a superb viewpoint commanding the coast.

BASQUE CUISINE
Typical ingredients in Basque cuisine are tomatoes, peppers, garlic and onions: mixed with eggs these make *piperade*, a Basque omelette. Chicken, kidneys and grilled tuna are often served *à la Basquaise*, with a sauce of red peppers, garlic and onions. Traditional *gâteau* Basque has lemon and black cherries from Itxassou (south of Cambo les Bains). The best Basque wine is Irroléguy, from the area around St-Etienne-de-Baïgorry.

157

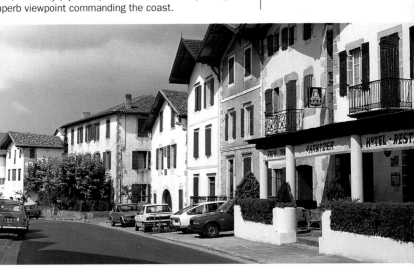

Espelette has a pimento fair (last weekend Oct) and is a market-place for *pottoks*, diminutive semi-wild horses which inhabit the local hillsides (fair: last Tue–Wed in Jan).

Soule (see page 166) cannot rival the coastal region for village prettiness but has magnificent countryside of forests and sheep pastures still managed, as they have been for centuries, by committees of communal representatives.

The red and white houses of Ainhoa, one of the most characteristic villages of the Labourd, founded in the 12th century

Carcassonne's magnificent defences

▶▶▶ Carcassonne 153E2

Set apart from a thriving modern town beside the Aude stand the towers and walls of a mint-condition medieval fortified city, one of the great sights of Europe. The defences were of little use in 1209, when Carcassonne lasted less than a month before opening its gates to the crusading army of Simon de Montfort. Tourism rules in the narrow streets, but nothing spoils the time-warp in the beautiful grassy area between the city's twin curtain walls. The massive towers buttressing the inner wall are a mixture of 13th-century and clearly visible Gallo-Roman masonry. The outer wall was built after the 1209 siege. Inside the city, the basilica of **St-Nazaire▶** has both a Romanesque nave and a Gothic choir.

▶ Cauterets 152B1

A 19th-century spa proud of its boiled sweets (*berlingots*), Cauterets is a good all-round resort: no great beauty as a village, but full of animation in midsummer and an excellent base for excursions into the Parc National des Pyrenees. The park information centre has a good exhibition of Pyrenean ecology (with a section devoted to the bearded vulture). A cable-car hoists skiers to the Cirque du Lys, known for the most reliable snow in the Pyrenees. For walkers, the classic excursion is by road past waterfalls to **Pont d'Espagne▶▶**, from where trails lead up to the highest peak in the French Pyrenees, the Vignemale (3,298m).

▶ Cerdagne 153D1

Cerdagne/Cerdanya is the beautiful upper Segre Valley, divided between France and Spain according to the terms of the 1659 Pyrenean treaty. It is a famously sunny region and its main resort, **Font-Romeu**, a sprawling ski resort, claims 3,000 hours of sun a year and boasts a solar oven. Much used for high-level athletics training, it is also a Catalan pilgrimage site, with an 18th-century hermitage on the site of a spring where a miraculous statue of the Virgin was uncovered by a bull. There are other interesting churches at **Llo▶**, the most picturesque old village in French Cerdagne, and Hix, near the border at Bourg Madame.

SOLAR OVEN
Built in 1969, the Odeillo solar oven at Font-Romeu consists of 9,500 mirrors forming a concave surface area of 1,800sq m, concentrating the sun's rays into an 80cm oven where the temperature can reach 3,500°C. Since 1986 it has not been used for power generation, but there are other highly technical scientific uses to which the mirrors are put, as explained in the permanent exhibition on site.

The Albigensian crusade, launched by Pope Innocent III in 1209 to eradicate the Cathar heresy which flourished in southwestern France, is one of the more compelling stories of internecine butchery and bravery in the annals of medieval history. Apart from wiping 400 villages off the map, it brought about royal control of Languedoc and the destruction of the Raymond dynasty of the Visigoths, a multi-cultural civilisation of great refinement, which had flourished at the court of Toulouse.

Kill them all! Promised remission for all sins past and future and the cancellation of all debts in exchange for 40 days' service, an army of land-grabbing northern French crusaders went south. Even contemporaries were shocked when Béziers was singled out for exemplary massacre on July 22 1209; Cathar and Catholic were slaughtered indiscriminately ('kill them all, for God will recognise his own' cried the Abbot of Cîteaux, no slouch with the sword); not even women and children sheltering in churches were spared.

Towns soon opened their gates to the crusaders but the Cathar *parfaits* and *parfaites* (the mystical corps of Cathar priests) retreated to remote fortresses in the foothills of the eastern Pyrenees.

The Cathar strongholds The two most exciting of these ridge-top eyries to visit are Peyrepertuse and Quéribus, north of the main Perpignan–Foix road (D117). **Quéribus** is set 500m above the main valley, with superb views of the Canigou and other high peaks to the south. Its siege in 1255, which succeeded only through treachery, was the last episode of the intermittent crusading effort. **Peyrepertuse** is a larger complex of ruins crowning a ridge, wild and overgrown and also commanding magnificent views. **Montségur** is equally impressive, but you are less likely to have it to yourself. There is a steep path to the ruins from the pass on its western flank. **Puivert** and **Puilaurens** are other good examples beside the Foix-Perpignan road near Quillan.

SIEGE OF MONTSÉGUR
The Cathars' headquarters on the rock of Montségur, south-east of Foix, was besieged by 10,000 Catholics throughout the autumn and winter of 1243–4. A truce was eventually concluded but all 207 Cathars declined to abjure their faith or escape, and walked calmly into the flames of a huge bonfire on the morning of March 16 1244.

A stronghold formed by Nature and by Man: Peyrepertuse

St-Bertrand-de-Comminges (above)

The Devil's Bridge at Céret (right)

EXTRA-CURRICULAR
Céret's sights include a monument to toreadors, and in July bull-running hits the streets. The traditional regional dance, *la sardane* peaks on the last Sunday in August with strict choreography to the sounds of an 11-piece band, *la cobla*, of tambourines and strident flageolets.

ST-LIZIER
At the northern edge of the Couserans lies the small town of St-Lizier with its 3rd-century Gallo-Roman ramparts still intact. Immediately to the south lie the church of St-Lizier, famous for its Romanesque cloister and its remarkable 9th-century apse frescoes, and the 18th-century pharmacy in the Hôtel-Dieu next door, still used as a stopover for pilgrims en route for St-Jaques de Compostela.

▶ Céret
153E1

An attractive, leisurely Catalan town at the heart of the fruit-growing region of the Tech Valley, Céret attracted leading Cubist artists at the turn of the century and has an excellent modern art museum, with works by Chagall, Dali, Picasso, Dufy and Braque. A canopy of plane trees adds to the pleasures of a stroll through the old part of town, south of the place de la République.

▶▶ Le Comminges
152C2

The heart of the Comminges region is the upper valley of the Garonne. In 72 BC Pompey founded a city, *Lugdunum Convenarum*, on an isolated hill at the entrance to the mountain valley. The old walled village of **St-Bertrand-de-Comminges▶▶** now stands on the site, dominated by its cathedral, which used to be an important stop on the pilgrimage road to Spain. All that survives of the original 12th-century building is the façade and three sides of the cloister, with beautiful capitals and an open gallery giving a fine mountain view. The choir has outstanding 16th-century carved wooden choir stalls and screen. At the foot of the hill there are some excavations of the Roman city and, beautifully set among cypresses near the quiet village of Valcabrère, the delightful 11th-century basilica of **St-Just▶**, largely built of recycled Roman masonry. Roman inscriptions and columns are easily identified.

Le Couserans
152C1

Between the Pays de Foix and the Comminges, the Couserans is an out-of-the-way region of quiet valleys without major sights or spectacular mountain scenery. The traditional local ways of life have survived better than in most places, but depopulation is as great an enemy as overdevelopment. The Bethmale Valley, well known for its local dress (including extravagantly upturned wooden footwear, see the Begouen Collection, St-Lizier), is now quiet holiday-home country. **Aulus-les-Bains**, a spa once known for its bear tamers, is now well past its prime but set among beautiful mountains near the Spanish border ridge and a good base for hikes to mountain lakes and waterfalls (the 110m Cascade d'Arse, notably). **Seix** is a centre for canoeing.

Pays de Foix

This tour combines the best Pyrenean cave with beautiful hill driving to the west of Foix.

Start at Foix.
Foix is less enchanting than a distant view of its picturesque three-towered castle suggests, but is a lively place, with a good choice of restaurants.

Take the N20 to Tarascon-sur-Ariège. Excursions possible to Grotte de Niaux (D8) and Grotte de Lombrives (N20).
Niaux is one of the finest prehistoric painted caves in Europe, with black bison and ibex in its Salon Noir, 'discovered' in 1906. Numbers are limited, book in advance: 05 61 05 88 37. You can always visit the replica in Tarascon-sur-Ariège's **Parc Pyrénéen de l'Art Préhistorique**. On the other side of the same mountain, **Lombrives** (2-hour guided tour and train ride) is an enormous network of caves used as a refuge and burial place since prehistory and covered with graffiti.

Take D618 to Massat and Biert, then D18/D17 via Col de la Crouzette, Sommet de Portel and Col des Marrous back to Foix.
The rest of the tour is a long scenic drive, 75km of beautiful woods, pastures and panoramas from high passes. It can be abbreviated by

taking the narrow road which climbs steeply from the Col des Caugnous (6km east of Massat) to the Col de Péguère near the Tour Laffont, a fine viewpoint a few minutes' walk from the road. The view from the Sommet de Portel (1,485m) is better still.

From Foix excursions can be made to Rivière Souterraine de Labouiche and Grotte du Mas d'Azil by D1 (30km each way).
Visiting the underground Labouiche River involves a 1.5km boat trip, with stalagmites, stalactites and a waterfall to admire. South of the village of le Mas d'Azil, the D119 runs through a superb 420m-long tunnel carved by the River Arize. Before sheltering 17th-century Protestants, side caves (guided tour) were inhabited by pre-historic man for thousands of years. Finds are well displayed on site.

►► Cirque de Gavarnie   *152B1*

The most celebrated mountain beauty spot in the Pyrenees is the huge theatre of cliffs, waterfalls and snowy peaks to the south of Luz-St-Sauveur. The classic way to see the cirque is by donkey (or on foot) along the 5km path from the car parks at the village of Gavarnie (where there is accommodation) to the foot of the cliffs.

BRECHE DE ROLAND
A tough three-hour walk from the Col de Gavarnie/Boucharo leads to the Brèche de Roland, a cleft in the rock wall where, according to the *Chanson de Roland*, Charlemagne's expiring lieutenant smashed his sword on the rock to prevent it falling into infidel hands.

► Isturits and Oxocelhaya (Grottes)   *152A2*

These two caves in the Basque country are within easy reach of the coast for a rainy-day outing. The higher chamber (Isturits) has yielded important evidence of occupation by prehistoric man; Oxocelhaya is more beautiful, with well-lit stalactites and stalagmites (*Open* mid-Mar–mid-Nov).

► Lourdes   *152B2*

Lourdes is an astonishing manifestation of contemporary faith. Queues of stretcher cases inch towards the holy taps, the candles and the screen of votive crutches at the entrance to the miraculous riverside grotto where a young country girl, Bernadette Subirous, saw the Virgin Mary on February 11 1858 and on 17 subsequent occasions. Shop after shop peddles plastic Virgins, bottles of holy water and exorbitantly priced candles to be lit at the shrine. The cavernous underground basilica has room for 20,000 pilgrims.

Lourdes was once an important strategic stronghold. An impressive fortress overlooks the Gave de Pau and houses a good regional museum.

LOURDES BUSINESS
The infrastructure for the world's leading pilgrimage is enormous: 300 hotels, 35 campsites, and scores of sanatoria, all dependent on voluntary helpers.

► Luchon (Bagnères-de-Luchon)   *152C1*

The Romans' favourite spa in the Pyrenees still has a certain chic, with tree-lined avenues, a casino and thermal baths set in a handsome park. At a junction of high mountain valleys, Luchon makes an excellent base for excursions. From the woods and waterfalls of the Val de Lys it is a splendid hairpin drive up to the mini-resort and lofty belvedere of Superbagnères (1,800m). The former Hospice de France refuge (10km south-east) and the Col de Pierrefitte (above **Bourg d'Oeil►**, 22km north-west) are better starting points for walks.

► Luz-St-Sauveur   *152B1*

This picturesque old village and modest resort between Lourdes and Gavarnie, is an attractive alternative to the larger resorts in the area. Once the capital of a self-governing republic, it has an unusual fortified **church►**. There is a national park information centre next door.

LUCHON'S DISTEMPERS
'Beastly dens ... sufficient to cause as many distempers as they cure.' – Arthur Young, on Luchon, 1787.

►►► Niaux, Grotte de   *153D1*

See **Pays de Foix Drive**, page 161

See **Pays de Foix Drive**, page 161

► Oloron-Ste-Marie and Vallée d'Aspe   *152B2*

Oloron-Ste-Marie is a busy market and chocolate-making town at the confluence of the Aspe and Ossau gaves, on the old pilgrimage route to Spain. Its showpiece is the 12th-century marble doorway of Sainte-Marie, richly carved with Biblical figures.

Running north from the Col du Somport (1,632m) is the beautiful **Aspe Valley►►►**. Its relative tranquillity

Accessible from June to early November, the D918 linking the valleys of the Gave d'Ossau and the Gave d'Arrens offers a scenic drive over the Col d'Aubisque

and its dwindling population of bears are threatened by a road tunnel under the Somport (end 1999). The Pyrenees national park office at Etsaut gives hiking information. Above the valley, the rough grey village of **Lescun** is a good hiking base with simple accommodation, beneath a superb circus of peaks including the Pic d'Anie (2,504m).

▶ Ossau, Vallée d' 152B2

One ridge east of the Aspe, the Ossau Valley runs north to Pau from the Spanish border at the Col du Pourtalet (1,794m); the two valleys combine to make a circuit via Jaca in Spain. The upper Ossau Valley is beautiful wild country, with a few bears lurking around Laruns, and rather more isards (Pyrenean chamois) on the slopes of the Pic du Midi d'Ossau (2,885m), centre-piece of the famous view from Pau. From Gabas, a narrow road climbs steeply to the artificial Lac de Bious (1,420m); from here it is a 2-hour walk to a cluster of natural **lakes▶▶** among splendid scenery at the foot of the Pic du Midi. Hiking trails link to form a full circuit of the mountain. On the other side of Gabas, a cable-car and mountain railway lead to the **Lac d'Artouste▶** via the panoramic Pic de la Sagette (2,031m). There is a hiking trail back to Gabas from the lake. From Laruns, it is a beautiful drive east over the Col d'Aubisque (1,709m).

▶▶ Pau 152B2

The one-time capital of Béarn has two claims to fame: Henri IV ('le Béarnais'), best loved of all French monarchs, was born there in 1553; and the boulevard des Pyrénées gives a famous view of the mountain range, best when the distant peaks are snowy (from November to April).

At the western end of the boulevard des Pyrénées, the much-restored château is a mixture of medieval, Renaissance and Second Empire. The interior (guided tours) has a collection of 17th- and 18th-century tapestries and many Henri-related items including his cradle, a turtle shell.

The High Pyrenees cover more than half the 400km length of the range, from the Pic d'Anie (2,504m) above Lescun in the Aspe Valley to the Pic Carlit (2,921m), east of Andorra. Apart from the Somport and Pourtalet passes in the west and the Garonne Gap (the Spanish Valle d'Aran) where the two Pyrenean chains overlap to the south of Luchon, there are no easy frontier passes in this wilderness area of spectacular peaks and rocky cirques mirrored in mountain lakes. The area has a rich and fascinating ecology, with the best examples of high-mountain flora and fauna in Europe.

A thin strip (110km by 15km at its widest) of the frontier mountains in the west, from Lescun to the Néouvielle Massif above St-Lary, is part of the Parc National des Pyrénées.

Climbers' challenges The highest Pyrenees are in Spain (due south of Luchon, the Maladeta Massif culminates at the 3,404m Pic d'Aneto), but the northern side has the most famous and beautiful peaks, including the Vignemale (3,298m), highest point of the frontier, the terraced cliffs and waterfalls of the **Cirque de Gavarnie** (see page 162), and the mighty **Pic du Midi d'Ossau** (2,885m), an isolated bastion which is the climber's favourite playground in the range. The Pic du Midi was first climbed in 1787 (the year after the first ascent of Mont Blanc) by a shepherd from the Aspe Valley.

South of Cauterets, the remotest of the Pyrenean spas, the uninterrupted 800m wall of the north face of the **Vignemale** is another formidable challenge for mountaineers. The Vignemale has the biggest glacier in the Pyrenees and was the adopted home of one of the more colourful characters in the history of mountaineering, Count Henry Russell (1834–1909), who dynamited seven caves (including one only a few metres below the summit) to inhabit and use for dinner parties. Russell climbed the Vignemale more than 30 times and had guides bury him to the neck in scree on the summit for closer communion with the mountain he described as his own. This was no exaggeration: Barèges gave it to him on a 99-year lease. Luchon Museum has a section devoted to Russell and there is a statue of him at Gavarnie.

A legendary mountaineers' challenge: the Vignemale

Pyrenean wildlife Bears, the most celebrated speciality of Pyrenean wildlife, do not inhabit the high mountains but instead choose to live on the fringe of human habitation at medium altitude (invariably below the tree-line). Other denizens of the mountains include marmots (numerous), isards (Pyrenean chamois) and desmans, nocturnal voles with webbed feet and a long trunk

Stunning Pyrenean mountain scenery in the Parc National des Pyrénées: guided hikes can be arranged through park offices in the main valleys

PYRENEAN TRAIL
Pont d'Espagne, south of Cauterets, is the point of departure for some of the most celebrated, not-too-arduous walks in the Pyrenees. You can take a chair-lift to the beautiful Lac de Gaube (otherwise an hour on foot). From the lake the GR10 continues up the valley to Les Oulettes refuge (2,151m) with increasingly impressive views of the north wall of the Vignemale. From there it climbs steeply to a high col (another two hours) on the mountain's eastern shoulder and down to the Barrage d'Ossoue. Another path from Pont d'Espagne follows the beautiful Marcadeau Valley to the refuge Wallon (1,866m, two hours from Pont d'Espagne). The trail, much used by travellers and smugglers down the centuries, continues over the mountains to Panticosa in Spain via the Port du Marcadeau (2,541m).

which are found only in the streams in the Pyrenees and the Caucasus.

Undisputed king of the Pyrenees, however, is the lammergeier or bearded vulture, the largest of European vultures (over 1m long and with a wingspan of up to 3m) and a unique link in the food chain – its favourite food is bone marrow, which it obtains by dropping bones on to rock from a great height. Lammergeiers nest on mountain ledges in the wildest locations and shun the company of other vultures at a carcass. When it is seen on the wing it is a magnificent sight, clearly distinguishable from other vultures by its size and narrow pointed wings and tail.

The hiker's Pyrenees An 8km rough road leads from **Gavarnie** to the **Barrage d'Ossoue** reservoir, along a valley where you might glimpse isards, marmots and (if you're lucky) bearded vultures. From the lake it is about three hours' walk to the foot of the Vignemale's Ossoue glacier and one of Russell's caves.

The **GR10** hiking trail crosses from Atlantic to Mediterranean on the northern side of the chain, passing through the national park via numerous refuges. No rock climbing is involved, but in many places the isolation and high altitude of the path brings it into the realm of mountaineering. A Pyrenean **Haute Route** (the HRP, for experienced climbers only) takes a higher line along the crest of the frontier mountains, crossing into Spain in several places.

There are national park information centres at Cauterets, Luz-St-Sauveur, St-Lary-Soulan, Etsaut and Tarbes.

BASQUE AMBUSH
From St-Jean-Pied-de-Port, the modern road to Roncevaux follows the Valcarlos road, where Charlemagne's rearguard, under Roland, Count of Blaye, with the valiant support of Olivier le Preux and Bishop Turpin, was ambushed and annihilated by rock-throwing Basques in 778. Legend, in the form of the great epic poem the *Chanson de Roland*, transformed Basques into Saracens and translated the action to the Ports de Cize route to the east, now open only to hikers (GR65).

St-Jean-Pied-de-Port huddles beneath the peak of Roncevaux

ON THE ROAD
The edible scallop takes its French name, coquille St-Jacques, from the emblem of the medieval pilgrimage to Compostela, Spanish burial place of the Crusaders' patron saint, Santiago (St James or St Jacques), on the scallop-rich coast of northwest Spain. Wearing the pilgrim's uniform (cap with cockle badge, stick and gourd) pilgrims crossed France on set routes from Paris, Arles, Le Puy, Vézelay and Tours. Pilgrimages continued throughout the Hundred Years' War but the vogue waned by the 16th century. So-called pilgrims were mistrusted as spongers, and the term 'coquelin' (now 'coquin' in colloquial French) took on a pejorative meaning.

▶ **St-Jean-Pied-de-Port**   *152A2*

An old Basque town with great charm and a long tradition of hospitality for passing travellers, St-Jean was where medieval pilgrimage routes converged before crossing the mountains ('Port' means mountain pass) to Roncevaux in Spain. Pilgrims walked down the delightful cobbled Rue de la Citadelle from the Porte St Jacques to Porte d'Espagne. Old pink sandstone houses and a fortified church (Notre Dame du Pont) built into the fabric of the ramparts overlook the right bank of the River Nive. The great military engineer Vauban added a citadel and a new system of defences on the left bank in the 17th century. Although full of tourists in summer, St-Jean is a cheerful place and a good base, with hotels both plush and simple, excellent restaurants, folklorish displays of Basque singing and dancing, and shops full of berets and Basque walking sticks.

▶ **St-Martin-du-Canigou**   *153D1*

This much-restored abbey is spectacularly sited on the western side of the Canigou above Vernet-les-Bains (see opposite).

▶ **Serrabone**   *153E1*

The 11th- to 12th-century abbey church here sits in a wild setting among scented scrub-covered hills to the south of the Prades–Perpignan road (see opposite).

▶ **Haute Soule**   *152A2*

Soule is the easternmost province of the Basque country and, in terms of village charm, the least interesting. **Mauléon-Licharre**, the capital, manufactures typical Basque products – espadrilles and pelota bats. The churchyard at Gotein (3km south) is characteristically Basque, with triple-crowned belfry wall and adjacent *fronton* (pelota court). Patient drivers can traverse the beautiful beech forests and wild pastures of the Haute Soule, still managed by the traditional collective syndicates of Soule communes, either driving 42km from St-Jean-Pied-de-Port to Larrau (via the Col Bagargiak 1,327m) through the fringe of the Iraty forest, or 36km from St-Jean to Tardets-Sorholus via Ahusquy, a more pastoral route. In wild country south of Tardets, the D113 leads past the entrance to the **Gorges de Kakouetta▶**, a narrow canyon accessible only to walkers (proper hiking boots are needed). At **Ste-Engrâce's** Romanesque pilgrimage church, the Queen of Sheba rides an elephant on one of the pillar capitals.

Medieval Catalonia was a prosperous and cosmopolitan region, with trade links all over the Mediterranean. Its architecture from the Romanesque period, before the lumpish northern Crusaders descended on the south-west to snuff out tolerance and invention, seems to reflect its open society. There is a remarkable and fruitful fusion of influences, from as far afield as southern Spain (so-called Mozarabic style) and Lombardy in northern Italy, home of many specialist masons.

Serrabone This is the most exciting church in the region, thanks to the contrast between the dour grey exterior of the 11th- to 12th-century priory church, which stands alone in a scrubby sub-mountainous wilderness, and the wealth of delicate carving on roseate marble inside.

St-Michel-de-Cuxa The 10th- to 11th-century buildings of the powerful abbey are red tiled, and there is a handsome four-storey crenellated tower. The 11th-century crypt has a remarkable central pillar similar to a palm tree. Half the cloister, found incorporated in surrounding buildings, was exported to New York to form The Cloisters Museum; the remainder has been reconstructed, with its delightful capitals. Concerts are held in the summer.

Corneilla de Conflent Ste-Marie here has good carved doorway and windows and 12th-century (wooden) and 14th-century (marble) Virgins inside (key next door).

St-Martin-du-Canigou This spectacularly sited rocktop monastery, over 1,000m above Vernet, has superimposed 10th- and 11th-century churches and a cloister of impressive rough simplicity. Much of St-Martin is obviously restored, but the spirit is authentic. Best reached on foot (half an hour) from Casteil above Vernet-les-Bains. Guided tours.

Eus A small Romanesque chapel (St-Vincent) sits at the bottom of an old village on a slope, with a good view of the Canigou. North of Prades by D35.

St-Martin-de-Fenollar This small chapel, with wonderful 12th-century frescoes, is signed from the N9, 6km north of Le Perthus. (*Open* daily; winter afternoons only.)

St-Génis-des-Fontaines Carvings of Christ and apostles stand over the doorway (dated 1020) of this church on the D618 between Le Boulou and Argelès.

167

Above: St-Michel-de-Cuxa; below: detail at Serrabone priory church

Cap d'Antibes, by Claude Monet

PROVENCE AND THE MEDITERRANEAN COAST

0	20	40	60 km
0	10	20	30 miles

THE FRENCH CALL it le Midi, where the sun is high in the sky and hot. The winter sun is warm enough for lemons at Menton, and launched the south of France as a winter playground. Now tourists prefer the white heat of the summer. It is a harsh climate, prone to the howling Mistral (north wind) which fans devastating fires every summer. Only the Riviera is sheltered from its forces.

It is an area of enormous diversity of life, landscape and history. The Mediterranean coast has the spectacular mountains and fashionable urban resorts (with urban traffic problems) of the Riviera; and the long tracts of featureless sands of the Languedoc coast.

The French make for the sea *en masse* in July and August. The marshlands of the Camargue and the high mountain country of the Maritime Alps have their own wilderness appeal. Between the two lies the hill country of rural Provence, an ideal retreat: bright colours and lavender-scented air, and scores of old villages which are ideal for sitting in the shade of a plane tree sipping *pastis* and watching a game of boules. The sightseeing glories of the south are Roman – great amphitheatres and triumphal arches to rival the best in Italy. There are medieval treasures, too – the Papal city of Avignon – and a wealth of artistic associations: scenery made famous by Van Gogh and Cézanne, and great modern art museums. Artists follow money and the sun. In the south, there is plenty of both.

The shifting marshy area, half land and half sea, of the Rhône delta is desolate but uniquely appealing. It is a wilderness full of potent, exotic images – wild horses, costumed cowboys (les gardians), migrant flamingos and flamenco festivals.

OTHER POINTS OF INTEREST

Mas du Pont de Rousty: an open-air museum, Musée Camarguais, beside the main Saintes-Maries to Arles road. A 3km walk through Camargue-scapes (*Closed Tue Oct–Mar*).

Pont de Gau: a big bird sanctuary and information centre near Les Saintes-Maries.

St-Gilles: a small pilgrimage town on the northern edge of the Camargue, with an old church; the façade is decorated with beautiful but damaged 12th-century sculptures.

Souvenir of Saintes-Maries, depicting a gardian (traditional cowboy of the region) astride a native Camargue horse. Directly descended from prehistoric horses, the coats of these horses turn white aged 4–7 years

Here land and sea have an unstable relationship. A fragile ecosystem exists, where wildlife and society are threatened by irrigation, agriculture and, of course, tourism. The Camargue is an ornithologist's pilgrimage, with over 100 migrating species, including flamingos. The best chance of seeing them is in the spring at **Etang de Fangassier** in the south-east. There is a good information centre at **la Capelière**, on the eastern side of the main lagoon (Vaccarès), with guided tours on request (*Closed* Sun). Several traditional Camargue ranches (manades) are open to visitors and run riding excursions. Méjanes, on the Etang de Vaccarès, has a highly commercialised example.

Towns and ports The main resort is **Les Saintes-Maries**, where the Holy Maries (Salomé and Jacobea) landed on the beach with a black servant girl Sarah, the patroness of gypsies. On May 24 and 25 gypsies flock from all over Europe for the pilgrimage, which is followed by a Camargue festival of dancing, costume displays, bullfights and rodeos. Les Saintes-Maries is a rather seedy resort, but worth visiting for its church, a windowless fortress full of ex-votos. There is a good sandy beach and boat excursions on the Petit Rhône.

At the western edge of the Camargue lies **Aigues-Mortes**, purpose-built by Louis IX in the 13th century as a fortified port. The grid of old streets is encircled by ramparts, which you can climb and tour, for views over the Camargue and empty marshes.

Two other modern resorts near by are **Port Camargue** and **Le Grau du Roi**.

▶▶ Aix-en-Provence 168C2

Chic and cultured, Aix is one of Europe's loveliest small cities, still seemingly inhabited by the spirit of Provence's last great ruler, *le bon roi* René d'Anjou (1409-80), who made Aix his base and a centre for all the arts. Once a spa (Aix is from Aquae), it is still a fountain-rich city of classical town houses. The only nightmare is parking. Café life and traffic jams centre on Aix's main boulevard, the **cours Mirabeau**▶▶, shaded by a magnificent canopy of plane trees, flanked by some of the best façades and most populated café-terraces.

Old Town To the north lies the old town, a maze of narrow cobbled streets, with a lot of restoration of old buildings. This is the most interesting part of town to explore, and there is an excellent daily market on Place Richelme.

St-Sauveur Cathedral▶ has elements from all periods, from Merovingian (the baptistery) to Renaissance, and a delightful Romanesque cloister. The great treasures are the triptych of *The Burning Bush*, painted by Nicolas Froment for King René, and the carved prophets and sibyls on the main doors. Both are kept shut, but a key holder is usually on hand.

Near the cathedral on the rue Saporta are two good museums. The former archbishop's palace has an excellent collection of 17th- and 18th-century **Beauvais tapestries**▶ (*Closed* Tue). The Museum of Old Aix's folklore collection includes Provençal *santons* (Christmas crib figurines, *closed* Mon).

On the south side of the cours Mirabeau in the quieter Mazarin quarter, the **Musée Granet**▶▶ has an outstanding collection of works by Ingres, Rubens, Bernini and Giovanni Bologna. A room is devoted to Cézanne, who was born at Aix in 1839 and died there in 1906. The nearby 17th-century Fontaine des Quatres Dauphins (rue Cardinale) is one of the most delightful of Aix's many fountains. (See also page 174.)

▶ Antibes 169E2

A lively old port at the heart of a big modern town, full of narrow back streets, pretty squares and a good market. Overlooking massive 17th-century fortifications, the Grimaldi Castle now houses a **Picasso museum**▶▶ (see page 174). The former cathedral dates from the 12th to 17th centuries and has a good Renaissance altarpiece (the local Brea school) in the south transept.

Aix's fountains witness a lively international music and opera festival every July

171

▶▶▶ REGION HIGHLIGHTS

Aigues-Mortes (Carmargue) *page 170*
Aix-en-Provence *page 171*
Arles *page 172*
Avignon *pages 172–3*
Les Baux *page 176*
Cannes *pages 178, 182*
Lubéron *page 180*
Nice *pages 175, 182–3*
Pont du Gard *pages 187, 189*
Porquerolles *page 180*
Verdon Gorges *page 192*

The flower market in Aix-en-Provence is held on Tuesday, Thursday and Saturday mornings on the place de l'Hôtel de Ville

Provence

END OF A DREAM
Van Gogh dreamed of establishing an artists' colony in Arles, with Gauguin as its 'abbot'. The two shared Van Gogh's 'yellow house', decorated with sunflower paintings, but after a quarrel and the severed ear incident, Gauguin left. Van Gogh entered an asylum in 1889. His house, later a café, was bombed in 1944.

►►► Arles   168B2

Spiritually, if not officially, Arles is the capital of Provence. The Gallic Rome was a city of 100,000, a busy inland port linked to the sea by canal. Now it is half that size, but still an important town. It is one of the great tourist centres of the south with spectacular Roman and medieval buildings, a beautiful old town centre, good museums, cultural events, costume festivals and bull-fights. Arles is also a good base for exploring.

The heart of town is the leafy place du Forum, which has a statue of the poet Mistral, café tables under the plane trees, live music in the evenings and the simple delights of Mon Bar Tabac, where posters of Olympic Marseille footballers and Camargue bullfighters vie for wall space. To the south, the boulevard des Lices monopolises promenaders.

A global entrance ticket covers all the town's museums and monuments (available in situ).

Amphitheatre and theatre see page 189

St-Trophime►► The 12th-century reliefs of the *Last Judgement* on the façade are a masterpiece of Romanesque carving. St-Trophime boasts one of France's most beautiful cloisters, a mixture of Romanesque and Gothic.

Museums The most unusual is the dusty old **Muséon Arlaten (Arles Museum)►**, the grandfather of folklore museums and still one of the best. Features include attendants in local costume, a bullskin rug with horns and re-created interiors. In 1995, a strikingly designed museum, **Musée de l'Arles Antique►►** opened near the Roman circus, west of the centre. Displays cover pagan art, including the Venus of Arles and Roman mosaics, and early Christian antiquities.

Les Alyscamps One of the most famous burial grounds in medieval Christendom is now rather a let-down. Most of the tombs lining the shaded avenue, once a thought-provoking approach to Arles, have gone (some to the archaeological museum).

Espace Van Gogh This is an initiative to transform the old Hôtel Dieu into a commercial and cultural centre, painted in Van Gogh's favourite primary colours, with flower beds to match. Van Gogh lives again, too, at the **Pont de Langlois**, an old wooden bridge painted by him, unobtrusively signed near the Sémence de Provence factory on the Salon road.

►►► Avignon   168C2

A historical heavyweight city beside the Rhône, its old centre still enclosed by 4km of medieval walls, Avignon is an essential stop on the Provençal sightseeing trail. It is often windswept and can seem a rather joyless place, but comes alive during the annual drama and dance festival (2nd week July for three weeks) when the **place de l'Horloge►** cafés work round the clock.

Avignon owes its fame to the 12th-century bridge, Pont St-Bénézet, of the popular song *Sur le pont d'Avignon*,

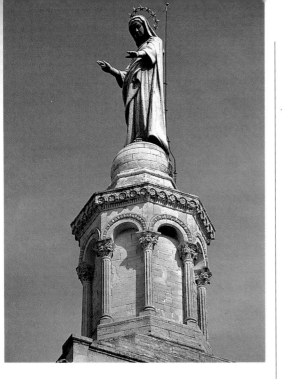

PAPAL PRESENCE
In the 14th century, Avignon was a Provençal city surrounded by papal land. Fed up with the insecurity of life in Rome, Pope Clement V brought the papal court to Avignon in 1309. Six French popes succeeded him, buying Avignon from the Countess of Provence in 1348 and building the magnificent Papal Palace. In 1377, Gregory IX took the curia back to Rome but in 1378 a group of cardinals returned to Avignon with a French rival to the Italian pope. Thus began the Great Schism, lasting until 1417.

A fresco by Simone Martini (now restored and in the Papal Palace) once adorned Avignon's cathedral, itself a fine example of Provençal Romanesque architecture

long reduced to four spans jutting out into mid-stream, and the 14th-century 'Babylonian Captivity', as the scandalous papal residence at Avignon was known. The bridge bears the name of a local shepherd boy who, in a vision, was told to build a bridge there.

The popes gave Avignon its walls and the magnificent **Papal Palace▶▶▶**. The palace has a rock solid façade, which defied all attempts to dismantle it after the Revolution. Its interior, though, was turned into a barracks. The rooms are unfurnished except for beautiful 14th-century frescoes, many inspired by *mille fleurs* tapestries. The monumental central courtyard is used during the festival for major theatrical productions.

Town and gown Outside the rule of French law, the city was a haven for outlaws and assorted disreputables so the 'town and gown' contrast of low life and the curia's ostentatious opulence was real enough.

There are good views from the Rocher des Doms Gardens and also two excellent museums: the **Petit Palais▶**, an old papal guesthouse with an outstanding collection of Gothic and Renaissance art; and the **Musée Calvet▶▶**, in a fine 18th-century town house, with good 18th- to 20th-century art, furniture and wrought ironwork (*Closed* Tue).

Villeneuve-lès-Avignon On the opposite bank, Villeneuve-lès-Avignon was an exclusive residential suburb much favoured by cardinals. French kings built impressive fortifications to remind the popes of French power. The handsome 19th-century buildings of Villeneuve's Carthusian monastery, **La Chartreuse▶▶**, are now a cultural centre (*Open* daily).

FOCAL POINTS
Away from the monumental centre, the most picturesque part of Avignon is the old gypsy quarter, where the cobbled rue des Teinturiers was the home of the 19th-century calico cloth dyers. The focus of café life is the place de l'Horloge. The main north/south axis of the walled town, the rue de la République, has the best shopping.

Towards the end of the 19th century, artists made their way to southern France, attracted by its special quality of light and colour. Avant-garde artists followed Van Gogh's and Cézanne's example by coming south to paint, and society artists followed society to Nice and Monte Carlo when the Riviera hit the social jackpot in the last quarter of the century.

In the first category, Signac discovered the old fishing port of St-Tropez in 1892; artists who followed him there included Bonnard and Matisse. In 1905, Matisse and André Dérain worked together at Collioure. 'The light here is very strong,' wrote Dérain, 'the shadows very luminous. I am learning to rid myself of the whole business of the division of tones.'

Matisse designed Vence's Rosary Chapel in gratitude to the nuns who looked after him between 1943 and 1948, when he withdrew there, overworked and exhausted

This approach earned Dérain, Matisse, Dufy and others working on the coast the name *fauves* – the wild beasts of colour. One of many to fall under the influence of Cézanne was Georges Braque, whose landscapes at L'Estaque, in the first decade of the 20th century, first elicited the term 'cubist'. Matisse and Dufy settled in Nice and recorded all the brilliance and *joie de vivre* of the Riviera. Picasso settled in the south of France in 1946, revived the flagging ceramic industry at Vallauris, and lived there, at Cannes, at Vauvenargues and finally at Mougins, until his death in 1973. Max Ernst was another painter seduced by Provence's charms at Seillans. As well as providing inspiration for many great modern artists, the south is a rich store of their works in private and public collections. Ironically, the two founders of the new art, Van Gogh and Cézanne, so closely associated with the south, are not represented there.

Aix-en-Provence Cézanne's studio is open to the public, but it is a sadly inadequate memorial. To admire the Mont Ste-Victoire, Cézanne's favourite subject, take the Le Tholonet road east from Aix and circle the mountain, taking in one of Picasso's abodes, the château at Vauvenargues on the way (not open to the public).

Antibes One floor of the Grimaldi château is filled with paintings, drawings, sculptures and ceramics by Picasso, most of it the inspired output of a single year (1947).

Biot An interest in ceramics brought Fernand Léger to Biot shortly before he died in 1955. The museum of his work is one of the best modern museums in the south.

Cagnes Renoir painted on despite arthritis so severe he was unable to wield the brush unaided. His home and studios at Les Collettes are open to visitors. The Château also displays collections of work by artists who worked and lived locally, including Dufy and Vasarely.

Fréjus The Chapelle de Cocteau (4km from Fréjus on the N7) (*Open* afternoons only, *closed* Tue) contains unfinished interior decoration by Jean Cocteau.

Menton Jean Cocteau designed a museum (*closed* Tue) to himself in a section of the old harbour fortifications and also decorated the Salle des Mariages in the town hall (Mon–Fri) with cheerful murals.

Nice The Cimiez district has museums devoted to Matisse (in the Roman arena) and Chagall (near the bottom of the avenue de Cimiez), the latter specifically designed for Chagall's biblical work. In the city centre, there are temporary modern art exhibitions in Les Ponchettes, at the eastern end of the beach, and a contemporary art museum near the theatre and acropolis conference/exhibition centre which covers European and American avant-garde art since the 1960s. There is some Warhol, César's squashed Renault, a portrait of a man via the contents of his waste paper basket, and striking blue dye on bronze portraits by Yves Klein. Avant-garde work is also shown at Villa Arson.

St-Paul-de-Vence There are dozens of mediocre art galleries within the walls and, outside, the exceptionally rich and architecturally intriguing Maeght Foundation, which stages exemplary summer exhibitions beside its permanent collection.

St-Tropez L'Annonciade Museum has a small but select private collection of Post-Impressionist paintings, many of St-Tropez, in a former chapel, including works by Signac, Bonnard, Matisse and lots of local scenes by Camoin, who worked at St-Tropez for over 60 years.

Vence The Rosary Chapel resembles a Provençal *mas* and was designed and decorated by Matisse (1947–51).

Villefranche The 14th-century Chapelle St-Pierre (*closed* Mon), beside the port once stored fishing nets. In 1957, Cocteau decorated it with scenes from the life of St Peter.

Nice is an art-loving centre: its contemporary art museum is the latest addition

'The future of the new art lies in the South. The painter of the future will be a colourist such as never existed.'
– Van Gogh, 1888.

'Sunlight cannot be reproduced, but must be represented by something else – by colour.'
– Paul Cézanne, native of Aix, 1876.

Provence

▶▶▶ Bandol   169D1
Bandol is a lively weekend resort between Toulon and Marseille, with marina, sandy beaches and the best of Provençal red wines. It is a few minutes by boat to the small island of Bendor, a purpose-built leisure centre with craft village, sailing and diving schools and an alcohol museum exhibiting 8,000 bottles (*Closed* Wed).

▶▶ Les Baux   168C2
'The Petra of France' (Augustus Hare) is a ruined citadel in a savagely romantic setting on a spur of the jagged Alpilles chain, almost invisible from below. Home of a notoriously rapacious medieval dynasty, which included the star of Bethlehem in its coat of arms, Les Baux later became a Protestant refuge. Richelieu demolished the fortress and, having supported a population of 6,000 during the Renaissance, Les Baux was all but deserted by the 19th century. It now teems with visitors. To stand any chance of appreciating the ghostly beauty of the place, visit at sundown or out of season.

▶▶▶ Béziers   168A2
A wine centre at the foot of the Minervois hills, Béziers stands for rugby, Spanish bullfights and the most savage atrocity of the Albigensian crusade: on July 22 1209 Simon de Montfort's crusaders massacred 30,000 inhabitants, not bothering to distinguish Catholic from Cathar. 'Kill them all,' said the Abbot of Citeaux, 'God will recognise his own'. The main points of interest are the former cathedral, prominently placed high above the River Orb, and the two museums nearby: the Musée du Vieux Bitérrois et du Vin (local history, archaeology and wine) and the **Musée des Beaux Arts**▶ (paintings).

▶▶▶ Biot   169E2
This picturesque and usually overcrowded old village in the scented hinterland of the Riviera is long famous for its ceramic industry and more recently for its glass and the **Fernand Léger Museum**▶▶ (*Closed* Tue, see page 174). You can visit the main glassworks (Verrerie) and watch the blowing process. There are potteries and galleries in the heart of the village, which has kept its 16th-century gates and arcaded square.

A relaxing game of boules at Bandol; a year-long pastime helped by Bandol's 320 days of sun

Provence is hill country, and on almost every hilltop there perches a village: a rhapsody of crumbling honeyed walls, pink tiled roofs and steep cobbled alleys too narrow for cars. A shady little square with a café and a fountain at the heart of the village, long views over vineyards, lavender fields, olive groves or the sea make each a paradise on earth.

The most spectacularly sited villages overlook the sea high above the Riviera – **Eze**, **Gorbio**, **Ste-Agnès**, **La Turbie** and **Roquebrune**, with its 10th-century castle. Even **Monaco** counts as a perched village, naturally pretty but about the most tawdry of them all. Other beauty spots near the coast, all often overcrowded, are **Biot** (famous for its pottery and glass), **Tourrette-sur-Loup** (a weaving centre), **Gourdon** (a souvenir village) and **St-Paul-de-Vence**, the most famous of all the artists' villages. For all its fame, St-Paul remains a place of style and irresistible charm, with a plane-shaded *boules* pitch outside the Café de la Place at the gates of the old walled village. Opposite the café, the prestigious Colombe d'Or hotel is full of masterpieces of modern art, accepted in lieu of payment by the proprietor, M Roux. Deeper into the mountainous hinterland of Nice, **Peillon** and **Luceram** are worth visiting for their church paintings. Strung across a precipice high above the Roya Gorge, **Saorge**'s setting is the most startling of all. It is easier to reach by car than looks likely from below, and fascinating to explore on foot.

Further west, the landscape of the interior is less wild, the hill villages more welcoming. **Bargème**, **Mons**, **Bargemon**, **Seillans** and **Fox Amphoux** all have great charm. In the fashionable Lubéron/Vaucluse area, **Gordes** and the red ochre village of **Roussillon** are the touristy beauty spots. Quieter villages include **Oppède le Vieux**, where the imposing Renaissance houses are now being rescued; and **Ménerbes**, recently invaded by Britons. **Le Barroux**, **Crestet** and **Séguret** are beautifully restored villages on the flanks of the jagged Dentelles de Montmirail.

HILL VILLAGES
Hill villages evolved for defence in the lawless centuries that followed Roman peace. Since the 18th century many of the hill villages have gradually been abandoned by their inhabitants. Most have been revived by tourism and new residents seeking a peaceful alternative to the coast. The most picturesque have now evolved from artists' colonies to popular beauty spots.

177

Eze, one of the most dramatic of the Provence hill villages

Provence

*Baroness Béatrice
Ephrussi-de-Rothschild's
collection is housed in
the Villa Ile-de-France,
Cap Ferrat, set among
seven hectares of gardens*

CASSIS CALANQUES
The coastal landscape
between Marseille and
Cassis is unexpectedly
wild and beautiful: cliffs
and inlets (*calanques*) of
bleached grey rock, clear
water and pocket hanky
beaches, accessible only
on foot (an arduous
marked GR path follows
the coast) or by boat.
Sormiou and Sugiton
calanques can be reached
on foot from Marseille
(start near the university).
Prehistoric depictions of
animals, similar to those
at Lascaux in Dordogne,
were discovered recently
in a cave at Sormiou. The
three eastern *calanques*
are served by boat trips
from Cassis: Port-Miou
(accessible by car); Port-
Pin; and En-Vau, the
prettiest of all. Forest
fires in 1994 sadly
destroyed much of the
surrounding vegetation.

▶▶ Cannes   169E2
Famous for its international film festival in May, Cannes
is the glamorous focus of the Riviera at any time of year,
with spectacular yachts and expensive beaches along the
palm-lined promenade, La Croisette (see page 182).

▶ Cap Ferrat   169E2
A beautiful walk makes a full circuit of this narrow
rocky cape covered with luxurious villas. Set in the Villa
Ile-de-France, in superb gardens, the Ephrussi de
Rothschild Museum houses Baroness Beatrice's rich art
collection. The small resort and marina of **St-Jean-Cap-
Ferrat** is in keeping with the cape's muted opulence.

Carpentras   168C3
Carpentras is a busy medieval market town at the heart
of the most fruitful area of Provence, famous for its truffles and sweets (*berlingots*). Sights include a 15th- and
16th-century cathedral, a small Roman triumphal arch
and the beautiful Hôtel Dieu.

▶ Cassis   168C2
This charming fishing port beneath the 400m cliffs of
Cap Canaille has waterfront cafés, fish restaurants and
small hotels – a Mediterranean idyll. Boats travel to the
rocky inlets, good for scuba diving and rock climbing.

▶▶ Esterel, Massif de l'   169E2
The 32km coast road between La Napoule and St-
Raphael offers the most spectacular scenery in the south.
Flame-red porphyry mountains drop to the rocky shores
and rough and narrow forest roads lead into the moun-
tains. A track branching south 3km west of the **Auberge
des Adrets**, a notorious brigand's hang-out in the late
18th century, takes you within walking range of the
Esterel's highest peak, the **Mont Vinaigre** (618m). The **Pic
de l'Ours▶▶**, near the coast (496m), is equally dramatic.
There are few bathing spots, but there is red sand at
Agay, a small resort on a sheltered horseshoe bay.

▶ Fréjus   169D2
Fréjus was the first big Gallo-Roman port, with a ruined
aqueduct, theatre and **amphitheatre▶** (see page 188). An
outstanding complex of cathedral buildings forms the
town centre: cloisters, a 5th-century **baptistery▶▶** (both
closed Mon), an archaeological museum (*closed* Tue), and
the Gothic cathedral itself. Fréjus Plage has a big marina
and good sandy beach.

The Dentelles de Montmirail and Mont Ventoux

Start at Malaucène.
Malaucène is a lively market town at the foot of **Mont Ventoux**, France's highest mountain outside the Alps and Pyrenees. Its bare scree slopes make the Ventoux look snow-capped all year; in winter it is, and there is skiing on both flanks.

D974 via Mont Ventoux.
The road loops round the summit (crowned by ugly towers and a café), giving enormous views. On the eastern side is a memorial where cyclist Tommy Simpson died during the 1967 Tour de France.

From Mont Ventoux continue to Bédoin.
The road down to Bédoin through thick woodland was long used for time trials and still has the skid marks to prove it. **Bédoin** is an attractive village with a naturist holiday zone nearby.

D138 as far as Caromb and the D13 up to Le Barroux.
Caromb and **Le Barroux**, the latter dominated by an ill-proportioned Renaissance château, both have excellent small hotels.

Continue north to Suzette.
The slopes above Le Barroux lead to the dramatic jagged crest of the **Dentelles de Montmirail**. There are good views of the crags from **Suzette**.

D90 to Beaumes-de-Venise.
The tour now takes in some Rhône wine villages: **Beaumes-de-Venise**, **Vacqueyras** and **Gigondas**. The Dentelles de Montmirail are signed from Gigondas. The road surface soon turns rough, climbing through vineyards to a pass at the foot of the central spine of the Dentelles, the Col du Cayron. From here it is a steep 15-minute walk up an obvious path to a breach in the rocks, giving spectacular views. There are many possibilities for extending the walk: paths along the eastern flank of the rocky crest, or through the vineyards from the Col du Cayron, a long hike to Séguret (see below).

D7 and D23 to Séguret; then the D88 and 977 to Vaison, taking the D938 back to Malaucène.
The circuit continues to **Vaison-la-Romaine** via the restored village of **Séguret**. On the other side of the hill, **Crestet** has a medieval castle, an arcaded square and fountain, and a fine view.

▶ **Fontfroide** *168A1*

This Cistercian abbey, set among the Corbières vineyards near Narbonne, was abandoned at the Revolution and was privately owned for most of this century. The buildings, a mixture of Romanesque and Ancien Régime styles, have been well restored and complemented by delightful gardens (*Open* daily).

Fontvieille *168C2*

Fontvieille is known for a pretty windmill on a wooded hillside to the south –– the Moulin of Alphonse Daudet's *Lettres de Mon Moulin*, although the author neither owned nor wrote from it. The mill has been restored to working order and houses a museum of Daudet memorabilia (*Closed* Jan).

Giens Peninsula *169D1*

Two 5km spits of sand enclose working salt pans and link the village of Giens to the motherland near Hyères. There are pine woods and some modest resort development (Hyères Plage) along the eastern sand bar. The biggish town of Hyères, once a health resort of some cachet, no longer attracts many tourists, although the old upper town around the place St-Paul has some charm and fine public gardens.

▶ **Grasse** *169E2*

The world capital of the perfume industry is an old town in a sheltered, south-facing setting. Queen Victoria wintered here, but modern Grasse has no trace of Riviera glamour. The old town centre has a tumbledown charm, though, with a narrow arcaded market place, the place aux Aires. Stalls surrounding the fountain are filled with local fruit, flowers and herbs.

The massive 12th-century **cathedral▶** boasts three Rubens and a rare religious work by Grasse's most famous son, Jean Honoré Fragonard (1732–1806). Fragonard left Grasse at six and returned only briefly in 1790, bringing with him a series of paintings, The *Pursuit of Love*, rejected as too frivolous by their intended owner. Copies of the originals are on display in the villa where he stayed, with one good self-portrait and a number of works by his son Alexander.

Several scent producers (including Fragonard) offer free factory tours. The International Perfume Museum charges for entrance and is less visited.

▶▶ **Lubéron** *168C2*

The 65km mountain ridge between the rivers Durance and Coulon is divided into Petit and Grand Lubéron by the only road over the ridge, between Bonnieux and Lourmarin. The Lubéron is wild country, protected by regional park status but developing nevertheless. Now ultra-fashionable, the quiet villages on the wooded north slope have become the latest corner of Provence to experience the questionable benefit of a second-home renaissance, spurred on by the phenomenal success of Peter Mayle's books. Ménerbes, Bonnieux and the Marquis de Sade's Lacoste are examples of reviving villages. Oppède-le-Vieux, a place of romantic ruins, is in the process of rescue from abandonment.

OFFSHORE HYERES
Easily reached by boat from Hyères and Giens, the lovely islands of Porquerolles, Port Cros and Levant offer forest walks, good beaches and no cars. The largest, Porquerolles, has a small village resort. Mountainous and luxuriant, Port Cros and surrounding waters are a national park. Its only hotel is booked months in advance. The Ile du Levant has naturists in the west, and a small resort (Héliopolis). The eastern half is a naval base.

THE NOSE KNOWS
Grasse took to perfumery when scented gloves came into fashion in the 16th century. It takes 500kg of roses to produce a litre of essential oil; many local plants are still used and a few are unique to the Var. A specialist sniffer (*le nez*) chooses the fragrances.

180

The Vaucluse Plateau

Start at Vénasque; take the D4 to Murs.
Vénasque is a fortified village on a ledge of the Vaucluse Plateau. It was a bishopric in the early Middle Ages and gave its name to the papal territory, Comtat Venaissin. Beside the church is an intriguing ancient chapel. The road climbs through oak woods to the **Col de Murs** before descending into the fashionable second-home territory of the Vaucluse/Lubéron.

D102 to Roussillon.
The red village of Roussillon is a tourist trap, but not to be avoided for

❏ When the noble Tricline Carbonnelle fell for the young poet Guillaume de Cabestan, her jealous husband killed him and had his heart served for supper. When the severed head was produced for pudding, Tricline realised what she had eaten and jumped out of the window. The earth of Roussillon was stained red for evermore. ❏

that. The vivid colour of the buildings and the sculptural ochre quarries of the surrounding hills is astonishing.

Back along the D102 and then the D2 to Gordes; D177 to Sénanque and back.
Gordes is another busy beauty spot, carefully restored and expensive, at the heart of *borie* country (see below). An imposing Renaissance château and turreted church command the plain and the steeply terraced village. A narrow road winds to the Cistercian abbey of Sénanque, set among fields of lavender.

D2/N100/D24 to Fontaine de Vaucluse.
Fontaine de Vaucluse was made famous by its romantic associations in Petrarch's love poetry. The site and nearby village are now thoroughly commercialised.

The Fort de Buoux

The ruins of the medieval fortifications are on the site of a much older citadel, south of the hamlet of Buoux (turn off the D113 at a *colonie de vacances*); later used as a Protestant refuge, it was dismantled in the 17th century. Walking possibilities include a two-hour tour. For a longer haul, follow marked paths across the Lubéron to Lourmarin or Vaugines; or along the crest of the Grand

❏ Dome-shaped dry-stone dwellings are found as far afield as southern Italy, the Balearics and Ireland. Dating back in origin to the Ligurian inhabitation of the region 4,000 years ago, the Vaucluse/ Lubéron area has thousands of these bories, some inhabited until the 19th century. Gordes is the borie capital, with a restored museum village of the dwellings. ❏

Lubéron to the Mourre Nègre (1,125m), and down to Auribeau (north side) or Cabrières (south).

*Menton's dowdy, Monte's brass
Nice is rowdy, Cannes is class*

The French Riviera has changed profoundly in the past few decades, primarily in becoming a summer instead of a winter playground. But the words of the old song still say plenty about the differences of style between the resorts which form an almost unbroken urban sprawl along the mountainous coastline between Cannes and the Italian border. This is the Riviera proper, although the term Côte d'Azur is often used to include the less densely developed coast between Cannes and Marseille.

ISLAND ESCAPE
If the Riviera buzz is getting too much, make an easy escape by using the regular boat service from Cannes to the tranquil Iles de Lérins, 15–30 minutes across the waves. The closest, Ste-Marguerite, offers walks through pine and eucalyptus woods, swimming off rocks and a marine museum. Smaller but equally seductive, St-Honorat has an ancient fortified monastery, part of which can be toured, and a new one still functioning – a favourite for retreats.

Larger-than-life musicians at the Nice Mardi-Gras

Cannes The Riviera at its most showy: the promenade of La Croisette, lined with palm trees and palatial hotels, is a perfect catwalk. Unlike many Riviera resorts, Cannes has a good sandy beach, parcelled up into expensive private concessions, many of them attached to hotels and with classy lunch restaurants.

There is a public beach at the west end of the Croisette, near the gleaming conference centre separating the prom from the port, which is full of expensive yachts. It is also naturally picturesque, overlooked by the trees and medieval towers of **Le Suquet**, a small hill where some traces of an old village survive. The Croisette, the rue d'Antibes and side streets between them have the best shops. Boat trips go from the port to the Lérins Islands, Ste-Marguerite and St-Honorat, both with dense woods. Ste-Marguerite has old prison buildings.

Juan-les-Pins A favourite with the Americans in the '20s: Frank Gould, Scott Fitzgerald, Hemingway, Harpo Marx, Mary Pickford and many others, Juan-les-Pins is less smart now, a young place with fast food and discos. A monument at neighbouring **Golf Juan** commemorates Napoleon's landing after his escape from Elba in 1815.

Antibes see page 171

Nice The capital of the Alpes Maritimes and the Riviera is, if not rowdy, a big city. The promenade des Anglais (endlessly due to undergo extensive restructuring for pedestrian benefit) is a roaring dual carriageway but has kept many of the domes and façades of its *belle époque* buildings (notably the Hotel Negresco).

An Italian city (Nizza) until 1860, and the home town of Garibaldi, Nice has kept more than a hint of Italian style in the gardens and arcaded neo-classical buildings around the place Masséna and the port, and especially in the narrow backstreets behind the quai des Etats Unis and the broad plaza of cours Saleya. This is Nice's open market and the best place for cafés and restaurants. This old quarter is separated from the port by the so-called château – a hill with gardens and views.

Many of Nice's Victorian visitors (including the Queen) stayed at Cimiez, a hill suburb and site of the Roman settlement, with good museums and ruins (see pages 175 and 188). The other museums are in the striking modern complex north of the place Garibaldi and, for Old Masters, the Masséna and fine arts museums. Nice goes mad for its two-week pre-Lent carnival, which ends with fireworks and a battle of flowers.

Cap Ferrat see page 178

Villefranche The most sheltered bay on the Riviera has an unspoilt fortified village above the fishing port (see also page 175).

Monaco/Monte Carlo Every inch of the Grimaldi family's tiny principality is occupied, and Monaco continues to grow upwards (skyscrapers) and outwards, on new man-made promontories. The old clifftop village of Monaco is now a toy-town pink and yellow tourist village with white-suited policemen, waxwork museums, the Grimaldi's Marzipan Palace (a Napoleon museum and some of the interior are open to visitors), a gruesome 19th-century cathedral with good Renaiss-ance paintings and an oceanographic museum. Traffic is strictly controlled: signs to Monaco lead into under-ground car parks, with lifts up to the centre.

Monte Carlo is the heartland of Monaco: plush jewellers, luxury hotels and the exuberant casino and Hôtel de Paris. A 3km circuit is used for the Grand Prix in May.

Menton Mild winters and lemons brought fame to Menton (it has a lemon festival in February). A baroque belfry and high, pastel-painted houses overlook the beach. Summer concerts are held on the small piazza outside the church of St-Michel (see page 175).

Despite its casino, Menton's atmosphere is the slowest of the Riviera

THE CORNICHES
Three corniche roads hug the mountainous coastline from Nice to Menton. The lower corniche (N98) runs through all the resorts: a 33km journey of many hours in summer. The middle corniche (N7) is much quicker and passes the perched village of Eze; the upper or Grande Corniche (D2564) goes through La Turbie and over the Col d'Eze. Both upper and middle corniches bypass Monaco. Above this there is now a fourth corniche, the A8 motorway. With its fast drivers, sharp bends, tunnels and multiple exits, the motorway demands full concen-tration. Grace Kelly was one of the cor-niches' many victims.

THAT SOUP
Quintessential product of the Mediterranean, *bouillabaisse* (fish soup) originally developed in Marseille as a fishermen's stalwart. Hundreds of pale imitations are offered along the Côte d'Azur, but there is a strict etiquette to its concoction (types and combinations of fish) and to its service: the fish must be dissected by the waiter at table.

▶ **Marseille**   *168C2*

The Mediterranean's biggest port and France's second city is an acquired taste – notorious for corruption and gangsterism, and a sure break from the tourist trail. The Greeks founded the city in the 6th century bc, but it is the modern life of the city which intrigues and repels in equal measure. The city is a melting pot of Arab, African and Latin cultures, with France's biggest community of Algerians. Racial tension simmers – National Front leader Jean Marie le Pen has his roots here.

The once celebrated **Canebière▶** is the main shopping street. There is an Arab market, a spectacular morning fish market at the **old port▶** (a good area for restaurants) and cheap souks near the Porte d'Aix.

Marseille's most famous monument is a former prison – the rocky island of **Château d'If▶** (boat trips from the old port). There are many excellent museums: archaeology and ethnography in the superbly restored 17th-century hospice, **La Vieille Charité▶▶**; fine arts; local history in the beautiful Renaissance **Maison Diamantée**; fashion; and natural history. The best of the smaller museums are the **Cantini▶▶** (20th-century art), the faïence museum at **Château Pastré** and **Grobet-Labadié▶**, a 19th-century collector's house and contents preserved intact. The port is dominated by a hilltop cathedral, but better still is the garden setting of the Parc and Palais du Pharo and **Parc Borély▶▶**.

Local produce from the Massif des Maures also includes strongly flavoured chestnut-tree honey

▶ **Maures, Massif des**   *169D2*

This wild hinterland of hill country between Fréjus and Hyères is named after its dark mantle of pines, chestnuts and cork oaks. The interior is little visited, mainly because the roads over the hills are narrow and very slow (except the D25 from Ste-Maxime to Draguignan) though scenic. The D558 Grimaud/La Garde crossing is more rewarding. To the west of the resorts on the bay of St-Tropez (see page 190) are peaceful beaches with campsites.

Le Lavandou/Bormes▶ is the main resort agglomeration, with a big marina. La Croix Valmer and Cavalaire are smaller centres. There are ferries and boat trips in the Hyères Islands (see page 180) from Cavalaire and Le Lavandou.

▶ Montpellier 168B2

A dynamic city of high-tech industry, bold new architecture and buzzing student life, Montpellier has cast off its traditional mantle of donnish stuffiness. One of the few big southern cities without a Roman history, its medieval growth was fostered by trade with the eastern Mediterranean.

The 17th- and 18th-century **promenade du Peyrou▶▶** is an impressive ensemble of triumphal arch, statue of Louis XIV and water tower at the head of the aqueduct that quenches the city's thirst. The view from the terrace is splendid. People congregate around the **place de la Comédie▶**, Esplanade Gardens and on the place Jean Jaurès in the fashionable **old town▶▶**, where elegant mansions line narrow winding streets.

Antigone, the new residential area, is a typically ambitious neo-classical project. The **Musée Fabre▶▶** has an outstanding collection of Old Master and 19th-century paintings. One of the benefactors was Alfred Bruyas, a rich patron of Courbet, Delacroix and others. There is an international dance festival at the end of June and an international wine fair in October.

Narbonne/Languedoc– 168A2
Roussillon Coast

This coastline, sandy from the Petit Rhône to the Pyrenees, is often thin strips separating sea from enclosed lagoons. The resort style is modern: the pyramid apartment blocks of **La Grande Motte** are an aggressive '60s monument, while newer resorts have adopted a less obtrusive style. **Port Camargue** is an interesting marina-based design. The biggest develop-ment of all is **Cap d'Agde**, with a 41-court tennis club and a naturist area (Port Nature). Between Montpellier and Béziers is the fishing port of **Sète▶**, built at the end of the Canal du Midi in the 17th century.

Southern resorts Further south, **Port Leucate** and **Port Barcarès** are big new resorts with marinas, on a sand bar between sea and salt lake. For 30km before the Spanish border, after the concentration of campsites at **Argelès sur Mer**, stretches the scenic **Côte Vermeille▶▶**. **Collioure▶▶** is an artists' favourite.

Other Areas of interest:

Agde Founded by Greeks when it was a sea port, Agde has a fortified black lava church.

Elne The cathedral has a beautiful medieval cloister.

Narbonne▶ This wine town once hit the news because of race riots. The twin towers of an unusual, unfinished Gothic cathedral dominate the town and surrounding vineyards. Excavations in the central square have unearthed part of the Roman road from Italy to Spain, the Via Domitia; there is an archaeological museum nearby.

Salses The well-preserved 15th-century fortress here was altered by Vauban.

Sigean Safari Park African wildlife; expensive.

MONTPELLIER MEDICINE
Pre-Renaissance Europe did not read Greek, and medical knowledge filtered in from the east via the spice trade, of which Montpellier was a centre from the 12th century. The university specialised in medicine and attracted Petrarch and Rabelais among its students.

HERBS
Herbs grow throughout the south of France; in Provence they are an important industry, and every market sells them in quantity. Buis-les-Baronnies, renowned for its *tilleul* fair in early July, has a good weekly *marché provençal* on Wednesdays.

185

BULL-TEASING
All summer the Roman amphitheatres at Nîmes and Arles and the modern arena at Béziers are the setting for the *corrida*, the traditional gory Spanish bullfight. The Camargue specialises in a more informal and slightly less cruel encounter, the Provençal *course à la cocarde*. In makeshift arenas bullfighters (*razeteurs*) try to snatch a rosette (*cocarde*) from the horns of Camargue bulls, which survive to fight again. The razeteur escapes by vaulting over the ringside hoardings.

Between the mouth of the Var and the Italian border, the Alps drop abruptly into the Mediterranean with no transition between mountains and coast. This cramps life by the sea and offers plenty of escape routes from the heat and crowds into the cooler, cleaner air of the mountains.

VALLEY MARVELS
The ancient artistic marvels of the Vallée des Merveilles date from the Bronze Age (1800–1500 bc). They were traced into the schist surface using silex or quartz tools and mostly represent human or bovine figures, pointing to the Ligurian people's cult for the all-powerful Mt Bégo and for bulls. To visit the 100,000-odd rock drawings you must be accompanied by a guide. There are several visits a day starting from the main refuges and from the Lacs Jumeaux (Jul–Aug; Jun & Sep, Sun only: 04 93 04 77 73). Less hardy walkers might find an overnight stay at the mountain refuge of Merveilles helpful.

Old perched villages of the immediate hinterland (**Eze, Peillon, Peille, Gorbio, Lucéram, Coaraze**) are the obvious short-haul targets. Longer journeys involve heading up any of the four main river valleys which have their sources at altitude near the Italian border: the **Tinée, Var** and **Vésubie** (which end up as one, the Var); and the **Roya**, which crosses into Italy about halfway down to the sea. Connoisseurs of river gorge drives will want to see the **Vésubie** Gorges (between Plan du Var and St-Jean-la-Rivière) and the **Cians** gorge between Pont de Cian and Beuil (tight driving). The source of the Tinée is near the **Col de la Bonette**, at the northern limit of the Maritime Alps; the **Bonette** road, Europe's highest, is a rugged and beautiful route north, for travellers who are not in a hurry.

The **Roya** Valley is of more varied interest; either follow the river up from Ventimiglia (Italy) or drive up from Menton to Sospel and over the Col de Brouis, joining the Roya near **Breil**, a small town with simple accommodation. North of Breil, the Roya cuts impressive gorges, especially below the balcony village of **Saorge**, well worth a detour to explore on foot. **La Brigue** is the best base in the upper valley with an interesting church and remarkable 15th-century frescoes in the nearby chapel. On the other side of the valley are **Lac des Mesches** and **Casterino**, reached from St-Dalmas-de-Tende, the start of hikes to the Vallée des Merveilles around Mont Bégo (2,872m). The valley is only accessible from July to early October.

The **Mercantour** is mainland France's youngest national park, covering a long stretch of high mountain country along the Italian border. Gateways to the park (with information centres) include the summer and winter resort of **Valberg** and **St-Martin-de-Vésubie**.

Le Boréon (near St-Martin) is a good starting point for hikers.

High mountain country in the Mercantour National Park

[photograph]

►► Nice   169E2

See pages 175, 182–3 and 188.

Swimmers in the Gardon River, near Pont du Gard, escape the stifling mid-summer heat

► Nîmes   168B2

The birthplace of denim (serge de Nîmes) is not one of the most charming towns of France. It is best known for extreme heat, its Roman amphitheatre and temple (see page 188) and a state-of-the-art contemporary art museum designed by Norman Foster.

► Orange   168C3

Orange, gateway to the south, has a fine Roman arch which, with its still finer **Roman theatre►►►**, is the most compelling reason for a visit (see page 189). Orange is an important market town for the Rhône Valley's fruit and wine output.

► Perpignan   168A1

The capital of French Catalonia, red-brick Perpignan was the medieval HQ of the kingdom of Majorca – an off-shoot of the ruling house of Aragon. Their low-rise fortress covers a large area at the heart of the city. The streets around the cathedral (Gothic) and medieval town gate (Castillet) are more entertaining. Catalan is spoken here, and there is Hispanic music and even dancing in the streets on summer evenings. The most beautiful building in the town centre, the Gothic Loge de Mer (a trading house), is now a burger restaurant.

►► Pézenas   168A2

Now a small town of under 10,000 inhabitants, Pézénas once enjoyed a glorious reputation as the Versailles of the south. It flourished in the Middle Ages, and later hosted the meetings of the Languedoc Estates General, which were the occasion for lavish festivities during the governorship of the Bourbon Prince de Conti, an early patron of Molière. The old town centre around the place Gambetta has kept many beautiful 17th-century houses and a medieval **Jewish ghetto►**. Outstanding among them are **Hôtel Lacoste►** and the **Hôtel d'Alfonce►**, where Molière's troupe performed in 1655. Abundant crafts shops and workshops add contemporary colour and interest.

►►► Pont du Gard   168B2

This fine Roman aqueduct near Nîmes is one of the greatest masterpieces of Roman architecture in France (see page 189).

187

EXPORT ORANGES
In the 16th century, the principality of Orange passed to the House of Nassau. The first prince of this House was William the Silent, who led the rebellion of the Netherlands against Spain, becoming the provinces' Stadtholder in 1580. A century later, William of Orange mounted the English throne as husband of Mary.

The Romans enjoyed the south of France. They colonised it early, romanised it intensively and adorned it with temples, theatres, amphitheatres, monumental arches, aqueducts and bridges. No other region outside Italy is so rich in Roman remains, many of which are still in use today.

Aix-en-Provence The first Roman town in Gaul, founded as *Aquae Sextiae* by consul Sextius, has little left to show for itself, apart from the Musée Granet's items from the pre-Roman settlement at Entremont.

Arles Once the capital of Gaul and Constantine's favourite base, Arles has a spectacularly well-preserved amphitheatre (Arènes), as well as the Théâtre Antique seating 12,000, still in use for bullfights and real drama. The amphitheatre (1st century ad) held more than 20,000 spectators, nearly half the town's present population. The structure was converted into a medieval fortress and later a town within a town, which was dismantled in the 19th century. The Musée de l'Arles Antiques groups Roman artefacts with early Christian exhibits.

Fréjus This Roman port with surviving fragments of theatre, aqueduct and Gaul's oldest amphitheatre now hosts bullfights and concerts. The 11th-century cathedral houses an archaeology museum.

Nice-Cimiez The hill town of *Cemenelum* was the capital of the Roman province of Maritime Alps. Between the monastery and the once grand hotels of Victorian Cimiez is an area of excavations, including a small amphitheatre, a museum and a large area of baths, used every July for Nice's great jazz festival.

Nîmes The amphitheatre (1st century AD) and temple known as the Maison Carrée (1st century BC) are the best preserved buildings of their kind in the Roman world. After a 1,500-year hiatus, the full three-storey structure again echoes with the roars of fighting bulls and an excited public. The Maison Carrée has done service as town hall, private home, stable, church and now a public monument.

188

ROMAN INVASION
Colonisation began in 125 BC when consul Sextius responded to an appeal from the Greek port of Massilis (Marseille) and destroyed a native power base on the Entremont plateau. A new *Provincia* (Provence) was establish-ed in 118. Marseille lost its privileges in 49 BC. Its commercial role was taken over by Arles, Fréjus and Narbonne, which became the capital of the renamed Provincia Narbonensis in 27 BC.

The 1st-century amphitheatre at Nîmes

Orange As at Nîmes, two outstanding Roman buildings attract tourists to an otherwise uncaptivating town. Founded in 46 BC, Arausio was three times as populous as modern Orange. The Roman theatre (1st century BC) is the only one with its backstage wall standing. A statue of Augustus is above the stage, still used for summer concerts. The triumphal arch (1st century BC) is a roundabout on the N7 at the northern gateway to town. In the interests of traffic flow, do not attempt to admire it from the wheel.

Pont du Gard This three-tiered section of the Uzès to Nîmes aqueduct, spanning the River Gardon, is made of massive stones without mortar. You can drive across the lower tier, walk across the unspectacular interior of the waterduct or, vertigo and Mistral permitting, across its 3m-wide unprotected roof, 50m above the water. New landscaping is designed to enhance access to the bridge's beautiful woodland setting, with information points and two museums.

St-Rémy-Glanum and Les Antiques Among trees to the south of St-Rémy, utterly uncluttered by fencing or graffiti, stand two beautiful Roman monuments (late 1st century BC). The triumphal arch has lost its top but not all its decoration of fruit and captives. Beside it stands a well-preserved and elegant memorial to two grandsons of Augustus. Not far away, on the other side of the road, lie the extensive excavations of Glanum, a pre-Roman town, probably a spa, which was later romanised, then abandoned in the 4th century.

La Turbie Only partial remains survive of the 50m Trophée des Alpes, built in 6 BC to celebrate Augustus' successful Alpine campaigns. There is a good museum on site with a magrette, photos of a similar trophy in Romania, and old engravings of the Trophée as a medieval fortress. There are tremendous views of the coast from the surrounding park.

Vaison-la-Romaine A Roman bridge spans the River Ouvèze and separates medieval Vaison from the dull modern town and the excavations of the Roman Vasio, in two sectors separated by the place Novembre 11. Ruins include a shopping street, a villa, public toilets, a theatre and a museum, all in an attractive setting of rosebeds and cypresses.

DEVELOPMENT
The many Alpine tribes resisted Rome longer than the rest of Gaul and were not conquered until the campaign of Augustus (24–12 BC). This success allowed the completion of the Via Aurelia from Rome to Arles and was commemorated with the 50m Alpine Trophy. Nîmes flourished throughout the first two centuries AD, while Arles emerged as the centre of the new Christian religion.

189

The Roman theatre in Orange comes to life every July during a prestigious opera festival

Port Grimaud   169D2

The Venice of the Riviera is an ingenious modern resort at the head of the Gulf of St-Tropez, designed for a yacht-owning (or renting) clientele. Its streets are waterways spanned by footbridges linking clumps of holiday homes, each with its own mooring outside the front door. The architecture is inspired by the local style and, with shady squares on many of the accommodation clusters, Port Grimaud achieves the simulation of ordinary village life, except that there are no ordinary villagers.

St-Raphaël   169D2

A big family resort at the foot of the Esterel, popular in Roman times and revived a century ago, modern St-Raphaël has no great cachet, but the Riviera ingredients are there – beaches, marina, palm trees, traffic jams and golf courses.

St-Rémy   168C2

This cheerful little plane-shaded town at the foot of the mini-mountainous range of Alpilles, has **Glanum▶** and Les Antiques (see page 189) on its doorstep. The main square is a good place for a drink in the shade, except on Wednesdays when the market takes over. On the edge of town is the former monastery of **St-Paul-de-Mausole▶**, the asylum where Van Gogh lived for a year from 1889. The restored Romanesque church and cloister are usually open to visitors, but there is nothing else to see: even the bust of Van Gogh by Zadkine has been stolen.

▶▶ St-Tropez   169D2

Among an arty élite, the old fishing port of St-Tropez and its surrounding coast and mountains have been no secret since the turn of the century, when the painter Paul Signac settled there. But it was Brigitte Bardot in the 1950s who made 'St Trop' a cliché for liberated youth. This it remains, although the original habitués are greying and liberated youth arrives in herds from nearby campsites. The port has exorbitant hotels, low-rise and studiously informal; stars hiding in high-walled villas; fat yachts in the port; lots of denim and leather and loud rock music; and lots of blondes. Out of season and early in the morning, the close-knit old port remains its old self, as portrayed on scores of canvases in the excellent museum. In the evening the Place des Lices at the back of the old town becomes a vast *boules* arena. The port has no beach to speak of, but the Ramatuelle peninsula has long tracts of sand, which are part of St-Tropez mythology (Tahiti, **Pampelonne▶**, **l'Escarlet▶**). The old hill villages set back from the coast (**Ramatuelle▶▶**, **Gassin▶** and Grimaud) now have more chic and less hubbub than St-Tropez itself.

Ste-Maxime   169D2

Facing St-Tropez across a wide bay, Ste-Maxime is a much quieter and more sheltered resort, originally a Phoenician colony. It has a fishing harbour, marina and a sandy beach. The bay provides safe sailing and good windsurfing.

St-Tropez still retains a sense of identity, despite its 'glam' status

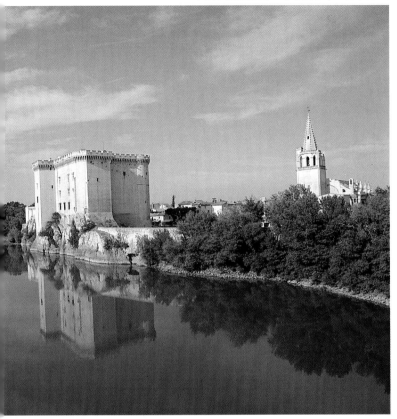

▶ Sisteron   169D3

Sisteron is one of the natural gateways of northern Provence, a fortress town with an impressive **citadel▶**, described by Henri IV as the most powerful in the realm. Its opposition was unfortunately strategic enough to attract heavy bombing in 1944. The citadel has been restored and is used for the summer festival of drama, dance and music. There is a 12th-century former cathedral in the town, and picturesque streets.

Tarascon/Beaucaire   168B2

Their imposing medieval fortresses confronting each other across the Rhône, Beaucaire and Tarascon vividly commemorate the medieval frontier between French Languedoc and Imperial Provence. The **Château de Tarascon▶ ▶** is one of the best preserved of its kind, and is open to visitors. The next-door **church▶** has a Romanesque door, paintings by Provence-based artists and the tomb of St Martha in the crypt. St Martha tamed the legendary monster La Tarasque, celebrated by a colourful June festival. Tarascon also has a popular museum, the so-called house of the fictional Tartarin de Tarascon, anti-hero of Daudet's comic novels. The **Musée Souleïado▶** displays examples of sunny Provençal fabrics, still made today by the Souleïado company.

The well-preserved Château de Tarascon, sitting on the bank of the River Rhône

TAMING THE BEAST
St Martha found Tarascon terrorised by a monster with a lion's head, six twisted bear claws and an unhealthy appetite for women and children. She tamed the beast and led it back to the Rhône. King René organised a celeb-ration in 1474, parading a model through the streets, knocking down anyone in its way. A less destructive version still takes place in June.

Toulon 169D1

France's main Mediterranean naval port features more prominently in history books than on holiday itineraries. The young Captain Bonaparte covered himself in glory during the eight-month siege of English-occupied Toulon in 1793, and in November 1942, 60 French ships were scuttled in the harbour when the Nazis moved into Vichy France. Ironically, in 1995 the city council became National Front.

The dingy backstreets of the old town centre of Toulon may have *louche* appeal and certainly have cheap restaurants, and you can count on finding a hotel room when the rest of the south of France (except Marseille) is taken.

Otherwise, Toulon's main attractions are the renovated Naval Museum at the eastern end of the arsenal complex and Mont Faron, the rocky mountain ridge dominating the city and reached either by cable-car or a narrow hairpin road. As well as a splendid view, there is a museum devoted to the Allied landings in 1944, and a run-down zoological museum. The 19th-century fort on the summit is still occupied by the military.

▶ Uzès 168B3

This dignified old town, robbed of its fortifications by Richelieu because of its Protestant leanings, stands on a high plateau of rocky garrigue, the southeastern ledge of the Massif Central. At the heart of the town, near the arcaded main square, is the **Ducal Palace**▶▶ (Duché), still inhabited, with a medieval tower and a fine Renaissance façade by Philibert Delormé. The round 12th-century **tower**▶▶ (Tour Fenestrelle) is all that remains of the Romanesque cathedral. In 1662, Jean Racine was sent to Uzès to forget dreams of a literary career and prepare for holy orders. Racine liked the town, but could not understand the people, who spoke southern dialect, not rhyming Alexandrine couplets. He returned to Paris, and the rest is tragedy.

Vence see opposite

▶▶▶ Grand Canyon de Verdon 169D2

Between Castellane and Moustiers is the most spectacular gorge in Europe, with limestone cliffs plunging 700m to the narrow river bed. The best way to see it from a car is by following the Route des Crêtes, a circuit which leads from La Palud on the north bank. The road passes the **Châlet la Maline**, one terminus of the tough day's walk (14km) along the bottom of the canyon, via numerous tunnels (torch essential), to a car park near the Point Sublime. For a quick taste of the gorge scenery, park at this end of the path and walk down to the water.

The main tourist centre is **Moustiers-Ste-Marie**▶, an interesting old village straddling a mountain ravine and waterfall. Long famous for its ceramics and lavender, Moustiers is well worth a stroll, if you can park. The church has an unstable look – bulging walls and unaligned Gothic choir and Romanesque nave. Below Moustiers, the Verdon is dammed to form a vast reservoir. There are a few villages and campsites beside the lake: only **Ste-Croix-du-Verdon** has any charm.

192

RACING DUKES
The dukes of Uzès have been the official first dukes of France since the 17th century. King Louis XIII announced that all peers should get their titles confirmed by chancery and that future precedence would reflect the speed at which this was achieved. In the ensuing race the carriages of Uzès and Luynes converged at speed in the narrow rue St-Thomas du Louvre. The Luynes team was overturned and Uzès was the first duke home.

TONS OF LAVENDER
Corduroy fields of lavender are favourite aspects of Upper Provence, for a brief mid-summer period between flowering and harvest: July is best. Lavender grows naturally above 600m and thrives on the climate and chalky soil. A hybrid plant (le lavandin, not la lavande) has been developed to grow at lower altitude. Provence produces 100 tonnes of lavender essence and a thousand tonnes of lavandin essence each year.

Vaison-la-Romaine, Nyons and the Baronnies

Start at Vaison-la-Romaine.
Vaison-la-Romaine is a good base for excursions. The Ouvèze separates medieval Vaison, beneath a hill fortress, from the modern and Roman towns.

D938/D538 to Nyons.
Nyons has an olive museum and oil mills open to visitors: most interesting during the winter pulping season. A jumble of vaulted lanes (Quartier des Forts) climbs from the place Bufaven to a tiny pilgrimage chapel.

D94 to Curnier; D64 to Buis-les-Baronnies.

A beautiful drive over the **Col d'Ey** to **Buis-les-Baronnies** passes a riverside lavender distillery at

Ste-Jalle. Buis-les-Baronnies is the main centre of trade for the popular lime blossom (*tilleul*) infusion.

D5 back to Vaison.

Vence, Col de Vence, Gourdon

Start at Vence.
Vence is a busy hill town with three medieval gateways and a square (place du Peyra) on the site of the Roman forum. The former cathedral has Roman inscriptions in the façade. Matisse's **Rosary Chapel** (see pages 174–175) is near the St-Jeannet road.

Follow D2 north-west to Col de Vence. There are fine views from the 970m **Col de Vence**.

D2 to Courségoules and Gréolières. Beneath the impressive walls of the Montagne du Cheiron, **Gréolières** and **Courségoules** have good Renaissance paintings in their churches. Enthusiasts of mountain motoring can continue towards the ski resort of **Gréolières les Neiges** or round the **Massif Cheiron**.

D3 to Gourdon and Gorges du Loup. **Gourdon** is a former Saracen stronghold in a superb setting dominating the Loup Valley and surveying the coast. The Loup has impressive views, but few safe stopping places except at a café that charges for a sight of a waterfall, the Saut du Loup.

D2210 via Tourrettes-sur-Loup. **Tourrettes-sur-Loup** a pretty, old hill village, a centre of the violet industry and now a thriving arts and crafts centre.

Return on D2210 to Vence.

Massif Central

THE MASSIF CENTRAL is no single mountain range, but an enormous highland region between the Loire and the Mediterranean, covering about one sixth of France. More southern than central, it is certainly massive. Diversity comes as no surprise.

HIGH GROUND The highest peaks are in the northern region, Auvergne, a land of rich pastures and a mountain diet of ham, hard cheese (Cantal) and dark bread: food built to last through a long winter of isolation. Its villages are grey and, as a holiday area, so is its image. The main resorts are spas and, by Alpine or Pyrenean standards, the mountains are unimpressive, with no glaciers, no snow-capped peaks in summer, few rock faces to excite climbers, and no great lakes. Just big hills, ugly hydro-electric reservoirs, and dreary old spas – albeit full of fading splendours.

QUIET SIMPLICITY On the other hand, Auvergne tourism is quiet, prices are low, and the value in simple hotels is often outstanding. There is a little skiing (more than a little, for cross-country skiers) but in general the slopes and rough old mountain villages have escaped the ravages of ski development. Summits are accessible to walkers and are quite high enough to be rewarding. With good fishing and canoeing, Auvergne is a fine area for an active outdoor holiday, with some sightseeing thrown in – hilltop castle ruins, beautiful old churches and a range of extinct volcanoes, small but perfectly formed.

WILD COUNTRY Further south, the Causses and Cévennes form less high but wilder and not as well-trodden country. For fishing rivers and green valleys, substitute white water and rocky gorges; for cow pastures, windswept limestone plateaux with no spring water, only dewponds and sheep; and for creamy St-Nectaire, razor-sharp Roquefort. This is wilderness France, an area of enormous appeal to a growing minority of travellers, second-homers and permanent refugees from the comforts and stresses of town life, who take their escapism seriously. If you find the charms of rural France a bit tame, try the southern Massif Central.

Massif Central

▶▶▶ REGION HIGHLIGHTS

Ardèche, Gorges de l'
page 196

Causse du Larzac
page 206

La Chaise-Dieu
page 199

Cirque de Navacelles
page 206

Conques *page 199*

Lot, Valée du *page 200*

Puy de Dôme
pages 201, 202

Le Puy-en-Velay
page 202

Tarn, Gorges du
page 206

Vichy *page 204*

Canoeists set off from the river beaches by the Pont d'Arc in the Gorges de l'Ardèche

▶▶ Aigoual, Massif de l' — 194B2

Aigoual means wet. For reasons to do with the convergence of Atlantic and Mediterranean air currents, the southern bastion of the Massif Central (1,567m) is the wettest place in France. The slopes have been reforested in an attempt to reduce flood damage. There are roads to the summit from north and south, big views from the top and an arboretum (**Hort de Dieu**) just below it, signed from the road. **Meyrueis▶** is a popular tourist base, well placed for excursions to **Aven Armand** and **Dargilan** grottoes and drives along the **Jonte** and **Tarn** gorges or south to **Dourbie gorge▶▶**. It has a Cévennes National Park information centre.

▶ Allier, Gorges de l' — 194B3

West of Le Puy-en-Velay, the Allier runs north through dark gorges of granite and volcanic rock, best seen from the train, between tunnels. It is an area for simple accommodation and outdoor holidays – riding, fishing, canoeing (information from the tourist offices at **Brioude▶** and **Langeac**). There are interesting churches (*Open* Jul–Aug) with frescoes near the river north of Langeac – **Peyrusses**, **St-Cirgues**, **Blassac**. **St-Ilpize** is a picturesque old village with ruined **fortress▶**.

▶ Anjony, Château d' — 194A3

A well-preserved 15th-century fortress overlooks the village of Tournemire (north of Aurillac) and its colourful volcanic-stone church, proud possessor of a thorn from Christ's crown. The château's four slender towers make an impressive landmark, and there are interesting Renaissance murals inside (*Closed* mid-Nov–mid-Feb).

▶▶ Ardèche, Gorges de l' — 194C2

The D290 from Vallon Pont d'Arc to Pont St-Esprit is the great Ardèche road, a succession of roadside belvederes hundreds of metres above the river. Objects in view include a natural archway (the **Pont d'Arc**) spanning the river and, usually, a dense traffic of canoeists doing the Ardèche properly. In summer, the pace of the river is comfortable; operators at **Vallon** rent out two-man canoes and organise return buses from **Sauze**, near **St-Martin d'Ardèche**, 32km and about six hours' paddling and drifting downstream, via many good sunbathing and picnic places. To the south of Vallon is the magnificent **Aven d'Orgnac▶▶** pothole (guided tours, long staircases). **Aven de Marzal▶** is a shorter detour from the Ardèche road, and is almost as spectacular, with a museum devoted to the underground world.

RAIN
The Massif de l'Aigoual has an annual rainfall of over 2m. Over 52cm of rain fell in 24 hours in February 1964. The 100-year-old Meteo-France departmental obervatory has stunning views across a quarter of France (*Open* to public May–Sep daily).

Drive

The Cévennes and Mont Lozère

Start at Florac.
This long circuit through some of the wildest country in France is easily abbreviated by using the D998 Florac/Pont-de-Montvert road along the upper valley of the Tarn. **Florac**, **Mende** or **St-Jean-du-Gard** will do as overnight stopping places. Mende is the largest, a quiet old cathedral town beside the Lot. Florac is the HQ of the Cévennes National Park and is the starting point of the classic drive down the Tarn gorges.

Take the D907 and Corniche des Cévennes road to St-Jean-du-Gard.
The western leg between **Mende** and **St-Jean-du-Gard** includes the Corniche des Cévennes road, which runs through camisard (18th-century outlawed Protestants) country.

Follow D983, 984 and 29 (crossing the N106), and the D35 to the Col de la Croix de Berthel, and Le-Pont-de-Montvert; then the D20 to the Col de Finiels and Le Bleymard.
The eastern leg from St-Jean to **Le Bleymard** is very slow driving: 90km of narrow mountain roads over the ridges

of the Cévennes and the granite mass of **Mont Lozère**. From the **Col de Finiels** and from the **Châlet du Mont**

Lozère (4km north) there are paths to the Finiels summit (1,699m), the top of the Lozère. The Col des Tribes (east of Le Bleymard on D901) marks the Mediterranean/ Atlantic watershed. From the road up to the pass, a path leads north to the source of the Lot.

Take the D901 and N88 to Mende and Balsièges, then the N106 via the Col de Montmirat to Florac.

Walk

Footpath across the Massif

One of the old transhumance trails is now the GR7 path, which crosses the massif from **Le Bleymard** to the **Col de la Croix de Berthel**, via the **Col de Finiels**. The best section is between **L'Hôpital** and **L'Aubaret** (about two hours). Both can be reached by car from **Le Pont-de-Montvert**. Along the GR7, farm

buildings and isolated bell-towers (to help travellers caught in a storm) have been restored as part of the Lozère Ecomuseum.

❏ Protestants were outlawed in 1685. In the Cévennes they took to the hills (*désert*). Passive resistance to conversion became guerilla warfare in 1702, and the Protestants became known as *camisards*, after their white shirts. There is a camisard museum at **Le Mas Soubeyran** (11km east of St-Jean-du-Gard by D50). ❏

CANTAL CHEESE

Auvergne's number-one cheese, Cantal, was already being made 2,000 years ago. Some 99 gallons of cow's milk are required to make a dense 99-pound cheese, which forms a huge 16-inch diameter cylinder. The best Cantal is said to be made at Salers, and for real sharp flavours always choose the riper variety (*vieux Cantal*, aged in cellars) as opposed to the young cheese or halfway-there variety (*entre deux*).

▶ Besbre, Vallée de la   194B5

Fertile country south-east of Moulins, with a rich concentration of small châteaux. The busy main-road town of **Lapalisse▶** has the most magnificent of them, rebuilt and decorated by a marshal who brought home a taste for Italian Renaissance art from the Italian war. Downstream there are other châteaux to admire: **Chavroches**, **Vieux Chambord**, **Jaligny** and **Toury**, a delicious pinkish château in miniature, with turrets and towers. There is a zoo, amusement park and train ride at **Le Pal**, and a Trappist monastery at Sept-Fons.

▶ Besse en Chandesse   194A4

With the ski slopes of Super-Besse 7km away, the picturesque old grey town of Besse is a year-round mountain resort, popular in summer as a base for hiking, fishing and cycling (cycles can be hired locally), and is worth visiting anyway for its old houses, town gates and church (a mixture of Romanesque and late Gothic), all built of black lava. The deep, round **Lac Pavin▶** (southwest of Besse) is one of the prettiest of Auvergne's volcanic crater lakes, and a popular local beauty spot. The summit of **Puy de Montchal** (1,411m) is about half an hour's walk from the lake.

▶ Bort-les-Orgues   194A4

This small town on the upper Dordogne sits beneath a remarkable cliff of massive pillars of volcanic rock, the **Orgues▶** (organ pipes), which are worth inspecting at close quarters. Walk to the foot of the cliff from the road, then drive on up to the plateau above for good views of the valley and the long reservoir above Bort's hydro-electric dam, the first of five on the Dordogne. When full, it makes an island of the picturesque turreted 15th-century **Château de Val▶** (guided tours), whose waterside setting seems quite natural. There is a small beach nearby, with boat trips.

Bourboule, La   194A4

Restful to a fault, La Bourboule is a big spa spanning the young Dordogne a few kilometres downstream from Le Mont-Dore. There are gardens and long hill walks down from the **Charlannes Plateau▶**, reached by gondola lift. French parents send their asthmatic children to benefit from La Bourboule's waters, rich in arsenic.

▶ Cère, Vallée de la 194A3

The most beautiful part of the Cère is its upper valley at the heart of the Cantal Mountains, from its source at **Le Lioran** to **Aurillac**. The old village of **Vic-sur-Cère** is a good base for driving tours and/or hiking, notably along the peaks from the **Plomb du Cantal** (1,855m), reached by cable-car from **Super-Lioran**, to the **Col de Curebourse** (997m) above Vic. On the other side of the valley, the **Puy de la Poche** (1,503m) and **Puy Griou** (1,694m) are rewarding targets, the latter hard-going near the top.

▶ La Chaise-Dieu 194B4

High up in logging country north of Le Puy-en-Velay, La Chaise-Dieu is a base for outdoor sports. It has a magnificent 14th-century **abbey church▶▶**. It is worth paying to enter the choir and see the tomb of Pope Clement VI, beautiful tapestries, a *Dance of Death* fresco and Gothic cloister. There is a music festival at the end of August.

▶ Clermont-Ferrand 194B4

An industrial city, Clermont-Ferrand's dark streets are dominated by the black lava cathedral, a soaring Gothic building. Nearby **Notre Dame du Port▶** is at least as interesting as Clermont-Ferrand. To the west, situated in a fine 16th-century house, the Musée du Ranquet boasts a calculator made by the scientist Blaise Pascal, born locally in 1623. Many elegant houses on and around the rue des Cordeliers have been restored and a fine arts museum displays their salvaged contents (*Closed* Mon). Search out the Maison de l'Annonciation, the Maison de l'Eléphant and the Hôtel des Fontenilhes in old Montferrand.

▶▶ Conques 194A3

Tucked away in a remote fold of hill country to the south of the Lot, Conques is a small village and a great pilgrimage church. Thanks to the relics of an early Christian martyr in Agen, St Foy, the monastery won a mention in the pilgrim's guide of the day, accumulated a rich treasure and went on to build the **church▶▶** in the late 11th century. Its glory is the Last Judgement carving over the main doorway, and the **treasury▶▶▶** (entrance charge), which includes a 10th-century gold statuette-reliquary.

Conques' name derives from the shell-like shape (concha in Latin) of its wild, hilly site

GRIMALDI POWER

For a century and a half before the Revolution, the Vallée de la Cère was controlled by the Grimaldis of Monaco, who are still viscounts of Carlat (a château, no longer standing, east of Aurillac). They stayed, as do many tourists today, at Vic sur Cère.

RUBBER INDUSTRY

Clermont Ferrand is the home of the French rubber industry, started by the Barbier (later Michelin) family in the early 19th century.

Lioran, Le   *194A3*

With nearby **Super-Lioran**, this is the Cantal's main ski resort, in a forest setting near the Col de Cère (1,294m): a watershed between the beautiful upper valleys of Cère and Alagnon, which feed the Dordogne and Loire respectively. Both upper and lower resorts are open for business in summer, as is the cable-car from Super-Lioran to the **Plomb du Cantal▶** (1,885m). On the other side of the pass, there is no mechanical help for the ascent of conical **Puy Griou** (1,694m). Its last stage is more arduous than most Auvergnat climbs (see page 199).

▶▶ Lot, Vallée du   *194A3*

The Lot is one of France's best-loved rivers, less touristy than the Dordogne, more welcoming than the wilder Tarn. A number of unspoilt small towns with medieval bridges reflected in the water complement the scenic drive along the middle reach of the river: **St-Cômé-d'Olt**, **Espalion**, **Estaing▶** and **Entraygues▶**, where the Lot is fed by the Truyère, all have great charm. A minor road continues along the right bank to the turn-off for **Conques** (see page 199). The landscape is at its loveliest along the **gorges▶▶** between Estaing and Entraygues, with steep wooded slopes above the river, swollen by the hydro-electric Golinhac Dam below Estaing.

▶ Le Mont-Dore   *194A4*

Charming is not the word that springs to mind first, but Le Mont-Dore is less depressing than most spas, thanks to its location at the foot of an amphitheatre of mountains. In winter, it is one of the massif's main ski resorts. The odorous baths, housed in a 19th-century temple-like building, are worth visiting (*Open* mid-May–mid-Oct), and car tours combine mountains, lakes (with bathing and watersports at **Lac Chambon**), churches (**St-Nectaire**, **Orcival**), châteaux (**Cordés**, north of Orcival, and **Murol**) and cheeses. Besse, Murol and Orcival are alternative bases for exploring the Monts Dore. A cable-car to the summit of **Puy de Sancy▶▶** gives total panoramas.

MOUNTAIN HIKE
Take the cable-car from the source of the Dordogne to a point not far below the summit of the Puy de Sancy, at 1,885m the high point of the Massif Central. From here you can hike along the hills to the Capucin (1,465m) and take a cable-car down to Le Mont-Dore. For the very fit, a full circuit of the amphitheatre, starting and finishing at Le Mont-Dore, is possible in a day. Take the Capucin lift and proceed anti-clockwise via the Puy de Sancy, descending to Le Mont-Dore at a 30m waterfall (Grande Cascade).

The lower section of the River Lot twists past villages with Romanesque churches, châteaux and vineyards which produce Cahors wine

MUROL
Murol is a small resort village beneath the ruins of a medieval fortress, which was strengthened and embellished during the Renaissance but used as a quarry after the Revolution. Enough remains for an interesting visit.

Unlike most landscapes of volcanic origin in Europe north of Naples, the area to the west of Clermont-Ferrand looks the part. The Monts Dômes, more than 100 abrupt conical peaks, form a chain on a north–south axis. Rising only a few hundred metres from the fertile surrounding landscape, some of the old volcanoes (puys) are grassy, others wooded.

Most of the volcanoes have craters, in some cases as neatly decapitated as boiled eggs. Vulcanologists warn that it is much too early to write them off as extinct. As indicated by the many hot springs (**Royat**, **Le Mont-Dore**, **Vichy** etc), underground Auvergne is far from tranquil. The spring water at **Chaudes Aigues** (south of St-Flour) is the hottest in Europe.

The Puy de Dôme The highest of the chain has a road spiralling to the summit, a superb viewpoint, albeit cluttered with weather station and tourist paraphernalia. There are also scant remains of a Roman temple. Hikers use the steeper track from the Col de Ceyssat. Immediately to the north, the **Puy de Pariou** and **Petit Puy de Dôme** both have twin craters. They stand inside the boundaries of a military firing range and access (on foot from the Puy de Dôme, or by car and footpath from the Clermont-Pontgibaud road) is at restricted times.

To the south of the Monts Dômes are surviving fragments of older and much larger mountains, the **Monts Dore** and the **Monts du Cantal**: the Cantal volcano probably reached at least 3,000m before explosion and glacier erosion. **Puy Griou**, near the Plomb du Cantal, is one of the chimneys at the centre of the original crater. On its northern flank beneath the Puy Violent, the village of Salers occupies one of many lava plateaux, known as *planèzes*.

All these volcanic massifs are included in a regional natural park, the Parc des Volcans. The main information centres are at **Aurillac**, **Montlosier**, **Volvic**, near Riom (a lava quarry), **Egliseneuve d'Entraigues**, between Besse and Condat, and **Riom ès Montagnes**. The area around **Le Puy-en-Velay** falls outside the boundaries of the park, but is also volcanic in origin (see page 202).

ANCIENT VIEW
Motorists wanting to combine a scenic drive and a short panoramic walk should head for the Pas de Peyrol, east of Salers by D680. From the car park it is less than half an hour's walk to the Puy Mary (1,787m) at the end of a crest of peaks commanding a magnificent view of the Cantal Mountains and valleys, like the ruins of a vast natural fortress, 20 million years old.

The high tops of Cantal can be very bleak, but meadows on the lower slopes are famous for their wild flowers and for butterflies (above: Scarce Copper)

Le Puy-en-Velay's medieval chapel of St-Michel-d'Aiguilhe reaches dizzy heights, perched precariously 85m up on an outcrop of volcanic rock

LACE-MAKERS
From Louis XIV's time until the 20th century, much of the female population of the Vélay region made lace. Now that machines do the work more cheaply, country village squares are no longer filled with women deftly manipulating their *fuseaux*. But Le Puy-en-Velay still has a lace-making conservatoire (rue du Guesclin), with a small display of old lace and craftswomen to demonstrate and explain techniques. Training for 'professional aptitude' takes three years of eight hours' practice a day. Lace-making courses for the public are also given in the gallery-cum-boutique at 38–40 rue Raphael.

▶▶ Le Puy-en-Velay   *194B3*

Le Puy-en-Velay fills an old crater punctuated by outcrops of volcanic rock, on the spikiest of which sits **St-Michel-d'Aiguilhe▶**. On the main hill, the lava-cobbled rue des Tables climbs to the **cathedral▶▶** (see page 203) passing tourist shops with costumed lace-makers in the doorway. Above looms a huge statue of a green-eyed *Virgin and Child*, made of melted Crimean cannon, with a viewing platform in the crown. North of Le Puy-en-Velay, look left for the ruins of the **Château de Polignac▶**.

Riom   *194B4*

Once Clermont's rival, Riom is now threatened by the sprawl of its neighbour. The old lava-built centre, ringed by boulevards, is of interest for its Renaissance **palaces▶**, the 14th-century statue of *Virgin, Child and Goldfinch* in Notre Dame du Marthuret (rue du Commerce) and a regional museum. There are superb fortress ruins at **Tournoël▶▶**, above Volvic, a source of mineral water and lava.

▶ Rodez   *194B4*

The departmental capital of remote Aveyron has recently benefited from a modest revival in its fortunes as disenchanted urbanites have acquired a taste for rustification. The pedestrian centre and ramparts here have been restored. The great red **cathedral▶** is a mixture of bare fortification and late Gothic and Renaissance ornament.

Royat   *194B4*

A Roman spa overlooking Clermont Ferrand, Royat was the height of Second Empire fashion. Now it is a comfortable suburb with unexceptional hotels, extensive sports facilities and Romanesque church. A toll-road leads up to the summit of the **Puy de Dôme▶▶▶**

▶ St-Guilhem-le-Désert   *194B1*

After a long career in the armed service of Charlemagne, William of Orange retired to found an abbey at the foot of the Causses. He brought a fragment of the Cross, which put St-Guilhem on the medieval pilgrimage map.

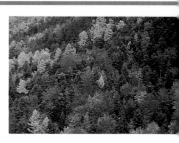

In a region of dour grey villages it may come as a surprise to find that the local version of the Romanesque style is full of colour and invention. The builders of these churches, one feels, had fun exploiting the range of local granite, sandstone and lava to create mosaics of geometric and speckled patterns decorating the walls of churches large and small.

Clermont and surrounding area

Clermont-Ferrand: Notre-Dame du Port. The most perfect example of the local style: colourful stonework, beautiful capitals, a reproduction black Virgin in the crypt.

Chauriat (east of Clermont-Ferrand): look out for colourful stonework and good capitals.

Marsat (near Riom): features include a severe black Virgin in a golden cloak, and a wheel around which 3km of wax (the distance from Riom) is threaded.

Mozac (on the edge of Riom): the church is no beauty, but the capitals (including Jonah and a group of acrobats) and reliquary are outstanding.

Monts Dore

Orcival: a harmonious grey pilgrimage church, with a 12th-century Virgin, set in a pretty village. Note the good capitals in the choir.

St-Nectaire: prominently set above a small spa, this handsome 12th-century church has outstanding capitals and treasure (*Open* Apr–Oct, Wed–Mon).

South of Clermont

Brioude: the biggest and most majestic of all, Brioude has colourful stonework even on the floor. Entertaining rustic themes can be made out in the carved capitals. Look for the 14th-century 'Leprous' wooden Christ.

Issoire: this grand town-centre church was done no favours by its 19th-century decorators; but it does boast a beautiful east end and fine capitals.

Lavaudieu (south-east of Brioude): a 12th-century former abbey church (entrance charge) with a cloister, frescoes and octagonal belfry.

Le Puy-en-Velay: set on a steep slope and constructed on several levels, the cathedral has a patterned west end and an unusual vault of oblong domes. There are good frescoes and a superb cloister (entrance charge). The earlier 10th- and 11th-century chapel of St-Michel d'Aiguilhe, erected on a spire of rock, has intricate scalloped decoration surrounding the door, apparently inspired by Moorish art.

VIEWING

The striking similarities with the spirit of oriental art probably reflect crusading contacts. Enjoyment of a Romanesque church is never complete without a good look at the back: a fan of chapels in a rhythmic interplay of curves. Inside the church, every capital tells a lively story.

Clermont-Ferrand's cathedral

▶ Salers   194A3

Salers is an outwardly well-preserved old village of grey turreted houses, ramparts and gateways on the western flank of the Cantal Mountains and at the heart of cheese country. With several good hotels, it is a good base for exploring the Cantal Mountains and Monts Dore. The **church▶** has a painted sculptural group of the Entombment (late 15th-century).

▶ Souvigny   195B5

Once an important Cluniac abbey, pilgrimage and burial place for the Bourbon dukes, Souvigny is now a peaceful place, with only the great abbey church▶▶ (Romanesque and Gothic) to remind visitors of its past glory. There is interesting sculpture inside the church (two splendid ducal tombs) and in one of the two museums housed in the adjoining abbey buildings. St-Ménoux (6km north) also has a beautiful 12th- to 13th-century church.

▶▶▶ Tarn, Gorges du see pages 206–7   194B2

▶ Thiers   194B4

Still dedicated to its traditional manufacture of cutlery, Thiers is remarkably old-fashioned in appearance. The old timbered houses lining the steep narrow streets still harbour traditional workshops, despite gradually losing out to factory mass production (visits: rue Durolle and rue de la Coutellerie). There is also a good cutlery museum (*Closed* Mon). The Vallée des Rouets (3km east of Thiers), where the knife sharpeners worked, can now be visited.

▶ Truyère Gorges   194A3

Once a tributary of the Allier, the Truyère now abruptly changes course near the old grey town of **St-Flour▶**, beneath a long railway bridge (Viaduc de Garabit) built, before his more famous tower, by Eiffel. Here it swells into the largest of a series of narrow reservoirs on its way to join the Lot at Entraygues. No road follows the valley, but the road from **Pierrefort** to the **Barrage de Sarrans** runs through some of the best scenery. The best thing about St-Flour, the highest cathedral town in Europe (887m), is its setting on a volcanic outcrop, well viewed from the Clermont-Mende road (N9). About 14km south, the ruins of the **Château d'Alleuze** overlook a finger of the top lake. At **Pont de Tréboul**, a submerged 14th-century bridge (superimposed by a modern replacement) resurfaces when water is low. **Entraygues▶** has a 13th-century bridge and château overlooking the confluence of the rivers Lot and Truyère.

▶ Vichy   194B5

The great spa has lost its share of the fizzy water market and most of its cachet as a resort, partly by association with the 1940–4 period of German occupation, which is often referred to simply as Vichy, and partly because staying at a spa is now a cheap holiday for those with a sympathetic doctor. In season, *curistes* still queue for a drink at the taps in the Parc des Sources, amble in gardens on the banks of the Allier and avail themselves of Vichy's many seasonal entertainments and sports facilities.

TAKING THE WATERS
The waters of Vichy were known to the Romans but its boom time was the 19th century, when it acquired most of its exotic architecture. Marshal Pétain lived at the Pavillon Sévigné, formerly the residence of the celebra-ted 17th-century correspondent Madame de Sévigné, who came for her rheumatism, found the water foul-tasting and described the cure routine as purgatory.

204

Stained-glass windows at Vichy's church join the town's Second Empire and Belle Epoque architecture

Drive

Mont Mézenc and the source of the Loire

The appeal of this tour is the scenery around Mont Mézenc (1,753m) and the Gerbier de Jonc, a cone of volcanic rock marking the source of the Loire.

Start at Le Monastier. D500/36 to Moudeyres, Les Estables.
Moudeyres has an excellent hotel; Les Estables has good cross-country skiing.

D274 to Croix de Peccata; D631/400/378 to Gerbier de Jonc (D122-215 to Ray Pic and back (see Walk, below).

The Ray Pic waterfall is 15 minutes' walk from the road by an easy path. *D122 to Le Béage, D16 to Lac d'Issarlès, Coucouron, and Auberge de Peyrebeille.*
The volcanic crater Lac d'Issarlès, has a beach and restaurants. Coucouron is a cheese-making village with a Wednesday market. Hoteliers with cash flow problems may sympathise with Pierre and Marie Martin, who ran the lonely highland inn, Auberge de Peyrebeille, and killed at least 53 guests in 26 years, pocketing their money and burning the bodies. Rumbled in 1833, they were guillotined in front of the inn.

N102/88 north to Costaros, D49/54 to Arlempdes.
Arlempdes has a simple hotel beneath a medieval fortress high above the Loire.

Return to Le Monastier.

Mont Mézenc and the Gerbier de Jonc

Marked paths lead to the summit of Mont Mézenc from the road at Croix de Péccata (half an hour) and Croix de Boutières (slightly longer). The Gerbier de Jonc is a steeper but shorter walk from the roadside, unmarked but obvious.

Alternatively, a round trip of the Mont Mézenc from Les Estables takes about three hours.

Most of the large area between the upper Lot Valley and the Mediterranean coast of Languedoc consists of a high limestone plateau, or causse, divided into four by rivers which have cut gorges like great wounds into the land. There are other causses in France, but these are the serious ones: high, wide, wild, windswept and empty.

LARZAC RESISTANCE
The Larzac is the best known of the Grands Causses, thanks to the outcry provoked by a government plan in the 1970s to expand its military camp at the expense of a few sheep farms. The farmers took their sheep to demonstrate in Paris; angry youth found the military a soft target, and Sauvons Le Larzac fitted nicely on a T-shirt. Suddenly everyone cared about one of the more desolate parts of the country. Worry about Roquefort output may also have influenced opinion. On his election President Mitterrand lost no time cancelling the project.

From north to south, the four Causses are: **Sauveterre**, between the Lot and the Tarn; **Méjean**, the highest and wildest, between Tarn and Jonte; the **Causse Noir**, between Jonte and Dourbie; and the **Larzac**, the largest, to the south of the Dourbie. The river gorges can be admired on foot, by boat (in a few places) and by car. Speleomanes can explore potholes equipped with lifts and staircases and artfully lit to show off delicate translucent curtains of rock and underground lakes.

Chaotic rocks Above ground, chaotic collections of rocks make natural imitations of ruined cities and give a small village like **Le Caylar** the look of a fortified town. **Montpellier-le-Vieux**, on the Causse Noir south of Le Rozier, is an overgrown maze of dolomitic rocks among which it would be easy to get lost without the plan available on site. Elsewhere, retreating rivers have left bends like natural theatres, or *cirques*: **Navacelles** is the finest example, near the small town of Ganges. Throughout, civilisation takes a back seat. Sheep are the most numerous inhabitants and their cheese, the pungent Roquefort, is the main output. Small dry-stone shelters for man and beast dot the landscape like lonely mausoleums.

Access Inhospitable as they are, the Causses are not inaccessible. A toll-free section of the A75 motorway travels across the Massif Central from St-Flour to Montpellier; a good road follows the Tarn Gorges; and the old pilgrimage route across the Causse du Larzac is now a fast main road (N9 from Millau to Montpellier), passing a series of villages with evocative names like **La Cavalerie** and **L'Hospitalet**, built by the Templars and Hospitallers, the area's medieval landlords. **Ste-Eulalie** was the original Templar base, but **La Couvertoirade** (north of Le Caylar, off the main road) is the least modernised, with much of its old ramparts, towers and gates intact. South of Le Caylar the road descends from the Causse in a few hairpins at the **Pas de l'Escalette**, where earlier travellers had to use a staircase in the 300m cliff.

Celebrated gorge The most famous river gorge, and the easiest gorge road, is the Tarn between **Ste-Enimie** and **Le Rozier**. There are cliffs of up to 500m on either side, vividly coloured when sunlit; caves in the rock

High and wild country: the Causse Méjean

walls, brilliantly clear water and occasional fertile openings in the narrow gorge, with small villages, orchards and riverside châteaux. From **La Malène** there are organised boat trips through a section of the gorge known as **Les Détroits** (the Straits) with beautiful caves, to **Baumes Hautes**. Canoeists can tackle the same section, but should not continue downstream, where a rocky chaos (the Pas du Souci) is a dangerous obstacle. **Le Rozier** is a good base for energetic hikers: there are spectacular cliff paths above the Tarn and Jonte, with exposed sections where ladders have been installed. From **Les Vignes** (below the Pas du Souci) a hairpin road scales the right bank wall and leads to the **Point Sublime**, one of the few easily accessible places where the gorge can be viewed from above.

Other options The other sections of gorge scenery, much less crowded but with slower driving, are the Jonte between **Meyrueis** and **Le Rozier**; and the Dourbie, where two sections of tight gorges are interrupted by a more open valley around the village of **St-Jean-de-Bruel**, a cheerful resort among orchards.

Potholes The Causses' potholes are the grandest in France, although lacking the extra dimension of pre-historic art. The most spectacular are **Aven Armand**, north of the Jonte near Meyrueis, with its 'Virgin Forest' of stalagmites; and the **Grotte des Demoiselles** near Ganges.

Other places to visit
Grotte de Dargilan (near Meyrueis), **Grotte de Clamouse** (near St-Guilhem-le-Désert): stalagmites and stalactites, almost as good as Aven Armand and less crowded.

Hyelzas (4km west of Aven Armand): restored traditional Causse farm.

La Jasse (beside the N9, between Millau and La Cavalerie): Larzac Ecomuseum, a splendid all-round presentation of the history and ecology of the Causse du Larzac (summer only).

Roquefort-sur-Soulzon: where the cheese comes from; caves open to visitors all year.

Sauveterre (north of Ste-Enimie): small village with typical old Causse houses.

BLUE-VEINED AROMAS
When it comes to blue-veined cheese made from the untreated milk of Lacaune ewes, there is Roquefort and Roquefort. These days most of it is made mechanically in southern France and Corsica. But a small amount is produced in the traditional manner at Roquefort-sur-Soulzon, south of Millau, using a natural mould from huge decomposed loaves of two-month-old bread. The cheeses are stored for many months in cold, damp natural caves beneath the village before being wrapped in tin foil and stamped with their red sheep insignia. The caves are open to visitors.

The Cirque de Navacelles, where the course of ancient rivers can still be seen in the land

The Alps & Rhone Valley

►►► REGION HIGHLIGHTS

Annecy, Lac d'
page 210

Aravis page 211

Chamonix page 214

Mejie Glaciers
page 219

Pérouges page 221

Queyras page 212

La Vanoise page 222

Vénéon Valley page 220

Vercors page 222

FROM LAKE GENEVA to the Mediterranean, the Alpine chain is dominated by the pinnacles and glaciers at the shoulders of Mont Blanc (4,807m), a pilgrimage for mountaineers from all over the world. The Alps have their place in the history books, but are primarily a region for sport and leisure in a context of natural beauty. In two uninhabited national parks (**Vanoise** and **Ecrins**) eagle, ibex and gentian enjoy protection and hikers have to make do with simple refuges. The Queyras and Vercors Regional Parks have been set up to foster traditional crafts and ecosensitive tourism.

FRENCH ACQUISITIONS The southern province of Dauphiné was sold to France in 1349 and traditionally ruled by the heir to the throne, or *dauphin*. Grenoble became its capital and remains the metropolis of the French Alps, a dynamic industrial and university city. **Savoie** was a transalpine independent duchy with capitals on either side of the chain at **Chambéry** and **Turin**. In 1860 Chambéry's half voted to join France.

THE ALPS AND THE RHONE VALLEY

The Alps & Rhone Valley

Savoie More accessible than Dauphiné, Savoie is greener in summer and whiter in winter, and more developed for tourism. There are old spas and lakeside resorts with casinos and windsurfing schools; pre-war resorts grafted on to old chalet villages among woods and pastures; and high modern resorts planned for convenient skiing, cheap self-catering and never mind the aesthetics.

Facelifts The current effort is to improve the looks of the new resorts and broaden their summer appeal. Climbing and hiking, golf, riding, mountain biking, tennis, paragliding, rafting and summer skiing are widely available. For the young and hyperactive, the high resorts are great. For cowbells and pretty chalets, look elsewhere.

Cable-cars and high roads bring the glories of the Alpine landscape within the reach of even the least energetic traveller. Fine weather (unfortunately never predictable in the mountains) is vital to a good holiday, and the high resorts and road passes open for a short summer season.

The Rhône Valley is a great thoroughfare, much travelled and little visited. Its capital, **Lyon**, is a city of merchants, bankers and gourmets. While others pass through on the way south, gastro-tourists target the Rhône Valley to feast at the tables of Blanc, Bocuse, Chapel and other high priests of gourmandise.

Annecy's 12th-century Palais de l'Isle

A CHEQUERED CHATEAU
Annecy's château, glowering from its hilltop site, represents four centuries of architectural history (12th–16th) and now, to reflect this chequered past, groups wide-ranging museum displays. Ultra-contemp-orary revamped exhibition halls explore alpine ecology (aquariums) and anthropology, as well as regional archaeology, painting, religious sculp-ture and contemporary art. Illustrious past owners of the château include the Counts of Geneva, the Dukes of Savoie and the military (1742–1947).

Nearly 14km long but rarely more than one kilometre wide, Lac d'Annecy's natural beauty has long magne-tised writers and artists

▶▶▶ Annecy, Lac d'   *208B3*

An old town at the head of a beautiful mountain lake, flanked by elegant villas and smart hotels, Annecy is the French showpiece of lakes-and-mountains beauty. The only complaint may be its popularity: Annecy itself, the most dynamic and prosperous town in Savoie, has industrial and residential suburbs spreading far beyond the old centre. And the banks and waters of the lake are approaching saturation with villas and boats. Once seri-ously polluted, the slow-draining waters are now clean enough for the prized local delicacies, *lavaret* (lake trout) and *omble chevalier* (char).

The heart of town is a delightful canal zone where the Thiou flows from the lake, overlooked by the towers of a vast 16th-century fortress. Strolling around is the main attraction (especially on market days, Tue, Fri and Sun mornings), but there are a few specific sights: Renaissance frescoes in the church of **St-Maurice**, and a renovated **regional museum** in the **château▶▶**. The Palais de l'Isle, a picturesque old prison in mid-stream, is open for visits. There are extensive gardens beside the lake, with boat trips from beside the Hôtel de Ville. The best place for bathing and watersports is at the eastern end of the long avenue of planes (**avenue d'Albigny**) near the splendidly restored Imperial Palace Hotel.

On the west bank, it is a fine drive up the wooded Semnoz Mountain to the **Crêt du Chatillon▶** (1,699m) and back to the lake at **Sevrier** via the **Col de Leschaux**, giving good views of the lake and the more interesting mountains climbing steeply from the eastern shore: the cliffs of **Mount Veyrier**, jagged **Dents de Lanfon** and tow-ering crags of **La Tournette** (2,351m). The best alternative way to enjoy the scenery is a boat ride from Annecy to **Talloires▶**, the most fashionable resort on the lake, with prestigious hotels and restaurants in an idyllic leafy set-ting, sheltered by the 150m **Roc de Chère** cliffs, a nature reserve of primarily botanical interest. Facing Talloires across the narrowest part of the lake, the picturesque **Château de Duingt** is not open to visitors.

▶▶ Aravis, Massif des   208C3

The Aravis is Haute Savoie at its most charming: high mountains, rich pastures, woods, old chalets with flowers on the balcony, creamy *reblochon* cheese. The **Cimetière des Glières** and **museum** commemorate the exploits of Resistance forces based on the Glières plateau (to the north) in 1944. **Thônes▶**, an attractive small market town, has a typically Savoyard onion-domed church, good cheese shops and a small local museum; **La Clusaz**, reached along the D909, is one of Haute Savoie's oldest and biggest ski resorts, with traditional chalet-style hotels, lots of sport and good walks from the Beauregard cable-car and the Col des Aravis (1,498m), which commands a famous **view▶▶** of Mont Blanc. From here, the return to Annecy, via **Manigod** (D16) and **Col de la Forclaz** (D12, N508, D42), is slower driving through particularly beautiful pastoral scenery with good views over the lake.

▶ Assy, Plateau d'   208C3

This institutional resort high above Le Fayet has a superb view of Mont Blanc. The former TB clinics are not a cheerful sight, but the modern church of **Notre Dame de Toute Grace▶▶** is well worth the long hairpin climb: its decorators included Lurçat (tapestry behind the altar), Léger (exterior mosaic), Rouault (windows), Chagall and Matisse. If you are bound for Chamonix, take the minor road via **Servoz** and the **Gorges de la Diosaz**, instead of driving back down to the valley.

Barcelonnette and the Ubaye   208C1

The 13th-century base of the Count of Barcelona is a rough mountain town, visibly old if not irresistibly charming, beneath modern ski resorts (**Pra Loup** and **Le Sauze**) at the heart of one of the most remote valleys of the French Alps. Until a road was cut through the tight Ubaye gorges around **Le Lauzet** in the late 19th century, the area's best connections were with Italy via the **Col de Larche**: Savoy ceded it to France in 1713.

MOUNTAIN ROADS SOUTH
All routes south to the Maritime and Provençal Alps are tortuous, slow and closed for a long winter: the 60km road to St-Etienne-de-Tinée peaks at the Cime de la Bonette, the highest main road in the Alps. The Col de la Cayolle road is even slower and very narrow. The Col d'Allos road is the least arduous. After the pass it follows the Verdon Valley south past the small resort of Allos, good for access to the Mercantour National Park. On the drawing-board is a projected *grande route des Alpes* connecting the highest Alpine passes with the Mediterranean.

ST BERNARD
High above Lake Annecy, the Château de Menthon (closed winter) is the birth-place of the 11th-century saint, Bernard, who gave his name to a dog.

Elegant Aix-les-Bains, a long-established Alpine spa, dates from the Roman occupation of Gaul

HIGH-ALTITUDE WALK
From St-Véran, drive 6km to the pilgrimage chapel Notre Dame de Clausis, beneath a splendid theatre of frontier peaks. A marked path leads to the border at the Col de St-Véran in about one and three-quarter hours. From here it is about an hour's walk north along the crest to the Col de Chamoussière, skirting the Pic de Caramantran (3,026m). Return to the Clausis Chapel by the GR58 trail. This walk requires sturdy footwear and good weather.

▶ **Bourget, Lac du, and Chambéry**   *208B3*

Like Lake Annecy, the slightly larger and deeper Lac du Bourget is long and thin. Much though it was admired by Romantic poets (notably Lamartine), its shoreline and surrounding mountains – long ridges towering above it on either side – are less varied than Annecy's. Its main town, **Aix-les-Bains**, an ancient spa and one of the grand Alpine resorts of the 19th century, is lively enough (as spas go), with a beach, gardens by the lake, plenty of sports on and off the water and boat trips to **Hautecombe Abbey▶▶**, mausoleum of the Savoyard dynasty. Most of the buildings are in neo-gothic style. The D914 runs high above the west bank through pretty farmland with good views from the **Chapelle de l'Etoile▶**.

Chambéry Now the busy prefecture of Savoie, Chambéry was the capital of the transalpine kingdom of Savoy until it lost its status and its Holy Shroud to Turin in the mid-16th century. Despite the high reputation of its herby vermouth, it hardly demands a visit, but there is a good regional **museum** not far from the cathedral and an amusing 19th-century **elephant fountain** at the central crossroads. The Italianate arcades of **rue de Boigne▶** lead to the ducal **castle▶** and late Gothic **Sainte-Chapelle**. On the south-east edge of town, the home of Madame de Warens (**Les Charmettes**), where Rousseau spent six years (1736–42), has been restored as a museum.

▶ **Briançon and the Briançonnais**   *208C1*

The highest town in Europe (1,320m) plugs a strategic junction of valleys at the heart of the Dauphine Alps. Above the anonymous modern town that sprawls around a tangled road junction, the walled **upper town▶** stands splendidly intact, a gaunt citadel built by Vauban for Louis XIV but subsequently much altered and reinforced with outlying forts on the heights above the town and the Col de Montgenèvre.

Alpine Crossroads At 1,850m, the Col de Montgenèvre is the easiest crossing of the western Alps, busy with armies and travellers throughout history and still kept open all winter. Since the opening of the Fréjus Road Tunnel the volume of traffic has declined, improving the quality of life at the border village and ski resort of **Montgenèvre**. A more picturesque route to Italy is via the peaceful **Névache Valley** and **Col de l'Echelle** (1,766m) to Bardonecchia. There are interesting churches at **Plampinet** (with frescoes; only open in summer) and Névache. Along the Guisane Valley to the west of Briançon, a succession of hamlets make up the ski resort of Serre Chevalier, named after a rounded peak (2,483m) accessible by cable-car. Lifts from downtown Briançon to **Mont Prorel** (2,572m) have opened up additional skiing and summer walks, with views of the Durance Valley and, from the summit, the peaks of the Ecrins.

Chalets and Sun To the south of Briançon, the remote lunar expanse and famously sunny **Queyras▶▶▶** (now a

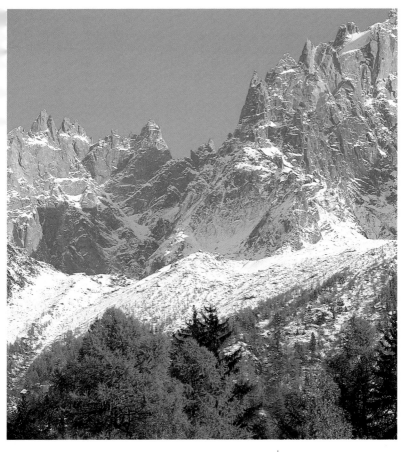

213

regional park) has a few small resorts. **St-Véran▶** is the most interesting of them, and at 2,000m is one of the highest villages in Europe. St-Véran's sundials, fountains, crosses adorned with the instruments of the passion, and houses crowned by wooden grain-stores, are typical of the region. One house with traditional Queyras interior is preserved as a museum. **Aiguilles** is the other main crafts centre. The massive fortress above the village of **Château Queyras▶** and the fortified town of **Mont Dauphin** (above Guillestre) are both mostly Vauban's work.

High roads Motorists who are neither in a hurry nor hairpin-shy can travel the length of the Alps via the high road: 80km from **Chamonix** to **Bourg St-Maurice** via the **Mont Blanc Tunnel** and **Col du Petit St-Bernard** (2,188m); 120km to **St-Michel-de-Maurienne** via the **Col de l'Iseran** (2,770m); 67km to **Briançon** via the **Col du Galibier** (2,646m) and **Col du Lautaret** (2,058m); 53km to **Guillestre** via the **Col de l'Izoard** (2,360m); 51km to **Jausiers** via the **Col de Vars** (2,111m); and 133km to **Nice** via the **Cime de la Bonette** (2,802m), from which point it is downhill all the way to the sea. All the high passes close for the winter.

Autumn colours stop short of the snow-covered 'aiguilles' above Chamonix

CABLE-CAR TO HEAVEN
Chamonix has the most spectacular lifts in the Alps. The most exciting trip is over the Massif Mont Blanc to La Palud in Italy via the Aiguille du Midi, and six stages of cable-car and telecabin (take passport, and return by bus through the tunnel). On the oppposite side of the valley, the Brévent and Flégère cable-cars give the best views of Mont Blanc and the snaking Mer de Glacé glacier respectively.

▶▶▶ Chamonix   208C3

Chamonix likes to add Mont Blanc to its name, and throws in 'world capital of Alpinism and skiing' for good measure. If it added that the grandeur of its setting is unrivalled in Europe, no one would argue. The white dome of the highest Alp (4,807m) officially occupies St-Gervais communal territory, but it was at Chamonix that the pioneers of Alpinism looked for a way to cross the chaotic mass of glaciers descending almost to the valley floor: the Glacier des Bossons drops 3,600 vertical metres at a gradient of almost 45 degrees.

Old and new A colourful, often overcrowded and traffic-plagued town of 10,000 inhabitants, Chamonix is a mixture of modern blocks, old-fashioned villas and bulky hotels. Clientele and population are remarkably diverse: old people, rugged mountaineers and sporty holiday-makers who come for the climbing, skiing, hang-gliding, golf and bar crawls. Near the central statue of Mont Blanc's 18th-century conquerors, Balmat and de Saussure, the **Musée Alpin** illustrates the history of the valley and Mont Blanc.

Chamonix now sprawls over the central section of the 15km valley, where heavy traffic (2,000 juggernauts a day) using the road tunnel through Mont Blanc to Italy is an added scourge. The tourist office issues useful maps of summer walks at less polluted altitudes. Above Chamonix, the valley is more peaceful. **Argentière**, skiing focus of the valley, is the main resort, but for peace and quiet the best bases are the hamlet of **Le Lavancher▶▶** (superb views of Chamonix's 'needle-like' rocky pinnacles, the 'aiguilles', and good walks) and the village of **Le Tour**.

Despite a few lingering traditions, Chamonix has been strongly cosmopolitan ever since a mainly English clientele flocked there over a century before skiing took off

Long walk The celebrated Tour du Mont Blanc (GRTMB) walk, via Italy, Switzerland and France, takes more than ten days to complete. It can be cut in half by taking the cable-cars or bus between **La Palud** and **Chamonix**, or joined briefly from any resort along the circuit. The best combination of easy walking and spectacular views is the south-facing balcony **walk▶** between **Planpraz** and **La Flégère**, both accessible by lift from Chamonix. It takes about two hours, and is nowhere arduous, although sturdy shoes are needed.

Among early mountaineering exploits, one of the most impressive was the conquest of table-topped Mont Aiguille in 1492, by royal command. Curiosity about reported sightings of angels on the summit provoked this expedition, but it was the Enlightenment's spirit of scientific enquiry which gave further impetus to high Alpine exploration.

Interest centred on Mont Blanc, visible from Geneva and increasingly well known for its glaciers. In August 1786, 25 years after Geneva scientist Horace de Saussure offered a reward to the first man up Mont Blanc, the climb was achieved by a local doctor and guide, **Paccard** and **Balmat**. **De Saussure** went up with 18 guides and no ropes in 1787. On his return, a **Colonel Beaufoy** set off immediately for the summit. This man 'was almost the first of the mountaineering race' wrote the English Alpinist **Edward Whymper**: he climbed to amuse himself.

New explorers Colonel Beaufoy's idea of fun did not catch on until the late 19th century, when the railway brought a new generation of explorers to the Alps. In 1864 and '65, Whymper climbed the Aiguille Verte and the Grandes Jorasses in the Massif Mont Blanc, the highest peak in the southern Alps (the Ecrins) and, in an expedition which killed four of his team, the Matterhorn in Switzerland.

Chamonix With its scores of rocky pinnacles, Chamonix was the mountaineers' headquarters. Hotels in the village had telescopes through which friends watched progress and, at the wave of a hat from on high, cracked a bottle of champagne. A smart advertiser set up a champagne hoarding on the summit, but under-estimated the power of the elements, as did **Dr Janssen** of Meudon, who was carried up Mont Blanc in a litter and devoted years to building an observatory on top. Completed in 1893, it registered a minimum temperature of -43°C before sliding off towards the valley as part of a glacier.

New tests Climbers have since continued to seek ever greater challenges – most recently, climbing without ropes or nails driven into the rock. At the same time, competitive climbing on indoor walls has become a TV sport. Traditionalists scoff, but dedicated climbers need the sponsorship that celebrity brings. Many mountain resorts now have these artificial climbing walls for practice.

GUIDES
Chamonards formed the first company of mountain guides in 1832.

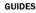215

Every year thousands of people climb Mont Blanc, still thought by most people to be Europe's highest peak; in fact, Mt Elbruz in the Caucasus tops it by 835m, at 5,642m

Chartreuse, Massif de la 208B2

Climbing abruptly from the Isère between **Chambéry** and **Grenoble**, the wettest massif in the Alps is thickly forested, and at its most beautiful in autumn. Roads are narrow and the main resort, **St-Pierre-de-Chartreuse**, is small. A road from the Col de la Porte leads to open pastures near the top of the **Charmant Som►**, a good viewpoint over the remote niche of **La Grande Chartreuse**, founded by St Bruno in 1084. The 17th-century buildings, inhabited by a few dozen monks, are not open to visitors and women are not supposed to enter monastic land; but there is an interesting museum at the entrance (**La Correrie►**) which also sells Chartreuse. The monks built the road along the gorge of the Guiers Mort from **St-Pierre** to **St-Laurent-du-Pont**.

Die 208A1

An ancient walled town beside the Drôme at the foot of the southern flank of the Massif Vercors, Die has a few fragments of its Roman buildings: a triumphal arch (Porte St-Marcel) at the southern edge of town; and Roman columns in the cathedral porch. The local sparkling wine (Clairette de Die) is one of the best champagne substitutes.

► Evian 208C4

Evian, a major supplier of mineral water, was transformed from old walled village to grand spa resort after Baron de Blonay gave his lakeside château and park to the town in 1865. Gardens, leafy promenade, domed casino and baths took their place; big hotels have followed as Evian has grown into a major conference centre. There is plenty to do: boat trips on the lake, exhibitions and a full range of sports.

► Grenoble 208B2

A go-ahead, high-rise, modern university city, Grenoble fills a broad gap in the mountains, with the massifs Vercors and Chartreuse to west and north, and the higher peaks of the Belledonne to the east. The centre of life is the pedestrian area around the places Grenette and St-André on the left bank of the Isère. A gondola lift spans the river to the rocktop **Fort de la Bastille**, a good viewpoint. Paths lead down to the Musée Dauphinois (regional history and crafts) and the church of St Laurent. The relocated Musée de Grenoble has an outstanding modern art collection.

► Léman, Lac (Lake Geneva) 208C4

The giant of the Alpine lakes is a 70km-long bulge in the course of the Rhône, which enters in the east near Montreux and exits via Geneva. From the frontier near Geneva, a minor road follows the shore of the narrow part of the lake (Petit Lac) to **Yvoire►►**, a picturesque medieval village. **Excenevex►** has the best beach on the lake. **Thonon►** is the main town of the French bank and Evian's great rival as resort and spring, with a more everyday lifestyle. Surrounded by its vineyards to the east of town, the splendid **Château de Ripaille** (*closed* winter) was the retreat of Amadée VIII, first duke of Savoy, who was pulled out of retirement to be anti-pope

GREEN LIQUEUR
The famous green and less potent yellow Chartreuse liqueurs, based on a secret herbal elixir whose recipe was imparted to the monks in 1605, are no longer produced at La Grande Chartreuse but at the small town of Voiron (north-west of Grenoble), where the vast cellars are open to visitors. All but the recipe is revealed, and free tasting is offered.

ARTFUL CITY
In, 1994, the fine arts museum, now called Musée de Grenoble, moved to its sleekly designed new home on Grenoble's place Lavalette. Its 20th-century art collections complement the avant-garde exhibitions held at Le Magasin in the cours Berriat. No less artful was Grenoble's former Gaullist mayor, Alain Carignon, indicted in 1995 for fraud and corruption after a lengthy investigation.

(Felix V) during the Great Schism. Between Evian and the Swiss border at **St-Gingolph**, mountains climb steeply from the lake's deepest waters. For a bird's-eye view of the lake, take the cable-car from **Thollon** (12km from Evian by the D24) to the **Pic de Memise▶** (1,677m). Thonon and Evian are good places for boat trips.

▶ Lyon   *208A3*

France's second city, famous for its trade fairs and bankers in the Renaissance and its silk and gastronomy industries ever since, spreads over the confluence of Saône and Rhône. On the narrow peninsula between the two rivers, the vast place Bellecour and the place des Terreaux are the twin poles of civic life. Between them, the rue de la République is the city's main shopping axis. There are excellent museums nearby, the **Musée des Arts Décoratifs▶**, the **Musée Historique des Tissus▶▶** and, most notably, the renovated **Musée des Beaux-Arts▶▶** with the Jacqueline Delabuc collection. The restored old quarter on the right bank of the Saône is now the focus of Lyonnais chic: Renaissance palaces (rue St-Jean and rue du Boeuf), designer shops and restaurants, lively *bouchons* (bistros). There are major remains of Roman **Lugdunum▶▶** near **Fourvière basilica** (**views▶▶**) and a good **Gallo-Roman museum▶▶**.

CULTURAL LIONS
Hustling hard to keep up with the Parisians and justify its possession of Europe's largest protected Renaissance quarter after Venice, Lyon is culturally very active, with its own Biennale d'Art Contemporain (summer 1999). In 1993, the 1831 opera house was completely revamped by architect Jean Nouvel, sprouting a voluminous glass top floor in the process (see below). In 1995, Renzo Piano designed the new Museum of Contemporary Art to the north of Lyon, in the Cité Internationale. Even the Roman amphitheatre at Fourvière sees rock concerts, and every evening over 150 monuments are bathed in illuminations.

217

Lyon's Fourvière basilica gives access—via 300 steps—to an observation point with views over the city to the alps

▶ La Maurienne — 208B2

The Arc Valley is the southernmost of Savoie's great thoroughfares. The main valley, from the dreary border town of **Modane** to the confluence of Arc and Isère near **Chambéry**, is dull, dark country, punctuated with power stations and factories. **St-Jean-de-Maurienne** (see margin and page 219) is worth a stop for the cathedral, with beautiful 15th-century choir stalls and an alabaster reliquary for three of the Baptist's fingers.

The most developed of the few resorts above the valley is **Valloire▶**, on the road to the Galibier Pass, well placed for an overnight stop. It has an ornate baroque church and has not lost all its village charm.

Above Modane, the upper Arc Valley (**Haute Maurienne**) is of greater interest. Apart from **Lanslebourg**, at the foot of the Mont Cenis Pass, the villages have charm and a wealth of baroque art in their churches. The best are at **Avrieux**, **Termignon**, **Lanslevillard** and **Bessans▶**, where the carving tradition is maintained. Termignon is the main gateway to the high mountains of the Vanoise. **Bonneval▶ ▶**, the last village before the long climb to the lofty Iseran Pass (summer skiing), is a showpiece unspoilt mountain village in a severe setting, with a few simple hotels.

A typical Maurienne chalet

Mont Aiguille — 208C3

A table-topped tower on the southern flank of the Vercors, Mont Aiguille (2,086m) is not remotely like a needle. Its previous name, Mont Inaccessible, had to go once an intrepid team had scaled the cliffs in 1492 by order of Charles VIII, to check for a colony of angels. All they encountered were flowers, birds and chamois. It is well seen from the N75 south of Grenoble.

▶ Morzine — 208C3

A large, traditional year-round resort at the heart of the Chablais between Mont Blanc and Lake Geneva, Morzine fills a complicated junction of narrow valleys and suffers from too much traffic. It does, however, have delightful surroundings, dotted with chalets and mountain restaurants – good walking country with or without the help of the various lifts above Morzine and its smaller neighbour, **Les Gets**. A hairpin road and cable-car take you to the clifftop modern resort of **Avoriaz▶** where cars are prohibited.

218

The Croix de Fer and Glandon passes

Start at St-Jean-de-Maurienne.
This splendidly varied 54km of mountain road presents few map-reading difficulties but demands full concentration from the driver at all times, climbing steeply via tunnels and hairpins from the Maurienne up the Arvan Valley before emerging into a beautiful landscape of open high pastures and the modest mountain resort of **St-Sorlin d'Arves**.

D926 as far as Col de la Croix de Fer. D927 to Col du Glandon and La Chambre.
The route switchbacks over the **Croix de Fer** (2,068m) and **Glandon** (1,924m) passes, close neighbours with differing views. To the south of the Croix de Fer, the spiky **Aiguilles d'Arves** (on the left) and the glaciated **Massif Grandes Rousses** together frame the more distant **Meije**.

The **Col du Glandon** gives a good view north to Mont Blanc. The descent to **La Chambre** is also narrow, mostly tortuous and in places steep, requiring careful attention to the road.

Take the N6 for the return journey to St-Jean.

219

Over the mountain from Morzine

Start at Morzine. D354 to Samoëns.
From Morzine it is a beautiful drive over the mountain to **Samoëns** (woods and orchards) via the **Col de Joux Plane**, a popular picnic spot with a view of Mont Blanc. At Samoëns, an old village once famous for its stone masons, a 550-year-old lime tree shades the central square. There are botanical gardens and summer and winter sports facilities, including river rafting and skiing.

D907 to Sixt-Fer-à-Cheval (for excursions to Cirque du Fer à Cheval and Cascade du Rouget).
At **Sixt**, 13th- to 17th-century former abbey buildings surround another fine lime tree. East of Sixt, the road ends beneath a magnificent horseshoe of cliffs and waterfalls (**Fer à Cheval**). To the south, the narrow D29 climbs to the **Cascade du Rouget**; hikers can continue uphill to more waterfalls.

D907 back to Samoëns and Taninges; D902 to Les Gets and Morzine.
The return from Samoëns to Morzine passes the small resort of **Les Gets**, with lifts to **Mont Chéry** (1,829m), a superb viewpoint.

Alpe d'Huez's easy access for today's skiers belies the remoteness of the Oisans, famous in the 19th century for itinerant salesmen, who spent the winter months carrying their village-crafted wares as far afield as the Orient

▶ L'Oisans 208B2

Facing each other across the dark Romanche Valley, **L'Alpe d'Huez** and **Les Deux Alpes** are the big ugly sisters of Dauphiné skiing, with high open snowfields in easy reach of Grenoble. In summer, both offer plenty of sport, including glacier skiing. L'Alpe d'Huez is reached by a famous hairpin climb (a punishing finale to one stage of the Tour de France) from the mineral-rich town of **Bourg d'Oisans**. A summer road continues over the Col de Sarenne to the picturesque old villages of **Clavans** and **Besse**. The narrow **Vénéon Valley**▶▶▶ road, the D530, leads south to the heart of the **Massif des Ecrins**, the highest mountains in the southern Alps and a famous climbing area. At the end of the dark road, **La Bérarde** is an austere village, mainly of interest to climbers. In winter the road is closed beyond **St-Christophe** and its population dwindles to one.

Beside river and main road to the west of the Lautaret Pass, the rough old village of **La Grave** and its Romanesque church are dominated by the mighty pillars and hanging glaciers of the **Meije**▶▶ (3,983m), which is best admired from the road up to **Le Chazelet**, a delightfully rustic village. La Grave has simple hotels, a good cheese shop and a tall, wild ski area.

Serre Ponçon, Lac de 208B1

When full, the V-shaped reservoir at the confluence of the Durance and Ubaye rivers is popular for watersports. **Savines-le-Lac** is the main lakeside resort but is a modern and characterless place. The old town of **Embrun**▶ makes a more appealing base, with simple hotels and an Italianate 12th-century cathedral, where marble lions support the columns of the main doorway. The tourist office is housed in a chapel with 15th-century murals.

A geological *spécialité du pays* is the **Demoiselle Coiffée** – a pillar of earth saved from erosion by the boulder on top. The best examples are beside the D453, the road climbing steeply from **Remollon** (on the Sisteron road) to **Mont Colombis**.

GLACIER CIRCUIT
A two-stage telecabin climbs from La Grave to the Col des Ruillans (3,200m) for a close-up view of the Meije and a distant one of Mont Blanc. The surroundings are glacier: not for walkers. However, in summer it is about an hour's walk from the mid-station up to the picturesque old Evariste Chancel refuge/ restaurant, via the Lac du Puy Vachier, rich in trout. A well-marked path leads down through woods to the river below the village. Stick to the path (cliff danger to the left). The descent from Chancel to La Grave takes about an hour and a half.

The Rhône Valley remains what it has always been: a north–south thoroughfare for travellers and traders. Motorway and railway follow the broad river past power stations, cement factories, unlovely towns and vineyards which produce muscular red and white wines. The motorway plunges through the middle of Lyon – a hazardous crossing in view of the Lyonnais' customary lunacy at the wheel.

Lyon (see also page 217) has had a long history of success, since its foundation in 43 bc and its subsequent elevation to the status of capital in Roman-occupied Gaul. Its strategic position on the banks of the Saône and Rhône rivers, on the route between Paris and the Mediterranean, has made this a prosperous city, and the focus of busy development. There are plenty of aesthetic attractions for visitors – mainly due to the commercial and industrial (silk and textiles) successes of the past: wealthy merchants and bankers of the 16th century built tall, elegant houses which still stand, some having been extended upwards with an extra floor.

To the south of Lyon the mountains of the Vercors and the eastern wall of the Massif Central enclose the valley before it opens out beyond **Montélimar**, city of nougat and gateway to the land of almonds and honey, Provence.

Valley cuisine Food is the main reason to visit the Rhône Valley, rather than pass swiftly through it. The most famous landmarks on a gastronomic itinerary are **Paul Bocuse** at Collonges, a northern suburb of Lyon; **Pyramide** at Vienne; and **Pic** at Valence. These are not the only outstanding restaurants in the region, and many would say they are no longer the best. But they are generally regarded as holy places in the modern history of French cooking.

Valley sights Sightseeing interest is contrastingly modest: an outstanding vintage vehicle museum at **Rochetaillée-sur-Saône**, north of Lyon; a Roman theatre and well preserved temple, and several medieval churches (the cathedral and St-André-le-Bas) at **Vienne**; the new museum and Roman site across the river at **St-Romain-en-Gal**; a restored Romanesque cathedral at **Valence**, where the museum has a fine collection of Roman drawings by Hubert Robert, leading exponent of this favourite 18th-century genre; a comprehensive shoe museum at Romans-sur-Isère; and a few well-sited fortress ruins, notably **Crussol**, near Valence.

North-east of Lyon, the film-set walled village of **Pérouges** (named after the colony of immigrants from Perugia who settled there in the Middle Ages) has been scrupulously restored and preserved, and its various crafts revived, albeit for tourists.

LOCAL POSTMAN HERO
Often overlooked are the pastoral hills of the Drôme, which rise from the Rhône valley east of Valence and Montélimar. Here, in the village of Hauterives, is an extraordinary monument built by one of France's most celebrated self-taught creators, the Facteur (postman) Cheval. His fantastical Palais Idéal freely mixes Hindu, Buddhist and Islamic temple features with European medieval elements. It took 33 years – from 1879 to 1912 – for this determined and inspired man to complete his life's masterwork.

LA VALLOUISE
La Vallouise is a tributary valley of the Durance to the south of Briançon, and one of many remote areas where Waldensian heretics hid from persecution in the Middle Ages. The village of Puy-St-Vincent, now a ski resort, commemorates the 15th-century visit of St Vincent Ferrer.

The valley is the main gateway to the Ecrins National Park, with the might of Mont Pelvoux towering above the small resort of Ailefroide. The road continues to a point where two glaciers (Noir and Blanc) once converged. Now they have retreated, and it is a long hike up to the ice. There is a national park exhibition/information centre near the village of Vallouise (04 92 23 32 31).

La Vallouise see panel   208C1

▶▶ La Vanoise   208C2

The oldest French national park, founded in 1963, is a wilderness of empty high valleys, glaciers and rocky peaks culminating at the 3,855m **Grande Casse**, and bordering the older Italian Gran Paradiso national park. The peripheral area has seen ski resort development on a scale unrivalled elsewhere in the Alps. **Val d'Isère**, **Tignes**, **Les Arcs**, **La Plagne**, **Courchevel**, **Méribel** and **Val Thorens** are the big resorts. More charming alternatives are the old villages of **Pralognan**, **Champagny** and **Peisey-Nancroix** on the Tarentaise side (north) of the park; **Bonneval**, **Termignon** and **Aussois** on the Maurienne side (south). The old village of Champagny-en-Vanoise is a centre of traditional Beaufort cheese, the best of hard French Alpine cheeses. Savoie's baroque churches have all undergone extensive restoration since 1992. Tours and information are available at the tourist office in Bourg-St-Maurice.

Hiking trails cross the park and refuges offer simple accommodation. At the heart of the park, the **Vallon de la Leisse▶** is rich in wildlife. The car park at Bellecombe, 9 miles north of Termignon, is the closest access point.

▶▶ Vercors   208A1

The unbroken walls of the Vercors rise abruptly to peaks of over 2,000m. Behind lies a tranquil, thickly forested highland region. Its striking limestone river gorges converge at **Pont-en-Royans▶** before feeding the Isère. **Villard-de-Lans** is the largest of the modest resorts, a good base for impressive drives: along the dark **Gorges de la Bourne▶** and **Grands Goulets▶▶** (very narrow) and the St-Jean-en-Royans to Vassieux road (D76). The Vercors was a Resistance base until 1944, when German forces launched an aerial assault on the region and the villages of **Vassieux**, **La Chapelle** and **St-Nizier** were razed. Vassieux has a Resistance museum (*Open* Apr–Oct).

Pont-en-Royans, where rivers converge

In 1874, a visiting lawyer recorded his impressions of Bonneval-sur-Arc, at the head of the Haute Maurienne: 'low grey houses, half buried and huddled tightly together for warmth. In winter the inhabitants live in the underground stables warmed by their animals. Wood being rare and coal too expensive, the usual fuel is sun-dried dung. Snow covers the ground for six or seven months a year, often cutting communications and trapping the villagers like marmots in their burrows.'

Sun and shelter Alpine architecture is adapted to the hardships of mountain life. Warmth, exposure to the sun and winter storage space for animals, grain and the staple ingredients of the Alpine diet – long-life cheeses, hams and big disks of dark bread – are the priorities.

In some places villages are widely spread across the steep sunny slope (*adret*) of a valley. **St-Véran**, in the Queyras, is a fine example. Elsewhere, as at **Bonneval**, where the slopes are too steep, the houses are clustered around the church on the valley floor at a safe distance from regular avalanche paths.

Wooden castles Except at high altitude, wood is generally plentiful in the Alps, and widely used in the construction of the chalet (the word is a diminutive of *château*). In the northern Alps, a few old chalets with wooden roofs and chimneys survive. More often, chalet roofs are constructed from rough stone tiles (*lauzes*), gently pitched to support a thick insulating blanket of snow for the winter. In the Vercors, steeper roofs are the custom, and the end walls are traditionallly stepped, to facilitate access to the roof. Most chalets have large, sheltered balconies exposed to the sun, for storing firewood and drying things. Grain is either stored under the eaves or in separate buildings, raised on stone stilts to keep the rats out and to allow air to circulate.

BONNEVAL-SUR-ARC
Although modernised, Bonneval has changed remarkably little (externally, anyway). In the absence of local forest, the houses are built almost entirely of stone, wood being reserved for the balconies. The Bonnevalains still dry dung as a fuel.

223

Alpine architecture at Bonneval

Burgundy & the Jura

▶▶▶ REGION HIGHLIGHTS

Arc-et-Senans
page 226–7

Autun *page 227*

Auxerre *page 227*

Beaune *page 230*

Brou *page 232*

Flavigny-sur-Ozerain
page 233

Fontenay Abbey
pages 231, 233

Tanlay, Château de
page 239

Tournus and Brancion
page 239

Vézelay *page 239*

224

THIS IS THE WARM HEARTLAND of gastronomic France, a welcoming and colourful landscape of dazzling mustard fields, rich pastures and golden villages. There are snails (France's finest) and smelly cheeses, best beef from the gleaming white Charolais herds, and the sumptuous wines of the Côte d'Or. The best wine tourism is at Beaune, headquarters of the industry. Great pageantry surrounds the climax of the wine calendar in November: a famous harvest festival and wine auction at Beaune.

The fancy dress and the noble brotherhoods of *vignerons* recall the golden age of Burgundy, when its 14th- and 15th-century Valois dukes lived in splendour appropriate to the Imperial status they craved. In the Hundred Years' War they skilfully switched allegiance between French and English camps. Their real power base was in the Low Countries. Only when the English were finally expelled could the French crown turn its attention to the problem of Burgundy. The struggle between the valiant knight, Duke Charles the Bold, and the arch manipulator, King Louis IX, can be seen as the clash of two eras. Charles went down fighting in 1477 and France took control. In an earlier age (10th to 12th centuries), Burgundy saw the foundation of two monastic orders: first at Cluny, later at Cîteaux near Dijon, where Bernard of Clairvaux led the reaction to Cluniac decadence. Burgundy has fine Romanesque churches and abbeys in unadorned Cistercian style.

The old county of Burgundy, or Franche Comté, is quite different – a remote region of forests, mountains (the Jura) and notoriously unruly inhabitants. The Jura offers its own unusual wines and an escape to the simple life.

The contents of Louis Pasteur's house in Arbois have been perfectly preserved

PASTEURISATION
Louis Pasteur (1822–95) was born at Dole and five years later moved with his family to Arbois. Pasteur discovered the causes of fermentation and developed the heat treatment of milk known as pasteurisation; his work opened a new era of preventative and curative medicine.

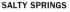
SALTY SPRINGS
The salt springs in Lons-le-Saunier and Salins-les-Bains have been exploited since prehistoric times.
At Salins, a handsome old town hemmed in between hills beside the fast flowing Furieuse river, the salt mine only ceased operating recently, but it is open to visitors. In underground galleries, salty brine was pumped from a depth of 250m. The brine was then reduced to salt in large cauldrons over a coal fire. These days the salt waters of Salins are used only for medicinal purposes (whence Salins-les-Bains).

Ain, Vallée de l' 225C1

The much-dammed River Ain feeds hydro-electric plants as it descends through rapids, gorges and reservoirs on the 190km journey from its source near Champagnole to the Rhône. In and around the upper valley, watery beauty spots include the **Gorges de la Langouette▶** and the **Perte de l'Ain▶**, where the river disappears into a rocky cleft. But the outstanding attraction is the **Cascades du Hérisson▶▶**, a series of magnificent waterfalls reached by the D326 (and subsequently on foot) from Doucier. There is fishing and boating on the Lac de Chalain, and a number of watersports centres on the long stretches of reservoir lower down the Ain.

▶ Ancy-le-Franc, Château de 224B3

A fine Renaissance château, Ancy-le-Franc was designed in the mid-16th century by the Italian Sebastiano Serlio, in a new classical style. The sobriety of the exterior is quite different from the exuberant ornamentation of earlier Loire châteaux, and contrasts with the more complex design of the inner court. Inside (guided tours), much of the furniture and decoration is original, designed by Primaticcio and the School of Fontainebleau (*Open* Apr–Nov daily).

▶ Arbois 225C2

The home of Louis Pasteur is an attractive honey-coloured small town beside the river Cuisance, close to some of the best Jura scenery. Arbois produces interesting, little-known wines, including one of the best of all rosés, much appreciated by Henri IV, and the exceptionally strong and expensive 'vin jaune' (from Château-Chalon and Arbois), which is not bottled for years and keeps for up to a century. *Poularde au vin jaune* is a ubiquitous local speciality. *Vin de Paille* is made from overripe grapes traditionally dried on straw. There is a small wine museum near the arcaded central square, and the main production house, Henri Maire, opens its doors to visitors and offers tastings (not of *vin jaune*!). Pasteur's house is beside the river on the edge of town (guided tours only; *closed* winter and Thu).

▶▶ Arc-et-Senans 225C2

Although incomplete, the monumental complex of buildings (Salines Royales) erected for the royal saltworks near Salins is a rare and fascinating survival of late 18th-century industrial architecture, by the visionary Claude Nicolas Ledoux (1736–1806). Eleven buildings of the ambitious project for an entire Utopian town, built on a concentric plan, form a semi-circle around the director's house, with a handsome colonnaded portico. It is flanked by the main salt evaporation halls, where salt was produced until the works were abandoned in the late 19th century. The buildings are now used for various temporary exhibitions, a superb museum of Ledoux's work and ideas and a salt museum (Open daily).

▶▶ Autun   224B2
Autun has interesting survivals from antiquity including two town gateways and fragments of the largest Roman theatre in Gaul. But its great treasure is the 12th-century cathedral of **St-Lazare**▶▶ with outstanding carved tympanum and a wealth of lively carving on the capitals inside. The nearby **Musée Rolin**▶ has a rich collection of Gallo Roman and Gothic statuary (a lovely polychrome Virgin), and the 15th-century Moulins Master's beautiful painting of the Nativity.

▶ Auxerre   224A3
An old town of cobbled streets and timbered houses, Auxerre makes a good first Burgundian halt for motorway travellers on the way south from Paris. The most central of the three churches turning their backs to the river is the Gothic cathedral of **St-Etienne**▶. Its elaborate lopsided façade was robbed of much of its sculptural decoration during the Wars of Religion. There are beautiful 13th-century windows inside, and 11th-century frescoes in the crypt. The **crypt**▶▶ of the former abbey of St-Germain is France's oldest, with frescoes from the mid-9th century, depicting scenes from the saint's life. The main square (place Leclerc) has a Renaissance gateway with a 17th-century astronomical clock.

▶ Avallon   224A3
Old Avallon, a well-preserved walled town, is a good place to stretch the legs at the end of a day at the wheel and has hotels and restaurants for most pockets in town and nearby. Inside the ramparts, all is convincingly old and cobbled. A 15th-century watch-tower spans the main street, the old church of St-Lazare has good carvings on the façade doorway and there are gardens outside the walls, looking out over rolling Burgundian countryside and the leafy **Cousin Valley**▶ (see page 233), which has good secluded hotels.

BURGUNDY CANALS
France's three greatest rivers, the Loire, Seine and Rhône, have added to Burgundy's navigable rivers to create a 1,200km network of waterways, now little used for commercial traffic (except for the Canal du Centre between Digoin and Chalon-sur-Saône) and ideal for slow-moving houseboat holidays. The best choices are the Canal du Bourgogne (at its best in the Auxois, between Tonnerre and Vénarey); and the Canal du Nivernais, which crosses wonderfully peaceful countryside between Decize and Cravant (south of Auxerre). Two of the main hirers are Bâteaux de Bourgogne at Auxerre (tel: 03 86 72 92 10) and Burgundy Cruisers at Cravant (tel: 03 86 81 54 55). Both offer bicycle hire.

227

The former abbey of St-Germain in Auxerre, founded in the 6th century, now houses a fine arts museum

The hills of Burgundy produce one of the world's greatest white wines (Montrachet), the most expensive red (Romanée Conti) and everyday Beaujolais by the unpretentious boatload. About four-fifths of all burgundy is red.

The medieval village of Berzé-le-Châtel, in the heart of the Mâconnais

228

The wines The greatest vineyards form a long narrow strip (only 4,000 hectares in total) along a south-east-facing slope extending south from Dijon and past Beaune. This is the Côte d'Or, of which there are two halves. Between Nuits St Georges and Dijon, the Côte de Nuits vineyards (including Gevrey Chambertin, Vosne Romanée and Vougeot) produce red wine. The southern half is the Côte de Beaune, which makes red and white. Villages include Aloxe Corton, Pommard, Meursault and the two Montrachets (Chassagne and Puligny).

Golden-green wines of a different style, but scarcely less prestigious, are produced at Chablis near Auxerre. Geographically and in the taste of its wines, Chablis is closer to Champagne than the Côte d'Or.

The output of the small Côte Chalonnaise, a few miles south of the Côte d'Or, is no match for the Grands Crus to the north but is fine wine by any other criterion. Mercurey and Rully are the best known appellations. South of Tournus, a large area of the Mâconnais and Beaujolais produces excellent everyday wines, mostly white in the Mâconnais, almost all red in Beaujolais. In north-western Burgundy, Pouilly-sur-Loire's white wines have more in common with those of its neighbour Sancerre than any burgundy. Pouilly Fumé is its best wine, not to be confused with Pouilly Fuissé, pride of the Mâconnais.

The grapes In Burgundy proper, the Chardonnay grape is used throughout for white wine, Pinot Noir for red. Pouilly Fumé is made from the Sauvignon grape, Pouilly-sur-Loire from the Chasselas. In the Beaujolais, the Gamay thrives on sandy ground, giving light and fruity wine which is drunk young – often within weeks of the harvest (*beaujolais nouveau*).

Vineyards and tasting Many of the finest vineyards belonged to the Church, whose estates were broken up after the Revolution. The high price of the best wines is another reason for fragmentation: prime vineyards cost as much as 5 million francs a hectare and change hands in tiny lots. The 50-hectare vineyard of Clos de Vougeot is split between 60 growers, who produce wines of different character and quality all called Clos de Vougeot.

Many of the big *négotiants* (Bouchard and Drouhin) are based at Beaune. A few welcome visitors and offer tastings but many charge a fee and there is pressure to buy. Much the best alternative is to pay to visit the Marché Aux Vins in Beaune, an association of private wine-growers, where a fine selection of bottles stand open at your disposal, in tasting order – from white to Beaujolais

A MONKS' CHATEAU
There are few impressive vineyard châteaux to rival those in the Médoc. Clos de Vougeot is one of the few exceptions to the no-châteaux rule. Originally a Cistercian property, it is now the headquarters of the proud Confrérie des Chevaliers du Tastevin, who hold banquets and initiation ceremonies there. The interior (guided tours) has vaulted cellars and old wine-presses.

to the big reds of the Côte d'Or – with only discreet supervision and a generous time limit to make sure you don't over-indulge. A *tastevin* and spittoons are provided. Tasting at the 16th-century Château de Meursault is organised similarly.

Beaujolais is higher and steeper hill country than Burgundy, almost mountainous in places. Driving is slow but pretty, and many of the villages have great charm, with tastings at wine growers' co-operatives. The best area to explore is south-west of Villefranche, although this is not Grand Cru country. There are picturesque ruins at Châtillon and Oingt, 9th-century murals and capitals in the church at Ternand.

Classification Burgundy production and labelling is strictly controlled and classified. On the Côte d'Or, the best vineyards (called *climats*) are designated Grands Crus (32, including Richebourg, Romanée Conti, Chambertin and Montrachet). Next comes a larger number of Premiers Crus, then vineyards entitled to use the communal name (Gevrey Chambertin, Beaune, etc), finally plain Bourgogne. Chablis also has Grands Crus and Premiers Crus, followed by Chablis and Petit Chablis. In the Mâconnais, Pouilly-Fuissé and St-Véran are the best appellations. Mâcon plus the name of a village (Mâcon-Viré, for example) indicates a better wine than Mâcon Villages, which is better than plain Mâcon. Beaujolais also has a superior subsection of Beaujolais-Villages and ten Grands Crus, of which Moulin à Vent is usually rated the best. Unlike most Beaujolais wines, it keeps.

OENOLOGICAL PATIENCE
The only problem with Burgundy's aromatic Pinot Noir red wines is that they require patience. Unimpressive when young, red burgundies only reach their optimum between five and eight years after harvest and so do not come cheap. The alternative is the fruity Beaujolais whose exaggerated world demand is such that a lot of mixing goes on…
Things look up, however, with the whites. These are delicious within two years of harvest, although a fine Chablis Premier Cru peaks at ten years. Recent exceptional years were 1990, 1993, 1995 and 1996.

If half a day en route is all you can afford for the region, devote it to Beaune, capital of burgundy with a small 'b' (the wine), at the heart of the area's most prestigious vineyards. Ducal capital until the 14th century, it remains a medium-sized town with its old walls and town gates intact. Its position at a motorway junction two-and-a-half hours south of Paris is ideal for a break in the journey.

BEFORE YOU LEAVE
The 12th- to 13th-century church of Notre-Dame has beautiful tapestries of the Life of the Virgin (not on show in winter). There is an excellent wine museum near the church, good wine and food shops on the pedestrian streets near the market square, and an unmissable wine-tasting opportunity at the Marché Aux Vins, opposite the Hôtel Dieu (see page 228).

230

Hôtel Dieu On the main square in the heart of the old town, the market hall houses the tourist office. Across the street is the Hôtel Dieu, an outwardly unspectacular charitable hospital founded in 1443 by Nicolas Rolin, Chancellor of Burgundy and great art patron.

A unique survival, the Hôtel Dieu functioned as a hospital until 1971 and is now an old people's home, partly staffed by a few remaining nuns and funded by the famous annual auction of the produce of its many Côte de Beaune vineyards. The auction sets the annual price level for burgundy and is the centre-piece of the 'Trois Glorieuses', a three-day wine festival on the third weekend in November. The other two events are banquets at Clos de Vougeot and Meursault.

From the entrance portico, you can glimpse the brilliantly colourful tiled roof of the Hôtel Dieu's beautiful courtyard, the most elaborate roof in Burgundy, but it is well worth entering to see the old pharmacy, the kitchens and, above all, the vaulted 70m ward, which remains in its original disposition: beds (with room for two in each) in the nave, curtained off from the choir and altar except for services. The original altarpiece, Van der Weyden's magnificent polyptych of the Last Judgement, is now displayed in a separate museum section, with tapestries also from the main ward.

Beaune lies in the very heart of Burgundy's most celebrated vineyards

In 910, 12 monks left the Abbey of Baume les Messieurs and founded a new community at Cluny, not far from Mâcon. Under abbots answerable only to Rome, Cluny's influence spread rapidly, and hundreds of dependent houses were founded throughout Europe.

The Abbey of Cluny The mother Abbey's 177m-long third church, built between 1080 and 1130 at the height of Cluniac power, was the largest and most splendid church in Christendom, unsurpassed by any Gothic cathedral. If the heavenly host could be content with earthly habitation, declared one impressed visitor, this would be the ambulatory of angels. Cluny later fell into decline under absentee abbots and was systematically dismantled after the Revolution, when the Cluniac order was suppressed. A single tower of the transept remains standing to give an idea of its scale and style. A grain store also survives, and is now a museum housing, amongst other things, a collection of capitals from the church.

Above: Berzé-la-Ville; below: Cluny

Cistercian austerity Cluniac churches were erected to glorify God; the more splendid, the better. In 1098, a new abbey was founded at Cîteaux near Dijon, in a spirit of reaction to the excesses of Cluniac life and art. A local nobleman, known to history as St Bernard of Clairvaux, went to Cîteaux in 1112 and later founded an abbey at Clairvaux (now a prison; tours May–Oct, Sat afternoon). Preaching a return to the frugal spirit of the Benedictine rule, he condemned ornamental figurative carving and the waste of money lavished on vast churches; for him, even bell-towers were superfluous. Life under Cistercian rule was austere in the extreme, and the architectural style of the monasteries is one of unadorned simplicity. There is no better example than **Fontenay** (see page 233). Cîteaux was suppressed in 1790 but revived in 1898 and rebuilt as the headquarters of the Trappist order.

CLUNIAC ARCHITECTURE
Of many examples of Cluniac architecture in Burgundy (especially in the Brionnais), Paray-le-Monial's church, contem-porary with Cluny, is almost a replica of the lost original on reduced scale. A chapel at Berzé-la-Ville (between Mâcon and Cluny) has a series of early frescoes, probably by the artists employed at Cluny itself (*Open* Apr–Oct).

Besançon lies in a deeply wooded basin, almost enclosed as the River Doubs loops around it. Its old centre is now entirely closed to cars – only buses whisk you around.

CHICKEN EXTRAORDINAIRE
King of chickens, chicken of kings: the *poulet de Bresse* is to the battery-reared oven-ready bird what a Grand Cru burgundy is to *vin ordinaire*. Bresse is in fact a poultry appellation, with limited output and strict production rules. The birds are sold with a seal, a numbered ring and a certificate of origin. In their early months they enjoy the freedom of the farmyard before spending two weeks in a 'finishing room' fed on a mixture of creamy milk and wheat. The result is peerless white meat, firm but succulent, with no fat.

▶ Besançon   225D3

The capital of Franche-Comté, Besançon is a place for sightseeing on a wet day. It is a dignified, if somewhat gloomy city, with fine façades along the Grande Rue, notably the Renaissance **Palais Grenvelle**, which, in honour of the city's renown as a clock- and watch-making centre is being transformed into a 'time museum' (Musée du Temps, due to open in June 2000). The cathedral dates from many periods, with equally varied contents, including a 19th-century **astronomic clock▶▶**, the 16th-century tomb of diplomat-cum-art patron, Ferry Carondelet, abbot of Montbenoît, and Fra Bartolommeo's *Virgin and Child* (1512) which he commissioned. The **Musée des Beaux Arts et d'Archéologie▶▶** has particularly rich collections of paintings, ceramics and sculpture, including works by Titian, David, Géricault, Renoir, Bonnard and many local Courbets. The **citadel▶▶** encloses a zoo and several museums.

Bresse   225C1

From the Saône to the Ain at the foot of the Jura, the Bresse plain is rapidly crossed now that there is uninterrupted motorway from Mâcon to Geneva. Travellers who prefer the slow road can admire its hand-some old barns and farm houses, their roofs almost reaching the ground. Its busy market town, **Bourg-en-Bresse▶**, is great fun on market day (Wed and Sat morning). The main attraction is the church at Brou (see below).

▶▶ Brou   225C1

A suburb of Bourg-en-Bresse, Brou contains rare treasures of late Gothic art in the 16th-century monastery church, behind which lies a story. Margaret of Bourbon vowed to upgrade the priory if her husband (Count of Bresse) recovered from a hunting accident. He did, but she died soon afterwards. When their son Philibert died young in 1504, his young widow, Margaret of Austria, took it upon herself to fulfil the promise. The choir contains the three beautiful marble tombs of Philibert and both Margarets, painted windows, and carved wood and stonework, all of breathtaking quality. The adjacent monastery is now a regional **museum▶**.

▶ Châtillon-sur-Seine   224B3

The **museum▶▶** of this peaceful little town has a huge (1.64m) 6th-century bc bronze vase, found with jewellery in a princess's tomb at Vix, 7km north of Châtillon.

The Auxois

Start at Avallon. Take the D86 to Noyers.
Noyers is delightful: admire its town gates, timbered houses and towers from the old fortifications.

D956 takes you to Rougemont.
Montbard near Rougemont was the home of 18th-century natural historian, the Comte de Buffon. The forge he founded near Buffon has been restored (*Open* Jun–Sep).

A detour on D905/D32 takes you to the Abbaye de Fontenay.
This is the outstanding example of Cistercian simplicity and peace.

Timbered house at Noyers

Back to D905 and on to Venarey-les-Laumes and Alise-Ste-Reine.
Alise-Ste-Reine has a museum with finds from a Gallo-Roman town, thought to be *Alesia,* site of the Gauls' heroic last stand against Rome in 52 bc. Vercingetorix's statue looms above.

233

D954 to Bussy-Rabutin.
The Château de Bussy-Rabutin (guided tours) has an entertaining collection of portraits of warriors and royal mistresses.

Take D19/D6 to Courceau, N71 to Chanceaux and D103C to St-Germain-Source-Seine.
The river issues from a cave 2km south of St-Germain. A Roman temple once stood near by.

Take D103C/D10 to Thénissey and Hauteroche, then D9 to Flavigny-sur-Ozerain.
Flavigny-sur-Ozerain is a walled village of tumbledown charm, known for its aniseed sweets.

Continue to Semur-en-Auxois.
Admirably set on a rocky spur almost encircled by the Armançon, this old town still bristles with towers. Take the D103B 4km south for bathing and watersports at the Lac de Pont.

Take the D954 to Cussy-les-Forges via Epoisses, N6 to Magny, D427 to Pontaubert , D957 back to Avallon.
A double row of fortifications encloses the elegant château at Epoisses, a village renowned for its cheese. The rest of the route follows the pretty Cousin Valley, skirting Avallon.

KIR

Bourgogne aligoté (local white wine made from the inferior *aligoté* grape) mixed with Dijonnais *crème de cassis* (blackcurrant liqueur) is a traditional regional aperitif, now named after Canon Kir, Mayor of Dijon during the 1940s. Kir served the drink at all public functions in a bid to boost flagging sales of *cassis*. In what many kirophiles would consider an excess of promotional zeal, the canon's recipe was one-third *cassis* to two-thirds wine; one-fifth to four-fifths is a more palatable mixture.

Part of the Palais des Ducs is sited on top of remains of the walls of the Roman castrum

▶ Dijon   225C3

The first Valois duke, Philip the Bold, made Burgundy a great independent power at the heart of Europe by marrying the heiress of Flanders. Dijon became his capital and here, with the help of Flemish artists, Philip and his successors built themselves a magnificent palace and an equally lavish necropolis, the Chartreuse de Champmol. Both have been transformed and now only hint at their original splendour. Dijon still has a core of picturesque medieval streets, but it is primarily a busy industrial city, great for gourmets (as you would expect of the Burgundian capital, famous for its mustard and *crème de cassis*) but short on charm.

The **Palais des Ducs▶** overlooks the semicircular colonnade of the elegant 17th-century place de la Libération, at the end of Dijon's main shopping axis, the rue de la Liberté. As well as the town hall, the palace houses the **Musée des Beaux Arts▶▶**, with medieval kitchens and an outstanding collection of sculpture, of which the highlights are two masterpieces of 14th- to 15th-century Burgundo-Flemish art, the tombs of Philip the Bold and John the Fearless (with consort) in the vast Salle des Gardes. Both the tombs and the beautiful altarpieces in the same room came from the chartreuse of **Champmol**, now a mental hospital (towards the A38 motorway). Most of its original buildings and works of art have been destroyed or removed, but it retains the **Puits de Moïse▶** (Moses' Well), a magnificent group of six prophets (Moses is the one with horns) by 15th-century sculptor Claus Sluter. Plans are underway to reconstruct the chapel, as only its doorway (with more Sluter Statues) still stands (access currently limited).

Dijon's churches are of minor interest. The cathedral has a round 10th-century crypt, and St-Michel a good Renaissance façade. Notre-Dame's Gothic façade has rows of grimacing monsters and a 14th-century Jacquemart (mechanical clock with figures hammering the chimes). The most interesting old streets in the **medieval zone▶** behind the palace are rue des Forges (where the 15th-century Hôtel Chambellan is the tourist office), rue Verrerie and rue de la Chouette.

▶ Doubs, Vallée du 225D2

From its source in a forest cave near the village of Mouthe, the River Doubs charts an indecisive course, flowing five times as far as a crow would fly on its way towards the Saône. The most beautiful stretch of the valley is where the river defines the Franco-Swiss border between the **Saut du Doubs▶▶** (a splendid 30m waterfall near Morteau) and the village of Goumois: impressive limestone gorges and good canoeing and trout fishing. In the upper valley, Malbuisson is a peaceful lakeside resort, also popular with fishermen. Between Pontarlier and Morteau, **Montbenoît's abbey church▶** has a richly decorated 16th-century choir with beautiful carved stalls.

Lons-le-Saunier 225C2

Lons-le-Saunier, an old Roman salt town, is now the prefecture of the Jura and still functions as a spa. Rouget de Lisle, composer of the *Marseillaise,* was born at No 24 rue du Commerce in 1760 and the town clock plays a few notes of the tune on the hour.

▶ Moulins 224A2

The capital of the dukes of Bourbon, big players in the politics of medieval and Renaissance France, Moulins is now a quiet market town. The cathedral has beautiful 15th-century stained-glass windows and the famous **triptych** by the Master of Moulins (1500), with donor portraits by the Duke and Duchess of Bourbon. The **Musée d'Art et d'Archéologie▶** in the old Bourbon château is worth a visit. Mechanical figures hammer the chimes on the 15th-century Jacquemart clock-tower.

▶ Nevers 224A2

A grey town at the confluence of the Nièvre and Loire, Nevers has been famous for its spun glass and faïence porcelain since the 16th century, when Lodovico Gonzaga of Mantua, Duke of Nevers, imported specialist artists from Italy. The industry survives, and there are good collections of both in the town **museum▶**. Other buildings of interest include the cathedral; the turreted 15th- to 16th-century ducal palace (housing the tourist office); the Porte du Croux; and **St-Etienne▶▶**. The tomb of Bernadette Subirous, visionary of Lourdes, is displayed in the convent of St Gildard.

THEATRICAL VIEWS
In the vineyard hills between Lons-le-Saunier and Arbois, erosion has carved a series of splendid valleys (*reculées*) ending in abrupt theatres (*cirques*) of cliffs with caves, resurgent streams, stalactites and underground lakes. The Cirque de Baume heads a valley occupied by the ancient abbey of Baume les Messieurs. There is a good viewpoint over the valley from the D471 east of Lons-le-Saunier. A similar clifftop belvedere over-looks the Reculée des Planches and Cirque du Fer à Cheval beside the D469 Arbois–to–Champagnole road.

235

When in Lons-le-Saunier, don't miss an improvised sandwich of Jura's celebrated hard cheese, Cómtè. Five hundred litres of milk are needed for a 50kg cheese

Nevers Cathedral is a composite of several centuries; the 6th-century baptistery was discovered in July 1944, after heavy bombing damaged the Gothic choir

GUSTAVE COURBET
In Parisian café society Courbet posed as a rough peasant, embraced revolutionary politics and professed an anti-everything philosophy of art, conveniently known as Realism. Returning often to Ornans, he painted local landscapes, hunting and village scenes, including the still disturbing *Burial at Ornans* (1850; Musée d'Orsay), executed on a grand scale. His favourite subject, however, was himself. After a spell in jail for helping to pull down Napoleon's column at place Vendôme in 1871, Courbet spent his last years in Swiss exile.

▶ Ornans   225D2

In this small Jura town between Besançon and Pontarlier, old ramshackle houses prettily overhang the waters of the River Loue against a backdrop of wooded escarpments that are instantly recognisable from the work of painter Gustave Courbet (1819–77). His birthplace on the left bank near the bridge has become a museum.

La Puisaye   224A3

South-west of Auxerrre lies the relatively unexplored region of La Puisaye, familiar to many through the writings of Colette (full name Sidonie Gabrielle Claudine Colette), who spent her early childhood at St-Sauveur-en-Puisaye (its château is now the **Musée Colette**).

Apart from the quiet beauty of the area, with its woodland, hedgerows, meadows and many lakes, the main reason for coming here is to visit the 20 or so churches decorated with exceptionally fine and unusual murals dating from as early as the 12th-century (see margin text).

La Puisaye has also been famous for its pottery since the 14th century, and numerous pottery fairs and markets still abound. Old earthenware is best seen at the **Musée d'Art Régional▶** at Villiers-Saint-Benoît, the **Chateau de Ratilly** and the **Musée du Grès de Puisaye** in Saint-Amand. At **Moutiers** you can visit the vast 18th-century horizontal kiln (75m3) used to fire Puisaye household earthenware, still operational today. Both the frescoes and the pottery made use of the locally-mined ochre, exported in vast quantity throughout the 19th century. Today only one mine remains and can be found at Saint-Amand.

Les Rousses   225D2

On a high (1,100m) plateau at the foot of the summit ridge of the Jura mountains, Les Rousses is a busy summer and winter resort, with watersports on its **lake▶**, walking and riding in the forest.

In winter there are long cross-country ski trails and the Jura's best downhill skiing (lifts up to 1,680m). Local cheese and butter is made at the dairy, which you can visit. There is more skiing at the Col de la Faucille (1,300m), 18km up the N5 towards Switzerland. Mont Blanc, 80km away, is visible on a clear day.

Saulieu and the Morvan 224B3

Saulieu is what the French call an *étape gastronomique*: a punctuation mark on an ancient thoroughfare, with a long-established reputation for good restaurants, ideal for an overnight of over-indulgence. It still lives up to its reputation. The town can also boast beautiful carved capitals in the 12th-century basilica (**St-Andoche▶**), and a bronze statue of a bull. This is the acclaimed masterpiece of the sculptor Pompon, born at Saulieu in 1855, who trained with Rodin.

To the west of Saulieu, the **Morvan hills▶▶** stretch north to Avallon and south to Autun. The Morvan is Burgundy's wilderness and a regional natural park, with fast-flowing rivers for canoeists and fishermen, reservoirs for watersports and hydro-electric power, rocky escarpments for climbers, and forests for walkers. However, its peaks scarcely soar, and the views from its finest belvedere (Mont Beuvray 821m, near Autun) do not take the breath away. For this sort of holiday, there are better regions – the Massif Central, for example. Château Chinon is the main accommodation centre.

▶ Sens 224A4

Northern gateway to Burgundy, Sens is a moderately attractive country town with the first pure **Gothic cathedral▶** to be built in France, begun in the mid-12th century. Sculptures around the main doorway, much damaged in the Revolution, include a statue of St Stephen, to whom the cathedral is dedicated. The interior has fine medieval and Renaissance stained glass; the oldest windows are on the north side of the choir, and include a depiction of the murder of archbishop Thomas à Becket of Canterbury, who had spent six years at nearby Pontigny hiding from the ill-disposed English king, Henry II. The **treasury▶▶** is unusually rich in vestments, tapestries and miscellaneous religious *objets d'art*.

▶ Solutré 224B1

The great rock of Solutré hangs over the best vineyards in the Mâconnais (Pouilly and Fuissé) like an unfurling wave. The foot of the cliff has been excavated to reveal the bones of 100,000 horses, from the period 15,000 to 12,000 bc, now known as the Solutrean age. A few human skeletons and artefacts from earlier and later periods have also been found. These are now housed in the Musée Départemental de Préhistoire at the foot of the rock (*Closed* Dec–Jan and Tue).

HORSEMEAT
Place of ritual sacrifice or prehistoric knacker's yard? The usual explanation for the hapless horses of Solutré is that the local inhabitants cornered wild horses on top of the rock and scared them with fire into jumping off the cliff. Down below, the dead animals were cooked and eaten, and their bones discarded. An early example of *boucherie chevaline*.

Sens lies on the banks of the Yonne which joins the Seine to the north, bringing heavy river traffic

Drive

The Charollais and the Brionnais

This is a tour of Burgundy at its most picturesque: pastures dappled with white Charollais cattle; golden churches (keys usually from the *patronne* at the café next door); beret-clad locals with baguettes under their arms pedalling rusty bicycles.

Start at Paray-le-Monial.
Paray-le-Monial's 12th-century basilica of Sacré-Coeur is no humble village church but a majestic example of Cluniac Romanesque architecture, a smaller version of the demolished abbey church at Cluny itself.

Take D34 then D10 to Marcigny. Continue on D989 to Semur-en-Brionnais and D9 to St-Julien-de-Jonzy and Iguerande.
The tour continues via a series of smaller churches in more rustic surroundings, with octagonal towers and richly carved doorways and capitals: Anzy-le-Duc, Semur-en-Brionnais, St-Julien-de-Jonzy and Iguerande.

Take the D482 to Pouilly-sous-Charlieu, then D487 as far as Charlieu.
Charlieu is a busy little market town with fragments of an old abbey. There are guided tours of the ruins, but the best part is the 12th-century carved doorway of the porch, visible from outside.

The route continues along the D987 to La Clayette and D193 as far as Drée.
Both La Clayette and Drée have interesting châteaux to admire from outside, but only Drée can be visited, in summer.

Take D325/D41 to Dompierre-les-Ormes and continue via D41 and D379 to Butte de Suin.
The route threads its way through the wooded hills and farmlands of the Charollais passing Pézanin arboretum, with hundreds of exotic species (near Dompierre-les-Ormes), and offering a choice of panoramic picnic spots – the Montagne de St-Cyr near Montmelard (771m) or the Butte de Suin (593m).

D17 and N79 take you back to Paray-le-Monial via Charolles.
Charolles has given its name to the finest provider of steak to French tables. Apart from this, unless your visit coincides with the weekly cattle market (Wed), the town is of little interest.

Further on, Perrecy-les-Forges has an old priory with beautiful carvings in the porch.

▶ Tanlay, Château de   *224B3*

A gracious moated Renaissance château near Tonnerre, Tanlay has elegant round towers, bell-shaped domes, and swans in the moat. The interior (guided tours) has period furniture, sculpted chimney-pieces and a *trompe l'oeil* gallery (*Closed* Tue and mid-Nov–Mar).

Ternant   *224B3*

This humble village church, in the middle of nowhere, contains two beautiful wooden **triptychs▶** donated in 1435 by Duke Philip the Good's chamberlain, Philippe de Ternant, who is portrayed in both works.

▶▶ Tournus   *224B2*

Tournus is a quiet town sandwiched between the motorway and the Saône, and dominated by the towers of **St-Philibert▶▶**, one of the oldest and finest of France's great Romanesque churches. In the cobbled centre, old houses and former abbey buildings cluster beneath the martial walls and towers of the 11th- to 12th-century church. Inside, massive unadorned pillars of salmon-coloured stone support a series of transverse barrel vaults. Oldest of all is the crypt with several Roman columns and 12th-century frescoes. From Tournus, the D14 west takes you to **Brancion▶▶▶** (15km), a picturesque semi-ruined fortified village.

▶▶▶ Vézelay   *224A3*

The single street of a picturesque old village with some fine old houses, usually overrun with tourists, climbs a steep hill towards a great **pilgrimage church▶▶▶**. By laying false claim to the relics of Mary Magdalen, the abbey at Vézelay became a popular stop on the pilgrimage to Compostela. St Bernard of Clairvaux launched the Second Crusade there in 1146. The present church, which was rescued from dilapidation by the much-maligned Viollet le Duc in 1840, dates mostly from the 12th century. Its most striking features are the colourful alternation of chocolate and golden stone in the arches and bands of the vault; and beautiful relief carving over the doorway leading from narthex to nave and on the capitals along the nave; as well as the sheer luminosity of the interior. Concerts are held in this magical setting in summer.

239

The highlight of Tanlay's château is the painted ceiling (School of Fontainebleau) in the Tour de la Ligue depicting courtiers as divinities

RECOMMENDED WALKS
Vézelay is an excellent starting point for walking, both in the countryside under the 'colline eternelle' and further afield in the Morvan Regional Park. The tourist office has all the necessary information. A good first stop is the Château de Bazoches, home of France's great founder of civil engineering, Vauban, 10km south of Vézelay (*Open* Apr–Oct).

Alsace-Lorraine & the North

▶▶▶ REGION HIGHLIGHTS

Amiens *page 242*
Arras *page 242*
Colmar *page 245*
Hunspach *page 259*
Nancy *page 251*
Reims *page 253*
Ronchamp *page 254*
Route des Crétes
page 246
Route du Vin *page 247*
Strasbourg *page 255*
Troyes *page 259*

THE NORTH PROSPERED in the Middle Ages, and the profits of the great trading towns were channelled into Gothic buildings of unequalled splendour in Amiens, Laon or Reims. There is fine building from other periods too, as in the Renaissance squares of Arras and Charleville-Mézières. While the Loire may be the natural habitat of the *château-de-luxe*, this border country is studded with fortress-châteaux of all ages, from fearsome feudal ruins like Coucy to the star-shaped strongholds of Louis XIV and the indestructible remains of Hitler's Atlantic Wall.

The countryside, too, is worth exploring, especially where the bare and spacious plateaux give way to the lush valleys of slow-moving rivers like the Somme. With its

ALSACE - LORRAINE AND THE NORTH

superb sandy beaches and high cliffs alternating with great sweeps of sand-dunes, the Channel coast is one of France's finest. Its ports, Calais, Boulogne and Dunkerque, are among the country's busiest. The chalk hills and escarpments of champagne country around Reims and Epernay lead to Lorraine, with heavy industry in the north and its elegant capital, Nancy, in the south. The wooded Vosges Mountains guard the way to the Rhine Valley and Alsace. Indisputably French, this easternmost province has a Germanic flavour expressed in its dialect, its food and wine, and in the utter charm of its half-timbered and flower-bedecked towns and villages, from Strasbourg, one of the capitals of the new Europe, to the humblest wine village along the Route du Vin.

ALSATIAN BEER FAME
Legend has it that France's patron saint of beer, Arnoldus, provided a miraculous draught of the foaming liquid for the pall-bearers at his funeral. Arnoldus was Bishop of Metz in Lorraine, and while his province still brews beers of reputation, it is neighbouring Alsace that has acquired international fame with Germanic-sounding and tasting brands like Kronenbourg. In the industrial North, as well as lagers the many breweries also make top-fermented ale-like beers in Belgian style, as well as a curious 'red' beer.

▶ Amiens
240A3

Much battered in two world wars and extensively modernised since, the ancient capital of Picardy on the banks of the Somme has a glorious Gothic **cathedral▶▶▶** with an array of sculpture adorning the glorious west front which captures the visitor's attention. This Bible story in stone focuses on the famous statue of Christ known as 'Le Beau Dieu'. The serene simplicity of the interior is enhanced by the incredible richness of the 16th-century choir stalls.

The city's other attractions include the **Musée de Picardie▶**, with statues and Greek and Egyptian antiquities, local history at the 17th-century **Hôtel de Berny**, Auguste Perret's extraordinary 1947 skyscraper, and a museum devoted to the author **Jules Verne**, buried in an evocative **cemetery▶**. In the flood-plain of the Somme are Amiens' watery **Hortillonnages▶**, a strange area of market gardens threaded by innumerable little channels and in part accessible only by boat.

▶ Ardennes, Les
240C3

These densely wooded uplands, most of them on Belgian territory, are the abode of deer and wild boar, a paradise for hunters and walkers. They form a high plateau penetrated by the deep valley of the meandering Meuse, best experienced by boat ('bateau-mouche' from Charleville-Mézières or Monthermé) or when viewed from the numerous crags along its course.

Industry found an early foothold along the banks of the river; engineering works and quarries are today complemented by a nuclear power station at Chooz. There are fine fortresses at **Rocroi▶** and **Sedan▶▶**, the largest fortified castle in northern Europe and a Protestant stronghold in the 16th century as well as at **Charleville-Mézières▶** with its splendid Renaissance square, the **place Ducale**.

▶▶ Arras
240B3

Renowned for its tapestries in the late Middle Ages, Arras spent its accumulated wealth on its 16th-century **town hall** and on adorning its two squares, the **Grand' Place** and the **place des Héros**, with the dignified town houses we see today. Flemish gables, harmonious brick and stonework, and continuous arcades combine to form one of the finest urban compositions in northern Europe. Beneath it all run the extensive cellars which sheltered the citizenry during the devastating bombard-ments of World War I.

Market produce on sale in a historic setting in the former tapestry town of Arras

Born in the Ile-de-France, the Gothic style flourished in the prosperous towns and cities of the North. Its liberating effect can be seen, not only in world-famous cathedrals like Laon, Reims and Amiens, but across the whole region, in great abbey churches like St-Riquier and urban basilicas like St-Omer and St-Quentin. There are less well-known cathedrals at Noyon and Soissons, both masterpieces in their own right, though the latter is upstaged by the majestic façade of the great monastery church of St-Jean des-Vignes.

The achievement of the Gothic architects is matched by that of the sculptors and craftsmen who collaborated with them. Fine-grained local limestone lent itself to masterly carving, as in the sculpted figures adorning the west front at Amiens. At Amiens, too, similar virtuosity is evident in the wood-carving of the splendid choir stalls.

Emergence of Gothic The style underwent constant development as the great master-masons sought to exploit its technical and symbolic possibilities. At 12th-century Laon, we see it still in an early stage of evolution; the cathedral has the many towers typical of earlier churches, and its minimally pointed arches seem to hark back to their rounded Romanesque predecessors, while the deeply modelled west front, with its bold projections, openings and deep shadows, has an extraordinary plastic quality.

Reims Cathedral

Flowering and flamboyance In the 13th century, the style reached its zenith; at Amiens, the use of flying buttresses enables the masonry of the walls to be reduced to an absolute minimum, making way for the great windows through which the daylight streams into the soaring spaces of the interior.

By the time Abbeville's **St-Vulfran** was built in the 15th century, decoration had become more important than structure; in this final, Flamboyant phase, window-tracery writhes, flame-like, and the west front carries an overload of ornament.

Occasionally a cooler influence is felt from across the Channel, as in the tall, soberly-decorated tower of St-Omer's Notre-Dame, an echo of English Perpendicular.

CHANNEL TO-ING AND FRO-ING

Boulogne and Calais both have longstanding connections with *la perfide Albion*, visible across the Channel. First was Julius Caesar in 55 bc, who used the site of Boulogne to launch his invasion of England; 18 centuries later, Napoleon planned to follow Caesar's example, but was waylaid skirmishing elsewhere. Calais' Burghers played a more defensive role but today, the Channel Tunnel has opened the floodgates to thousands of holidaying Brits. In the other direction go, not the French, but carloads of wine and beer snapped up at Calais' burgeoning alcohol supermarkets, many of which are British-owned.

Old Boulogne's basilica replaced a cathedral destroyed by Revolutionary zeal but still contains a Romanesque crypt

▶ Ballon de Guebwiller — 241E1

At 1,424m, this (also called the Grand Ballon) is the highest of the *ballons*, the bare rounded mountain-tops rising impressively from the tree-clad slopes of the southern Vosges. No one should shirk the short walk up from the car park to the summit: at your feet the Alsace plain; beyond the Rhine, the wooded heights of the Black Forest; to the south the Jura and the distant Alps.

Belfort — 241E1

Connoisseurs of station names on the Paris Métro will remember Denfert-Rochereau, named after a hero of the Franco-Prussian War. Besieged in Belfort's citadel by superior force, this doughty colonel and his men withstood the German assault for 103 days, only giving up after the armistice. Their heroism is commemorated by the **Belfort Lion**, a great beast in red sandstone guarding the way up to the **citadel▶▶** and overlooking the workaday town on the banks of the Savoureuse far below.

▶ Bergues — 240B4

Sitting serenely behind its protective walls and elaborate moats, this is one of the prettiest little places in French Flanders. Built in yellow brick, it has resisted many an attacking army.

▶ Boulogne — 240A4

With its old core, the Vieille Ville, still surrounded by medieval ramparts and dominated by its idiosyncratic 19th-century cathedral, Boulogne beats its rivals Calais and Dunkerque for character. Nausicaà, France's largest aquarium, makes an additional reason to visit. Its harbour lands more fish than anywhere else in France. To the north of Boulogne stretch the cliffs, dunes and beaches of the **Côte d'Opale▶▶** (Opal Coast), culminating in the mighty headland of **Cap Gris Nez**. Further north still, at Cap Blanc-Nez is the amusing Musée du Transmanche, relating serious and utopian projects for crossing the Channel.

Calais — 240A4

Wrecked in World War II and unstylishly rebuilt, this busy port is a mere 38km from the English coast, whose chalk cliffs are clearly visible on a fine day. The English siege of 1346–7 is commemmorated by Rodin's celebrated and moving bronze of the **Burghers of Calais**, at the foot of the tall town hall tower. Nearby, an old German bunker has been converted into a war museum.

▶ Cambrai — 240B3

Famed since medieval times for its fine linen known in English as 'cambric', Cambrai suffered terribly during the German retreat of 1918. An industrial town, it is also the centre of a rich agricultural area and is famous for its tripe and sausages, as well as for the minty titbits called *bêtises* ('nonsenses'). Gates and cobbled streets form the old centre with its striking Spanish house and recently revamped municipal museum. At Le Cateau-Cambrésis is a large collection of Matisse paintings.

▶ Cassel 240B4

The flat farmlands of French Flanders are relieved by a number of isolated knolls, the 'Monts de Flandres'. On the highest of these (176m) perches this exquisite little Flemish town, its elongated and cobbled **Grande Place** lined with fine old buildings. From the summit of the knoll, with its 18th-century windmill, there are terrific views towards the far-off Channel and into Belgium.

▶▶ Colmar 241E1

Large numbers of visitors come to Colmar to savour the special character of Alsace. High-gabled, timber-framed houses front the old streets and squares of the perfectly preserved town centre; outstanding are the galleried **Ancienne Douane▶** (Old Customs House), and the **Maison Pfister▶**, adorned with frescoes and medallions. The **Krutenau district▶▶**, Colmar's 'Little Venice', is particularly picturesque.

But Colmar's greatest treasure is kept indoors, in the tranquillity of the chapel in the **Musée d'Unterlinden▶▶▶**. Here, in all its terrifying intensity, is the *Issenheim Altarpiece*, the masterwork of Matthias Grünewald. The folding panels of the altarpiece were painted around 1515 for the Prior of the Monastery of St Anthony at nearby Issenheim. Its visionary evocation of the suffering in the *Redemption of Christ* still has the power to move the most casual observer; seldom has the agony of the dying Saviour been more forcefully portrayed.

The impact of the altarpiece is such that it is best left to the end of your visit to the museum, which has much else to offer. Apart from the Orlier altarpiece by Grünewald's near-contemporary, Martin Schongauer, and the 24 panels of the *Passion* altarpiece attributed to his workshop, there are local collections of 16th- to 19th-century decorative and traditional arts, and an array of modern French paintings (by Braque, Picasso, Léger, etc). Schongauer's work can be seen again in the **Dominican Church**, where his *Virgin in the Rose Bower* has pride of place.

ALSATIAN DELICACIES
Alsace is one of France's gastronomic provinces, serving Germanic food with a French accent, like *choucroute* (Sauerkraut), garnished with Strasbourg sausages or pork chops. From Strasbourg, too, comes *foie gras*, goose liver eaten *au naturel* or as pâté. Pork plays a big role, but so do delicately flavoured poultry and trout (from the Vosge) and eel. Munster cheese is renowned, as is *kougel-hopf* cake.

Colmar's narrow streets are rich in immaculately restored houses some dating from the 16th and 17th centuries

Drive

Route des Crêtes

broad plain of the Rhine, the wooded Vosges Mountains are among France's most attractive uplands. From rugged sandstone heights in the north to the gently rounded forms of the *ballons* in the south, this superb walking country extends for 170km between the German border and the Belfort Gap. The Route des Crêtes was built during World War I to serve the French front line; it now forms a magnificent drive.

Start at Saverne. Take the D132 south-west and turn left on to D98 at Lutzelbourg. At Haselbourg follow the D45 and at the little resort of Obersteigen turn right on to the D218.
This part of the Vosges has romantic landscapes of woods, pretty valleys and castle ruins commanding fine views.

Just beyond Niederhaslach with its great Gothic church, turn right on to the N420 along the picturesque valley of the Bruche. At Lutzelhouse you can either head south via Muhlbach up to the panoramic viewpoint at the Signal de Grendelbruch or continue along the valley past Schirmeck to Rothau and turn left up the D130 towards Le Struthof.
The approach road to **Le Struthof** was built by the slave labourers of the Nazi concentration camp. Chilling remains still stand with a museum.

The alternative routes rejoin near the Neuntelstein viewpoint. Head east on D130 and D426 towards Mont-Ste-Odile.
Vistors crowd the mountain-top convent dedicated to **St Odile**, above all on her feast day (December 13). Alsace's patron saint lived in the 8th century; the imposing masonry of the great defensive earthwork known as the **Mur Païen** (Pagan Wall) harks back to much earlier times, when Gaul was ruled by the mysterious Celts.

Return westward via D109. Turn left on to D426 towards the little upland

Rising gently eastwards from the Lorraine plateau, then dropping abruptly through the vineyards to the

resort of Le Hohwald, then go south-west on D425, turning right after the Col du Kreuzweg to the Champ du Feu.
From the **Champ du Feu** observation tower there are staggering views which can extend as far as the Black Forest, or even as far as the Swiss Alps on a clear day.

Return to D425 and continue south to Villé, then to Fouchy and the pretty Col de Fouchy. Down in the valley again at Lièpvre, turn right towards the small industrial settlement of Ste-Marie-aux-Mines. At the Col des Bagenelles, follow signs to Le Bonhomme, where you turn right to travel towards the Col du Bonhomme. The **Col du Bonhomme**, traversed by one of the main routes linking Alsace with Lorraine, marks the northern end of the Route des Crêtes.

The Route winds along for 83km from here as far as Thann in the south. Splendid forests alternate with high pastures, while far below are

attractive lakes. All along the route are spectacular viewpoints, the most celebrated being that of the **Grand Ballon** (1,424m). A sombre reminder that the ridgeline was bitterly contested by the opposing armies is the National Memorial at **Vieil-Armand**. The Route descends sinuously to Cernay and then 6km west to Thann.

Route du Vin d'Alsace

This second tourist route of Alsace, some 180km long between Thann in the south and Marlenheim in the north, is well signposted. Its winding course is best taken at a leisurely pace, with ample time for tasting – details available locally or from the tourist office, 4 rue d'Unterlinden, in Colmar.

From Thann, follow the Route via Eguisheim, past Colmar to Kaysersberg.
The vines grow in a narrow north–south band along the foothills of the Vosges. Here are immaculate villages, whose cobbled streets and squares and high-gabled timber houses

epitomise Alsace. Many, like three-towered **Eguisheim** or triangular **Turckheim**, have all the airs of miniature towns. The favourite town is probably Riquewihr, almost unbearably crowded on occasion. Kaysersberg, with its fortified bridge, was the birthplace of the great humanitarian, Albert Schweitzer.

Continue north past Sélestat and Obernai to Marlenheim.
Castles abound in this frontier province, most of them in romantic ruin. One exception is **Haut-Koenigsbourg**, its formidable silhouette rising imperiously over the forested slopes above Sélestat. It was reconstructed for Kaiser Wilhelm II in the early years of this century, when Alsace was ruled from Berlin. Disillusioned by the course of the Great War, the Emperor left a brief but telling comment here on his last visit in 1918, an inscription reading: 'I did not want this'.

STORK SHORTAGE
One of the emblems of Alsace is the stork's nest atop a chimney-stack or steeple. Weighing up to half a ton, these form annually refurbished residences, occupied each summer. Courtship is noisy, with much flapping of wings and clattering of bills. Eggs can number up to half a dozen. Sadly, the stork population has declined dramatically in recent years, though efforts are now being made to augment their numbers by breeding them in captivity.

DUAL IDENTITY
Long-settled by German-speakers, Alsace was assimilated into France as Louis XIV pushed eastward to the 'natural' frontier along the Rhine. While accepting French rule, the population felt uneasy with Paris' centralising tendencies, and not everyone regretted being reabsorbed into the German Reich after the Franco-Prussian War of 1870–1. Re-annexation by Nazi Germany in 1940 was a less happy experience. Today's Alsatians are content to live in a Europe where Germany and France are partners and where their own identity can flourish.

► Coucy-le-Château 240B3
In the Middle Ages, this ridgetop castle was one of the greatest strongholds in the land. Towards the end of World War I, the retreating Germans added to the depredations of the centuries by blowing up the massive keep. But enough remains of walls, towers and massive gateways to enclose completely the modern village of Coucy and to leave an unforgettable memory of medieval might. The usual approach winds up from the south to the Porte de Soissons; inside the gateway is a little museum.

Douai 240B4
War-damaged in 1914–18 and again in 1940, Douai nevertheless retains a good number of 18th-century houses as well as its 64m Gothic **Beffroi►** (bell-tower), one of the finest in the North. In the 17th century, the town became a refuge for English Roman Catholics. Driven out by the anti-religious fervour of the Revolution, their descendants returned to England, where they founded Downside Abbey and, later, its famous school.

Douai was the administrative centre for France's great northern coalfield; at nearby Lewarde, in an old mine, is the **Centre Historique Minier►**, which gives a good picture of mining life (*Closed* mid–end Jan).

► L'Epine 240C2
Pilgrimages have taken place here ever since shepherds saw a statue of the Virgin Mary in the middle of a burning thorn (*épine*) bush. The great late-Gothic church erected to commemorate the miraculous apparition easily dominates the humble half-timbered houses of the village huddling at its foot. Its grandeur is relieved by its many gargoyles.

► Langres 241D1
The **Plateau de Langres** is a vast rolling upland straddling the headwaters of three of France's great rivers, the Marne, the Meuse and the Seine. Perched on one of its limestone promontories is the ancient town of Langres itself, still intact within its well-preserved walls. The most rewarding walk leads round the ramparts, passing towers and gateways and offering fine views over the valley of the Marne. Within the town are many splendid old houses, some of them of Renaissance date. Important vestiges of the Gallo-Roman town, Andematunum, are housed in the **Musée d'Art et d'Histoire**, including the Bacchus mosaic unearthed in 1985.

►► Laon 240B3
It is 1,000 years since Laon was France's capital, but this walled and gated city still dominates the flatlands all around from its spectacular ridgetop site. The glorious Gothic **cathedral►►►**, begun in the late 12th century, rises grandly over the rooftops. With deeply inset porches and windows, the west front is a triumph of early Gothic drama and ebullience, while the interior has a monumental simplicity and dignity. The figures of oxen high up in the towers commemorate the beasts who hauled the heavy stone. Below the bluff lies the new town, linked by an innovative overhead tram, the Poma.

Laon, once the capital of France, is an attractive town surrounded with medieval ramparts and imposing entrance gates

► Lille
240B4

Lille is the undisputed capital of the North, the focus of a sprawling industrial conurbation of more than a million inhabitants. While much of this sprawl lacks allure, the city's pedestrianised centre is full of style and vigour, a fascinating mix of French and Flemish influence, though the huge **Citadel** is entirely French, built by Louis XIV's military engineer Vauban. The enlarged and revamped **Musée des Beaux Arts►►►** displays Flemish and Dutch masters through to Impressionists. General de Gaulle's birthplace, **Maison Natale du Général de Gaulle**, includes the great man's christening robe and the car in which he narrowly escaped assassination in 1962.

Lunéville
241D2

In the early 18th century, the Duke of Lorraine built a château here to rival Versailles. His **palace►►**, somewhat the worse for wear, houses a porcelain museum (*Closed* Tue).

► Marmoutier
241E2

Just to the south of Saverne stands the splendid monastery of Marmoutier. Built in red Vosges sandstone, begun in the 11th century, its complex and commanding west front forms one of the finest examples of Romanesque architecture in Alsace.

► Metz
241D2

Strategically located not far from France's eastern frontier, Metz has been a fortress city for most of its long existence. Between 1871 and 1918 it belonged to Germany, and buildings dating from this period, like the huge **railway station**, have a distinctly Germanic air. But the **cathedral►►** is characteristically French, with a lofty interior and sumptuous stained glass, including modern work by Marc Chagall. Metz's riverside is worth seeking out, not least for the formidable gateway known as the **Porte des Allemands**. The history museum, the **Musée de la Cour d'Or►►**, is exemplary.

LUNÉVILLE'S SON
Little is known of the life of painter Georges de la Tour, born at Vic-sur-Seille near Lunéville in 1593. It appears that he pursued his career as court painter to both the Duke of Lorraine and King Louis XIII with a worldly and ruthless determination, certainly not reflected in his pictures, which have a mystical stillness and tranquillity never since equalled. He is the master of nocturnal interiors peopled by serene figures whose calm features are lit by the concealed flame of a single candle. Few works survive, but examples can be seen in the Musée Historique Lorraine at Nancy.

VOSGES SPAS
Lorraine is world-famous for its water – few can fail to recognise the name Vittel – and any number of spas have grown up in the south of the province. As well as Vittel and its neighbour Contrexville (both with bottling plants open to the public, Apr–Oct), there are several places (Plombières, Luxeuil, Bourbonne, for instance) tapping the waters springing from the fringe of the Vosges Mountains. Pretty surroundings, parks and gardens, elegant old-fashioned spa architecture and a general atmosphere of leisure and pleasure make these little resorts as attractive to the casual visitor as to those in search of a cure.

HEAVENLY VOICES
Among the Meuse's attractions is the tiny village of Domrémy-la-Pucelle, near Neufchâteau, famed for being the birthplace of Joan of Arc (*la pucelle* in question). Her family home, despite extensive alterations, remains a good example of a 15th-century peasant house and is open to the public. By the woods where the 13-year-old Joan first heard heavenly voices, there now stands a less inspiring 1900s basilica, a magnet for pilgrims. Four years after receiving her divine instructions, Joan left the Vosges, never to return.

Meuse   240C2

Some 900km long from its source near Bourbonne-les-Bains to its mouth in the North Sea, the Meuse is part of the extensive system of canalised waterways linking France to her neighbours to the north-east. For nearly 160km between Neufchâteau and Stenay, it flows in a trench-like valley marked to the east by the high limestone hills of the Côtes de Meuse. Fortress-cities like **Verdun▶** guard this section of the river, and some of France's most fateful battles have been fought along its banks, at Sedan in 1871 and again in 1940, and above all at Verdun (see page 259).

Moselle   241D1

A river of contrasts, the Moselle starts its life as a mountain stream high in the Vosges near the Col de Bussay. The most attractive part of its course is between here and Epinal, where it flows through rich farmlands. From Neuves-Maisons near Nancy, however, it becomes one of Europe's great industrial waterways, particulary around Thionville, France's 'Pays de Fer' ('Land of Iron').

▶ Mulhouse   241E1

The dynamic industrial town of Mulhouse attracts visitors less for its townscape than for its outstanding museums and its symbol of modernity, the lofty **Tour de l'Europe▶**. The **Musée de l'Automobile▶▶** has an extraordinary collection of vehicles, French and foreign, from pioneering prototypes to famous racers. The **Musée du Chemin-de-Fer▶▶** is the national collection of railwayana, featuring the French steam locomotives of yester-year, perhaps the most beautiful machines of their kind ever made. The **Musée de l'Impression-sur-Etoffes▶▶** has brilliant explanations of the processes of printing on cotton, complemented by an unsurpassed display of fine fabrics. Electropolis is a recent attraction devoted to the story of electricity. At the open-air **Ecomusée d'Alsace**, off the D430 to the north, dozens of traditional buildings have been reconstructed to show the domestic life and crafts of past generations.

Munster   241E1

This little resort in the vine-clad and wooded valley of the Fecht in the southern Vosges is famous for the pungent and semi-soft Munster cheese. Nearby is the **Petit Ballon▶**, 1,267m high and one of the province's most spectacular viewpoints.

Capital city of the Duchy of Lorraine before becoming part of the kingdom of France on the death of its last duke, Stanislas, Nancy prides itself on its classical townscape, product of the urban planning of its enlightened rulers.

Elegance and harmony Stanislas had been King of Poland. When he was deposed in 1736, his son-in-law, Louis XV, managed to engineer him the dukedom of Lorraine. Full of architectural enthusiasm, Stanislas set about linking the rectilinear 'New Town' laid out by his predecessor, Duke Leopold, to the old town around the Ducal Palace. Together with his architect, Héré, he planned an urban composition of unsurpassed elegance and harmony (now **place Royale** (now **place Stanislas**).

Flanked by lesser buildings in the same richly ornate but dignified style, the monumental **Hôtel de Ville** dominates the square, facing north towards an **Arc de Triomphe**. The exits from the square are guarded by Jean Lamour's gilded ironwork grilles of the utmost sumptuousness. The best view of the whole ensemble is from the Hôtel de Ville's upper floor, reached by a splendid staircase, also the work of Héré.

Museums and galleries Beyond the Arc de Triomphe extends the lengthy place de la Carrière, lined by fine 18th-century town houses and terminated by the colonnaded Palais du Gouvernement. Beyond is the austere Ducal Palace containing the **Musée Historique** Lorraine, with much material on the history of Lorraine and its capital as well as engravings by local artist Jacques Callot depicting the horrors of war. In contrast is the mood of peacefulness in the luminous interiors by the painter Georges de la Tour (see panel page 249).

Nancy's other museums include the **Musée des Beaux-Arts** with collections of European art from medieval to modern times, and the not-to-be-missed **Musée de l'Ecole de Nancy**. The city was France's most important centre of art nouveau outside Paris, and the fascinating collections of this museum, housed in an elegant residence of the period, make this one of the best places to experience the heady luxuriance of the decorative arts of the turn of the century.

Gallé Emile Gallé established his glass workshop in Nancy in the early 1870s. He excelled in making exquisitely beautiful vases in translucent cameo glass, inspired by the motifs and techniques of Japanese art. Gallé was also a designer of extravagant furniture, like the extraordinary bed inlaid with a huge mother-of-pearl moth which can be see on display in the Musée de l'Ecole de Nancy.

THE DAUMS
The Daum brothers, Jean and Antonin, developed complex techniques for giving glass ever greater subtleties of colour and texture.

251

Guibal's Neptune fountain and Lamour's magnificent gilded ironwork grilles frame the western end of place Stanislas, Nancy's classical architecture showpiece

KIWIS ALOFT!
Le Quesnoy's ingenious design failed to protect its German defenders from the New Zealand Rifle Brigade in 1918; they employed medieval siege tactics and scaled its walls with ladders.

252

Neuf Brisach 241E1

In 1697, the French were forced to withdraw from Alt ('old') Breisach, one of the chain of strongholds they had built on the east bank of the Rhine. The fortress-town of Neuf ('new') Brisach was its replacement. Sited among the flat farmlands of the frontier river, it is a perfectly preserved example of the genius of Louis XIV's military engineer, Vauban, who has a museum devoted to him.

▶ Obernai 241E2

Among the vineyards at the foot of the sacred mountain of Mont-Sainte-Odile, Obernai is the epitome of an Alsace wine village, with crumbling walls and ancient, narrow streets lined with timber-framed houses. In the place du Marché stand the 15th-century **town hall** and the 16th-century **Corn Hall▶**, overlooked by the tall **Tour de la Chapelle**. A statue of Ste Odile graces the fountain in the centre of the square, and not far away stands the pretty **Puits aux Six-Sceaux**, a little Renaissance well whose six buckets hang in pairs.

▶ Le Quesnoy 240B3

Still intact after more than three centuries, the extensive moats and bastions of this quiet little fortress-city are a masterpiece of baroque military engineering and a potent reminder of the vulnerability of France's northern frontier. The moats are now a leisure park.

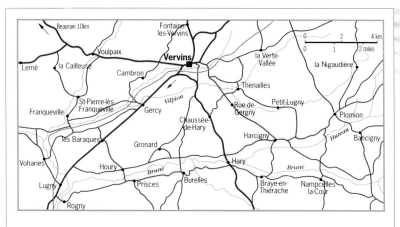

Drive

La Thiérache

This lush green frontier countryside with its rich pastures and cider orchards was always vulnerable to the ravages of invading armies. The harassed locals' response was to fortify their parish churches, many of which still stand.

A drive through La Thiérache can be centred on the town of Vervins. From here a number of fortress churches are within easy reach: brick-built **Burelles**, twin-towered **Plomion**, 12th-century **Prisces** with its massive tower, lonely **Beaurain** on its isolated eminence. The churches' interiors were adapted to withstand a siege, with a well, a bread-oven, and upper floors to house the villagers.

World-famous for its great Gothic cathedral, Reims owes its name to St Rémi, the saint who, in the year 498, baptised the heathen Clovis, King of the Franks. Later, Reims became France's coronation city, with 25 rulers crowned here.

Treasures of Reims The cathedral was begun in 1211, and all but ruined during World War I. Expertly restored, it has an inspiring west front: high up above the great rose window is the Gallery of Kings; down below, in the left porch, is the Smiling Angel. Inside, the stained glass is among the finest in France. Adjoining the cathedral is the old Bishops Palace, the **Palais du Tau**, housing the Cathedral Treasury as well as a number of statues from outside. Not far away is the **Basilica of St-Rémi**, whose monastic buildings are a storehouse of medieval art, arms and armour. In July and August free classical music concerts are held in Reims' monuments.

Champagne The process by which champagne acquires its sparkle was invented, almost accidentally, by a 17th-century monk, Dom Perignon. The caves (premises with famous names such as Veuve-Cliquot, Piper-Heidsieck, Taittinger and Pommeroy) can be visited and a discreet *dégustation* enjoyed.

On the flanks of the Montagne de Reims, just to the south of the city, vines give way to woods of beech, oak and chestnut, a regional park harbouring deer and wild boar. The vines spread out along the valley of the Marne to either side of Epernay, and south of the town are the slopes known as the Côte des Blancs. A sojourn hereabouts may convince you of the justification for the staunch refusal by the French to let any other drink be marketed under the name of champagne. Over-possessive? Perhaps, but you are likely to come away convinced that no other sparkling wine, however carefully produced, can ever match the refinement of the product of France's northernmost vineyard.

REIMS
The chalky rock on which Reims stands is as hollow as a Swiss cheese, with mile upon mile of caves providing ideal conditions for the production and storage of the region's most renowned product.

253

Reims' Musée des Beaux-Arts, in the Abbaye St-Denis, has some rare Renaissance painted hangings, paintings and sculpture. Below: Tête de Brigand, bronze bust by Camille Claudel (Rodin's lover)

Sélestat's Bibliothèque Humaniste is an impressive symbol of the town's educational prowess during the Middle Ages and later as the cradle of Alsatian humanism

►► Ronchamp   241D1

High up on its hilltop, the pilgrimage chapel of Notre-Dame-du-Haut is one of the most atmospheric of modern churches (*Open* daily). Designed by Le Corbusier in 1955, it is as much a sculpture as a building, with a billowing roof covering the mysterious interior, which is lit by stained-glass windows deeply set into the massive concrete walls. The old mining town has a mining museum.

► St-Omer   240A4

Now bypassed by the A26 motorway, this small town was once the first stop for visitors heading inland from Calais. It is a dignified place with fine old 17th- and 18th-century houses and a network of canals, the **watergangs►** (boat-trips). The imposing **Basilica of Notre-Dame►►** has a tall tower in English Perpendicular style and an interior which is a veritable museum of ecclesiastical art. The **Hôtel Sandelin►►** has collections of furniture, Flemish paintings, local ceramics and Delft ware, together with the extraordinary gilt and enamel pedestal for a medieval crucifix known as the Pied de Croix de St-Bertin (*Closed* Mon, Tue).

▶ St-Riquier 240A3

The village is dominated by its great abbey church, founded by the Benedictines in the 7th century. The present building dates mostly from the 15th and 16th centuries; built in pale local limestone in Flamboyant Gothic style, it has the scale and presence of a cathedral, with a massive tower and a calm interior of great dignity (tours daily; *closed* mid-Nov–mid-Feb).

Sélestat 241E1

The cramped network of medieval streets here is contained within Sélestat's ring of long-since demolished walls. It has two good churches, Gothic St-Georges and 12th-century **Ste-Foy▶**; the latter, with its three towers, is one of the finest Romanesque buildings in the province. The **Bibliothèque Humaniste▶▶** contains collections of books and manuscripts dating back to the 7th century.

▶ Somme 240A3

Despite witnessing some of the bloodiest battles of World War I, the Somme flows peacefully and languidly through a lush valley set among open chalklands. It reaches the sea at the wide Baie de la Somme, an attractive estuary well endowed with crustaceans and other forms of marine life, much of which is consumed by visitors to the little port-resorts of **Le Crotoy** (to the north) and **St-Valéry▶** (to the south). Vintage trains run from Le Crotoy via St-Valéry to the sandy beaches of Cayeux-sur-Mer.

▶▶▶ Strasbourg 241E2

Seat of the Council of Europe and the European Parliament, Strasbourg is the jewel in the crown of Alsace. Sited between the branches of the River Ill just west of the Rhine, the ancient city centre is dominated by the single soaring spire of the superb medieval **cathedral▶▶▶**, a building particularly rich in sculptural decoration. Inside, a three-tiered triumph of Gothic carving depicts the drama of the Last Judgement, while close by is a 19th-century astronomical clock, a favourite for its midday performance; 330 steps lead up the tower to a platform with fabulous views.

Strasbourg is well endowed with museums. The **Musée de l'Oeuvre Notre-Dame▶** has original sculpture from the cathedral. Three museums (Beaux-Arts, Archéologique, Arts Décoratifs) are grouped in the **Palais de Rohan▶▶**; the ceramics collection is one of the best in France. The **Musée Alsacien▶** (folk culture) spreads over three 16th- and 17th-century dwellings, and the **Musée d'Art Moderne et Contemporain▶** (European painting and sculpture from Impressionism onwards) is now in its new purpose-built home alongside the château.

At the west end of the 'island' formed by the arms of the Ill is **La Petite France▶▶**, with winding streets, half-timbered houses and turreted bridges, best observed from the **Barrage Vauban** with its viewing terrace.

EUROPEAN CROSSROADS
Strasbourg's Palais de l'Europe houses the Council of Europe; but the European Parliament now has its own brand-new home in the same district, the Quartier Européen. Other institutions, like the European Court of Human Rights and the European Science Foundation, have found Strasbourg's location on the border between western and central Europe a congenial place to be.

255

The cathedral square, Strasbourg, at the centre of a vast pedestrian area served by a mini-train

Many of the most dramatic struggles in the course of French history have taken place in this region whose gently rolling countryside offers few natural barriers to invasion from the north-east.

HOMAGE TO THE GREAT WAR

At Péronne, south of Arras, a striking new museum, the Historial de la Grande Guerre, presents the experiences of the three main contenders. A short film gives archival background to the Commonwealth volunteers while a free guide to the Circuit du Souvenir (the main battlefields, memorials and museums of the Somme) emphasises Britain's contribution. The museum is closed from mid-December–mid-January, and on Mondays for the rest of winter.

World War I saw a tenth of France's population dead or missing (1.4 million) and nearly three million injured

Early days The English – called *les goddons* (meaning God damn!) for their peculiar habit of continuous swearing – were the perennial enemy, and some of the decisive battles of the Middle Ages were fought here, such as **Crécy** and **Agincourt** (Azincourt in French). Later, French anxiety about the exposed frontier fuelled successful attempts to push the kingdom's border north-eastwards, cementing it in place with chains of fortresses and fortified towns. Many of them designed by Louis XIV's ingenious military engineer, Sebastien Le Prestre de Vauban, these baroque strongholds were the ultimate deterrent of their day, with few financial constraints inhibiting the lavish layout of places like **Le Quesnoy** or the Citadel at **Lille**.

The war to end wars The outcome of the Franco-Prussian War of 1870–1 was decided by Napoleon III's humiliating defeat at Sedan. His successors laboured for decades to create an impregnable chain of huge forts along the Meuse. But in 1914, in the opening weeks of World War I, the river was crossed again as the German armies marched south-westwards. Stalemate followed the successful French counter-attack on the Marne, and for four long years the opposing armies attempted to bleed each other white in a series of lumbering and indecisive offensives. The scenes of greatest devastation, both of landscape and of human life, took place along the Somme (where the British attack in 1916 cost 600,000 casualties before grinding to a halt), in the soggy fields of Flanders, and at Verdun, where relentless German pressure was countered by equally determined French resistance.

Afterwards, memorials arose all over the now silent battlefields to commemorate the unprecedented slaughter. The cemeteries of the British War Graves Commission, much of their classical architecture designed by the great Edwin Lutyens, have a serene, timeless air. They are thickest on the ground in the windswept fields north of the Somme around the rebuilt town of **Albert**, from which a waymarked 'Circuit de Souvenir' guides the visitor around the killing grounds. A stretch of trenches has been preserved at the Newfoundlanders' Memorial at **Beaumont-Hamel**. Further north, at **Vimy Ridge**, dramatically visible from the A26 motorway, the Canadian Memorial towers over the hilltop. Here, the land has been given in perpetuity to the Canadian nation, a tribute to the 60,000 sacrificed in its capture. The clash of arms in the titanic struggle which raged for eighteen months around **Verdun** finds no echo today in the eerie forest now covering the land deep-ploughed by shellfire. Here are some of the most poignant memorials of the war, like the white-towered **Ossuary** of Douaumont, as well as the **Memorial Museum** at nearby Fleury (*Closed* mid-Dec– mid-Jan).

World War II Haunted by memories of the carnage, inter-war French governments sought to protect the nation from a recurrence by building a 20th-century equivalent of Louis XIV's frontier fortresses along the Franco-German border. As in the time of Vauban, no expense was spared, but when the test came in 1940, the ultra-modern defences of the Maginot Line were simply outflanked by the Wehrmacht's blitzkrieg through the 'impenetrable' Ardennes to the coast. Remains of this costly deterrent which failed to deter can be seen at **Fermont** near Longwy or at **Lembach** in Alsace.

Fighting in the North, both in the spring of 1940 and in the Liberation of 1944, was brief compared with the long drawn-out battles of 1914–18. The epic of **Dunkerque** is recalled by exhibits in the town's Musée des Beaux-Arts; the fate of Calais during the war and occupation, by the Musée de la Guerre housed in a German bunker. The most tangible remains from World War II are the formidable concrete coastal defences built to repel the Allied invasion which the Wehrmacht had convinced itself would be launched against the beaches of the Pas de Calais rather than in Normandy. One of the blockhouses of this 'Atlantic Wall' at **Audinghen** on the cliffs between Calais and Boulogne has been converted into a private museum. Germanic mastery of reinforced concrete is demonstrated again in what is supposedly the biggest such structure ever built, the bunker rising ominously over the tree-tops at **Eperleques** near St-Omer. Constructed by slave labour, this was to serve as one of the launching-ramps for the V2 rocket bombardment of London, but was put out of action by air attack.

DUNKERQUE'S NEW FACE
Dunkerque was bought back from the English by Louis XIV in 1662. In 1945, 90 per cent of the town was destroyed but since then it has been rebuilt and revitalised to become France's third largest port. Boat tours of the harbour leave from the Bassin du Commerce. The walk past the two locks to the lighthouse gives views over the vast docks.

257

The town centre, Toul, much of which was rebuilt after World War II destruction. Toul once had the status of an independent enclave within the duchy of Lorraine

STAINGLASS-MAKING
Known as the 'Ville Sainte du Vitrail', Troyes' exceptional heritage of stainglass windows, dating from the 13th–19th centuries, provides in-situ restoration laboratories whose methods remain essentially unchanged despite improved techniques (better quality leads, more sophisticated soldering and a 3,000-strong palette as opposed to the original 12 colours). The School of Troyes' last known great master was Linard Gontier (17th century), specialist in *grisaille*, a technique of shading (Eglise St-Martin-ès-Vignes). The 19th century saw a revival of the art.

FLYING CARS
Le Touquet airfield, now only used by the private planes of the prosperous, was busy in the 1950s with the bulky Bristol Freighters of Silver City Airways, whose pioneering attempts to fly travellers' cars across the Channel eventually came to nothing.

▶ **Thann**   *241E1*
This little industrial town, southern terminus for both the Route des Crêtes and the Route du Vin (see pages 246–7), is overlooked by the ruins of its medieval castle, the Engelsbourg. The demolition of the fortress in 1673 left a massive cylindrical chunk of the keep lying on its side. Seen from a distance it resembles a huge eye staring down the valley – hence the local name, *L'Oeil de la Sorcière* (Witch's Eye). Thann's imposing Gothic **church▶** is called 'The Cathedral' by locals; beneath its tall spire it has an ornately sculpted porch, while inside, the carving of the choir stalls is equally lively. *The Madonna of the Vineyards* is the name given to the church's painted wooden statue of the Virgin and Child, a reminder of the famous Rangen wine produced here.

Toul   *241D2*
Long a fortress city, Toul's strategic importance was suddenly reinforced when Alsace-Lorraine was lost following the Franco-Prussian War of 1870–1. Huge sunken forts like the one open to the public at nearby **Villey-le-Sec**, were hurriedly built to protect France's shrunken eastern frontier. But the star-shaped moats and bastions which still ring the old centre are of much earlier date, as is the Porte de Metz, a creation of Louis XIV's engineer, Vauban. Toul's **cathedral▶** has an ornate west front and pretty cloisters, the latter a feature, too, of the town's other principal church, **St-Gengoult▶**.

▶ **Le Touquet**   *240A4*
Known as 'Paris-Plage' (Paris Beach) when first laid out in the 19th century, this seaside resort with its 12km sandy beach soon became popular with wealthy visitors from the far side of the English Channel, and its chic shops, 'Club Nautique', and many other sports and leisure facilities still attract the would-be smart set. Behind the main part of the town, its roads laid out grid-fashion, are villas set among the pine trees of a planted forest.

Past glories are characteristic, too, of enchanting little **Montreuil▶**, a short way inland up the pretty valley of the Canche. Its population may only be a fraction of what it was in the Middle Ages, but its citadel and ramparts still stand, a fascinating mixture of medieval and Renaissance defence works.

The flower-filled streets of Hunspach, near Wissembourg, one of northern Alsace's most delightful villages. Picturesque half-timbered houses, often intricately carved, line

▶▶ Troyes 240C1

The ancient capital of the Province of Champagne, Troyes has a wealth of half-timbered houses and medieval streets and passageways. A stroll around the old centre evokes the atmosphere of medieval times when merchants congregated from all over Europe to attend the great fairs held here. Beyond the elegant Gothic façade of the Basilica of St-Urbain stands the **cathedral**, its interior bathed in the light streaming in through the magnificent stained glass.

Troyes has almost as many museums as churches, all of them housed in venerable buildings. They include collections of tools and implements, hosiery, and an apothecary's jars and boxes. Outstanding among them is the **Museé d'Art Moderne▶**, which includes work by Soutine, Rodin, Vlaminck, Van Dongen, and above all, Derain.

▶▶ Verdun 241D2

The name of Verdun seems fated to be forever associated with the attempt by the German High Command to decide the course of the World War I by 'bleeding France to death'. A tour of the battlefield extending along the Meuse to either side of the city is a powerful reminder of the futility of war. The most evocative monuments are on the right bank, among the new-grown forest blanketing the scenes of devastation (though even the coarsest weeds refuse to grow in places). There are great fortifications like **Fort de Vaux**, or **Fort Douaumont**, captured almost accidentally in February 1916 by a German platoon in the early stages of the 18-month battle. Near by is the **Ossuary** with its tall, white Tower of the Dead rising over the countless graves. The course of the struggle is compellingly recreated in the **Mémorial-Musée de la Bataille de Verdun▶**, built on the the site of the village of Fleury.

▶▶ Wissembourg 241E2

In a pretty position on the banks of the River Lauter, this is one of the most charming little places in Alsace, with old houses, ancient ramparts and a big Gothic church in red sandstone. Wissembourg makes a good base from which to explore northern Alsace. Nearby are some of the province's most delightful villages, Oberseebach, Hoffen, and rustic perfection itself, **Hunspach▶▶▶**. To the west is the rugged, wooded country of the northern Vosges, with ruined medieval castles like **Fleckenstein** and **Falkenstein** glowering from their crags. A later age contributed one of the key strongholds of the Maginot Line, the fort near Lembach known as the **Ouvrage du Four à Chaux▶** (guided tours mid-Mar–Nov).

CONVERSION CHARTS

FROM	TO	MULTIPLY BY
Inches	Centimetres	2.54
Centimetres	Inches	0.3937
Feet	Metres	0.3048
Metres	Feet	3.2810
Yards	Metres	0.9144
Metres	Yards	1.0940
Miles	Kilometres	1.6090
Kilometres	Miles	0.6214
Acres	Hectares	0.4047
Hectares	Acres	2.4710
Gallons	Litres	4.5460
Litres	Gallons	0.2200
Ounces	Grams	28.35
Grams	Ounces	0.0353
Pounds	Grams	453.6
Grams	Pounds	0.0022
Pounds	Kilograms	0.4536
Kilograms	Pounds	2.205
Tons	Tonnes	1.0160
Tonnes	Tons	0.9842

MEN'S SUITS

UK	36	38	40	42	44	46	48
Rest of Europe	46	48	50	52	54	56	58
US	36	38	40	42	44	46	48

DRESS SIZES

UK	8	10	12	14	16	18
France	36	38	40	42	44	46
Italy	38	40	42	44	46	48
Rest of Europe	34	36	38	40	42	44
US	6	8	10	12	14	16

MEN'S SHIRTS

UK	14	14.5	15	15.5	16	16.5 17
Rest of Europe	36	37	38	39/40	41	42 43
US	14	14.5	15	15.5	16	16.5 17

MEN'S SHOES

UK	7	7.5	8.5	9.5	10.5	11
Rest of Europe	41	42	43	44	45	46
US	8	8.5	9.5	10.5	11.5	12

WOMEN'S SHOES

UK	4.5	5	5.5	6	6.5	7
Rest of Europe	38	38	39	39	40	41
US	6	6.5	7	7.5	8	8.5

Arriving

All visitors to France must have a valid passport, but only some need a visa. Visas are not necessary for visitors from the EU, Canada, New Zealand or the US staying less than three months, but they are necessary for Australians. Regulations do change, so check with your French Consulate.

Air The national airline is Air France, (including the now-defunct Air Inter), which operates worldwide. France's largest airport by far is Roissy (Charles de Gaulle) in Paris, to which most inter-national carriers fly. Other airports used for direct scheduled international flights include: Bordeaux, Lyon, Marseille, Nantes, Nice, Orly (Paris), Strasbourg and Toulouse.

Coach Eurolines operates services from the UK to over 60 destinations in France – information from any National Express agency or from 52 Grosvenor Gardens, London SW1 (tel: 0990 143219).

Rail British Rail International (tel: 0990 848 848) can give information about travelling by train from the UK to any station in France by train. Eurostar (tel: 0345 30 30 30), via the Channel Tunnel, connects London, Waterloo with Paris, Gare du Nord in three hours, and with Lille and Roissy (Charles de Gaulle) for connections south and south-west. A large number of passes are available offering a wide and complex range of rail travel options in France and Europe. Inter-Rail passes (under and over 26 versions) and Euro-Domino passes (adult, youth and child versions) are available to European citizens, but must be bought outside France for travel in France. Eurail passes or Europasses (1st class for adult, 2nd class for youth versions) can be bought from French Railways by non-European residents, and in North America, France Railpass, France Rail'n'Drive and France Youthpass offer yet more possibilities and permutations.

For more detailed information contact your travel agent, or, in the UK, SNCF (next to the French Tourist office at 179 Piccadilly, London WIV 0BA) or the Rail Shop (tel: 0990 300 033). In the

US, contact Rail Europe Inc, 226–230 Westchester Avenue, White Plains, New York, NY 10604; tel: (800) 438-7245. In Canada, Rail Europe Inc is at Toronto – 2087 Dundas Street East, suite 105, Mississauga, Ontario L4X 1M2; tel: (905) 602-4195 or 1-800-361-7245.

Sea Numerous ferry, hovercraft and catamaran services link France with the UK and Ireland. Current operators include P&O European Ferries, Hoverspeed, Sea France, Brittany Ferries and Condor Ferries (seasonal). The fierce competition presented by the Channel Tunnel has caused an upheaval in ferry tariffs and services. The cost of crossings varies widely according to time, day and month of travel, and many special deals are available for car and foot passengers, including package deals with selected accommodation or planned routes. Hovercraft and catamaran services, while much faster than conventional car ferries, are more easily disrupted by bad weather. Play safe and take the tunnel, Le Shuttle (tel: 0990 35 35 35). Cars are loaded on to trains and the crossing takes 35 minutes – hence the telephone number!

Camping
There are over 11,000 campsites throughout France. They have to be registered and are then graded (by the Fédération Française de Camping et Caravanning, 78 rue de Rivoli, 75004 Paris (tel: 01 42 72 84 08)) from one to four stars, depending on the facilities provided. A four-star site will have communal indoor recreation areas, hot water, lock-up for valuables and washing machines; one-star sites are more crowded and sometimes have only cold water. Local farmers often let out their fields to campers – *camping à la ferme* – with basic or non-existent facilities.

A camping *carnet* is useful; some sites won't let you in without one, and they include some third-party insurance cover. They are obtainable by members from motoring organisations and affiliated caravan and cycling clubs. One *carnet* covers up to 12 people.

Children
The French tourist industry shows a keen interest in children and several cities provide amusement parks and museums designed to attract them. **Disneyland Paris** (32km east of Paris) offers not only a theme park but also hotels, a campsite and a golf course (for parents). **Parc Astérix** (38km north of Paris) is a long-established popular attraction. Poitiers' **Futuroscope** is a hit with more technologically aware children and adolescents. The mega **aquarium** at La Rochelle is a favourite and Boulogne's **Nausicaa aquarium** is also a splendid attraction.

Many large towns have museums, often with hands-on exhibitions, parks, circuses, water parks (*parcs et centres aquatiques*) and zoos. In Paris, **Le Musée en Herbe** (Jardin d'Acclimatation) and **Cité des Sciences**, with its Argonaut, Géode and Techno Cité will appeal.

In general, children are welcome in restaurants, hotels and bars, often with special rates. Some hotels provide a baby-listening service.

Sabots on sale in Chinon

Climate

The south of France, including the Mediterranean coast, has hot, dry summers and warm, wet winters. Showers are short and sharp, often in the middle of the day. Summer winds are cooling and gentle but the colder and fiercer Mistral, which comes from the north, can swirl around for days.

North-west France is affected by the Atlantic, often rainy, yet with mild winters and rather cool summers. The south-west area of Aquitaine, including the Dordogne, has hot summers.

Eastern France has a more continental climate with hot summers and cold winters.

In the mountains, altitude is an important factor. While the Vosges are hot in summer, the Massif Central is stormy and the southern Massif very dry. In contrast, the Cévennes get a lot of rain and the northern Massif can become very hot.

As for Paris, late April to early May is the best time for a visit – neither too hot, too wet nor too crowded. In July and August, many restaurants close and the city can be muggy, but accommodation is cheaper.

UK Customs regulations

Tax/duty-paid goods: within the EU, anyone can import or export any reasonable amount of goods for personal use, including gifts. The following quantities are given as guidance levels only:

Tobacco: 800 cigarettes or 400 cigarillos or 200 cigars or 1kg tobacco.

Alcohol: 10 litres of spirits over 22 per cent vol (38.8 proof); 20 litres of alcohol under 22 per cent vol; 90 litres of wine, of which no more than 60 litres can be sparkling wine; 110 litres of beer.

Tax/duty-free goods: strict legal limits apply. Anyone may import, amongst other things, the following into the UK:

Tobacco: 200 cigarettes or 100 cigarillos or 50 cigars or 250g tobacco.

Alcohol: 1 litre of spirits over 22 per cent vol or 2 litres of alcohol under 22 per cent vol or sparkling wine; 2 litres of wine.

Other: 60ml of perfume; 250ml of

PARIS

July & August

May · August

NICE

October · December

April · September

GRENOBLE

August · November

May · August

263

toilet water; and £75 of other goods including gifts and souvenirs.

People under 17 may not import alcohol or tobacco into the UK.

Non-EU visitors should check with their local customs and excise departments as to what they can take home with them.

Crime

Holidaymakers are often more careless abroad than at home and leave tents open, luggage visible in cars and personal property unattended on beaches, making life easy for the opportunist thief. Pickpockets travel on public transport and visit fairs and other busy places. If your money or belongings are stolen, contact the police immediately (tel: 17). You'll also need to report the theft in person and sign a statement at the nearest police station for insurance purposes.

Cycling

Ride on the right-hand side of the road unless there are cycle paths.

Cycles can be hired from cycle shops, some tourist offices and also from about 25 SNCF stations. Cycles can be transported free in the luggage van of some trains and as hand-baggage on TGVs and some other trains. Alternatively you can send it registered from one station to another, but it will not travel with you so send it a few days in advance. The leaflet *Guide du train et du vélo* lists stations and prices.

More information from The Touring Department, Cyclists Touring Club, Cotterell House, 69 Meadrow, Godalming, Surrey GU7 3HS (tel: 01483 417217) or from the Fédération Française de Cyclotourisme, 8 rue Jean-Marie Jégo, 75013 Paris (tel: 01 44 16 88 88).

Disabled travellers

Facilities for the disabled have improved greatly over the past few years, and now many hotels, public buildings, toilets, airports and the railway system have been modified to facilitate access.

RADAR in the UK (Royal Association for Disability and Rehabilitation) can provide several useful annual guides, including *European Holidays and Travel Abroad and Access in Paris. Paris–Ile de France for Everyone* is available from CNRH – see addresses opposite.

Concessions and special help are available from airlines, railways and ferry companies (eg free travel for companions etc). The FGTO can provide further details and the SNCF issues a leaflet, *Le Guide du Voyageur à mobilité réduite*, which is especially useful for wheelchair travellers.

Useful addresses

Australia: ACROD, PO Box 60, Curtin, ACT 2605 (tel: (02) 6282 4333).
Canada: Canadian Rehabilitation Council for the Disabled, Suite 810, 45 Sheppard Avenue East, Toronto ON M2N 5W5 (tel: (416) 250 7490).
France: APF, 17 boulevard Auguste-Blanqui, 75013 Paris (tel: 01 40 78 69 00); CNRH, 236 bis rue de Tolbiac, 75013 Paris (tel: 01 53 80 66 66).
Ireland: Irish Wheelchair Association, Blackheath Drive, Clontarf, Dublin 3

Costumes and gifts on display in a central Strasbourg shop

(tel: 01 833 8241); National Rehabilitation Board, 25 Clyde Road, Dublin 4 (tel: 01 668 4181); Northern Ireland: Disability Action, 2 Annadale Avenue, Belfast BT7 3JH (tel: (01232) 491 011).
New Zealand: Disabled Persons Assembly: PO Box 27–524, Level 4, Wellington Trade Centre, 173–175 Victoria Street, Wellington (tel: 0–4 801 9100).
UK: RADAR 12 City Forum, 250 City Road, London EC1V 8AF (tel: 0171 250 3222); Tripscope, The Courtyard, Evelyn Road, London W4 5JL (tel: 0181 994 9294); Mobility International, 228 Borough Hill Street, London SE1 1JX (tel: 0171 403 5688).
US: Mobility International, PO Box 10767, Eugene, Oregon OR 97440 (tel: (514) 343 1284); SATH (Society for the Advancement of Travel for the Handicapped), 347 Fifth Avenue, Suite 610, New York, NY 10016 (tel: (212) 447 7284).

Driving

Accident Contact the police immediately (tel: 17 – this calls the ambulance too), particularly if someone is injured. You and the other parties involved must complete and sign an accident statement form (*constat à l'amiable*) and exchange insurance details. Try to persuade witnesses to stay in order to make statements.

Age You must be at least 18 years of age to drive in France.

Breakdown If your car breaks down, try to move it to the side of the road and flash your hazard warning lights. If the fault is electrical or the car is on a bend or on a hill, place a red warning triangle on the road 30m behind your car (100m on motorways).
   Emergency phones (*postes d'appel d'urgence*), linked to a local police station, are placed at 4km intervals on main roads and every 2km on motorways.

Children Children aged 10 and under must sit at the back of the car, belted up. If, however, a specially approved fitted seat facing backward is fixed in the front of the car, a baby may use it.

Documents You must bring with you a full valid national driving licence, the vehicle's original registration document and insurance certificate. If you've borrowed the car, you'll need a letter of authorisation from the owner. You'll also need a nationality plate or sticker. You can bring in any vehicle for up to six months in a year without customs documents.

Drink Maximum permissible alcohol levels are very low, and it is much wiser not to drink at all. The penalties are high and the French police carry out random breath-testing. Any driver found to be above the legal limit (0.05 per cent) can be fined on the spot, and visitors may be banned from driving in France.

Fines Drivers can be fined on the spot, although for some infringements the police may accept vouchers from people with insurance cover. If a motorist considers he is innocent, he can pay a deposit (*amende forfaitaire*), and the police will issue a receipt.

Fuel Leaded petrol (*essence super*) is sold in one grade (98 octane), while unleaded is sold in two: 95 octane (*essence sans plomb*) and 98 octane (*super sans plomb*). The minimum amount of petrol you can buy is five litres. Diesel (*gazole*) is cheaper and readily available. Petrol is cheapest at hypermarkets and exorbitant on the motorways.

Petrol stations There is no shortage of petrol stations in France: on motorways they are placed about every 24km. In some rural areas of the country they may be shut on Sundays. You can usually pay for petrol with a credit card. Garages displaying the *Bison Futé* (wily buffalo) sign give away a free road map of France produced by the French Ministry of Transport. This shows less congested routes and information centres and lists restaurants, garages and hotels.
   Useful phrases at garages include *faîtes le plein* (fill her up) and *vérifiez l'huile* (check the oil).

265

Setting the world to rights: women in traditional Breton dress

Insurance Fully comprehensive insurance, which will cover you for some of the expenses incurred after a breakdown or an accident, is advisable; motorists can easily extend their national cover to go abroad. The best policies provide you with accommodation while your car is being repaired, or replace your vehicle if it's a write-off. Policies are likely to cover spare parts, and labour charges up to a certain amount.

Lights Drivers of right-hand drive vehicles (from the UK and Ireland) must adjust their headlights, in order not to dazzle oncoming drivers, by fitting headlight converters (black masking tape in pre-cut shapes) over the headlamps. If another driver flashes his headlights at you, this can mean that he is claiming priority and that you should give way to him.

Renting a car Car rental may be included in a fly-drive package holiday, or in co-operation with French Railways, which can work out cheaper than arranging it in France. Most companies offer weekly rates with unlimited mileage. Although the minimum age of car rental is 18, many companies insist on drivers being 21–3. Cars can be rented from about 200 railway stations and at airports.

Road signs Driving is on the right (*serrez à droite*). Unless otherwise indicated, give way to traffic coming from the right (*priorité à droite*): watch out in towns and on small roads!

Outside built-up areas, traffic on main roads usually has precedence over traffic from side roads.
vous n'avez pas la priorité you do not have priority
cédez le passage give way
toutes directions route for through traffic
sens interdit no entry
sens unique one way street
déviation diversion
passage protégé main roads having priority
rappel restriction continues (lower speed limit, for example).

Seat belts It is obligatory to wear these, in the back too, if they are fitted. If you are stopped by the police for not wearing them, you can be fined on the spot.

Speed limits In dry weather a higher speed limit applies than in wet weather. Unless otherwise indicated, maximum speed limits are as follows with wet weather maximums in brackets. Motorways with tolls (*autoroutes à péage*), 130kph (110kph); on dual carriageways and motorways without tolls 110kph (100kph); other roads, 90kph (80kph); in built-up areas, 50kph under all conditions.

On motorways there is a minimum speed limit of 80kph in the outside (overtaking) lane during daylight on flat roads with good visibility.

For a year after passing their test, drivers may not drive faster than 90kph.

Toll roads Most motorways in France impose tolls. Payment can be made by credit card.

Electricity
In France, the supply is 220 volts and the frequency is 50 Hertz (Hz), including electricity on graded campsites. As plugs and sockets rarely conform, travel adaptor plugs are often necessary for gadgets such as hairdryers and shavers. Because of different voltages and frequencies used in Canada and the US, a transformer may also be required.

Embassies and consulates

Only in extreme circumstances do you contact your country's embassy. It is the Consul who issues emergency passports, contacts relatives and advises how to transfer funds.

American Embassy: 2 rue St-Florentine, 75001 Paris (tel: 01 43 12 22 22). There are Consuls-General in Bordeaux, Strasbourg and Marseille.

Australian Embassy: 4 rue Jean-Rey, 75724 Paris Cedex 15 (tel: 01 40 59 33 00).

British Embassy: 16 rue d'Anjou, 75008 Paris (tel: 01 44 51 31 00). There are British Consulates or Honorary Consulates in many other towns, including Amiens, Biarritz, Bordeaux, Boulogne, Calais, Cherbourg, Dunkerque, Le Havre, Lille, Lyon, Marseille, Montpelier, Nantes, Nice, Perpignan, St-Malo/Dinard, Toulouse and Monaco.

Irish Embassy: 4 rue Rudé, 75116 Paris (tel: 01 44 17 67 00). There are Honorary Consuls in Antibes, Cherbourg, Lyon and Monaco. Canadian Embassy: 35 avenue Montaigne, 75008 Paris (tel: 01 44 43 29 00). There are consulates in Lyon, Nice, Strasbourg and Toulouse.

New Zealand Embassy: 7 ter rue Léonard de Vinci, 75116 Paris (tel: 01 45 00 24 11).

Emergency phone numbers

Police – 17

Fire (*Pompiers*) – 18

Emergency medical aid is available through SAMU (*Service d'aide médicale d'urgence*) – 15. Local numbers are on the first page of local phone directories (*l'annuaire*).

Health

No vaccinations are required for visitors from Europe, the US, Canada, Australia or New Zealand. The cost of urgent medical treatment, after an accident, say, will be covered by normal holiday insurance, but a non-urgent visit to a doctor may not be. Visitors from EU countries can receive emergency treatment more cheaply if they have completed the requisite forms (E111).

Reciprocal health agreements do not cover the cost of non-emergency medical treatment – a visit *from* a doctor will cost more than a visit *to* a doctor. To find a doctor, ask at your hotel or campsite or enquire at a local pharmacy. For minor problems, you can go to a pharmacy (see **Pharmacies**).

Visitors from non-EU countries should take out a personal health insurance policy before travelling to France.

Hitch-hiking

It is forbidden to hitch-hike on motorways but permitted on other roads.

Insurance

If you go on a package holiday, the tour operator will offer an insurance policy, but you are under no obligation to buy it, although you may have to buy equivalent cover from another insurer.

A holiday insurance policy should cover (at least) medical expenses; loss of luggage and money; cancellation or curtailment of your holiday; delayed departure and delayed baggage.

If you are taking your car to France, you need to be covered for accidents and breakdowns.

267

Language

Two separate Romance languages evolved within France: in the north, the *langue d'oïl* and in the south, the *langue d'oc*, or Occitanian, which included dialects spoken in Limousin, Auvergne and Gascony, as well as in Provence. Today, many Provençal words survive and the **Institute of Occitanian Studies** strives to promote the language, in which some vowel sounds differ from the French

Haras du Pin stud, Normandy

and the last syllable is often pronounced.

Roman influence was felt less in Brittany, which had been invaded by Celts driven out of Britain by the Saxons hundreds of years earlier. The Breton language, closely related to Welsh, is spoken in the west, and there is a strong movement to promote it.

In the south, the Pyrenees divide two groups of people from their more politically active counterparts in Spain, with whom they would like to form a separatist nation. In the west are about 50,000 Basques; in the east are the Catalans. Both groups speak their own languages: Basque is unlike any other, while Catalan is similar to Provençal. In Alsace, which for so many years bounced between Germany and France, the local language is more akin to High German.

Meanwhile, the **Académie Française** works hard to preserve the purity of the French language; but speech changes faster than the written word, and, to their great annoyance, many words of English and American derivation (*le parking*, *le weekend*) are now firmly part of the language.

Basic phrases
yes oui
no non
thank you merci
please s'il vous plaît
hello bonjour
good evening bonsoir
goodnight bonne nuit
goodbye au revoir
can you show me the way to...? pouvez-vous m'indiquer la direction de...?
where is...? où se trouve...?
I would like/we would like... je voudrais/on voudrait
how many/much? combien?
this one ceci
that one cela
that's enough ça suffit
left à gauche
right à droite
near près
straight on tout droit
opposite en face de
what time? à quelle heure?

Numbers

one un/une		**seven** sept	
two deux		**eight** huit	
three trois		**nine** neuf	
four quatre		**10** dix	
five cinq		**20** vingt	
six six		**100** cent	

first premier/première
second seconde/deuxième
third troisième
fourth quatrième
fifth cinquième

Days of the week
Monday lundi
Tuesday mardi
Wednesday mercredi
Thursday jeudi
Friday vendredi
Saturday samedi
Sunday dimanche

Maps
For planning a holiday in France, and when you get there, good maps are essential. Two useful country maps to have are the Michelin Route Planning Map 911 and the AA Road Map France.

Once you are in France, you need maps on a larger scale (1:200,000).

The French equivalent of the Ordnance Survey is IGN (*Institut Géographique National*), which publishes a series of large-scale maps of long-distance footpaths (*Grandes Randonnés*): the largest scale maps are the blue ones (*Série Bleue* – 1: 25,000).

Local information offices or tourist offices may supply free town plans.

Media
English language newspapers are on sale in most towns, but the further south you go, the more likely they

are to be a day or two late. *Le Monde* is the most distinguished French newspaper; *Le Figaro* is the longest established, *Libération* the youngest in spirit; several news magazines cover a broad range of emphasis and bias.

Local and regional press is well-developed in France and can be a useful source for local events.

Any type of music can be found on the crowded French airwaves; tune in to France Infos (105.5MHz) for news.

The BBC World Service broadcasts in English on medium wave 648KHz.

For entertainment in Paris, buy the weekly listings magazine *Pariscope* which has an English section.

Money matters

The French franc (FF) is made up of 100 centimes. There are coins of 5, 10, 20 and 50 centimes and 1, 2, 5, 10 and 20 francs. Banknotes come in denom-inations of 20, 50, 100, 200 and 500 francs. (On 1 January, 1999, the euro became the official currency of France, and the franc became a denomination of the euro. French franc notes and coins continue to be legal tender during a transitional period. The introduction of euro bank notes is likely to start by 1 January, 2002.)

To change foreign currency into francs, find a bank displaying a *Change* sign or go to foreign exchange bureaux; avoid changing money at hotels, as the rate is poor.

Major credit cards – Carte Bleue (Visa/ Barclaycard) and Eurocard (Access/MasterCard) and charge cards (Diners and American Express) are widely accepted in larger hotels and restaurants, shops, garages and hyper-markets. Smaller establishments may not accept them.

Museums

National museums usually charge an entrance fee but allow free entry to permanent collections for those under 18, reduced price for people between 18 and 25 and free for some disabled.

Municipal and private museums usually charge an entrance fee. Reduc-tions or free entry, depending on the museum, are often available for children, students, groups, people over 60, the disabled and visits on Sundays.

National holidays

Most shops and banks are shut on the days listed below. If any falls on a Sunday, the holiday is taken on the Monday.
New Year's Day – 1 January
Easter Monday
Labour Day – 1 May
VE Day – 8 May
Ascension Day
Whitsun (Monday)
Bastille Day – 14 July
Assumption Day – 15 August
All Saints' Day – 1 November
Armistice Day – 11 November
Christmas Day – 25 December.

Opening hours

Banks Hours vary, but banks are gen-erally open 9–noon and 2–4. They are closed on Sundays and either Monday or Saturday. Banks close early the day before a public holiday.

Museums Museums usually close on Tuesdays; exceptions include the Trianon Palace, Versailles and the Musée d'Orsay, which close on Mondays. Each museum has its own hours which vary according to season; most close on some public holidays.

Shops Hours vary depending on the type of shop, location and season. For example, lunchtime in summer

Detail of a fountain in Evreux, Normandy

in the south of France may extend to 4pm and the shops then stay open later in the evening.

Food shops are open Tuesday to Friday 7/8–6.30/7.30. Most close all day Monday but some may open in the afternoon. On Saturday and Sunday they may open mornings only. Smaller shops may close at lunchtime (noon–2). Bakers are open on Sunday mornings. Supermarkets and hypermarkets open from about 9am until 9 or 10pm. They are closed on Sunday and some hypermarkets also close on Monday mornings.

Pharmacies
Easily recognised by the illuminated green cross, pharmacies are mostly privately owned and run by highly trained staff who can give first aid and advice about ailments. They are not allowed to dispense prescriptions from a foreign doctor.

Pharmacies are usually open six days a week, and on Sundays at least one pharmacy in a town is open (*pharmacie de garde*). Its name and address will be displayed

The 15th-century Hôtel Dieu in Beaune, founded as a hospital

outside other shops, announced in the local paper and available from the local *gendarmerie*.

Places of worship
Every town and village has a Catholic church though not all of them offer Sunday masses – priests often officiate in more than one village. Protestant churches exist in most large towns, particularly in Paris and the Dordogne, which was once a Huguenot area.

Jews, Buddhists and members of non-conformist churches may have more difficulty in finding out whether there is a place of worship in town.

Muslims are well catered for throughout most of France because of the large North African population.

Tourist offices, town halls and notice boards can give information on religious services.

Post offices
Open: 8–5, 6 or 7 weekdays, 8–noon Saturday. Small offices close for lunch weekdays.

La Poste, French post offices, deals with post and telecommunications. You can buy stamps (**timbres de poste**) and phone cards (**télécartes**) and cash postcheques and send telexes or faxes. You can also collect letters (showing your passport as proof of identity), which you should have addressed to yourself, c/o Poste Restante, Poste Centrale, followed by number of the *département* and the name of the town.

Letter boxes are mustard yellow and often fixed on walls. For posting abroad, use the slot marked *départements étrangers*.

Public transport
Air A comprehensive and frequent air network links major French cities with each other. Air France operates services to about 50 business and holiday destinations, mostly from Paris. For information, contact Air France (tel: 0181 742 6600).

Deregulation has spawned numerous smaller operators who compete on the main routes and fill in the gaps on the cross-country routes. Check with local travel agents.

Road Where bus services do exist outside of the main towns, they tend to serve a specific purpose: taking children to and from school, serving a local market – often weekly – or connecting with trains. The timetables are therefore often sporadic, seasonal and inconvenient. Long-distance buses are almost non-existent in France.

Tickets are bought on the bus and must be cancelled (*composter*). If you are in a group or making several journeys, it's worth buying a book of tickets (*carnet*).

Rail French Railways or SNCF (*Société Nationale de Chemins de Fer*) operates a 33,000km network throughout France. The flagship of the rolling stock is the fleet of high-speed **TGV** trains (*trains à grande vitesse*), which holds the world train speed record (515.3kph); normal passenger services operate at about 300kph.

The TGV network now extends through much of France: west to Brest, Quimper and Le Croisic; south-west to Bordeaux, Toulouse, Tarbes and Irun; south-east to Lyon, the Alps, Nice, Marseilles and Béziers; north to Lille, Calais and the Channel Tunnel.

Although all routes converge on Paris, it is now possible to by-pass the capital through connections at Roissy (Charles de Gaulle) and Lille.

Euro City trains, which require a reservation, are fast, comfortable, international trains which go to over 200 towns, including 14 European capitals.

Within France the *rapide* and *express* trains (first and second class) stop more often, and there are even slower local trains. The RER (*Réseau Express Régional*) rail service runs on suburban routes around Paris.

For longer distances, you may decide to travel at night. Many trains have couchettes holding up to six people, both sexes, second class (four people first class), with washing facilities at the end of the carriage. Two- or three-bedded sleepers are more comfortable, with their own washbasins, but first-class sleepers can cost nearly five times as much as a couchette.

Marker flags for oysters, the Atlantic Coast's special delicacy

Tickets

TGV: there are three levels of TGV depending on time of day, day of week and time of year. Reservation on these trains is obligatory and the fee is included in the price.

Other: these are divided into white periods (more expensive, normally at weekends and holidays) and blue periods (cheaper, normally weekdays). Reservations are sometimes necessary.

'*Train Verts*' (Green trains), including some TGVs, offer 15 per cent reductions with, normally, no reservation required.

All tickets must be validated (*composté*) at machines on the platform before boarding the train. Discounts are available for senior citizens, travellers under 26, people travelling with children, large families and advanced booking. Contact the Rail Shop (see page 262), or SNCF for more information).

Paris For travelling on the Métro (underground) it's cheapest to buy a book (*carnet*) of ten tickets; one ticket can be used for journeys of any length. Tickets from the same *carnet* can be used on buses, but here, the longer your journey, the more tickets you must use. (Tickets from some tabacs, bus terminals or Métros).

A tourist ticket called *Paris Visite* is valid for one, two, three or five days and allows unlimited 1st class train and bus travel; half price for children under 12. The *Mobilis* card, for which a photo is required, is a 2nd class version but is only valid for one day at a time. The *Carte Orange* – photo also needed – enables you to buy coupons valid for a week (Monday to Sunday) or a calendar month. If you have a *Carte Jeunes* (see below), you can get a Ticket Jeunes which gives you cheap travel at weekends and public holidays.

Student and youth travel

Several types of reasonably priced cards are available to young people under 26, giving discounts on accommodation, meals and travel as well as to cultural and sporting events. You will need identification and a photo for all of them.

The International Student Card (ISIC), for which you also need a student card, also entitles you to cheaper museum entry and beds in university residences.

Honfleur Harbour

The International Youth Travel Card, also known as the GO 25 Card, is for anyone under 25. Buy it in France from OTU Voyages, 119 rue St-Martin, Parvis 2 Beaubourg, 75004 Paris (tel: 01 40 29 12 12); it is valid in about 60 countries.

The *Carte Jeunes* (Youth Card) is available for those under 26 and can be bought from around 5,000 outlets including railway stations.

A booklet, *Youth Tourism*, is available from the French Tourist Office.

Accommodation France has 200 youth hostels. Members of national associations can stay at French hostels if they have a membership card with photo. Write to Fédération Unie des Auberges de Jeunesse, 27 rue Pajol, 75018 Paris (tel: 01 44 89 87 27) for a list of hostels.

International Accommodation Centres, providing 11,000 beds, give another cheap alternative; they also offer sports and sightseeing programmes. They go by different names in different areas of France. All the centres belong to an organisation called UCRIF and a list of them is available, free, from the FGTO or La Maison de l'UCRIF, 27 rue de Turbigo 75002 Paris (tel: 01 40 26 57 64).

Other accommodation information is available from the Paris Tourist Office at 127 avenue des Champs-Elysées, 75008 Paris (tel: 01 49 52 53 54/5) and OTU (see above) in Paris, and from OTU offices, tourist offices and CRIJ (Youth Information Centres) offices throughout France.

Travel There are various rail passes for people under 26 and the SNCF also has discounts available for those under 25. See **Arriving** under **Rail** and **Public transport** under **Rail**.

Telephones

Most public phone booths now require phone cards; buy them from post offices, tobacconists and railway stations. If you do find a payphone that accepts coins, feed it one, two, five or ten franc pieces. The old *jeton* system has disappeared.

You can receive calls in a booth if a blue bell sign is displayed.

Caen Cathedral

All French numbers now have ten digits. The following prefixes have been added to the old 8-digit numbers:

Ile de France: 01
North-west: 02
North-east: 03
South-east: 04
South-west: 05

To call abroad from France, dial 00 then dial the country code:

Australia: 61
Canada: 1
Ireland: 353
New Zealand: 64
UK: 44
US: 1

Then dial the area code (omitting the first 0), followed by the number.

Time

France is one hour later than GMT from October to late March, two hours later the rest of the year.
The time in other countries compared with France, October to March, is as follows:

Australia: Central – eight hours ahead; Western Australia – seven hours ahead; Eastern – nine hours ahead.
Canada: Eastern – six hours behind; Western – nine hours behind.
Ireland: one hour behind.
New Zealand: 11 hours ahead.
UK: one hour behind.
US: Eastern – six hours behind; Western – nine hours behind.

Toilets

Men are *Messieurs*; women are *Dames*. Public toilets vary from the older, smelly ones with footrests and a hole, to the high-tech self-flushing variety.

In Paris, the large department stores have clean toilets. It's always a good idea to take your own paper.

Tourist offices

There are over 5,000 tourist offices, in France, called either *Offices de Tourisme* or *Syndicats d'Initatives*. Larger towns have tourist offices called Acceuil de France. In some places the tourist offices only open seasonally.

The French Government Tourist Office (FGTO) publishes a great deal of literature in English, which is available from the following addresses:

Australia: French Tourist Bureau, BNP Building, 12th Floor, 12 Castlereagh Street, Sydney NSW 2000 (tel: (02) 9231 5244).
Canada: Représentation Française du Tourisme, 1981 Avenue McGill College, Suite 490, Montréal Québec H3A 2W9 (tel: (514) 288 4264).
Ireland: FGTO, 35 Lower Abbey Street, Dublin 1 (tel: 01 703 4046).
UK: FGTO, 178 Piccadilly, London W1V 0AL (tel: premium line: 0891 244 123).
US: FGTO, 444 Madison Avenue, New York, NY 10022 (tel: (212) 838 7800).

Hotels and guest houses

The French Government Tourist Office (FGTO) publishes lists of approved hotels, which are rated on a scale from one-star to four-star. Some local tourist offices can help with last-minute hotel bookings.

Although it is possible to stay throughout the country in hotels belonging to perfectly reputable hotel chains (including Campanile, Ibis, Mercure, Novotel Sofitel and the new chain of robotic Formule 1), which provide convenient and often high-standard bases for business or passing-through travellers, it is generally the traditional French hotel which offers the chance of combining picturesque charm and ambience with a memorable gastronomic experience. Many of the simpler (one- and two-star) family-run hotels, mainly in rural areas, belong to the Logis de France marketing organisation, and can be recognised by a distinctive yellow fireplace logo.

Following inspections, they are classified with one, two or three 'chimneys'. A guide to the 3,700 or so Logis hotels is available from the FGTO, bookshops, or La Fédération Nationale des Logis de France, 83 avenue d'Italie, 75013 Paris (tel: 01 45 84 70 00; fax: 01 45 83 59 66).

At the opposite end of the spectrum, some well-established luxury hotels belong to the Relais et Châteaux organisation; their annual brochure is available from the FGTO.

Staying in a château can be a more personal experience, and not necessarily an inordinately expensive one. The association Château Accueil covers 64 privately owned castles, mansions and historic buildings which offer accommodation, either on a bed-and-breakfast basis or with an evening meal (taken en famille) (tel: 02 32 33 78 87; fax: 02 32 39 30 42).

More modest guest-house accommodation is available in thousands of country houses, farms and even châteaux, through the organisation Gîtes Chambres d'Hôte/Gîtes Tables d'Hôte, identified by the yellow and green Gîtes de France logo, which features a cockerel and a roof, together with a Chambres d'Hôtes sign. Information is available from the Fédération National des Gîtes de France, 59 rue St-Lazare, 75009 Paris (tel: 01 49 70 75 75).

Some establishments place the emphasis on their restaurant and offer bedrooms as an ancillary service. The following list of recommended hotels gives a selection of places where the standard of cooking is above average in its category.
Restaurants are listed separately for Paris and other cities.

Self-catering France is extremely well-endowed with self-catering holiday accommodation of all kinds, largely as a result of the very high level of second home ownership. The Gîtes de France organisation offers thousands of simple rural properties all over the country; many are converted farm buildings, and may be remote. All are inspected and graded into three categories (tel: 01 49 70 75 75).

PARIS

Accommodation
Expensive
L'Abbaye St-Germain, 10 rue Cassette, 75006 Paris (tel: 01 45 44 38 11). Fine 17th-century town house with charming courtyard and sophisticated décor. There is an airy, open-plan bar/salon area, but no restaurant.
Hôtel Costes France et Choiseul 239 rue St-Honoré 75001 (tel: 01 42 44 50 25). Opened in 1995 and styled in a modernised French-provincial mode, this hotel has a more contemporary feel than many others in Paris. There are charming nooks facing on to the courtyard and the rooms are equipped with marble-topped basins and brocade walls. The chic restaurant is a current favourite in the city.
Le Crillon, 10 place de la Concorde, 75008 Paris (tel: 01 44 71 15 00). One of the world's great hotels, classical and elegant throughout, with the most lavishly decorated restaurant in Paris (lunch menus are good value for the quality of the surroundings).
L'Hôtel, 13 rue des Beaux-Arts, 75006 Paris (tel: 01 44 41 99 00). Truly idiosyncratic, sophisticated left bank hotel, frequented now, as always, by the famous. You can choose Oscar Wilde's or Mistinguett's bedroom; all are individually decorated, some very eccentrically. Piano bar; popular small restaurant.
Le Pavillon de la Reine, 28 place des Vosges, 75003 Paris (tel: 01 42 77 96 40). On Paris's most beautiful old square, a comfortable hotel with garden and courtyard. Parking. No restaurant.

Moderate
Les Deux Iles, 59 rue St-Louis-en-l'Ile, 75004 Paris (tel: 01 43 26 13 35). Beautiful 18th-century town house on the island, charmingly furnished. Cosy bar and elegant little sitting room. No restaurant.
Des Grands Hommes/ Panthéon, 17/19 place du Panthéon, 75005 Paris (tel: 01 46 34 19 60; fax: 01 43 26 67 32). Neighbouring buildings, hotels since the 18th century, with glassed-in garden, on quiet (at night) square. Smart bedrooms with good bathrooms. No restaurant.
Hôtel des Jardins du Luxembourg 5 impasse Royer-Collar 75005 (tel: 01 40 46 08 88). This no-frills, well-maintained and comfortable, 23-room hotel is in a very quiet street. Some of the rooms have balconies with wonderful views of Paris.
Latitudes St-Germain, 7–11 rue St-Benoît, 75006 Paris (tel: 01 42 61 53 53). Large hotel, converted from former printing house in heart of St-Germain; spacious bedrooms in classic style. Piano bar. No restaurant.

Hotels & Restaurants

Hotels & Restaurants

Lenox St-Germain, 9 rue de l'Université, 75007 Paris (tel: 01 42 96 10 95). In street of antique shops in St-Germain, a stylish and classic little hotel with small bedrooms. Bar, chintzy salon. No restaurant.

Des Marronniers, 21 rue Jacob, 75006 Paris (tel: 01 43 25 30 60). Popular little hotel with small garden and colourful verandah. Small rustic-style bedrooms with some tiny bathrooms. No restaurant.

Budget

Esméralda, 4 rue St-Julien-le-Pauvre, 75005 Paris (tel: 01 43 54 19 20). Views of Notre Dame; objets d'art; and an eccentric style in this 16th-century building. No restaurant.

Le Jardin des Plantes, 5 rue Linné, 75005 Paris (tel: 01 47 07 06 20). Opposite the botanical gardens, with flower themes in bedrooms. Roof terrace, tea-room (and light meals), bar.

Place des Vosges, 12 rue de Birague, 75004 Paris (tel: 01 42 72 60 46). Just around the corner from the glorious square, a 17th-century house decorated and furnished in rustic style. No restaurant.

Prima Lepic, 29 rue Lepic, 75018 Paris (tel: 01 46 06 44 64). Pretty, plant-filled hotel in the heart of bohemian Montmartre.

Hôtel des Trois Colleges 16 rue Cujas, 75005 (tel: 01 43 54 67 30). Picturesque and cosy hotel in the shadow of the mighty university colleges, within sight of the Panthéon. There is a view of the Sorbonne and the Panthéon from the beamed attic rooms.

Restaurants
Expensive

Alain Ducasse 55 avenue Raymond Poincaré (tel: 01 47 27 12 27). The iconic Michelin-starred chef Alain Ducasse's Parisian outpost is one of the most sought-after dining experiences in the city. The modern French food is understated, but the prices are certainly not.

L'Ambroisie, 9 place des Vosges, 75004 Paris (tel: 01 42 78 51 45). Always booked well ahead, small and exclusive, with superb décor and highly talented cooking by chef Bernard Pacaud.

Grand Vefour, 17 rue de Beaujolais, 75001 Paris (tel: 01 42 96 56 27). Arguably the most attractive restaurant in Paris, an historic monument under the arcades of the Palais Royal. Dining in formal elegance.

Joël Robuchon, 59 avenue Raymond Poincaré, 75016 Paris (tel: 01 47 27 12 27). Palatial quarters for one of France's greatest living chefs, a superb art nouveau setting and magnificent food.

Moderate

Le Boeuf sur le Toit, 34 rue du Colisée, 75008 Paris (tel: 01 43 59 83 80). Elegant brasserie with '20s décor, near the Champs-Elysées. Good seafood, choucroute, foie gras.

Brasserie Flo, 7 cour des Petites-Ecuries, 75010 Paris (tel: 01 47 70 13 59). Jolly and authentic turn-of-the-century brasserie.

La Cantine des Gourmets, 113 avenue de la Bourdonnais, 75007 Paris (tel: 01 47 05 47 96). A place for serious foodies who appreciate what's on their plate more than the décor (however comfortable, even elegant). Excellent value for memorable standard of cooking.

La Closerie des Lilas 171 boulevard du Montparnasse, 75006 (tel: 01 43 26 70 50). Famous old Montparnasse bar/brasserie/restaurant where a piano tinkles in the background, and the atmosphere is sophisticated and bustling.

La Coupole, 102 boulevard du Montparnasse, 75014 Paris (tel: 01 43 20 14 20). Famous and noisy brasserie with literary and artistic associations, still atmospheric. Open till 2am.

La Ferme St-Simon, 6 rue Saint-Simon, 75007 Paris (tel: 01 45 48 35 74). Cramped and popular (with writers, editors, politicians), a plush and elegant small restaurant with excellent food.

La Fermette Marbeuf 1900, 5 rue Marbeuf 75008 Paris (tel: 01 53 23 08 00). Glorious Belle Epoque décor. Good value menu and wine list.

La Guirlande de Julie, 25 place des Vosges, 75003 Paris (tel: 01 48 87 94 07). Fresh, winter garden décor, with terrace, on beautiful square.

Au Pied de Cochon, 6 rue de Coquillière, 75001 Paris (tel: 01 40 13 77 00). Pork, pork and more pork. A Parisian institution on the site of the former Halles market, now more popular with tourists than early-morning porters, but still open 24 hours a day and still good.

Le Procope, 13 rue de l'Ancienne-Comédie, 75006 Paris (tel: 01 40 46 79 00). One of the oldest café/restaurants (1686) in the world, another with literary associations (Racine, Voltaire, Rousseau...). Agence France Presse telex, fax; piano and pianola. Open till 2am.

Restaurant Curieux 14 rue Saint-Merri, 75004 (tel: 01 42 72 75 97). Curious baroque interior. Clients are kept in line by strict, buttoned-up waitresses, but there's an excellent choice of classic cuisine.

Budget

La Canaille, 4 rue Crillon, 75004 Paris (tel: 01 42 78 09 71). Attractive bar-restaurant decked with revolutionary posters. Friendly atmosphere and well-cooked food.

Le Petit Mabillon, 6 rue Mabillon, 75006 Paris (tel: 01 43 54 08 41). Picturesque old bistro, with terrace. Menu has simple dishes of the day.

Le Petit Saint-Benoit, 4 rue Saint-Benoit, 75006, Paris (tel: 01 42 60 27 92). Traditional, genuine cooking attracts a loyal band of patrons in this 1930s-style bistro. Outside tables add fair-weather charm.

Le Royal Belleville 19 rue Louis-Bonnet, 75011 (tel: 01 43 38 22 72). Vast, canteen-like Chinese restaurant with an endless menu of fine specialities. On the first floor with a different entrance is Le Président, which is slightly more up-market.

Thoumieux, 79 rue St-Dominique, 75007 Paris (tel: 01 47 05 49 75). Country cooking and provincial style in bustling bistro.

NORMANDY

Accommodation
Expensive
Château d'Audrieu, Audrieu, 14250 Calvados (tel: 02 31 80 21 52). Fine 18th-century château, in large grounds with swimming pool. Excellent and inventive cooking complemented by an extensive wine list.

Grand Hôtel, Promenade Marcel Proust, Cabourg, 14390 Calvados (tel: 02 31 91 01 79). Enviable position right on the beach, with terrace and lots of bustle. Some bedrooms are enormous.

Manoir d'Hastings et la Pommeraie, 18 avenue de la Côte-de-Nacre, Bénouville, 14970 Calvados (tel: 02 31 44 62 43). Renowned restaurant, now with rooms (though that should not suggest meagre comforts; merely that the bedrooms, in a rather dull modern block in the garden, came after the restaurant). A particularly fine tarte chaude normande.

Moderate
Auberge de l'Abbaye, Le Bec-Helloüin, 27800 Eure (tel: 02 32 44 86 02). Exceptionally charming Norman village house. Resolutely Norman cooking – veal, apple tart, cheese, and lashings of cream with everything.

Auberge du Vieux Puits, 6 rue Notre-Dame-du-Pré, Pont-Audemer, 27500 Eure (tel: 02 32 41 01 48). A splendid, timbered property – formerly a 17th-century tannery. The focal point is the restaurant – all gleaming copper, polished wood and fragrant flowers.

Le Dauphin, place de la Halle, L'Aigle, 61300 Orne (tel: 02 33 84 18 00). Old post house, renovated with care, in traditional style. There's also a fine collection of Calvados (apple brandy) on offer, both in the restaurant and in a little shop.

France et Fuchsias, St-Vaast-La-Hougue, 50550 Manche (tel: 02 33 54 42 26). Well run, simple town hotel with an excellent restaurant popular with the yachting fraternity from the nearby marina.

Hostellerie Lechat, place Ste-Catherine, Honfleur, 14600 Calvados (tel: 02 31 14 49 49). Right in the bustling heart of town, with a lovely terrace looking out over the church.

Le Lion d'Or, 71 rue St-Jean, Bayeux, 14400 Calvados (tel: 02 31 92 06 90). Still the best-known hotel in town, with bedrooms around a flowery courtyard, and a busy restaurant. You may not hear much French, though.

Le Manoir du Lys, route de Juvigny, Bagnoles-de-l'Orne, 61140 Orne (tel: 02 33 37 80 69). A 19th-century hunting lodge in spacious grounds (with tennis). Very comfortable with good cooking.

Relais des Gourmets, 15 rue de Geôle, Caen, 14000 Calvados (tel: 02 31 86 06 01). High standard of comfort behind a dull exterior, just by the grounds of the château (and museums), and with a very attractive restaurant.

Saint Pierre, rue Principal Intra Muros, Le Mont-St-Michel, 50170 Manche (tel: 02 33 60 14 03). Historic rampart building on the way up to the great abbey church (you'll need to leave your car way below). Well modernised bedrooms and a perpetually bustling restaurant.

La Verte Campagne, le Hameau au Chevalier, Trelly, 50660 Manche (tel: 02 33 47 65 33). This old farmhouse is profoundly peaceful, and the dining and sitting rooms (complete with log fires) are extremely cosy.

Budget
Hotel de France, 15 rue Emile Demagny, Isigny-sur-Mer 14230 Calvados (tel: 02 31 22 00 33). Small friendly hotel in a picturesque fishing port, serving excellent, good-value meals.

Mon Castel, 1 boulevard des Belges, Houlgate, 14510 Calvados (tel: 02 31 24 83 47). Good-value seafood is the mainstay of this unpretentious small hotel restaurant three blocks from the sea.

277

BRITTANY

Accommodation
Expensive
Le Bretagne, 13 rue St-Michel, Questembert, 56230 Morbihan (tel: 02 97 26 11 12). If you're tired of seafood platters, this ritzy place offers a gastronomic pilgrimage. Georges Paineau is one of France's foremost chefs. A few elegant little bedrooms.

Château de Locguénolé, route de Port-Louis, Hennebont, 56700 Morbihan (tel: 02 97 76 29 04). Another 19th-century château, rather formal in parts, with a renowned restaurant. Situated in extensive wooded grounds.

Les Maisons de Bricourt, 1 rue Duguesclin, Cancale, 35260 Ille-et-Vilaine (tel: 02 99 89 64 76). One of France's top hotel-restaurants. Some rooms are in an elegantly furnished old stone manor house on clifftops with windows overlooking the bay of Mont-St-Michel. The Maisons de Bricourt restaurant, equally elegant, is in a separate building. Gorgeous seafood a speciality.

Manoir de Lan-Kerellec, Trébeurden, 22560 Côtes-d'Armor (tel: 02 96 15 47 47). Sophisticated and elegant little manor house situated in leafy residential area with path down to the beach.

De la Plage, Ste-Anne-La-Palud, Plonévez Porzay, 29550 Finistère (tel: 02 98 92 50 12). Isolated at the edge of an enormous expanse of sandy beach. High standard of cooking, with a well-chosen wine list.

Hotels & Restaurants

Moderate

D'Avaugour, 1 place du Champ Clos, Dinan, 22100 Côtes-d'Armor (tel: 02 96 39 07 49). Thoroughly well-established old town-house hotel with rampart gardens and an airy restaurant overlooking place Du Guesclin in the heart of historic Dinan. Bedrooms comfortable, if a little dull. Very convenient for sightseeing.

Les Bains de Mer, 11 rue de Kerguelen, Bénodet, 29950 Finistère (tel: 02 98 57 03 41). Modern hotel near sea with a swimming pool. Some family rooms and plenty of seafood in restaurant.

Central, 6 Grande-Rue, Saint-Malo, 35400 Ille-et-Vilaine (tel: 02 99 40 87 70). In the old town (intra-muros). Comfortable little bedrooms; popular restaurant (La Frégate).

Le Goyen, place J Simon, Audierne, 29770 Finistère (tel: 02 98 70 08 88). Solid, port-side hotel, impeccably run. Adolphe Bosser, the owner, is one of the best chefs in Brittany.

Kastel-Moor and Ker-Moor, avenue de la Plage, Bénodet, 29950 Finistère (tel: 02 98 57 05 01 and 02 98 57 04 48). Twin hotels sharing large garden, with swimming pool and tennis, just across the road from the beach resort.

Manoir de Moëllien, Locronan, Plonévez Pozray, 29550 Finistère (tel: 02 98 92 50 40). Austere old stone manor, in isolated setting 2.5km north-west of Locronan. Ten ground-floor rooms with French windows.

Repaire de Kerroc'h, 29 quai Morand, Paimpol, 22500 Côtes-d'Armor (tel: 02 96 20 50 13). 18th-century manor overlooking bay with limited rooms but with generous seafood gastronomy.

Le Roof, Presqu'île de Conleau, Vannes, 56000 Morbihan (tel: 02 97 63 47 47). Fine situation by a small beach on the Morbihan gulf. Part of the Best Western group.

Budget

Chez Pierre, Raguenès Plage, Névez, 29920 Finistère (tel: 02 98 06 81 06). Delightful family hotel in a rural setting close to the beach. New annexe across the garden has duplex rooms. Children can eat early and are well catered for.

Du Port, Port-Manech, Névez, 29920 Finistère (tel: 02 98 06 82 17). Neat and compact hotel up a short hill from the port and beach of this bustling little resort.

Thalamot, Le Chemin-Creux, Beg-Meil, Fouesnant, 29170 Finistère (tel: 02 98 94 97 38). Straightforward little establishment, near beach and harbour.

LOIRE

Accommodation

Expensive

Château d'Artigny, Montbazon, 37250 Indre-et-Loire (tel: 02 47 34 30 30). Arguably one of the finest château hotels in France (1919; loaded with marble, gilt, frescoes...). Comfort

and facilities cannot be faulted, provided you like the style.

Domaine des Hauts de Loire, Onzain, 41150 Loir-et-Cher (tel: 02 54 20 72 57). Sober and elegant 18th-century mansion, with very large and beautiful bedrooms and apartments.

Grand Hôtel du Lion d'Or, 69 rue G Clemenceau, Romorantin, 41200 Loir-et-Cher (tel: 02 54 94 15 15). Didier Clement is one of France's finest chefs. If you're fearful of over-indulgence, you can opt for half portions. Old coaching inn around courtyard.

Moderate

Angleterre et Central, 1 place des Quatre Piliers, Bourges, 18000 Cher (tel: 02 48 24 68 51). Very central, traditional old hotel near Palais Jacques Coeur.

Le Bon Laboureur, Chenonceaux, 37150 Indre-et-Loire (tel: 02 47 23 90 02). An attractive and peaceful establishment, with bedrooms in annexes or around the flowery courtyard.

La Caillère, 36 route des Montils, Candé-sur Beuvron, 41120 Loir-et-Cher (tel: 02 54 44 03 08). Small country house, with the emphasis on the restaurant – one of the best in the area.

Gargantua, 73 rue Voltaire, Chinon, 37500 Indre-et-Loire (tel: 02 47 93 04 71). Fine restaurant with rooms in beautiful 15th-century town mansion in the old part of town.

Grand St-Michel, 103 place St-Michel, Chambord, 41250 Loir-et-Cher (tel: 02 54 20 31 31). The position is everything - isolated at the edge of a forest clearing opposite the great château. The hotel is comfortable enough, but rather unexciting.

Hotel Château des Tertres, route de Monteaux, Onzain, 41150 Loir-et-Cher (tel: 02 54 20 83 88). Comfortable 19th-century château in large grounds – very tranquil. No restaurant but free bike-rental.

Jeanne de Laval, 54 rte Nationale, Les Rosiers-sur-Loire, 49350 Maine-et-Loire (tel: 02 41 51 80 17). One of the best-known eating establishments in the Loire, its reputation created by the current owner's father some 50 years ago. Bedrooms are more simple.

Budget

Le Bussy, Montsoreau, 49730 Maine-et-Loire (tel: 02 41 38 11 11). Fine views of the powerful white château; rustic-style bedrooms.

Hôtel de la Sologne, place St Firmin, Beaugency, 45190 Loiret (tel: 02 38 44 50 27). Traditional hotel on main square, overlooking ruined castle. Breakfast is served in the garden.

Aux Naulets d'Anjou, 18 rue Croix-de-Mission, Gennes, 49350 Maine-et-Loire (tel: 02 41 51 81 88). Modern house in residential area, with garden.

Moulin Fleuri, Veigne, 37250 Indre-et-Loire (tel: 02 47 26 01 12). Charming family-run restaurant-with-rooms in converted watermill by the Indre. Acclaimed restaurant.

Splendid, 139 rue du Dr Gaudrez,

278

Montreuil-Bellay, 49260 Maine-et-Loire
(tel: 02 41 53 10 00). Small and pretty
bedrooms, some with château views; annexe
Le Relais du Bellay has swimming pool and
relaxing garden.

ATLANTIC COAST

Accommodation
Expensive
Château Cordeillan-Bages, 61 route des
Vignerons, Pauillac, 33250 Gironde (tel: 05 56
59 24 24). Paradise for oenophiles among the
world's finest vineyards. Charming, light
bedrooms.
Hôtel de Chantaco, route Ascain, Saint-Jean-
de-Luz, 64500 Pyrénées–Atlantiques (tel: 05
59 26 14 76). Basque-style house, with gardens looking over the famous golf course.
Hôtel du Palais, 1 avenue de l'Impératrice,
Biarritz, 64200 Pyrénées–Atlantiques (tel: 05
59 24 09 40). Empress Eugénie's villa, high
above the sea, furnished in appropriate style.
The cooking does justice to its surroundings.

Moderate
Au Bon Coin du Lac, 34 avenue du Lac,
Mimizan, 40200 Landes (tel: 05 58 09 01 55).
Elegant restaurant-with-rooms in lakeshore gardens. Shady courtyard setting for memorable
food.
France-Angleterre et Champlain, 20 rue
Rambaud, La Rochelle, 17000 Charente-
Maritime (tel: 05 46 41 23 99). Fine old town
house, in heart of old town (noisy in the morning, quiet at night); pretty garden. No restaurant.
Plaisance, place du Clocher, Saint-Emilion,
33330 Gironde (tel: 05 57 55 07 55).
Renovated old building alongside the bell
tower. Competent cooking, and a large wine
list.

Budget
Florida, 3 place Ste-Eugenie, Biarritz 64200
Pyrenees-Atlantiques (tel: 05 59 24 01 76).
This central hotel provides solid value, not
least at the Grill Eugenie, where you can
enjoy hearty cooking overlooking the main
square.
Logis de la Couperie, La Roche-sur-Yon,
85000 Vendée (tel: 02 51 37 21 19).
Romantic, personally run hotel in large 19th-
century country house with extensive grounds.
Very peaceful and elegantly furnished. No
restaurant.
Au Marais, 46–8 quai L Tardy, Coulon, 79510
Deux-Sèvres (tel: 05 49 35 90 43). Riverside
inn, well placed for canal boat trips. Very good
regional cooking; peaceful rooms in an annexe.

Restaurants
Expensive
Le Chapon Fin, 5 rue Montesquieu, Bordeaux,
33000 Gironde (tel: 05 56 79 10 10).
Extravagant décor. Weekday lunch menus offer
outstanding value.

Moderate
Le Vieux Bordeaux, 27 rue Buhan, Bordeaux,
33000 Gironde (tel: 05 56 52 94 36). One of
the best of Bordeaux's many fine restaurants.

Budget
A Côté de Chez Fred, 32 rue St-Nicholas,
La Rochelle 17000 Charentes-Maritime (tel: 05
46 41 65 76). Cheerful fish restaurant with
blackboard menus of whatever's freshest.
André, 5 rue Saint Jean du Pérot, La Rochelle
(tel: 05 46 41 28 24). At base of ramparts with
terrace overlooking port and serving a good
variety of seafood specialities.

DORDOGNE

Accommodation
Expensive
Des Beaux-Arts, 1 place du Pont Neuf,
Toulouse, 31000 Haute-Garonne (tel: 05 61
23 40 50). Well-kept small hotel, with a neighbouring brasserie open till the small hours.
L'Esplanade, Domme, 24250 Dordogne (tel:
05 53 28 31 41). Very traditional old hotel situated within the fortifications of the village of
Domme. The rustic restaurant has been
awarded many accolades for its outstanding
cuisine.
Grand Ecuyer, rue Voltaire, Cordes-sur-Ciel,
81170 Tarn (tel: 05 63 53 79 50). Wonderful
medieval mansion, sumptuously restored, with
renowned patron/chef.
Le Vieux Logis, Trémolat, 24510 Dordogne
(tel: 05 53 22 80 06). Very peaceful old buildings set in immaculate gardens (with its own
helipad).

Moderate
Auberge du Sombral, St-Cirque-Lapopie,
46330 Lot (tel: 05 65 31 26 08). Very old
house, beautifully restored, in high medieval
village. Simple country style with cooking to
match.
De Bordeaux, 38 place Gambetta, Bergerac,
24100 Dordogne (tel: 05 53 57 12 83). On
main square. Terrace for eating out.
De la Bouriane, place du Foirail, Gourdon,
46300 Lot (tel: 05 65 41 16 37). Simple, traditional hostelry in small market town. Above
average cooking.
Du Centre, place de la Mairie, Les Eyzies,
24620 Dordogne (tel: 05 53 06 97 13). Better
value than some of its competitors in this
major tourist centre, with riverside setting and
good cooking.
France, avenue F de Maynard, Saint-Céré,
46400 Lot (tel: 05 65 38 02 16). Modern,
rustic-style hotel with fine garden. Good value
menus.
Les Griffons, Le Pont, Bourdeilles, 24310
Dordogne (tel: 05 53 03 75 61). Fine 16th-
century house on the banks of the Dronne, with
popular restaurant.
Laborderie, Tamniès, 24620 Dordogne (tel: 05
53 29 68 59). Village-centre hotel with
annexes. Traditional Perigordian cooking.

L'Oustal del Barry, place du Bourg, Najac, 12270 Aveyron (tel: 05 65 29 74 32). Fine old house in medieval village; some bedrooms have excellent views. Good value menus.

Moulin de la Beune, Les Ezies-de-Tayac, 24620 Dordogne (tel: 05 53 06 94 33). Converted mill with large, comfortable rooms and a good restaurant. Good value in this honeypot tourist centre.

L'Univers, 2 place de la République, Villefranche-de-Rouergue, 12200 Aveyron (tel: 05 65 45 15 63). Simple, central hotel with views over hills and old town. Good value menus.

Budget

Au Déjeuner de Sousceyrac, Sousceyrac, 46190 Lot (tel: 05 65 33 00 56). Simple auberge in remote village, with small bedrooms. Excellent cooking and good value local wines.

France, 3 rue Marc-Dufraisse, Ribérac, 24600 Dordogne (tel: 05 53 90 00 61). Revitalised old building, with small garden. Good value menus.

Pagès, route de Payrac, Calès, 46350 Lot (tel: 05 65 37 95 87). Simple stone hostelry on the Causse de Gramat, with popular and good value restaurant.

Relais du Touron, route de Sarlat, Carsac-Aillac, 24200 Dordogne (tel: 05 53 28 16 70). Peaceful 19th-century manor in wooded countryside. Elegantly simple food.

De la Tour, place de l'Eglise, Aubazine, 19190 Corrèze (tel: 05 55 25 71 17). Central, with good value menus. Fine tower room with views.

PYRENEES

Accommodation
Expensive

Hostellerie des Sept Molles, Sauveterre-de-Comminges, 31510 Haute-Garonne (tel: 05 61 88 30 87). In a secluded rural setting 3km from Sauveterre. Elegant but informal, with large garden.

Les Prés d'Eugénie, Eugénie-les-Bains, 40320 Landes (tel: 05 58 05 06 07). Michel Guérard's luxury and very expensive restaurant/hotel/health farm. Bedrooms in a Second Empire mansion or in a converted convent.

Pyrénées, 19 place Charles de Gaulle, St-Jean-Pied-de-Port, 64220 Pyrénées-Atlantiques (tel: 05 59 37 01 01). Busy, traditional hostelry in the centre of this halt for Santiago-bound pilgrims. Excellent value restaurant serving dishes which reflect the colours and flavours of the regional cuisine.

Moderate

Angleterre, route Luchon, Arreau, 65240 Haute-Pyrénées (tel: 05 62 98 63 30). 17th-century inn amid fast-flowing rivers and mountain scenery. Good rustic cooking.

Arraya, Sare, 64310 Pyrénées-Atlantiques (tel: 05 59 54 20 46). Glorious old Basque village house, beautifully furnished and maintained, with pleasant small garden. Sophisticated atmosphere, good choice of regional dishes.

Auberge Atalaya, Llo, 66800 Pyrénées-Orientales (tel: 04 68 04 70 04). Delightful old converted farmhouse in tiny Cerdagne village. Attractive restaurant serves outstanding cuisine.

La Deviniere, 5 rue Loquin, St-Jean-de-Luz, 64500 Pyrénées-Atlantiques (tel: 05 59 26 05 51). Exquisitely furnished, tiny hotel.

Budget

Auberge du Poids Public, St-Félix-Lauragais, 31540 Haute-Garonne (tel: 05 61 83 00 20). Old inn in hill-top village. Local reputation for good cooking and wine list.

Brèche de Roland, Gèdre, 65120 Hautes-Pyrénées (tel: 05 62 92 48 54). Village centre, 8.5km from Garvanie, in fine walking country. Cheerful, rustic-style.

Hôtel Chilo, Barcus, 64130 Pyrénées-Atlantiques (tel: 05 59 28 90 79). Characteristic old Basque house situated in the heart of a village surrounded by the breath-taking scenery of the Pyrenees. Individually styled attractive bedrooms provide a soothing atmosphere for a relaxing stay. Gardens and playground. Good restaurant.

Lons, 6 place G Duthil, Foix, 09000 Ariège (tel: 05 61 65 52 44). Comfortably modernised posthouse in town centre, with spacious rooms and riverside views from the dining room.

Nivelle, St-Pée-sur-Nivelle, 64310 Pyrénées-Atlantiques (tel: 05 59 54 10 27). Little Basque auberge. Small, simple bedrooms (plus some in modern annexe across field). Good food.

Pic d'Anie, Lescun, 64490 Pyrénées-Atlantiques (tel: 05 59 34 71 54). Simple old mountain hotel in centre of walking village.

L'Oustal, Unac, 09250 Ariège (tel: 05 61 64 48 44). Pretty auberge in tiny village (13km north-west of Ax-les-Thermes) with views. Cooking well above average.

Les Sources de la Nive, Esterençuby, St-Jean-Pied-de-Port, 64220 Pyrénées-Atlantiques (tel: 05 59 37 10 57). Pretty riverside house in idyllic setting. Good value and excellent regional cuisine.

PROVENCE COAST

Accommodation
Expensive

Abbaye Sainte-Croix, route du Val-de-Cuech, Salon-de-Provence, 13300 Bouches-du-Rhône (tel: 04 90 56 24 55). Twelfth-century abbey buildings, beautifully converted, in a splendid rural setting between Aix and Arles. Beautiful swimming pool, cool and elegant public rooms, very good cooking.

d'Europe, 12 place Crillon, Avignon, 84000 Vaucluse (tel: 04 90 14 76 76). Just outside the city walls, but near the sights, an elegant 16th-century mansion with formal atmosphere.

La Réserve de Beaulieu, boulevard Général Leclerc, Beaulieu-sur-Mer, 06310 Alpes-Maritimes (tel: 04 93 01 00 01). Scott Fitzgerald, Greta Garbo... the pre-war atmosphere of this Italianate palace lingers on.

Moderate

Les Antiques, 15 avenue Pasteur, Saint-Rémy-de-Provence, 13210 Bouches-du-Rhône (tel: 04 90 92 03 02). Very charming 19th-century mansion near the centre. No restaurant.

Arène, place des Langes, Orange 84100 Vaucluse (tel: 04 90 11 40 40). In the heart of the old town, on a delightful shady square. Your car is parked for you. No restaurant.

D'Arlatan, 26 rue du Sauvage, Arles, 13200 Bouches-du-Rhône (tel: 04 90 93 56 66). Fine and very old mansion near the place du Forum. Your car is parked for you. No restaurant.

Auberge de la Madone, Peillon, 06440 Alpes-Maritimes (tel: 04 93 79 91 17). Astonishing situation, perched high in an isolated medieval village 18km behind Nice.

Le Beffroi, rue de l'Evêché, Vaison-la-Romaine, 84110 Vaucluse (tel: 04 90 36 04 71). Wonderful 16th-century building up a steep hill in the town's medieval quarter.

Clair Logis, 12 avenue Centrale, St-Jean-Cap-Ferrat, 06230 Alpes-Maritimes (tel: 04 93 76 04 57). Very simple establishment in large and lush gardens at the heart of the Cap. No restaurant.

D'Entraigues, place de l'Evêché, Uzès, 30700 Gard (tel: 04 66 22 32 68). Fine old town house; small bedrooms, a few self-catering apartments, and a wonderful restaurant terrace with a view of the Tour Fenestrelle.

L'Etrier Camarguais, chemin bas des Launes, Les Saintes-Maries-de-la-Mer, 13460 Bouches-du-Rhône (tel: 04 90 97 81 14). An ideal base to explore the Camargue, with its own horses for hire. Informal, friendly service and good food.

Les Florets, route des Dentelles-de-Montmirail, Gigondas, 84190 Vaucluse (tel: 04 90 65 85 01). Located at the foot of the rugged Dentelles de Montmirail and surrounded by the famous wine village of Gigondas. Excellent starting point for many country walks. Good cooking and quality wine list (the patron has his own vineyards).

Lou Troupelen, chemin des Vendanges, St-Tropez, 83990 Var (tel: 04 94 97 44 88). Modern, Provençal-style buildings, at the back of town, with garden and views. No restaurant. One of the cheapest St-Tropez hotels.

Le Manoir, 8 rue de' l'Entrecasteaux, Aix-en-Provence, 13000 Bouches-du-Rhône (tel: 04 42 26 27 20). Former cloister in quiet situation near centre. No restaurant.

Mas d'Aigret, Les Baux-de-Provence, 13520 Bouches-du-Rhône (tel: 04 90 54 33 54). The best value of all the luxury hotels in this extraordinary resort, below the medieval village.

La Table du Comtat, Séguret, 84110 Vaucluse (tel: 04 90 46 91 49). Attractive old house set in picturesque hillside village, comfortable and sophisticated. Excellent cooking and commendable wine list.

Budget

Auberge des Seigneurs, place du Frêne, Vence, 06140 Alpes-Maritimes (tel: 04 93 58 04 24). Simple, inexpensive rooms with character in a delightful 17th-century building, and an excellent Provençal restaurant.

Les Géraniums, place de la Croix, Le Barroux, 84330 Vaucluse (tel: 04 90 62 41 08). Impeccable little hotel in picturesque hilly hamlet, with terrace and views of olive trees, vineyards and orchards. Cosy bedrooms and good value country cooking.

Le Lisita, 2 boulevard des Arènes, Nîmes, 30000 Gard (tel: 04 66 67 66 20). Small but charming hotel in a street lined with plane-trees. Regional country furniture and a recommendable restaurant.

Médiéval, 15 rue Petite Saunerie, Avignon, 84000 Vaucluse (tel: 04 90 86 11 06). Old building with pretty courtyard; self-catering studios for stays of a week or more.

Le Vieux Fox, place de l'Eglise, Fox Amphoux, 83670 Var (tel: 04 94 80 71 69). Eleventh-century priory in delightful tiny hilltop village.

Restaurants
Moderate

Dar Djerba, 15 cours Julien, 6e, Marseille, 13000 Bouches-du-Rhône (tel: 04 91 48 55 36). A good place to sample some of Marseille's ethnic cooking, in a Tunisian restaurant with lovely Moorish tiling.

Don Camillo, 5 rue des Ponchettes, Nice, 06300 Alpes-Maritimes (tel: 04 93 85 67 95). Small and simple, with some of the best local dishes in the old town (raviolis, cheeses and puddings are particularly good).

La Merenda, 4 rue de la Terrasse, Nice, 06300 Alpes-Maritimes. No telephone. Take pot luck for a table in this tiny, traditional old-town bistro.

Budget

Le Bistrot Latin, 18 rue de la Couronne, Aix-en-Provence, 13100 Bouches-du-Rhône (tel: 04 42 38 22 88). Just off the Cours Mirabeau. Excellent local dishes and wines. Very good value menus.

MASSIF CENTRAL

Accommodation
Expensive
Château de la Caze, La Malène, 48210 Lozère (tel: 04 66 48 51 01). Medieval atmosphere, if not comfort, in this solid castle set in shady

281

grounds about 5.5km from the village; some additional apartments in converted farm buildings.

Château de Codignat, Bort-l'Etang, Lezoux, 63190 Puy de Dome (tel: 04 73 68 43 03). Turreted Renaissance château in pleasant wooded park. Antiques and candlelit dinners. All comforts.

Manoir de Montesquiou, La Malène, 48210 Lozère (tel: 04 66 48 51 12). A handsome little 15th-century manor house, with attractive well-maintained accommodation. It is conveniently situated for Tarn gorge. Restaurant serves a classic cuisine based on the best regional produce.

Michel Bras, route de l'Aubrac, Laguiole, 12210 Aveyron (tel: 05 65 51 18 20). A restaurant-with-rooms, rather than a hotel – but what a restaurant! Michel Bras, one of France's great chefs, makes dreams come true. Fifteen ultra-modern rooms.

Moderate

Auberge Pré Bossu, Moudeyres, 43150 Haute-Loire (tel: 04 71 05 10 70). Former farmhouse, in remote village of pretty thatched stone houses. Renowned cooking by patron/chef.

Château d'Ayres, Meyreuis, 48150 Lozère (tel: 04 66 45 60 10). Converted monastery in parkland on the edge of the Causses. Elegantly furnished bedrooms. Lavish breakfasts and welcoming owners.

Hostellerie de la Maronne, Le Theil, St-Martin-Valmeroux, 15140 Cantal (tel: 04 71 69 20 33). Nineteenth-century house in an idyllic valley setting near the hill-village of Salers. Excellent food and service. Ideal venue for lovers of architecture and culture.

Hôtel Beauséjour, 4 rue Basse, 15800 Vic-sur-Cère (tel: 04 71 47 50 27). Large hotel and garden in attractive medieval village. Modernised rooms. Auvergnat food.

Parc, 47 avenue J Monestier, Florac, 48400 Lozère (tel: 04 66 45 03 05). Peaceful, large hotel surrounded by extensive grounds.

Sainte-Foy, Conques, 12320 Aveyron (tel: 05 65 69 84 03). Eighteenth-century building in a splendid location in the heart of the village, which was once one of the main resting places on the pilgrimage route to Santiago de Compostela. Pretty bedrooms and two apartments in neighbouring former convent.

Budget

Auberge Fleurie, place du Barry, Montsalvy, 15120 Cantal (tel: 04 71 49 20 02). Ivy-covered auberge at the edge of the village, with cheerful country-style restaurant (excellent value).

Manoir, Arlempdes, 43490 Haute-Loire (tel: 04 71 57 17 14). Very simple inn in tiny village, affording splendid views.

Midi-Papillon, place A Lemasson, St-Jean-du-Bruel, 12230 Aveyron (tel: 05 65 62 26 04). Well run village hotel in a picturesque valley amidst hills and chestnut trees, offering

excellent value menus combined with more innovative dishes prepared with the finest local produce.

THE ALPS & RHONE VALLEY

Accommodation
Expensive

L'Abbaye, Talloires, 74290 Haute-Savoie (tel: 04 50 60 77 33). Elegantly furnished and very atmospheric former abbey building in beautiful situation on Lake Annecy.

Château de Coudrée, Bonnatrait, 74140 Sciez-sur-Leman (Haute Savoie) (tel: 04 50 72 62 35). On shores of Lake Geneva, 12th-century château elegantly furnished, family-owned.

Le Fer à Cheval, 36 route du Crêt-d'Arbois, Megève, 74120 Haute-Savoie (tel: 04 50 21 30 39). Hearty Savoy ambience with dinner round the fireplace.

Ostellerie du Vieux Pérouges, Pérouges, 01800 Ain (tel: 04 74 61 00 88). Medieval hostelry, a film-maker's dream.

Moderate

Beausoleil, Le Lavancher, Chamonix, 74400 Haute-Savoie (tel: 04 50 54 00 78). Simple little hotel, 6km from Chamonix, in mountain village; pretty garden, tennis.

Chalet Croix-Fry, la Croix-Fry, Manigod, 74230 Haute-Savoie (tel: 04 50 44 90 16). Cuckoo-clock chalet and delightful annexes, high on mountain pass.

Michel Chabran, 29 avenue du 45e-Parallèle, Pont-de-l'Isère, 26600 Drôme (tel: 04 75 84 60 09). Acclaimed restaurant-with-rooms just outside Valence.

Budget

Chalet-Hôtel du Cucheron, Col du Cucheron, St-Pierre-de-Chartreuse, 38380 Isère (tel: 04 76 88 62 06). Pass-top chalet, restaurant-with-rooms, in picturesque hiking country.

Grand, 60 rue de l'Hôtel de Ville, Crest, 26400 Drôme (tel: 04 75 25 08 17). Simple family-run establishment situated right in the centre of this small medieval village. Popular and good value restaurant in a fine 19th-century building serving a choice of specialities from the region.

La Marmotte, Bonneval-sur-Arc, 73480 Savoie (tel: 04 79 05 94 82). Totally peaceful, in fine surroundings. Pleasant terrace and hearty mountain cooking.

Restaurants
Expensive

La Tour Rose, 22 rue du Boeuf, Lyon 69005, Rhône (tel: 04 78 37 25 90). Extremely elegant hotel, in a glorious 17th-century former convent in the old town. The guest accommodation is exquisitely furnished and offers a high level of comfort. The standard of cooking is as exalted as the surroundings.

The restaurant, in the former chapel with its glass roof, serves an extensive array of imaginative dishes.

Budget
Café des Féderations, 8 rue du Major-Martin, Lyon 69000 Rhône (tel: 04 78 28 26 00). Popular eating house with cheerful service and rustic décor. The Lyonnaise classics here are such good value it's advisable to book.

BURGUNDY & THE JURA

Accommodation
Expensive
Le Cep, 27–29 rue Maufoux, Beaune, 21200 Côte-d'Or (tel: 03 80 22 35 48). Beautiful Renaissance mansion with courtyard, in town centre (your car is parked for you). Elegant restaurant, with terrace for eating out.
Château d'Igé, Igé, 71960 Saône-et-Loire (tel: 03 85 33 33 99). Medieval castle appropriately converted and furnished. Spacious bedrooms and gardens.
L'Espérance, St-Père-sous-Vézelay, 89450 Yonne (tel: 03 86 33 39 10). Restaurant-with-rooms. Food produced by one of France's top chefs, Marc Meneau. Some rooms in restored mill. Cheaper bistro opposite – same owner.
Host. du Vieux Moulin, Bouilland, 21420 Côte-d'Or (tel: 03 80 21 51 16). Jean-Pierre Silva offers gourmet eating and a welcome for families. Romantic setting.

Moderate
Le Bourgogne, place de l'Abbaye, Cluny, 71250 Saône-et-Loire (tel: 03 85 59 00 58). Stylish little hotel on the site where the Benedictine Abbey of Cluny originally stood. Restaurant serves superb imaginative dishes, complemented by an excellent choice of wines.
Jean-Paul Jeunet, 9 rue de l'Hôtel de Ville, Arbois, 39600 Jura (tel: 03 84 66 05 67). A chef in the ascendant, combined with a charming and tasteful hotel, makes this pretty place in the wine-growing Jura a satisfying stay.
Le Parc des Maréchaux, 6 avenue Foch, Auxerre, 89000 Yonne (tel: 03 86 51 43 77). Stylish B&B in a quiet part of the city. Warm welcome and generous breakfasts.
Paris et Poste, 97 rue de la Republique, Sens, 89100 Yonne (tel: 03 86 65 17 43). Old-fashioned town-centre hostelry (next to the cathedral).

Budget
Le Castel, Mailly-le-Château, 89660 Yonne (tel: 03 86 84 43 06). Turn-of-the-century house, convenient for stop-overs for south-bound travellers. Attractive garden and shady terrace.
Les Capucins, 6 avenue Paul-Doumer, Avallon, 89200 Yonne (tel: 03 86 34 06 52). Cosy restaurant-with-rooms on a quiet square. Excellent regional cooking and breakfast in the garden.

Hôtel-Restaurant Taillard, Goumois, 25470 Doubs (tel: 03 81 44 20 75). Chalet-style hotel in village on Swiss border. Good sports, fishing, riding and mountain biking.
Poste, Charolles, 71120 Saône-et-Loire (tel: 03 85 24 11 32). Right in the centre of this small market town. Offers very good regional cooking.
Relais du Maconnais, La Croix-Blanche, Berzé-la-Ville 71960 Saône-et-Loire (tel: 03 85 36 60 72). Unassuming little hotel in tiny village 14km from Macon, with elegant restaurant.

ALSACE-LORRAINE & THE NORTH

Accommodation
Expensive
Château de Montreuil, Montreuil-sur-Mer, 62170 Pas-de-Calais (tel: 03 21 81 53 04). Family-run, privately owned country house in English style, within the walled historic town of Montreuil-sur-Mer, just opposite the Roman Citadel. Excellent cooking; fine gardens.
Les Crayères, 64 boulevard Henri Vasnier, Reims, 51100 Marne (tel: 03 26 82 80 80). Gérard Boyer's palatial restaurant and hotel, in a 19th-century château located in Epernay's suburbs.
Grand Hôtel de la Reine, Nancy, 54000 Meurthe-et-Moselle (tel: 03 83 35 03 01). Eighteenth-century palace on the superb place Stanislas.

283

Moderate
Aux Armes de Champagne, place de la Basilique, L'Epine, 51460 Marne (tel: 03 26 69 30 30). Opposite the basilica, this renowned hostelry offers a warm welcome in an informal atmosphere. The cuisine offers a wide selection of delicately flavoured dishes from the region.
La Chatreuse de Val St-Esprit, 1 rue des Fouquières, Gosnay, 62199 Pas-de-Calais (tel: 03 21 62 80 00). 18th-century château set in peaceful wooded grounds. Original furniture in the rooms and a fine restaurant which specialises in seafood.
Le Cheval Blanc, Sept-Saulx, 51400 Marne (tel: 03 26 03 90 27). Traditional coaching inn in quiet village centre. Bedrooms (in annexe) in rustic style.
Les Vosges, 2 Grande Rue, Ribeauvillé, 68150 Haut-Rhin (tel: 03 89 73 61 39). In the heart of a pretty wine village, an elegant restaurant-with-rooms.

Budget
Les Alisiers, Lapoutroie, 68650 Haut-Rhin (tel: 03 89 47 52 82). Converted hill-top farmhouse; small and cosy bedrooms. Robust cooking.
Grand Hôtel de l'Europe, 23-25 rue Diderot, Langres, 52200 Haute-Marne (tel: 03 25 87 10 88). In town centre, busy and traditional, with generous cooking.

Index

Bold figures denote the main entry of a subject.

A

Abbeville 243
Abélard 101
Aber Wrac'h 92
Les Abers 92
Abri du Cap Blanc 143
accommodation **274–83**
Agde 185
Agen 136
Aigoual, Massif de l' 196
Aigues-Mortes 170
Ain, Vallée de l' 226
Ainhoa 157
airports and air services 70, **260**, 270
Aix-en-Provence **171**, 174, 188
Aix-les-Bains 212
Albâtre, Côte d' 74
Albert 256
Albi 136
Alençon **74**, 79
Alise-Ste-Reine 233
Allier, Gorges de l' 196
L'Alpe d'Huez 220
Alpes Mancelles 74
Alps **186**, 208
Alps & Rhône Valley 208–23
accommodation 282–3
Alsace-Lorraine & the North 240–59
accommodation 283
Les Alyscamps 172
Ambleteuse 79
Amboise **108**, 125
Amiens **242**, 243
Ancy-le-Franc, Château de 226
Les Andelys 80
Andorra 154
Anet, Château d' 60
l'Angenardière 88
Angers **108**, 109
Anjony, Château d' 196
Annecy, Lac d' 210
Antibes **171,**, 174
Apremont, Gorges d' 62
Aquitaine 127
Aravis, Massif des 211
Arbois 232
Arc-et-Senans 226-7
Arcachon 128
architecture **26–7**
Alpine 223
Gothic 243
Norman 82
Romanesque 82, 167, 203
rural 223
Les Arcs 222
Ardèche, Gorges de l' 196
Les Ardennes 242
Areines 117
Argent, Côte d' 128
Argentat 136
Argentière 214
Arlempdes 205
Arles 29, **172**, 185, 188, 189
Arles-sur-Tech 154
Arras 242
Arreau 154
Arromanches 79
Ascain 157
Asnelles 79
Aspe, Vallee d' 162–3
Assy, Plateau d' 211

Astérix, Parc **60**, 262
Atlantic Coast 126–33
accommodation 278
Aubazine 151
Aubeterre 128
Aubusson **136**, 141
Audierne 102
Audinghen 257
Aulnay 128
Aulus-les-Bains 160
Auray 101
Aure, Vallée d' 154–5
Aussois 222
Autoire 140
Autun 227
Auvergne 195
Auxerre 227
Auxois 233
Avallon 227
Aven Armand 207
Aven d'Orgnac 196
Aven Marzal 196
Aveyron Valley 149
Avignon 172–3
Avoine 114
Avon-les-Roches 115
la Avoraiz 218
Avrieux 218
Azay-le-Rideau 113
Azay-sur-Indre 122
Azur, Côte d'182

B

Bagnères de Bigorre 154
Baie des Trépassés 93
Balleroy, Château de 74
Ballon de Guebwiller 244
Balzac, Honoré de 124
Bandol 176
banks 269
Barbizon 62
Barcelonnette 211
Barèges 155
Barfleur 78
Bargème 177
Barnenez 95
Barneville-Carteret 78
Le Barroux 177, 179
Barsac 129
Basque country 153, **156–7**
Basse Navarre 156
bastides 139
Bastille 56–7
Batailley, Château 132
battlefields 256–7
Batz 104
La Baule 92
Les Baux 176
Bayeux **75**, 79, 82
Bayonne 128, **155**, 157
Bazas 129
Bazoches, Château de 239
Beaubourg 56
Beaugency 108
Beaulieu 149
Beaulieu-sur-Dordogne 138
Beaumes-de-Venise 179
Beaumont 139
Beaumont-Hamel 256
Beaune 224, 228, **230**
Beauregard, Château de 110
Beauvais 60
Le Bec-Hellouin 84
Bédoin 179
Beg-Meil 102
Belcastel 140
Belfort 244
Belle-Ile **92**, 93
Bellou 85

Bélon 92
Belvès 145
Bendor 176
Bénodet 102
La Bérarde 220
Bergerac 138–9
Bergues 244
Bernières 79
Berven 97
Berzé-le-Châtel 228
Berzé-la-Ville 231
Besançon 232
Besbre, Vallée de la 198
Bessans 218
Besse en Chandesse 198
Bétharram, Grottes de 155
Bethmale Valley 160
Beuvron-en-Auge 85
Beynac-et-Cazenac 137
Béziers 159, **176**
Biarritz **128**, 156, 157
Bibliothèque Nationale de France 26, 59
La Bigorre 155
Biot 174, **176**, 177
Biron 137
Blois **110**, 113, 125
Blonville 76
Bois de Boulogne **58**, 125
Bois de Vincennes **59**, 125
Bonaguil 137
Bonneval 218, 222, **223**
Bonnieux 180
Bordeaux 27, 29, 127, **128**, 132
Bort-les-Orgues 198
Bosc, Château de 136
Boudin, Eugène 76
Boulogne 244
La Bourboule 198
Bourcefranc-le-Chapus 133
Bourdeilles 147
Bourg-en-Bresse 232
Bourges 110
Bourget, Lac du 212
Brancion 239
Brantôme 147
Brasparts 97, 100
Brèche de Roland 162
Bréhat 93
Bresse 232
Brest 92
Briançon 212
Bricquebec 78
Brière Regional Park 94
La Brigue 186
Brinon-sur-Sauldre 123
Brioude 196, **203**
Brissac, Château de 110–11
Brittany 90–105
accommodation 277–8
Brou 232
Brouage 133
Bruniquel 149
Le Bugue 143
Buis 193
Buis-les-Baronnies 185, 193
bull-fighting 185
bull-running 160
Burgundy & Jura 224–39
accommodation 283
Bussy-Rabutin, Château de 233

C

Cabourg 76
Cadillac 129
Cadouin 139
Caen **77**, 79, 82

Cagnes 174
Cahors 139
Calais 244
Camargue 170
Cambrai 244
Cambremer 84
camping 262
canals 70, 227
Cancale 94
Candes-Saint-Martin 111
Le Canigou 155
Cannes 174, 178, **182**
Cantal 201
Cap d'Agde 185
Cap Ferrat 178
Cap Fréhel 98
Carcassonne 153, **158**
Carennac 139
Carnac **94**, 95, 101
Caromb 179
Carpentras 178
Carrouges, Château de 77
Cascades du Hérisson 226
Cassel 245
Cassis 178
Castelnau 140
Castelnaud 137
Cathars 159
Caudebec-en-Caux 82, **89**
Causse Noir 206
Causses 195, **206–7**
Cauterets 158
Le Caylar 206
Caylus 149
Centre Pompidou 26, 56
Cerdagne 158
Cère, Vallée de la 199
Céret 160
Cérisy 82
Cévennes 195, **197**
Cézanne, Paul 171, 174, 175
Chaillé 131
La Chaise-Dieu 199
Chambéry 208, **212**, 218
Chambord 111
Chambord, Château de 113
Chamonix **214**, 215
Champ-de-Bataille, Château de 77
Champagny 222
Champigny-sur-Veude 115
Champs-Elysées 53
Chancelade 147
Chantilly, Château de 60
Chapelle de Jérusalem 174–5
Charente 127
Charlannes Plateau 198
Charleville-Mézières 242
Charlieu 238
Les Charmettes 212
Charollais 238
Charolles 238
Chartres 61
La Chartreuse 173
Chartreuse, Massif de la 216
Chateaubriand 94, 105
châteaux, Renaissance 112–13
Châtillon-sur-Indre 122
Châtillon-sur-Seine 232
Chaudes Aigues 201
Chaumont-sur-Loire 111
Chauriat 203
Chauvigny 111
Chavroches 198
Le Chazelet 220
Chemillé-sur-Indrois 122
Chenonceau, Château de 112–3
Chenonceaux 111, 113

Cherbourg **78**, 79
Cheverny, Château de 114
children **262**, 265
Chinon 114, 115
Cians gorge 186
Cirque de Baume 235
Cirque de Gavarnie **162**, 164
Cîteaux 231
Clamouse, Grotte de 207
La Clayette 238
Clécy 87
Clermont-Ferrand **199**, 203
climate 263
Clos de Vougeot 228
Cluny 231
Cluny, Musée de 54
La Clusaz 211
coaches, international 260
Coaraze 186
Cocteau, Jean 62, 175
Cognac 131
Col du Tourmalet 155
Colette 236
Colleville 79
Collioure 174, 185
Colonges-la-Rouge 151
Colmar 245
Combarelles, Grotte des 143
Combourg 94
Le Comminges 160
Compiègne 61
Concarneau 94
Conques 199
conversion charts 260
Cordes 149
Corneilla de Conflent 167
Corniche Bretonne 96
Corniche de l'Armorique 96
Corseul 98
Cos d'Estournel, Château 132
Cotentin 78
Coucouron 205
Coucy-le-Château 248
Coupesarte 85
Courances 62
Courbet, Gustave 236
Courboyer 88
Courchevel 222
Cournouaille 102
Courségoules 193
Courseulles 79
Le Couserans 160
Coussac-Bonneval 137
Coutances 82
La Couvertoirade 206
credit cards 269
Crestet 177, 179
Creuse, Vallée de la 141
Crèvecoeur 85
Creysse 140
crime 264
Croisset 86, 89
Croix de Fer 219
Le Crotoy 255
Crouzilles 115
Crozant 141
Crussol 221
Culan 141
Cunault 114
Curemonte 141
customs regulations 263
cycling 264

Dargilan, Grotte de 207
Daudet, Alphonse 180
Dauphiné 208
de la Tour, Georges 249

Deauville 73, **76**
La Défense 58
Dentelles de Montmirail 177, **179**
Denezé-sous-Doué 114
Les Deux Alpes 220
La Dévinière 114
Die 216
Dieppe 78
Dijon 234
Dinan 98
Dinard 98
disabilities, travellers with 264
Disneyland Paris **61**, 262
Dives-sur-Mer 76
Doissat 145
Dol de Bretagne 99
dolmens 95
Domfront 78
Domme 141
Domrémy-la-Pucelle 250
Dordogne 134–51
accommodation 279–80
Douai 248
Doubs, Vallée du 235
Doué-la-Fontaine 114
Dourbie gorge 196
Drée 238
Dreux 61
Dunkerque 257

Ecomusée d'Alsace 250
Ecouen, Château d' 61
Ecouis 80
Ecrins National Park 208, 222
l'Eglise du Dôme 55
Eguisheim 247
Eguzon 141
electricity 266
Elne 185
embassies and consulates 267
Embrun 220
Emerald Coast 98
emergency phone numbers 267
Eperleques 257
L'Epine 248
Epoisses 233
Erquy 98
Espalion 200
Espelette 157
Les Estables 205
Estaing 200
Esterel de l'Massif 178
Etang, de l'Fangassier 170
Etelan, Château d' 89
Etretat 74
Eus 167
Evian **216**, 217
Evreux **80**, 82
Excenevex 216
Eymet 139
Les Eyzies-de-Tayac 142–3
Eze 177, 186

Falaise 80
Le Faou 100
Fécamp 74
Fédrun, Ile de 94
Felletin 141

Fermont 257
ferry services 74, **262**
La Ferté-Loupière 236
Fervaques 85
Les Feugerets 88
Finistère 93
Flaubert, Gustave 86
Flavigny-sur-Ozerain 233
Fleurie, Côte 72–3, **76**
Fleury 257, 259
Florac 197
Foix 161
Le Folgoët 97, 105
Font-de-Gaume, Grotte de 143
Font-Romeu 158
Fontaine de Vaucluse 181
Fontainebleau 62
Fontenay, Abbaye de 231, 233
Fontevraud 116
Fontfroide 180
Fontgombault 141
Fontvieille 180
food and drink **22–3**
Alsace cuisine 245
armagnac 136
Basque cuisine 157
Benedictine liqueur 74
bouillabaisse 184
calvados 85
champagne 253
Chartreuse 216
cheeses 84, 85, 198, 207
cognac 131
crêpes 96
foie gras 150
kir 234
Loire cuisine 120
ortolan buntings 128
oysters 92, 94, 101
pineau 131
poulet de Bresse 232
truffles 148
walnuts 145
wines 118, 132, 226, 228–9, 259
Fort de Buoux 181
Fort de la Latte 98
fortresses 137
Fougères 99
Fox Amphoux 177
Fragonard, Jean Honoré 180
Franche Comté 225
Fréjus 174–5, **178**, 188
Futuroscope **121**, 262

Gaillard, Château 80
gardens 125
Gargilesse 141
Gassin 190
Gaube, Lac de 165
Gauguin, Paul **103**, 172
Gavrinis Island **95**, 101
Genillé 122
Gerbier de Jonc 205
Gien 116
Giens Peninsula 180
Gigondas 179
Giverny 80
Glandon pass 219
Glane, Vallée de la 148
Glénan, Iles de 93
Gluges 140
Gorbio 177, 186
Gordes 177, **181**
Gotein 166
Gouffre de Padirac 140

Gourdon 177, **193**
Grand Andelys 80
Grand Bé 105
Grand-Palais 52
La Grande Chartreuse 216
Grande Corniche 183
Grande Côte 133
La Grande Motte 185
Granville 78
Grasse 180
La Grave 220
Grenoble 29, 208, **216**
Gréolières 193
Groix 93
Guéhenno 97
Guesclin, Bertrand du 98
Guimiliau 97
Gujan Mestras 128

Hambye 82
Haras du Pin 88
Haut-Koenigsbourg 247
Haute Soule 166
Hautecombe Abbey 212
Hautefort, Château de 141
Hauterives 221
Le Havre 81
health matters 267
Héliopolis 180
Hendaye 157
Henri IV 163
High Pyrenees 164–5
hill villages 177
history of France 31–47
Hix 158
Hoëdic 93
Honfleur 76
Hort de Dieu 196
Hortillonnages 242
hotels and guesthouses 274–83
Houat 93
Houlgate 76
Hourtin 132
Huelgoat 100
Hugo, Victor 56, 89
Hunaudaie, Château de la 98
Hunspach 259
Hyelzas 207
Hyères 180

If, Château d' 184
Les Iffs 94
l'Ile Bouchard 115
Ile de la Cité 56, 57
Ile de France 48, 49
Ile de Ré 131
Ile St-Louis 56, 57
Indre river 122
Indrois river 122
insurance 267
Issan, Château d' 132
Issarlès, Lac d' 205
Issoire 203
Isturits 162

Jaligny 198
Jardin du Luxembourg 54
La Jasse 207
Joan of Arc 35, 86, 108, 114, 120, 141, **250**

285

Index

Josselin 99
Juan-les-Pins 182
Jumièges 82, 89
Jura see Burgundy/Jura

K

Kakouetta, Gorges de 166
Kayserberg 247
Kerfons 96, 97
Kerguehennec 105
Kermaria 97
Kernascléden 97
Kérouat 100

L

Labouiche, Rivière
   Souterraine de 161
Labourd 156–7
Lacanau 132
Lacave 140
lace-making 202
Lacoste 180
Lagatjar 95
Lampaul-Guimiliau 97
Les Landes 130
Langeais, Château de 116
Langres 248
language 267–8
Languedoc/Roussillon
   coast 185
Lannion 96
Lanrigan 94
Lanslevillard 218
Laon 243, **248**
Lapalisse 198
Larzac 206–7
Lascaux 142–3, 178
Lassay, Château de 81
Laval 81
Le Lavancher 214
Le Lavandou/Bormes 184
Lavardin 117
Lavaudieu 203
lavender 192
Le Nôtre 64, 65, 125
Léger, Fernand 174, 211
Léman, Lac 216–17
Lembach 257
Léon 97
Leonardo da Vinci **108**,
   113
Lérins, Iles de 182
Lescun 163
Lessay 82
Levant 180
Lieue de Grève 96
Le Liget 122
Lille 249
Limoges 144
Lion-sur-Mer 79
Le Lioran 200
Lisieux **81**, 84
Livarot 84, 85
Llo 158
Loches 116
Locmariaquer **95**, 101
Locronan **99**, 105
Le Loir 117
Loire 106–25
   accommodation 278–9
Loire river 107
Lombrives 161
Lons-le-Saunier 226, **235**
Lorient 99
Lot, Vallée du 200
Loubressac 140
Loudenne, Château 132
Louis XIV **38–9**, 65

Loup Valley 193
Lourdes 152, **162**
Louvre 52
Lubéron 180
Lucéram 177, 186
Lucerne 82
Luchon (Bagnères de)
   162, 164
Lude, Château du 117
Lunéville 249
Lurçat, Jean **109**, 140,
   146, 211
Luxey 130
Luynes 118
Luz-St-Sauveur 162
Lyon 29, **217**, **221**
Lyons-la-Forêt 81

M

La Madeleine 143
Maillezais 131
Maison Picassiette 61
Malartie, Château de la
   146
Malaucène 179
Malle, Château de 129
Manoir de Tarde 146
Le Mans 118
maps 268
Le Marais 56
Marais Poitevin 131
Marans 131
Marcadeau Valley 165
Marennes 133
Margaux, Château 132
Marmoutier 249
Marquèze 130
Marsat 203
Marseille 184
Martainville 81
Martel 144
Marthonie, Château 147
Mas du Pont de Rousty
   170
Le Mas Soubeyran 197
Massif Central 142,
   194–207
   accommodation 281–2
Matisse, Henri 174,
   175, 211
Mauléon-Licharre 166
Maures, Massif des 184
Mauriac, François 129–30
La Maurienne 218
medical treatment 267
Médous, Grotte de 155
megaliths 95
Meije 220
Meillant, Château de 118
Méjanes 170
Méjean 206
Mende 197
Ménerbes 177, 180
Ménez-Hom 100
Ménez-Meur 100
menhirs **95**, 99
Menthon, Château de 211
Menton 169, 175, **183**
Mercantour 186
Méribel 222
Merlande 147
Merveilles, Vallée des 186
Metz 249
Meuse 250
Meyronne 140
Meyrueis 196
Milly-la-Forêt 62
Mistral, Frédéric 172
Moines, Ile aux 96
Moissac 144
Monaco 177, **183**

monasteries 231
Monbazillac, Château de
   144
Monet, Claude 80
money 269
Monflanquin 139
La Mongie 155
Monpazier 139
Mons 177
Mont Aiguille 218
Mont Blanc **214**, **215**
Mont Cenis 218
Mont Dauphin 213
Le Mont-Dore 200
Mont Lozère 197
Mont de Marsan 130
Mont Mézenc 205
Mont-St-Michel 82, **83**
Mont-Ste-Odile 246
Mont Ste-Victoire 174
Mont Ventoux 179
Mont Vinaigre 178
Montal 140
Montauban 144
Montbard 233
Montbenoît 235
Montbrun 137
Monte Carlo 183
Montélimar 221
Montgenèvre 212
Montgeoffroy, Château de
   119
Montignac 142
Montmartre 59
Montmuran 94
Montoire 117
Montparnasse 58
Montpellier 27, 29, **185**
Montpellier-le-Vieux 206
Montpezat de Quercy 145
Montpoupon, Château de
   119
Montrésor, Château de
   122
Montreuil 258
Montreuil-Bellay 119
Montrichard 119
Monts d'Arrée 100
Monts Dore 201, 203
Montségur 159
Morbihan, Golfe du 101
Moret 62
Mortagne-au-Perche 88
Mortemer 81
Morvan hills 237
Morzine 218
Moselle 250
Moudeyres 205
Mougins 174
Moulins 235
mountaineering 215
Le Moustier 142
Moustiers-Ste-Marie 192
Moutier d'Ahun 145
Les Moutiers 78
Moutiers 236
Mouton-Rothschild,
   Château 132
Mozac 203
Mulhouse 250
Munster 250
Murol 200
museums, charges 269

N

Najac 149
Nancy 251
Nanterre 49
Nantes 102
Napoleon Bonaparte **41**,
   55, 75, 131, 182

Narbonne 185
national holidays 269
Navacelles 206
Néouvielle 155
Neste d'Aure 154
Neuf Brisach 252
Névache Valley 212
Nevers 235
newspapers 269
Niaux, Grotte de 161
Nice 174, 175, **182–3**
Nice-Cimiez 175, 183,
   188
Nîmes 19, 185, **187**, **188**
Nohant, Château de 119
Noirlac, Abbaye de 119
Noirmoutier 131
Normandy 72–89
   accommodation 277
Notre-Dame 57
Notre-Dame du Crann 97
Notre Dame du Port 199
Notre Dame de Toute
   Grace 211
Nouans-les-Fontaines 122
Noyers 233
Nyons 193

O

O, Château d' 88
Obernai 252
Oceanopolis 92
L'Oisans 220
Oléron 131
Oloron-Ste-Marie 162
Opale, Côte d' 244
opening hours 269–70
Opera House, Paris 53
Oppède-le-Vieux 177, 180
Oradour-sur-Glane 145
Orange **187**, **189**
Orangerie 52
Orcival 203
Orléans 120
Ornans 236
Orsay, Musée d' 54
Ossau, Vallée d' 163
Ouessant 93
Oxocelhaya 162

P

Pagode de Chanteloup 108
Paimpol 102
Le Pal 198
Le Palais 92
Palais de Chaillot 58
La Palmyre 133
Paray-le-Monial 231, **238**
Parc National des
   Pyrenees 158
Parc Pyrenéen de l'Art
   Préhistorique 161
Parc Régional de Morvan
   239
Parçay-sur-Vienne 115
pardons 101, 104, **105**
Paris **48–71**
   accommodation 69,
      274, 276
   eating out 67, 276–7
   nightlife 68
   practical points 70–1
   public transport 70–1,
      271
   shopping 66
   sightseeing 52–65
parish closes 97
Pas de la Case 154

passports and visas 260
Pasteur, Louis 226
Pau 163
Pauillac 132
Pavin, Lac 198
Pays d'Auge 73, **84–5**
Pech-Merle 143
Pegasus Bridge 79
Peille 186
Peillon 177, 186
Peisey-Nancroix 222
pelota 156
Penne 149
people and culture
  architecture 26–7
  the arts 21
  cuisine 22–3
  economy 16–17
  fashion 18–19
  French society 13
  government 12
  modern art 174–5
  multiculturalism 14–15
  work and leisure 24–5
Perche 88
Père-Lachaise 59
Périgord 135, 142
Périgord Vert 147
Périgueux 142, **146**
Peronne 256
Pérouges 221
Perpignan 187
Perrecy-les-Forges 238
Perros-Guirec 96, 105
Peyrepertuse 159
Pézenas 187
pharmacies 270
Pic du Midi d'Ossau 163, **164**
Pic du Midi du Bigorre 155
Pic de l'Ours 178
Picasso, Pablo 174
place des Vosges 56
places of worship 270
La Plagne 222
Plampinet 212
Plancoët 98
Plessis Bourré, Château du 120
Plessis Macé, Château du 120
Pleyben 97
Plougasnou 96
Plougastel-Daoulas 97
Ploumanac'h 96
Ploumilliau 96, 97
Pointe du Raz **93**, 102
Pointe de Pen-Hir 93
Pointe de Primel 96
Poitiers 121
police 267
Pont l'Abbé 102
Pont-Audemer 84
Pont-Aven 103
Pont d'Espagne 158, **165**
Pont-l'Evêque 85
Pont du Gard 187, **189**
Pont de Gau 170
Pont d'Ouilly 87
porcelain 64, 144
Pornic 131
Porquerolles 180
Port Barcarès 185
Port Blanc 105
Port Camargue 185
Port Cros 180
Port-en-Bessin 79
Port Goulphar 92
Port Grimaud 190
Port Leucate 185
Port Navalo 101
Port Racine 78
Port Tudy 93

post offices 270
Le Pouldu 103
Pralognan 222
Préhistoparc 143
prehistoric sites 142–3
Primel-Trégastel 96
Proust, Marcel 76
Provence coast 168–93
  accommodation 280–1
public transport 270–1
Puilaurens 159
La Puisaye 236
Puivert 159
Puy de Dôme 201
Le Puy-en-Velay **202, 203**
Puy-St-Vincent 222
Puyguilhem 147
Puymirol 136
Pyrenees 152–67
  accommodation 280

Q

Quéribus 159
Le Quesnoy 252
Queyras Regional Park 208, **212–13**
Quiberon 102
Quimper 102

R

Rabelais, François 114
rail travel **260, 262,** 271
Rais, Gilles de 102
Ramatuelle 190
Rambouillet, Château de 63
Rance estuary 98
Reims 253
Rennes 103, **104**
Renoir, Pierre Auguste 174
Rétaud 133
Rhône Valley 209, **221**
Richelieu 115
Riom 202
Rioux 133
Ripaille, Château de 216
Riquewihr 247
Riva Bella 79
Rive Droite 52
Rive Gauche 54
Riviera 169, **182–3**
Roc Trévézel 100
Rocamadour 146
La Roche 97
La Roche aux Fées 95
La Roche Courbon 133
Roche d'Oëtre 87
Rochechouart, Château de 148
Rochefort 131
La Rochelle 127, **131,** 262
Rochers-Sévigné, Château des 105
Les Roches-Tranchelion 115
Rochetaillée-sur-Saône 221
Rocroi 242
Rodez 27, **202**
Rodin, Musée 55
La Roque-Gageac 146
Roland 162, 166
Roman remains 188–9
Romans-sur-Isère 221
Romorantin 123

Ronchamp 254
Rochères 263
Roque-St-Christophe 143
Roquebrune 177
Roquefort-sur-Soulzon 207
Roquetaillade, Château de 129
Rosary Chapel 175, 193
Roscoff 104
Rouen 27, 82, **86**
Rouffignac 143
Les Rousses 236
Roussillon 177, **181**
Route des Crêtes 246–7
Route du Vin 247
Roya Valley 186
Royan 133
Royat 202
Rumengol 105
Russell, Count Henry 164
Ry 81

S

Sable d'Or Les Pins 98
Sablonceaux Abbey 133
Saché, Château de 124
St-Aignan 121
St-Antonin-Noble-Val 149
St-Aubin 79
St-Benoît-sur-Loire, Abbaye de 121
St-Bertrand-de-Comminges 160
St-Brieuc 98
St-Cast-le-Guildo 98
St-Céré 140
St-Cirq-Lapopie 146
St-Côme-d'Olt 200
Saint-Denis 63
St-Emilion 127, 129
Saint-Fargeau 236
St-Fiacre 97
St-Flour 204
St-Fort 133
St-Génis-des-Fontaines 167
St-Germain 54
St-Germain-des-Vaux 78
St-Germain-en-Laye **63,** 130
St-Germain-de-Livet 85
St-Germain-Source-Seine 233
St-Gildas-de-Rhuys 101
St-Gilles 170
St-Guénolé 102
St-Guilhem-le-Désert 202
St-Herbot 97, **100**
St-Honorat 182
St-Jacques-des-Guérets 117
St-Jean-de-Bruel 207
St-Jean-Cap-Ferrat 178
St-Jean-de-Côle 147
St-Jean-du-Doigt 105
St-Jean-du-Gard 197
St-Jean-de-Luz 156, **157**
St-Jean-de-Maurienne 218
St-Jean-Pied-de-Port 166
St-Joachim 94
St-Junien 148
St-Lary-Soulan 154–5
St-Laurent 79
St-Léonard-des-Bois 74
St-Lizier 160
St-Maclou 82
St-Malo 105
St-Martin 117
St-Martin-de-Boscherville 82, 89

St-Martin-du-Canigou **166,** 167
St-Martin-de-Fenollar 167
St-Michel 100
St-Michel-de-Cuxa 167
St-Michel-en-Grève 96
St-Nectaire 203
St-Omer 243, **254–5**
St-Paul-de-Mausole 190
St-Paul-de-Vence 175, **177**
St-Pol-de-Léon 105
St-Quay-Portrieux 98
St-Quentin-sur-Indrois 122
St-Raphaël 190
St-Rémy-Glanum **189, 190**
St-Riquier 255
St-Rivoal 105
St-Romain-en-Gal 221
St-Savin 121
St-Sernin 150
St-Thégonnec 97
St-Tropez 174, 175, **190**
St-Trophime 172
St-Vaast-la-Hougue 78
St-Valéry 255
St-Véran **213,** 223
St-Wandrille 89
Ste-Agnès 177
Ste-Anne d'Auray 101, 105
Ste-Anne-la-Palud 100, **104,** 105
Ste-Céneri-le-Gérei 74
Sainte-Chapelle 57
Ste-Croix-du-Mont 129
Ste-Croix-du-Verdon 192
Ste-Engrace 166
Ste-Eulalie 206
Ste-Margeurite 182
Ste-Maxime 190
Saintes 131
Les Saintes-Maries 170
Salers 204
Salignac, François de 139
Salins les Bains 226
Salses 185
salt flats 94
salt springs 226
Samoëns 219
Sand, George **119,** 141
Saorge 177, 186
Sare 157
Sarlat 142, **148**
Saulieu 237
Saumur 123
Saut du Doubs 235
Sauternes 129
Sauvage, Côte 92, 133
Sauveterre 206, 207
Savoie 208, 209
Sceaux 64
Sedan 242
Sées 87
Séguret 177, 179
Seillans 174, 177
Sein 93
Seine valley 89
Seix 160
Sélestat 255
Semur-en-Auxois 233
Senlis 64
Sens 237
Sentier des Douaniers 96
Sept-Fons 198
Sept Iles 96
Serrabone **166,** 167
Serrant, Château de 123
Serre Ponçon, Lac de 220
Sète 185
Sévigné, Madame de 105, 204
Sèvres 64

287

Index/Acknowledgements

shops 269–70
Sigean Safari Park 185
Signal d'Ecouves 88
Sisteron 191
Sixt 219
Sizun 97
Solférino 130
Sologne 123
Solutré 237
Somme **255, 256**
Sorbonne 54
Sorges 147
Sormiou 178
Souillac 148
Soulac 128
Soule 156, 157, **166**
Souvigny 204
Souvigny-en-Sologne 123
spas 131, 204, 250
Strasbourg 29, **255**
Le Struthof 246
student/youth travel 272
Suisse Normande 87
Sully, Château de 124
Super-Lioran 200
Superbagnères 162
Suscinio 101

T

Talloires 210
Talmont 133
Tanlay, Château de 239
tapestries **109**, 136,
   171
Tarascon/Beaucaire 191
Tarn, Gorges du 206–7
Tavant 115
Le Teich Bird Reserve 128
telephones 272–3
Termignon 218, 222
Ternant 239
Thann 258
Thérèse de Lisieux 81
La Thiérache 252
Thiers 204
Thiviers 147

Thônes 211
Thonon **216**, 217
Le Thot 142
Tignes 222
time differences 273
toilets 273
Toul 258
Toulon 192
Toulouse 150
Toulouse-Lautrec 136
Le Touquet 258
Tour Eiffel 55
tourist offices 273
Tournoël 202
Tournus 239
Tourrettes-sur-Loup 177,
   193
Tours 124
Toury 198
Trappe, Abbaye de la 88
travelling to France 260,
   262
Trébeurden 96
Trégarvan 100
Trégastel-Plage 96
Tréguier 105
Trémalo Chapel 103
Treyne, Château de la
   140
Trôo 117
troubadours 176
Trouville 76
Troyes 258–9
Truyère Gorges 204
La Turbie 177, **189**
Turckheim 247
Turenne 151

U

Ubaye 211
Unterlinden, Musée d'
   245
Ussé, Château d' 124
Uzerche 151
Uzès 192
Uzeste 129

V

Vacqueyras 179
Vaison-la-Romaine 179,
   189, 193
Val, Château de 198
Val d'Isère 222
Val Thorens 222
Valcabrère 160
Valençay, Château de 124
Valence 221
Valentré Bridge 139
Vallauris 174
Valloire 218
Vallon de la Leisse 222
La Vallouise 222
Valois, Château des 131
Van Gogh, Vincent **172**,
   175, **190**
Vannes 101, **105**
La Vanoise 208, **222**
Vassieux 222
Vaucluse Plateau 181
Vaucocour, Château 147
Vauvenargues 174
Vaux-le-Vicomte, Château
   de **64**, 125
Vénasque 181
Vence 1/5, **193**
Vendée 127
Vendôme 117
Vénéon Valley 220
Ventadour 151
Ver-sur-Mer 79
Vercors Regional Park
   208, **222**
Verdon, Grand Canyon du
   192
Verdun 250, 256–7, **259**
Vermeille, Côte 185
Versailles 65, 125
Vésubie Gorges 186
Vézelay 239
Vic-sur-Cère 199
Vichy 204
Vieil-Armand 247
Vienne 221
Vienne river 115

Vierville-sur-Mer 79
Vieux-Bourg-de-Cravant
   115
Vieux Chambord 198
Vignemale 158, **164**
Villandraut 129
Villandry, Château de 124
Villard de Lans 222
Villars, Grottes de 147
Villefranche 175, 183
Villefranche-du-Périgord
   139
Villefranche-de-Rouergue
   149
Villeloin 122
Villeneuve-lès-Avignon
   173
Villequier 89
Villeréal 139
Villers-sur-Mer 76
La Villette 58-9
Villiers Saint-Benoît 236
Vimoutiers 85
Vimy Ridge 256
vineyards **132**, **228–9**
Vire 87
Vitré 105
Vittel 250
volcanoes 201
Vosges 246, 250

W

wildlief, Pyrenean 164–5
William the Conqueror 75,
   76, 77, 80
Wissembourg 259

Y

Yeu 131
youth hostels 272
Yquem, Château d' 127,
   129
Yvoire 216

Picture Credits

The Automobile Association would like to thank the following photographers, libraries and associations for their assistance in the preparation of this book.

J ALLAN CASH PHOTOLIBRARY Spine: Frenchman; CDT CANTAL 201 Chaines des Puys; CDT CHARENTE 128 Aubeterre; CHAMONIX TOURIST BOARD 209 Walkers, 211 Climbers, 215 Paragliders; CHASTEL & COURTOIS 236 Moutiers; HAUTE SAVOIE 25 Skiing; HULTON PICTURE LIBRARY 45 Général de Gaulle, 47 François Mitterrand; MARY EVANS PICTURE LIBRARY 34 Fighting Spanish, 34/5 French in Flanders, 37 Cardinal Richelieu, 39 Louis XIV, 40 Napoleon, 41 Women marching to Versailles; Napoleon, 42 Lafayette; poster, 44 Signing of Treaty of Versailles cartoon; POWERSTOCK/ZEFA spine; SCOPE 164 Gave des Oulettes de Gaube, Vignemale, 167 St-Michel de Cuxa, Prieuré de Serrabone; SPECTRUM COLOUR LIBRARY 26 Lyon, 28 Carnac, 47 Lyon, 109 Tapestry, 150 St-Sernin, Toulouse;TONY STONE Front cover: cyclists and farmhouse; GLYN WILLIAMS Front cover: man with wine; ZEFA PICTURES LTD 31 Megaliths, Gavrinis, 43 Yvette Gilbert, 46 Lyon, 103 Paul Gauguin, The Gossipers, 161 Garvanie, 168 Monet, Cap d'Antibes, 175 Museum of Modern Art, Nice

All remaining pictures are held in the Automobile Association's own library (© AA Photo Library), with contributions from:

P Atterbury, P Bennett, S Day, J Edmunson, P Enticknap, P Kenward, R Moore, D Noble, T Oliver, K Paterson, N Ray, B Rieger, D Robertson, C Sawyer, M Short, B Smith, A Souter, R Strange (and back cover), R Victor

Contributors

Revision copy editor: Andrew Renshaw   Original copy editor: Nia Williams
Revision verifiers: Philippa Richmond, Nicholas Wood (Anglo.Doc)